THE ROYAL HORTICULTURAL SOCIETY

WATER GARDENING

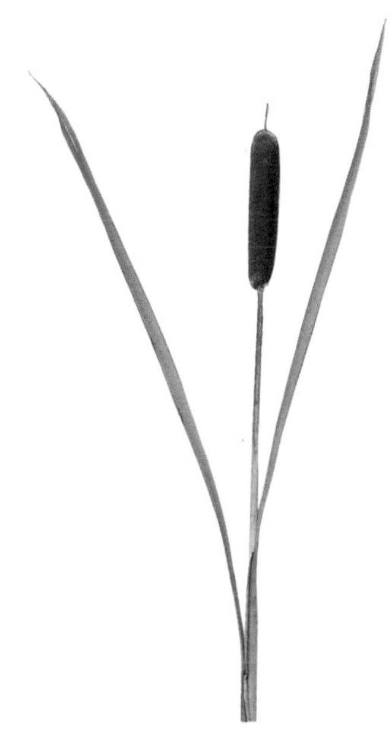

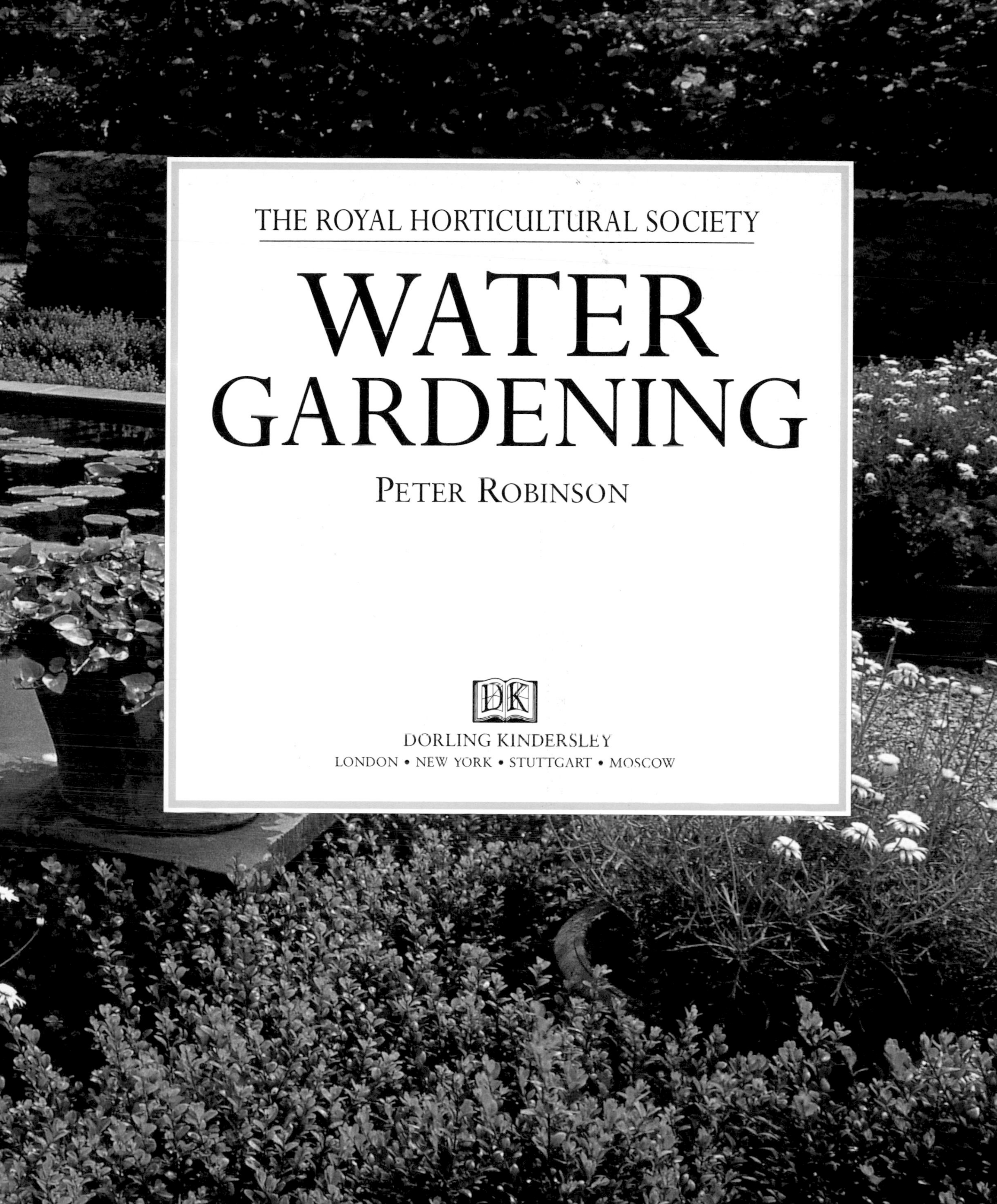

THE ROYAL HORTICULTURAL SOCIETY

WATER GARDENING

PETER ROBINSON

DK
DORLING KINDERSLEY
LONDON • NEW YORK • STUTTGART • MOSCOW

A DORLING KINDERSLEY BOOK

PROJECT EDITOR Cangy Venables
PROJECT ART EDITOR Gillian Andrews

MANAGING EDITOR Louise Abbott
MANAGING ART EDITOR Lee Griffiths

DTP DESIGNER Chris Clark
PRODUCTION Ruth Charlton

PHOTOGRAPHY Peter Anderson, Steven Wooster
ILLUSTRATIONS John Woodcock, Karen Cochrane, Valerie Hill

First published in Great Britain in 1997
by Dorling Kindersley Limited,
9 Henrietta Street, London WC2E 8PS
Visit us on the World Wide Web at http: / / www.dk.com

A CIP catalogue record for this book is available from the British Library

ISBN 0 7513 0304 6

Colour reproduction by Bright Arts, Hong Kong
Printed and bound in Italy by A. Mondadori, Verona

KEY TO PLANTING PLANS

In planting plans accompanying water garden designs, colour coding indicates whether plants are growing in water, in moist soil, or in ordinary garden soil.

- WATER PLANTS
- MOISTURE-LOVING PLANTS
- OTHER PLANTS

KEY TO SYMBOLS

The following symbols accompany plant descriptions, indicating the type of plant and its cultivation requirements.

- Prefers a sunny position
- Prefers partial shade
- Tolerates full shade
- Submerged plant
- Floating-leaved plant
- Free-floating plant
- Water lily
- Lotus
- Marginal plant
- Award of Garden Merit
- Well-drained but moisture-retentive soil
- Moist soil
- Wet soil
- Frost-tender
- Half-hardy (to 0°C/32°F)
- Frost-hardy (to –5°C/23°F)
- Fully hardy (to –15°C/5°F)

CONTENTS

AUTHOR'S FOREWORD 7
INTRODUCTION TO WATER GARDENING 8

WATER GARDEN DESIGNS

DESIGNING WITH WATER 16
RAISED DOUBLE POOL 18
LARGE FORMAL POOL 22
CONTAINER GARDENS 26
ORIENTAL-STYLE WATER GARDEN 28
COURTYARD POOL 32
INFORMAL POND FOR A TOWN GARDEN 34
MILLSTONE FOUNTAIN 38
WILDLIFE POND WITH BOG GARDEN 40
STREAM FOR TOWN OR COUNTRY GARDEN 44

CREATING WATER FEATURES

PLANNING AND PREPARATION 50
CHOOSING A WATER FEATURE 52
ENCOURAGING WILDLIFE 54
SITING A WATER FEATURE 56
EXCAVATION AND DRAINAGE 58
MEASURING AREAS AND VOLUMES 60
CONSTRUCTION TOOLS AND MATERIALS 62
CONSTRUCTION TECHNIQUES 64
PUMPS AND FILTERS 70

Features with Still Water 74

Ponds with Flexible Liner 76

Beaches and Islands 80 • Independent Bog Gardens 82

Rigid Pool Units 84

Raised Pools with Flexible Liner 86

Semi-raised Rigid Pool Units 88

Sunken Concrete Pools 90 • Clay-lined Ponds 92

Water Gardens in Containers 94

Features with Moving Water 96

Simple Streams With Waterfalls 98

More Ideas for Stream Construction 100

Header Pools and Spillways 102

Rigid Stream Units 104 • Concrete Canals 106

Fountains 108 • Cobblestone Fountain 112

Other Reservoir Features 114 • Wall Fountains 116

Finishing Touches 118

Stepping Stones 120 • Bridges 122

Lighting Water Features 124 • Edging Materials 126

Timber Decking 130

Stocking & Maintenance

Maintaining a Healthy Pond 134

A Balanced Ecosystem 136 • Seasonal Changes 138

Routine Tasks for Pond Health 140

Cleaning out a Pond 142 • Pond Repairs 145

Plants for Water Gardens 146

Planting Environments 148

Soils and Containers 150

Planning Planting Schemes 152

Buying Plants 154 • Planting Techniques 156

Routine Plant Care 158

Division and Propagation 160

Plant Pests and Diseases 164

Fish for Water Features 166

Fish Species and their Requirements 168

Buying and Introducing Fish 170

Routine Fish Care 172

Fish Pests and Diseases 174

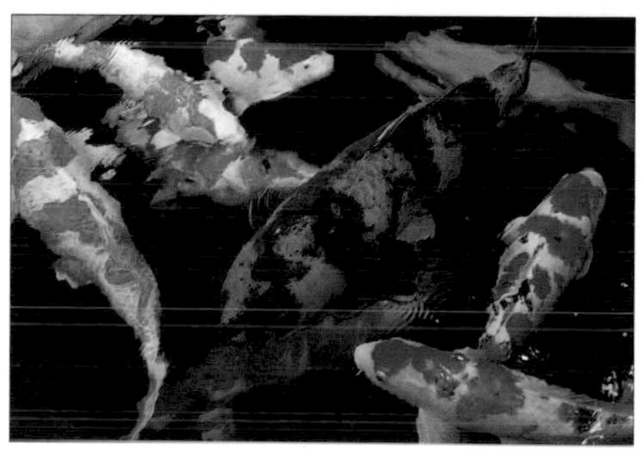

Plant Catalogue

Submerged Plants 178 • Floating-leaved Plants 180

Water Lilies 182 • Lotuses 188

Marginal Plants 190 • Moisture-loving Plants 196

Glossary 208 • Plant Index 210

General Index 214 • Acknowledgments 216

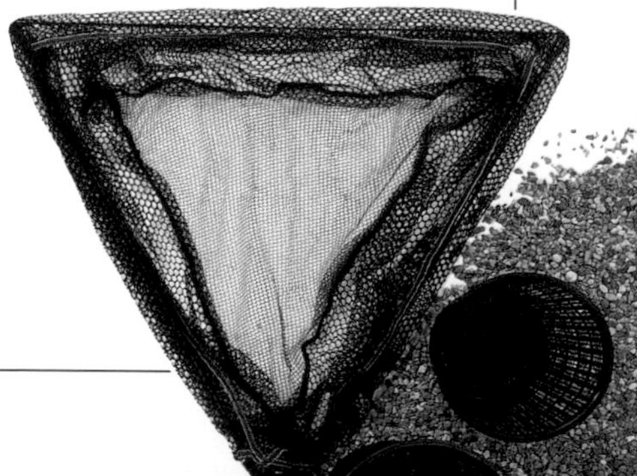

AUTHOR'S FOREWORD

THE CURRENT RISE in popularity of water gardening is not difficult to understand. This most beguiling element can be introduced to every size and style of garden, and in areas and at times of year when water is a precious resource, water gardening is, perhaps surprisingly, one of the most practical and least wasteful ways of transforming a garden into a cooling retreat with lush plant growth.

Without adequate care being given to the design and construction of a water feature, its full potential may be tantalizingly elusive. The intention of this book is to inspire and inform gardeners at every stage. For the garden owner contemplating a new water feature, it provides a complete practical guide to design and siting, construction, planting, stocking, and maintenance, but it has equal value to the owner of an existing water feature, offering ideas for improvement, care, and introduction of new plants. As with so many other aspects of ornamental gardening, a careful mix of science and art is required to ensure that a water garden achieves, then maintains, visual harmony and ecological balance. The aim here has been to explain and overcome all of the myths and problems so often associated with water.

Throughout this book, particularly in the section on water garden design, photographs and plans show how water features in a variety of styles may be integrated into overall garden plans. My thanks are due to the designers and owners of these gardens. The practical step-by-step sequences, showing exactly how features are built and equipment installed, were also photographed in private gardens. In order to provide realistic guides to construction, the projects shown were actually built as permanent features, and continue to provide considerable pleasure. I am especially grateful to the owners of these gardens for their help in producing a book that will, I hope, be both a visual and practical inspiration to its readers.

Peter Robinson

PETER ROBINSON

INTRODUCTION

THROUGHOUT HISTORY, WATER has been valued and even revered all around the world – in some cultures rivers, springs, and streams possessed their own deities. The name of France's river Seine, for example, comes from that of the Celtic goddess Sequana. The earliest tradition of building structures that conserved and channelled water is seen in areas where water was scarce – canals that conducted water away from reservoirs to irrigate fields and settlements have been found dating back as far as the 6th century BC.

FORMAL ORIENTAL WATER GARDEN
Artful naturalism in Oriental gardens was often balanced with the formal use of water, as in this contemporary interpretation of a straight-edged pool with symmetrical planting and pergolas.

But even in these very early times, water features gradually assumed roles in addition to their strictly practical use, forming centres for community life, ornamenting the pleasure gardens of the rich and powerful, and, in the far East, assuming symbolic significance in the private garden of the philosopher. The decorative possibilities of associating water with plants and ornamental materials were explored in ever greater depth; with its potential to add atmosphere and visual beauty, water has had a profound influence on the development of garden design, and it is surprising to discover just how central the use of water features is to gardens worldwide at all times in history.

ENCLOSED CHINESE POOL
The traditional Chinese courtyard garden was an enclosed, intimate space for scholarly contemplation, often heightened by the tranquil presence of still, reflecting water.

WATER GARDEN DESIGN AS AN ART FORM

The Oriental style is one of the oldest and most influential in water gardening. The Chinese strove to imitate their natural landscape: like poetry or painting, gardening became an artistic emulation of natural form. Great care was taken in designing gardens in which water and rocks represented the central principles of *yin* and *yang*, their placing crucial in attaining harmony. From the 3rd century AD, the pattern for the Oriental garden, with a lake, island, arched bridges, and subtle planting, was established. By the early 15th century this had become an art form that was a source of inspiration worldwide.

In Japan, garden design was first influenced by Chinese culture; then, the philosophies of Buddhism and Shinto introduced a strong element of religious symbolism. While Japanese design is much admired and imitated in the West, few Westerners have succeeded in understanding the delicate precision that governs the placing and combining of plants, water, and rock, based on religious, historical, and romantic associations.

THEMED LANDSCAPE
At Coombe Wood in Dorset, England, the planting around this pond appears informal, yet is a skilful balance of Japanese maples, rhododendrons, and other evergreens, all classic components of Oriental schemes. A fountain animates the elegant statues of cranes and the matching pair of Oriental bridges and, in Japanese style, all is immaculately well-kept.

The Early Islamic Water Garden

In addition to containing water essential for practical uses, early Islamic water gardens provided the serenity of still water and the refreshment of gently splashing fountains. In common with the early Egyptians, their enclosed, walled gardens were designed to provide relief from the relentless heat of the sun. In contrast with that of the Far East, design was formal and non-representational, with tiling and elaborate stonework often taking the place of plants that would have used up precious water reserves. Gardens were often arranged in four divisions, intersected by canals representing the four rivers of Paradise.

Canal at Generalife, Granada
This narrow canal with its arching jets, a brimming dish fountain at its head, highlights the beauty of the stone and ceramic tiling used in this 13th-century Moorish garden.

The Spread of Islamic Influence

From the conquest of the Middle East, Islam spread through Egypt and North Africa and from there into southern Spain. Again, the arid climate necessitated water to be transported to gardens, to be used for decorative and practical purposes. Among the most outstanding water gardens are those at the fortress palace of Alhambra, in Granada, where Moorish gardens and surrounding buildings are subtly integrated. Water for the Alhambra, built in the mid-13th century on a hillside, had to be elevated by aqueduct from the river Darro.

Formal Courtyard
The talent for creating perfect gardens with limited water resources is found throughout the Islamic world. The interrelationship of restrained planting and architecture is enhanced by the gentle movement of running water. This small fountain and shallow basin and pool, central to the garden's design, is surprisingly economical with precious water.

The Islamic use of water in the garden was to make a significant impact in the gardens built by the Mogul emperors in northern India between the 15th and 18th centuries. Again, fountains and large sheets of still water were introduced to provide refreshment from the continual heat. Similarly, the gardens were divided into four by canals, which were surrounded by sunken flower beds and raised paths. Gardens such as those of the Taj Mahal and at Nishat Bagh took traditional Persian design to new heights, associating water with spectacular architecture and harnessing water pressure for aesthetic effect.

Moorish Influence in Modern America
The use of decorative materials rather than plants to frame water is equally practical in this dry Californian garden. A tiled pool is surrounded by brick terracing, whose abstract patterning is typical of Islamic art and architecture.

Ancient Rome

In contrast to the crisp simplicity and decorative functionality of Islamic gardens, records reveal that the Romans were early pioneers of the modern concept of ornamentality. Water was brought into the garden solely for the pleasure it gave, particularly when associated with lavish, well-tended planting. Many affluent Roman citizens became early "gentleman gardeners", taking a keen interest in cultivation techniques and in new plants brought back from far parts of the Empire. Statuary, not permitted in the Islamic world but central to the Roman system of beliefs, was often used further to ornament gardens and water features.

The Water Garden in Renaissance Italy

Rome also became a centre for the exuberant use of water that characterized the gardens of the Renaissance. The hilly terrain north of the city provided ample water pressure, making it an ideal location for water gardens that rapidly became ever grander in scale. Movement and sound could be exploited to the full, and fountain design was spectacular, often incorporating statues of human figures, animals, or mythological creatures to create dramatic tableaux. The Villa d'Este remains the most outstanding and imaginative example of the technical brilliance and extravagance of the period: ingenious hydraulics produce a pathway of 100 fountains, a water organ, and a spouting dragon.

Pepsico Gardens, New York
Throughout the world, designers now realise the benefits, long recognized in the Arab world, of introducing water as a cooling and refreshing element in public spaces.

Post-Renaissance Europe

The influence of the Italian Renaissance reached France in the latter part of the 15th century, when Charles VIII invaded Italy. However, it was not until

the 17th century that classical formality in France really came to the fore. Louis XIV's Versailles, designed by Le Notre, exemplified tasteful flamboyance, and was the model to which garden designers all over Europe aspired for the next century or so. No expense was spared to create an extravaganza of water in a garden setting. It was combined with sculpture and architecture, and in many cases with the creation of broad, elaborate parterres, in order to achieve grand formality.

Le Notre's work inspired other grandiose schemes in Europe. In Russia, his disciple Le Blond created a garden with water tumbling down marble stairways into a huge marble basin. In Spain, Louis XIV's grandson Philip V created a magnificent water garden at La Granja, with impressive fountains and cascades. At Herrenhausen, in Germany, water was used to animate and link formal areas within a strictly geometric pattern that epitomizes the more rigid contemporary German and Dutch styles.

STATELY STYLE
In Europe, ornamental gardening was for centuries practised purely for the pleasure of the wealthy; as technical and mechanical skills developed, water features became ever more powerful and elaborate, reflecting the status of their owners. By the mid-19th century, few large houses were without awe-inspiring jets and cascades to welcome and impress the visitor, as here at Herrenhausen in Germany.

A MORE NATURALISTIC APPROACH

During this period many formal water features were brilliantly executed in England, notably at Chatsworth, in Derbyshire. The break with the formal use of water came towards the middle of the 18th century, with the landscape movement in Great Britain. William Kent (1685–1748) was one of the great pioneers of the movement, using Classical buildings in the landscape to great effect. His management of water was his greatest skill, replacing formal features such as fountains with three-dimensional compositions of woodland, lawn, and water. Contrasts of light and shade superseded tight architectural form. Craggy waterfalls, grottoes, and other follies became popular, taking their cue from the Romanticism evident in Germany during the 18th century. Monet's garden at Giverny, combining extensive informal planting and stretches of water on which reflections, light and shade, and floating water lilies interplay, is a landmark in the movement towards planting rather than architecture, which was to gather momentum in the 20th century.

ENGLISH VERSATILITY
At Shute House in Dorset, a formal vista with statue is seen beyond a foreground of dense, informal waterside planting in a brilliant and inventive blending of styles.

WATER GARDENS IN THE AMERICAS

Water features began to make an impact in America at the turn of the 19th century, after the upheaval of the Civil War, in a period known as the "Country House Era". Private wealth enabled ornamental gardening to surge forward, and Islamic features were incorporated with the styles of the Renaissance and the French gardens of the late 16th to early 18th centuries, dominated by still pools and fountains. The Country House Era came to an end as planting became more significant. Gardens filled with bulbs, perennials, and annuals appeared as the domestic garden developed. In the period between the two wars, American gardens developed their own sense of identity, often based on abstract form and landscaping.

MONET'S GARDEN AT GIVERNY
This naturalistic pond with rustic bridge encapsulates the move towards informality that now characterizes most domestic gardens, where water serves to enhance the beauty and colour contrasts of luxuriant planting.

CONTEMPORARY WATER GARDENS

As ornamental gardening has become more accessible to a widening section of society, the average size of garden has decreased. Modern materials and techniques allow water features to be used in gardens on a small domestic scale. Perhaps the most essential development in the 20th-century water garden, though, has been the breakdown of the traditional differentiation between formal and informal styles. Elements may be freely borrowed from other cultures and eras, then combined and adapted to today's gardens in individualistic and innovative style, making water gardening one of the most exciting aspects of garden design.

WATER GARDEN DESIGNS

DESIGNING WITH WATER

RAISED DOUBLE POOL • LARGE FORMAL POOL
CONTAINER GARDENS
ORIENTAL-STYLE WATER GARDEN
COURTYARD POOL • INFORMAL POND FOR A TOWN GARDEN • MILLSTONE FOUNTAIN
WILDLIFE POND WITH BOG GARDEN • STREAM FOR TOWN OR COUNTRY GARDEN

ORIENTAL-STYLE WATER GARDEN *(LEFT)*
The careful placement of water, plants, rocks and other materials, the subtle use of colour and foliage, and the contemplative atmosphere of the Oriental garden make it a popular landscaping style.

DESIGNING WITH WATER

WATER FEATURES CAN BE accommodated in any garden, in either a town or country setting. Although the site may dictate certain constraints, it is surprising how flexible these limits are. The following pages feature examples of excellent water design in gardens large and small, in formal or informal style – some combining elements of both. All are different, yet all share a marvellous sense of the exceptional role water can play in a garden setting, having the potential to animate and transform a landscape or corner with sound and movement or with stillness and reflection, and above all creating settings for new and beautiful plants.

DECIDING ON A DESIGN

To be really satisfying, a water feature requires an initial and quite searching appraisal of what you intend it to bring to your garden. Unlike lawns and borders, which are relatively easy to enlarge, reduce, or alter in shape, a water feature is less easy to change once installed. Each of the features here succeeds through a mix of elements that interrelate, above all, to the satisfaction of the owner. Some use water to enhance the colours and textures of decorative materials, while in others the water is there to lure wildlife. Some reflect a keen sense of plantsmanship, while others use planting simply as a textural element, to break or highlight line and colour.

FORWARD PLANNING

A new garden provides the perfect opportunity to incorporate water in a new and complete design. There is a huge advantage, for example, in the construction of a pond if mechanical equipment is able to manoeuvre freely, achieving in a few hours

REFLECTING FEATURE
Waterside areas open up exciting planting opportunities: Gunnera manicata *is ideally placed where its huge leaves can be seen reflected in the water surface.*

ROCKY STREAM
A level garden can be landscaped to create a cascading stream; the new versions of small, self-contained submersible pumps are much easier than older models to install and maintain.

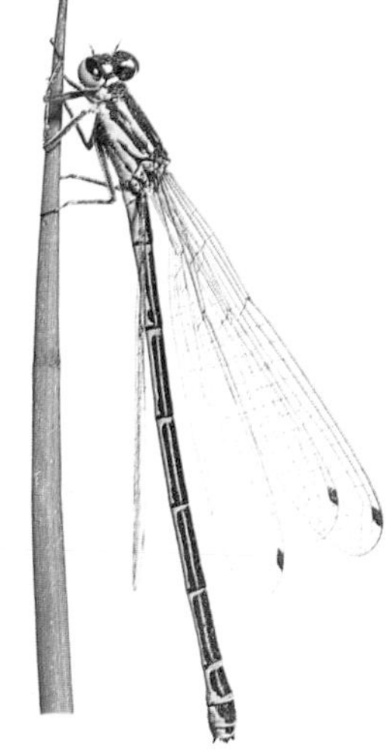

ATTRACTING WILDLIFE
For many, the sight of wildlife around a pond is one of the most rewarding features of a water garden. Providing a feature that is attractive to insects and other creatures needs thought at the planning stage.

LUSH LANDSCAPE
Creating a dedicated area of moist or boggy ground allows moisture-loving plants to grow with a vigour that is especially satisfying, and very practical, in areas where steady and gentle rainfall is, or is becoming, a luxury.

of excavation what would take days of hand digging. The placing of large boulders by mechanical means, as with those used in the Oriental-style garden *(see pp. 28–31)*, would be extremely difficult once the surrounding garden had been made, but they are an essential ingredient if the design is to work well.

But while a new garden is an ideal blank canvas, it is more common to want to add a water feature to an existing garden. There is no reason why this should not work well, provided that care is taken to integrate it well into its surroundings; a pond that suddenly appears in a border or lawn invariably looks like an afterthought or impulse decision. Try, therefore, to envisage and plan your water garden in its entirety from the start. A feature that is built and added to piecemeal over the years never has the assurance of one designed and installed as a whole.

LOOKING FOR INSPIRATION

When planning a design, although you may not be ready to purchase, visits to garden centres and aquatic specialists pay dividends: they often have demonstration gardens where new materials and the latest technology can be seen in action. Visit, also, as many gardens containing water as you can in search of ideas. Do not be daunted by large gardens, where abundant resources and protection from mature trees will have made it easy to create and maintain beautiful compositions. Scrutinize the detail, looking for attractive materials and the way these are juxtaposed with water and plants, then relate these to your own site and requirements.

DESIGNING WITH CONFIDENCE

While designs should not be overambitious (bearing in mind the limitations of your site and climate, and that the skills needed to install and maintain the feature should be comfortably within your capabilities), there is no need for designs to be timid. Successful designs demonstrate a strong theme; when executed with confidence, they are satisfying from the day the last stone or plant is in place, and improve with time as plants grow. The designs on the following pages have become expressions of their owners' individuality or interest, be it wildlife, plants, or a combination of elements. Their success reflects the thought, investment, and interest that the owner has put into them.

Raised Double Pool

In this mature, stylish garden the two interlinked pools in turn link the paved terrace area to the rest of the garden. Yet more skilful connections are made in the planting, with leaf shapes and colours echoed and blended perfectly in and around the water and beyond.

Interplay of Shapes and Colours

The general impression here is of calmness and continuity. The double pool, its formal edges softened by plants, is well built using materials that are in keeping with the paving and other stonework. Containers filled with alpines and tender perennials continue the gradation towards ground level. A pump sends water from the lower to the upper pool via a conduit in the shared wall and up through a millstone fountain. Skilful bricklaying is needed to construct double waterfalls of exactly equal height, as here: the slabs over which the water spills can be filed or ground down to perfect the effect. Flowering plants are few; harmony is created by confident positioning of complementary foliage – spiky irises, for example, are echoed by the white-variegated grass to the right, the red cordyline on the left, and the spikes of foxgloves and delphiniums in the bed beyond.

The Garden Plan

Seen from the house and terrace, the pool has its own surround of planting, which has largely been kept low so that views of the lawn and borders beyond are not blocked. Paving stones leading up the garden continue the theme of the terrace and stonework. The planting, using plenty of bold greenery, capitalizes on the backdrop of trees in neighbouring gardens.

PLANTING PLAN FOR THE RAISED POOLS

WITHIN THE POOLS, restrained planting leaves areas of open water, displaying gleaming pebbles on the pool floor. These are heaped up around planting baskets positioned in the lower pool, helping to disguise them and preventing soil from being dislodged. Underwater, small clumps of *Lagarosiphon major* and *Potamogeton crispus*, together with the splashing action of the fountain and waterfalls, keep the water oxygenated and clear. The soil surrounding these contained pools is not wet, but by using plants in these beds that are often seen in moist ground – willow, astilbes, hostas, ferns – and keeping them well-watered for lush growth, the illusion is created of natural waterside planting.

DYNAMIC PLANTING WITH FORMAL POND

This scheme is dominated by foliage: contrasting shades of green interspersed with bright patches of red, yellow, and purple. Water bubbles and trickles in the pools just enough to add movement, while not disturbing plants. A non-return valve prevents the upper pool draining through the delivery pipe when the pump is turned off.

SOFTENING LINES
Plants are positioned informally, so that they do not look too regimented against the rectangular shapes of the two pools. Vertical-leaved plants such as irises give height and break the lines of straight edges well.

KEY TO PLANTING PLAN

WATER PLANTS

1 *Lobelia* 'Compliment Blue' x 3
2 *Iris pseudacorus* 'Variegata' x 1
3 *Lobelia cardinalis* x 3
4 *Iris laevigata* 'Colchesterensis' x 2
5 *Aponogeton distachyos* x 3
6 *Iris laevigata* 'Snowdrift' x 3
7 *Acorus gramineus* 'Pusillus' x 3
8 *Lobelia* 'Queen Victoria' x 5
9 *Carex elata* 'Aurea' x 3
10 *Iris ensata* x 6
11 *Houttuynia cordata* 'Chameleon' x 3
12 *Eriophorum angustifolium* x 3
13 *Typha minima* x 3
14 *Iris laevigata* 'Dorothy' x 3
15 *Calla palustris* x 2
16 *Saururus cernuus* x 2
17 *Menyanthes trifoliata* x 3
18 *Eichhornia crassipes* x 5
19 *Caltha palustris* 'Flore Plena' x 2
20 *Houttuynia cordata* 'Flore Pleno' x 3
21 *Nymphaea* x *helvola* x 1
22 *Caltha palustris* x 2
23 *Juncus effusus* 'Spiralis' x 1

OTHER PLANTS

24 *Hedera helix* x 2
25 *Salix hastata* 'Wehrhahnii' x 1
26 *Viola odorata* x 3
27 *Potentilla fruticosa* 'Princess' x 1
28 *Astilbe* 'Sprite' x 1
29 *Asplenium scolopendrium* x 1
30 *Polystichum setiferum* 'Divisilobum Densum' x 1
31 *Lobelia* 'Cinnabar Rose' x 5
32 *Onoclea sensibilis* x 1
33 *Asplenium trichomanes* x 1
34 *Lysimachia nummularia* x 3
35 *Uvularia grandiflora* x 3
36 *Epimedium* x *youngianum* 'Roseum' x 2
37 *Omphalodes cappadocica* 'Starry Eyes' x 1
38 *Hepatica nobilis* 'Rubra Plena' x 3
39 *Hosta venusta* x 3
40 *Persicaria tenuicaulis* x 3
41 *Rubus pentalobus* x 1
42 *Geranium macrorrhizum* 'Album' x 3
43 *Paeonia mlokosewitschii* x 1
44 *Astilbe* 'Deutschland' x 5
45 *Yucca flaccida* x 1
46 *Astilbe* 'Irrlicht' x 10
47 *Hemerocallis* 'Frans Hals' x 1

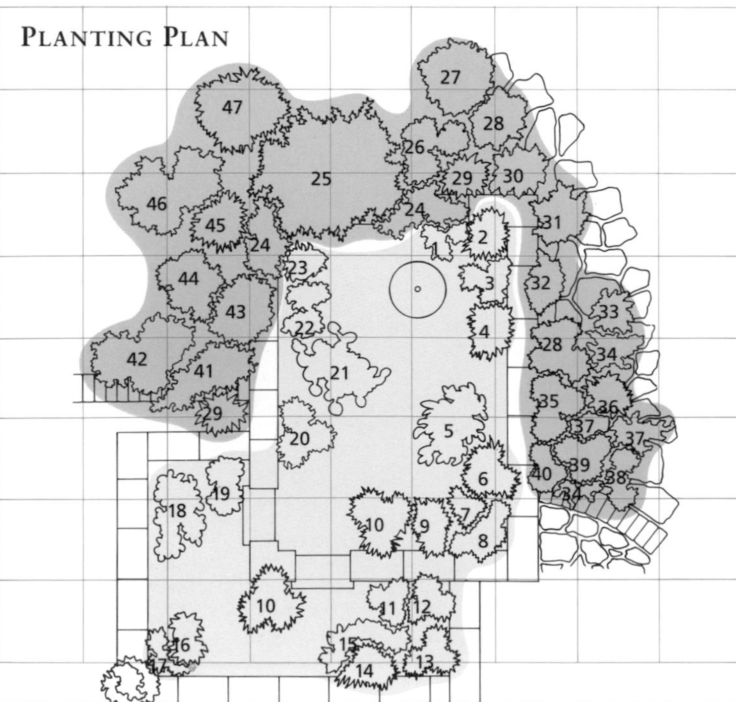

Salix hastata 'Wehrhahnii'
Deciduous shrub for free-draining or moist soil. White catkins are borne on polished stems in early spring. Oval, green leaves then appear. Propagate from cuttings, semi-ripe in summer or hardwood in winter. H and S 1.5m (5 ft).

Millstone Fountain
Millstones are attractive surrounds for fountainheads. They can be used within pools or over concealed reservoirs *(see p. 114)*.

Lobelia cardinalis (cardinal flower)
Herbaceous, short-lived, clump-forming perennial producing tall spikes of two-lipped, scarlet flowers from mid- to late summer. Stems are usually smooth, and the lance-shaped leaves either fresh green or reddish-bronze. This plant dislikes very wet winter conditions and, if grown in boggy soil, must be lifted before the onset of winter. Propagate from seed or by division in spring. H 1m (3ft), S 25cm (10in).

Houttuynia cordata 'Flore Pleno'
Vigorous, deciduous, spreading perennial marginal plant that grows well in shallow water or moist soil, where the foliage is not submerged. It is a useful ground-cover plant. The leaves are leathery and aromatic, and small, white flowers are produced in summer. Grown in soil, it may benefit from a protective winter mulch in cold climates. Separate new plantlets that root from spreading stems in spring. H 10cm (4in), S indefinite.

LARGE FORMAL POOL

FLOWERHEADS AND SPIKY LEAVES are lit up by late afternoon, late summer sunshine, while this formal pool, earlier in the day a mirror for the sky, assumes mysterious depths, with glimpses of submerged plants and fish. Weathered stone, a trickling fountain, and plants that mingle and tumble over path edges combine to give a languid air of faded grandeur.

CLASSIC SIMPLICITY

This is a design that perfectly combines the surfaces of water and stone and the soft colour palette of plants that are suited to both aquatic and arid conditions. The large, concrete-lined pool was built some time ago using the skilled and laborious "shuttering" method *(see p. 91)*. Today, new materials allow a more easily constructed concrete block shell to be covered with a thin layer of cement mixed with reinforcing fibres *(see p. 90)*, making a strong and waterproof lining. The small, gently brimming fountain sits within its own small concrete pool, completely independent of its larger neighbour.

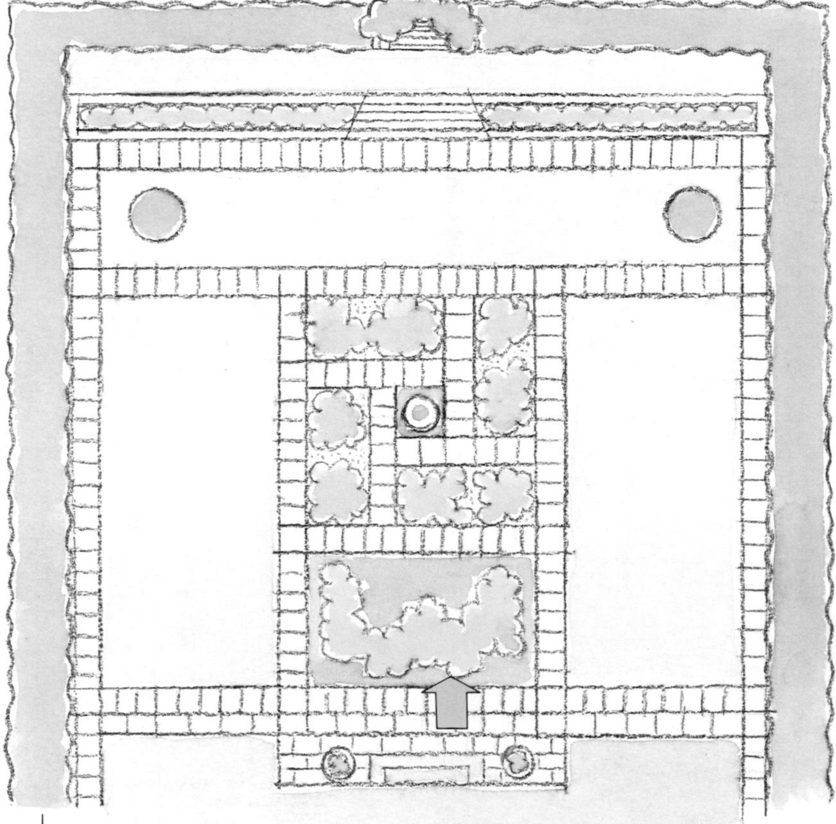

THE GARDEN PLAN

Classically European yet suitable for a range of climates, this design echoes that of grand country houses, where a formal pool was often situated near to the house. Regular paths, trimmed lawns, and an enclosing screen of well-kept formal hedging contribute to the "stately home" illusion.

Planting Plan for the Large Formal Pool

In the dry beds surrounding the small pool, a planting palette of pinks and greys is set off by natural stone, water, and the refreshing greens of the aquatic plants. All the plants chosen for these beds tolerate arid conditions, and enjoy the reflected heat from the paving. In the large pool, fish may take refuge in the shade of several water lilies. Together, beds and pool form a feature that is easy to maintain, and where the plants thrive even in the hottest summer. Plants in the dry beds and, in the pool, the oxygenating plants have been allowed to spread informally, while the water lilies and marginal plants are contained in planting baskets. Marginal shelves are easy to incorporate in concrete pools, allowing a shallower planting depth. Plants in baskets can also be perched on stacks of bricks, which allows more flexibility in moving plants around; this can be convenient when perfecting the final look of a pool. In cool climates, planting baskets also allow, as here, tender plants such as cannas to be lifted from the pool and stored over winter to protect them from frost damage.

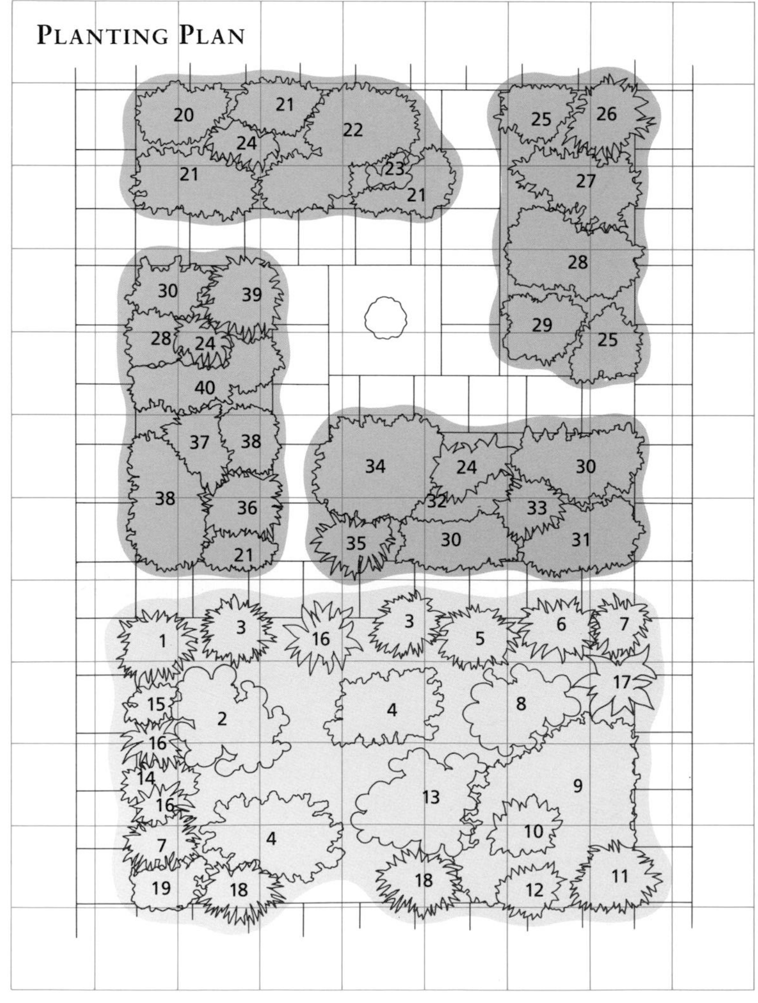

Influence of the Past

Flat terraces make excellent settings for formal pools and beds surrounded by wide paths, traditionally sited near the house in large country-house gardens. Here more relaxed, low-maintenance planting has replaced the labour-intensive, formal parterres of the past. This arrangement of pool and planting beds could also easily be reduced in scale for a smaller, similarly sheltered patio or terrace, using plants either singly or in groups of two or three instead of the larger, intermingling drifts planted here.

Regular Shapes
A small, square, unplanted pool echoes the shape of the pavers yet forms a small oasis in the middle of the dry beds and pathways.

Iris laevigata 'Snowdrift'
Deciduous perennial forming upright clumps of smooth, swordlike leaves and sparsely branched, erect stems that each bear, in early to mid-summer, two to four beardless, double white flowers. All cultivars of *Iris laevigata* will also grow well in permanently moist soil. Propagate by dividing rhizomes in late summer. H 60cm–1m (2–3ft), S indefinite, water depth to 7–10cm (3–4in).

Key to Planting Plan

WATER PLANTS
1 *Iris laevigata* 'Snowdrift' x 1
2 *Nymphaea* 'Escarboucle' x 1
3 *Schoenoplectus lacustris* x 2
4 *Lagarosiphon major* x 2
5 *Iris laevigata* 'Variegata' x 1
6 *Pontederia cordata* x 1
7 *Iris sibirica* x 3
8 *Nymphaea* 'William Falconer' x 1
9 *Myriophyllum verticillatum* x 1
10 *Menyanthes trifoliata* x 2
11 *Iris ensata* x 1
12 *Lysichiton camtschatcensis* x 1
13 *Nymphaea* 'Marliacea Albida' x 1
14 *Orontium aquaticum* x 1
15 *Caltha palustris* x 1
16 *Canna flaccida* x 3
17 *Canna glauca* x 1
18 *Glyceria maxima* var. *variegata* x 2
19 *Juncus effusus* 'Spiralis' x 1

OTHER PLANTS
20 *Lychnis coronaria* Oculata Group x 1
21 *Dianthus* 'La Bourboule' x 6
22 *Lavandula angustifolia* x 5
23 *Colchicum speciosum* x 1
24 *Allium christophii* x 7
25 *Saxifraga cotyledon* x 5
26 *Iris* 'Matinata' x 1
27 *Ptilostemon afer* x 1
28 *Erodium manescaui* x 3
29 *Centaurea hypoleuca* 'John Coutts' x 1
30 *Diascia flanaganii* x 4
31 *Dianthus* 'Pink Jewel' x 1
32 *Silene vulgaris* subsp. *maritima* x 1
33 *Allium giganteum* x 3
34 *Artemisia alba* 'Canescens' x 1
35 *Iris* 'Brannigan' x 1
36 *Iris* 'Langport Wren' x 1
37 *Dierama pulcherrimum* x 1
38 *Dianthus* 'Old Square Eyes' x 4
39 *Iris sibirica* x 1
40 *Diascia rigescens* x 3

Iris laevigata 'Variegata'
Deciduous perennial forming clumps of swordlike leaves and sparsely branched, erect stems that each bear, in early to mid-summer, two to four blue, beardless flowers. This cultivar has variegated leaves; there are others with different flower colours. Will grow in moist soil. Propagate by dividing rhizomes in late summer.
H 60cm–1m (2–3ft), S indefinite, water depth to 7–10cm (3–4in).

Canna glauca
Rhizomatous perennial with exotic leaves and showy, pale yellow flower spikes. Given full sun, it grows well in shallow water but in cool climates (where it is also a popular summer bedding plant) it must not overwinter in water, but be lifted and stored as for plants growing in soil. Thrives in a rich, loamy planting medium. Propagate by dividing rhizomes in spring.
H to 1.2m (4ft), S 60cm (2ft).

CONTAINER GARDENS

A MINIATURE POND in a pot, barrel, trough, or sink can be the central feature on a terrace or balcony, or tucked into a corner of a garden. Watertight containers *(see pp. 94–95)* can be used in cool climates to make indoor pools for tender plants such as lotuses and tropical water lilies, and also provide a still, humid atmosphere for delicate plants such as *Colocasia*. It is surprising how many plants can be fitted in. There are both tropical and hardy dwarf water lilies. Include tall plants to prevent a squat appearance; paper reeds *(Cyperus)*, for example, grow well in containers. Containers also restrain the growth of some beautiful but, in open water, highly invasive plants, such as *Eichhornia* and *Azolla*. Remember that oxygenating plants will still be necessary.

FIBREGLASS PLANTER

This small, lightweight tub is the centrepiece of a sun room used to grow and display frost-tender plants. Warmth and the humidifying effect of the water intensify the scent of the water lily and other flowers. *Myriophyllum* is a good choice of oxgenator, as it also contributes some visible attractive foliage.

PLANTER IN ITS SETTING
A backdrop of glossy ficus leaves and vivid bougainvillea heightens the tropical look of this container planting. Asparagus fern and a cycad blend with the trailing, feathery stems of Myriophyllum.

Eichhornia crassipes
(water hyacinth)
Evergreen or semi-evergreen free-floater that may root in muddy shallows, forming rafts of foliage on spongy stalks. May survive light frosts, but only flowers in warmer conditions. Separate new plantlets in spring or summer. S indefinite.

PLANTING PLAN

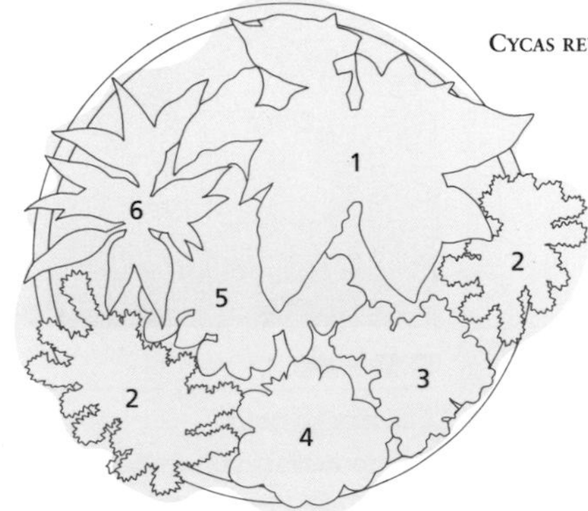

KEY TO PLANTING PLAN

WATER PLANTS
1 *Colocasia esculenta* 'Fontanesii' x 1
2 *Myriophyllum aquaticum* x 2
3 *Pistia stratiotes* x 1
4 *Nymphaea mexicana* x 1
5 *Eichhornia crassipes* x 1
6 *Thalia dealbata* x 1

Nymphaea mexicana (banana water lily)
Species that freely produces fragrant, deep yellow flowers that open around noon. Leaves, olive-green when young, are splashed with purple or brown. Can spread rapidly in open ponds. S 1–1.2m (3–4ft), water depth 45–60cm (18–24in).

HALF-BARREL

Prepared barrels *(see pp. 94–95)* make excellent miniature ponds. They can be free-standing, surrounded by other plants and perhaps a few cobbles at the base, or partially or completely sunk into the ground, which gives some frost protection. A variety of planting depths has been achieved here by standing planting baskets on brick stacks of various heights, enabling both marginal and deeper-water plants to be grown. To maximize space, tall, slender plants have been used, with attractive straplike leaves or unusual stems, such as the *Juncus*, *Isolepis*, and *Equisetum*, leaving room for a miniature water lily and free-floating plants; these should be thinned regularly.

BARREL IN ITS SETTING
In this sunny corner, cheerful planting surrounds the barrel with pelargoniums and fuchsias. Bidens and plumbago enjoy the sun, while a golden grass lights up the shadier side and echoes the variegated leaves of the Acorus.

PLANTING PLAN

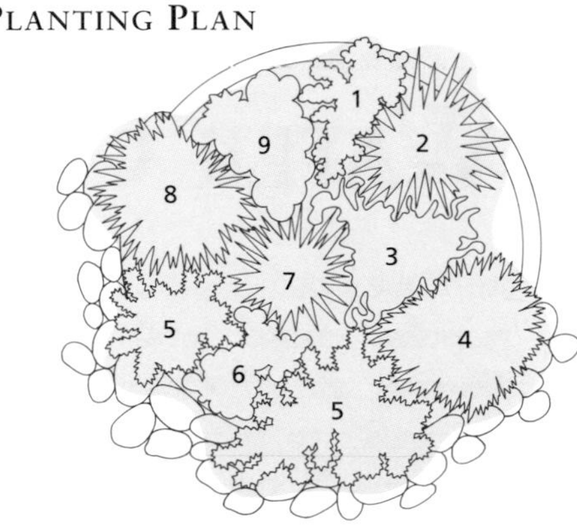

KEY TO PLANTING PLAN

WATER PLANTS
1 *Azolla filiculoides* x 1
2 *Acorus gramineus* 'Variegatus' x 1
3 *Juncus effusus* 'Spiralis' x 1
4 *Isolepis cernua* x 1
5 *Myriophyllum aquaticum* x 2
6 *Hydrocharis morsus-ranae* x 1
7 *Equisetum japonicum* x 1
8 *Acorus calamus* 'Variegatus' x 1
9 *Nymphaea* x *helvola* x 1

Juncus effusus 'Spiralis' (corkscrew rush)
Contorted variant of evergreen, tuft-forming perennial, which grows well in shallow water or moist soil. Its semi-prostrate, dark green, leafless stems twist and curl. Dense, greenish brown flower tufts form in mid-summer. Propagate by division in spring. H 1m (3ft), S 60cm (2ft).

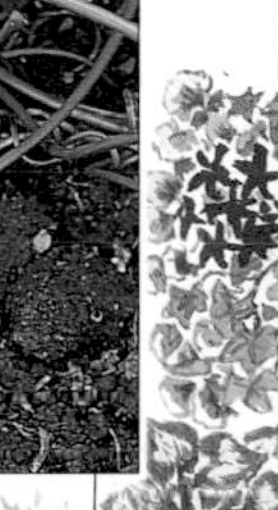

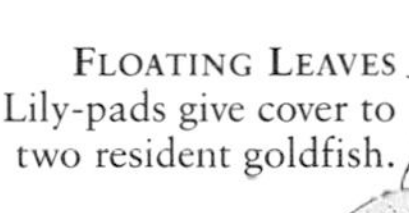

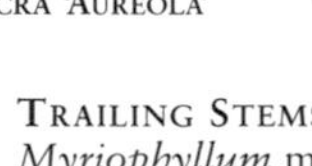

Myriophyllum aquaticum (parrot's feather)
Deciduous perennial for any depth of water, with stems covered in finely divided leaves. These can grow to up to 2m (6ft), becoming woody at the base, and will extend above the surface of shallow water, scrambling and softening water edges. Thin regularly. Propagate from cuttings. S indefinite.

Oriental-style Water Garden

The Oriental-style garden is probably the most popular exotic landscaping style in the West. Moving and still water, rocks, and gravel surfaces have major roles to play in its representation of nature. There is great subtlety in the layout and planting, with space, light, shadow, subtle harmonies and contrasts of colour, and viewing angles all given great consideration.

Balance and Harmony

In this garden, although all the elements seem artlessly placed, a perfect balance exists between the simplicity of the partly raised formal pool and the more naturalistic pond. It is an ambitious design, lit up at night, involving rock terracing and heavy boulders that need foundations and plenty of padding beneath to protect the butyl liner. While the liner has been taken under rocks in the foreground to create an informal outline with planting pockets, the raked shingle terrace on which the bonsai sits needs a rigid edge for support; a solid retaining wall lies behind the liner on this side. The liner is also taken up under the timber decking *(see pp. 130–131)*, so that it seems to overhang the water.

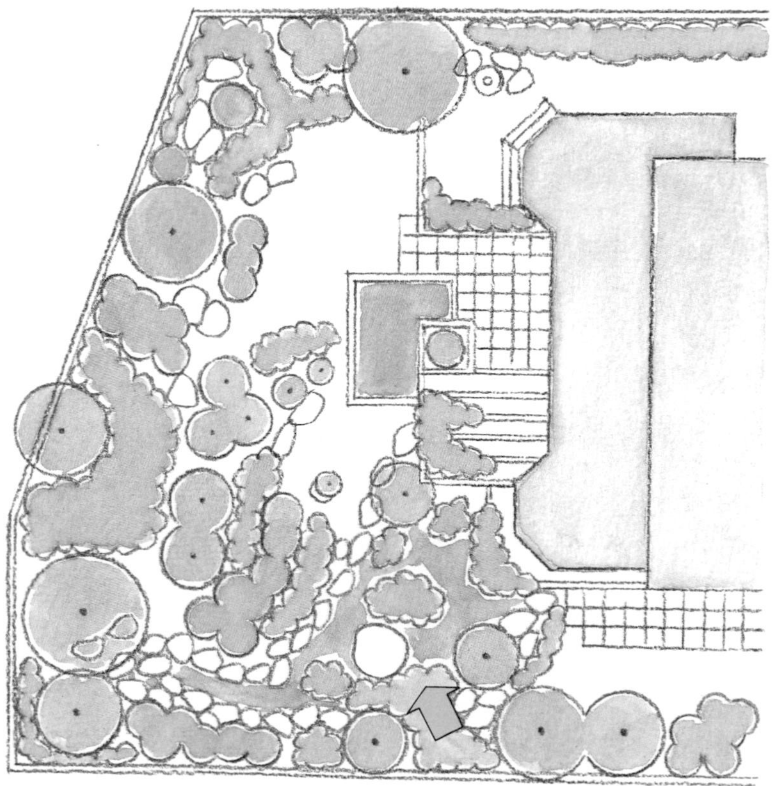

The Garden Plan

The overall plan demonstrates the importance placed on views from the windows and decking terrace around the house. Although the areas of clear water are small, they open up this enclosed garden by bringing reflections of the sky and surrounding trees into a very private domain.

PLANTING PLAN FOR THE ORIENTAL POND

THE PLANTING SCHEME is low key, with the occasional burst of bright colour. Trees and plants are set out asymmetrically in order to imitate the wildness of nature. Planted terraces slope up to tall trees at the perimeter of the garden, providing both privacy and shelter. While soft greens and browns predominate, harmonizing with the colours and textures of the brick, gravel, and boulders and the wooden fences, decking, and pergola, the permanency of the large rocks and the evergreens is given greater impact by the scattering of occasional flowers that help to highlight the passing of the seasons. Rocks lead the eye across the pool to the planting beyond; this line of stepping stones also extends across the gravel, kept free of plants because, in Japanese gardens, these carefully raked dry areas are a symbolic representation of water.

PLANTING FOR EFFECT

Mountain trees such as rowans and silver birch look appropriate among the upper rocks, while the elegant foliage of the Japanese maples gives a classically eastern feel. A dry island *(see pp. 80–81)* in the pond near the pergola pillar enables one of the maples to be planted so that it appears to float on the water surface.

Foliage colour is critical in achieving the subtle variations essential to Oriental schemes, where flower colour is traditionally limited. The pinky-purple and red tones provided by azaleas, rhododendrons, and a Chinese wisteria are complemented by the maples. The oxygenating plants here are all completely submerged, leaving the water surface clear for the clean outlines of lily-pads and the leaves of water hawthorn *(Aponogeton distachyos)*.

ENCLOSING OPEN SPACE

The formal pool is clear of plants to give a still, reflective surface, complementing the flat raked shingle. However, around the informal pond and leading up the rock terracing and on the fences, dense planting enfolds the open space.

Polystichum setiferum 'Divisilobum Densum'

Evergreen or semi-evergreen fern with soft, spreading, finely divided fronds that are white-scaled when young and unfurling, then mature to a matt mid-green. Remove faded fronds regularly. Propagate by division in spring. H 60cm (24in), S 45cm (18in).

Hosta undulata var. *albomarginata*, syn. *H.* 'Thomas Hogg'

Clump-forming, shade-tolerant perennial grown chiefly for its foliage. The leaves have irregular cream or white margins, sometimes extending to produce a streaked effect running toward the midrib. Slender-stalked, pale violet flowers are produced in summer. Prone to slug and snail damage. Propagate by division in early spring. H 75cm (30in), S 1m (3ft).

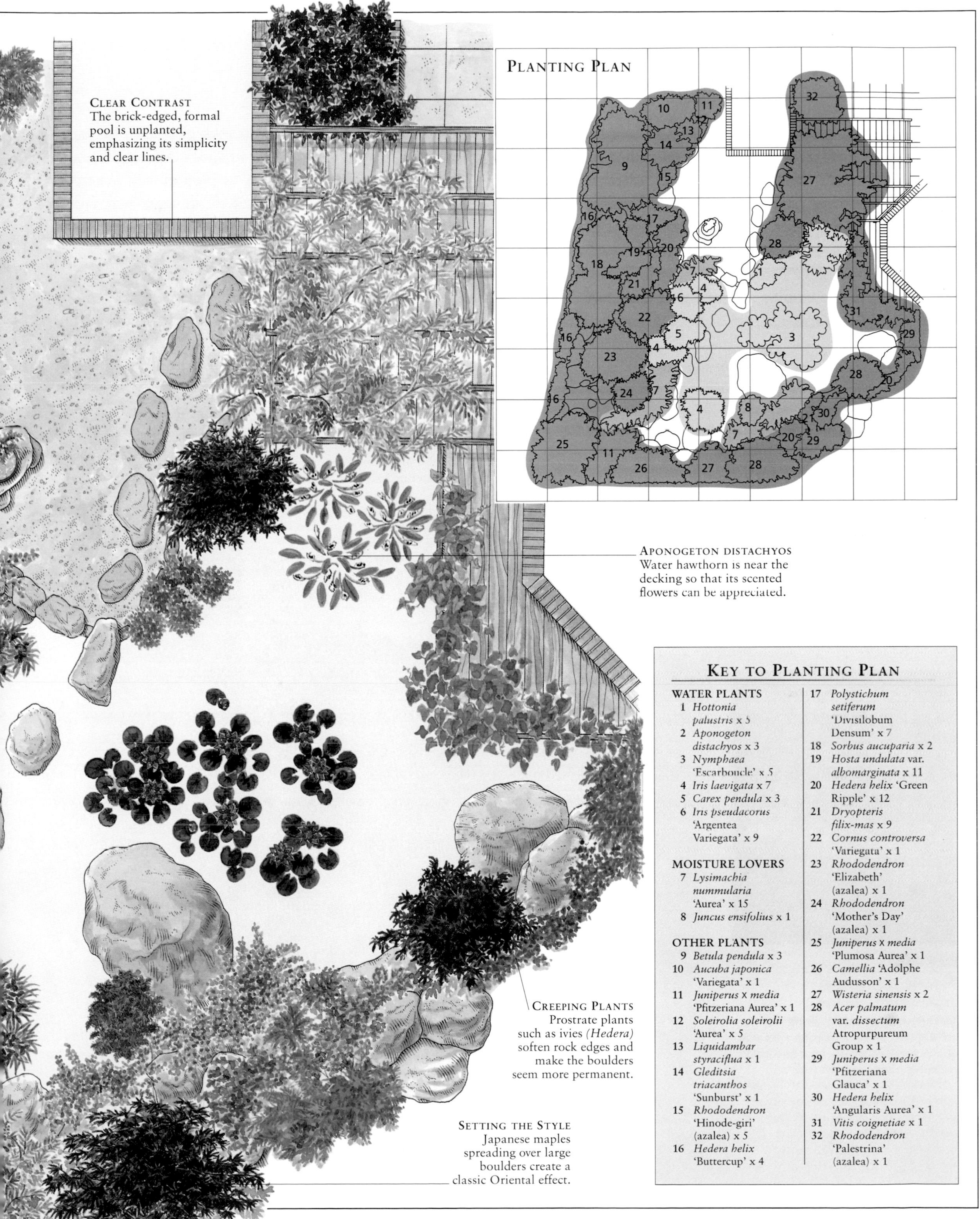

CLEAR CONTRAST
The brick-edged, formal pool is unplanted, emphasizing its simplicity and clear lines.

APONOGETON DISTACHYOS
Water hawthorn is near the decking so that its scented flowers can be appreciated.

CREEPING PLANTS
Prostrate plants such as ivies *(Hedera)* soften rock edges and make the boulders seem more permanent.

SETTING THE STYLE
Japanese maples spreading over large boulders create a classic Oriental effect.

KEY TO PLANTING PLAN

WATER PLANTS

1 *Hottonia palustris* x 5
2 *Aponogeton distachyos* x 3
3 *Nymphaea* 'Escarboucle' x 5
4 *Iris laevigata* x 7
5 *Carex pendula* x 3
6 *Iris pseudacorus* 'Argentea Variegata' x 9

MOISTURE LOVERS

7 *Lysimachia nummularia* 'Aurea' x 15
8 *Juncus ensifolius* x 1

OTHER PLANTS

9 *Betula pendula* x 3
10 *Aucuba japonica* 'Variegata' x 1
11 *Juniperus* x *media* 'Pfitzeriana Aurea' x 1
12 *Soleirolia soleirolii* 'Aurea' x 5
13 *Liquidambar styraciflua* x 1
14 *Gleditsia triacanthos* 'Sunburst' x 1
15 *Rhododendron* 'Hinode-giri' (azalea) x 5
16 *Hedera helix* 'Buttercup' x 4
17 *Polystichum setiferum* 'Divisilobum Densum' x 7
18 *Sorbus aucuparia* x 2
19 *Hosta undulata* var. *albomarginata* x 11
20 *Hedera helix* 'Green Ripple' x 12
21 *Dryopteris filix-mas* x 9
22 *Cornus controversa* 'Variegata' x 1
23 *Rhododendron* 'Elizabeth' (azalea) x 1
24 *Rhododendron* 'Mother's Day' (azalea) x 1
25 *Juniperus* x *media* 'Plumosa Aurea' x 1
26 *Camellia* 'Adolphe Audusson' x 1
27 *Wisteria sinensis* x 2
28 *Acer palmatum* var. *dissectum* Atropurpureum Group x 1
29 *Juniperus* x *media* 'Pfitzeriana Glauca' x 1
30 *Hedera helix* 'Angularis Aurea' x 1
31 *Vitis coignetiae* x 1
32 *Rhododendron* 'Palestrina' (azalea) x 1

Courtyard Pool

THIS SMALL GARDEN has been transformed by a pond which dominates the limited ground space, yet opens up the vertical dimension of the courtyard, adding another planting level to the surrounding beds and trellising. A pool such as this, where the edging doubles as a path, must have solid walls; as the pool is small, a concrete block shell waterproofed with flexible liner *(see pp. 78–79)* is the easiest construction method. The floor need not be concreted, but a central patch of hardcore foundation enables strong concealed brick plinths to be built *(see pp. 120–121)* to support an archipelago of "floating" stepping stones. A unified colour scheme and continuity in the materials used prevents a fussy look, always a danger in small spaces. The pavers are softened by marginal plants in the water. Careful maintenance, removing faded or untidy foliage, and thinning and dividing plants whenever they threaten to crowd the pool, will preserve the clean lines of this cooling retreat.

Planting Plan for the Courtyard

Courtyards are often warm and sheltered, enabling a wide range of plants to be grown, but it helps to keep the planting restrained in such a small space, allowing areas of clear water and paving to open up the design. Vertical-leaved plants enhance the clean, straight lines of the paving and the still water surface, while the lily-pads echo the stepping stones and the curved contours of the Ali Baba pot. The stepping stones also make the water plants accessible and easy to maintain.

❋❋❋

Typha minima

Deciduous perennial forming slender tufts of elegant foliage at the water's edge. Rust-brown flower spikes in late summer mature into decorative, cylindrical seed heads. Although happy in shallow water, it also grows well in wet soil. Propagate in spring from seed or by division. H 60cm (2ft), S 30cm (12in), water depth to 15cm (6in).

Repeated Plants
Repeated use of a small selection of plants helps to tie the planting scheme together.

Plants in Baskets
Marginal plants in planting baskets are supported on brick stacks to obtain the correct planting depth, allowing the water lily to enjoy the full depth of the pool.

❋❋❋

Myosotis scorpioides
(water forget-me-not)

Deciduous, marginal, perennial wildflower with a creeping rhizome. Stems are first prostrate, then erect, forming sprawling mounds of narrow, mid-green leaves. Flowers in early to mid-summer, sometimes in two flushes; the loose clusters of small, bright blue flowers have a central eye of pink, yellow, or white. H 15–22cm (6–9in), S 30cm (12in), water depth 0–15cm (0–6in).

POTENTIAL FOR VARIETY
While the strong design of the formal pool with its stepping stones is permanent, the plants in their baskets could be moved around or substituted to vary the effect and extend the season of interest. Changing the colour of the trellis and the colour-washed pot would also dramatically alter the mood.

KEY TO PLANTING PLAN

WATER PLANTS
1 *Iris sibirica* x 3
2 *Nymphaea* 'Gladstoneana' x 1
3 *Lobelia cardinalis* x 1
4 *Myosotis scorpioides* x 1
5 *Iris pseudacorus* x 1
6 *Schoenoplectus lacustris* subsp. *tabernaemontani* 'Albescens' x 1
7 *Iris pseudacorus* 'Variegata' x 1
8 *Typha minima* x 1
9 *Carex elata* 'Aurea' x 2

OTHER PLANTS
10 *Cryptomeria japonica* 'Spiralis' x 2
11 *Anthemis punctata* subsp. *cupaniana* x 1
12 *Sisyrinchium striatum* 'Aunt May' x 3
13 *Hosta fortunei* var. *aureomarginata* x 1
14 *Elaeagnus* x *ebbingei* x 1
15 *Hosta* 'Hadspen Blue' x 1
16 *Iris pallida* 'Variegata' x 1

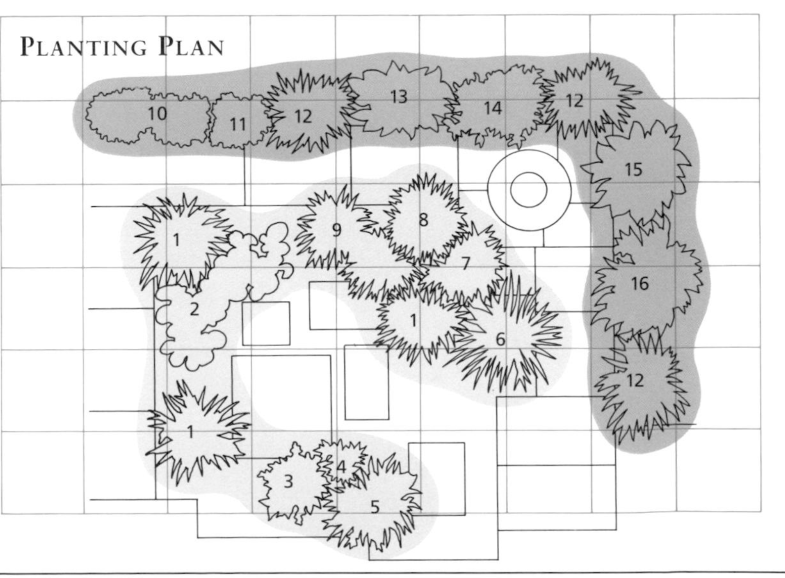

INFORMAL POND FOR A TOWN GARDEN

THIS TOWN GARDEN has been transformed by an informal pond and lush planting into a green paradise. While drifts of plants seem to spill down from the verandah to the poolside and merge around it, the tended lawn and clean lines of the well-scrubbed pebbles and decking prevent any sense of neglect.

A VIEW FOR ALL SEASONS

Planting opportunities have been maximized at the waterside by using a flexible liner to form not only a pool with a variety of planting levels, but also wide areas of damp planting ground around it *(see p. 78)*. In summer, the graduated heights of aquatic plants and vigorously-growing moisture-lovers combine to produce a verdant oasis. Lighting *(see pp. 124–125)* allows the feature to be enjoyed as the long evenings darken. However, on winter days, the view from the house windows skips over the poolside planting, now not at its best, to the more resilient trees and shrubs around the lawn and beyond, overturning the usual received wisdom that ponds belong at the bottom of the garden.

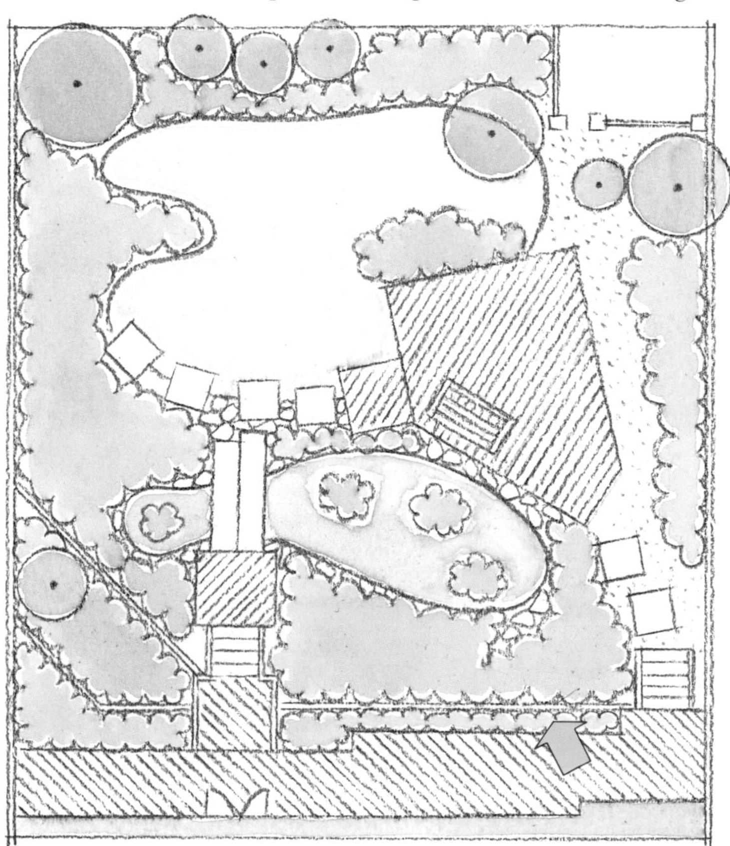

THE GARDEN PLAN
Curving lines, distinct planting areas, and the matching, weathered shades of decking, steps, bridge, and bench are crucial to making this garden seem much bigger than it really is. Steps on the right, with a gravel path leading to the utility area, give more practical access between house and garden.

Planting Plan for the Informal Pond

This water feature derives its impact from the skilful choice and placing of plants against the glassy, still water surface and the subtle colours and textures of the hard landscaping materials. Plants and pebbles leading gradually down into the pond, and the echoed roundness of the cobbles and lily-pads, blur the distinction between land and water. Plants with striking foliage, such as gunnera and hostas, are interplanted with soft, feathery ferns, sword-like irises, and slender grasses. These form a predominantly rich, green canvas persisting throughout the season on which vivid splashes of colour appear: the yellows of irises, ligularias and marsh marigolds, scarlet *Geum* 'Borisii' and the plumes of a crimson astilbe, and, in the water, a sequence of white, red, and magenta-toned water lilies.

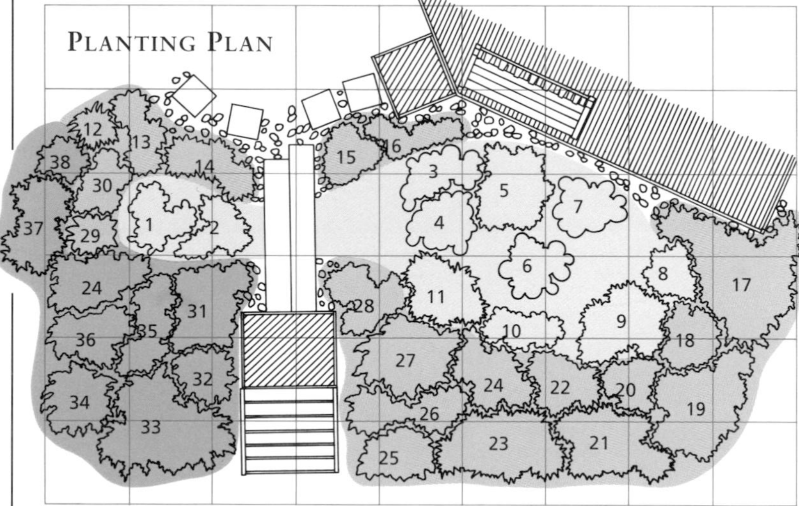

Key to Planting Plan

WATER PLANTS

1. *Hydrocharis morsus-ranae* x 3
2. *Callitriche hermaphroditica* x 3
3. *Nymphaea* 'Attraction' x 1
4. *Nymphaea* 'Firecrest' x 1
5. *Lagarosiphon major* x 7
6. *Nymphaea* 'Laydekeri Fulgens' x 1
7. *Nymphaea* 'Marliacea Albida' x 1
8. *Scrophularia auriculata* 'Variegata' x 3
9. *Iris laevigata* x 6
10. *Caltha palustris* x 3
11. *Iris pseudacorus* 'Variegata' x 5

MOISTURE LOVERS

12. *Glyceria maxima* var. *variegata* x 1
13. *Hosta ventricosa* 'Alba' x 3
14. *Hosta fortunei* var. *albopicta* x 3
15. *Geum* 'Borisii' x 3
16. *Astilbe* 'Fanal' x 4
17. *Lysimachia nummularia* x 10
18. *Rheum palmatum* x 1
19. *Filipendula ulmaria* 'Aurea' x 8
20. *Osmunda regalis* x 3
21. *Miscanthus sinensis* 'Gracillimus' x 6
22. *Carex pendula* x 3
23. *Miscanthus sinensis* 'Zebrinus' x 7
24. *Matteuccia struthiopteris* x 5
25. *Ligularia dentata* 'Desdemona' x 1
26. *Ligularia* 'The Rocket' x 2
27. *Gunnera tinctoria* x 1
28. *Onoclea sensibilis* x 3
29. *Hosta sieboldiana* var. *elegans* x 1
30. *Heuchera sanguinea* x 5

OTHER PLANTS

31. *Origanum vulgare* 'Aureum' x 7
32. *Juniperus* x *media* 'Pfitzeriana Aurea' x 1
33. *Fargesia murieliae* x 3
34. *Cedrus deodara* x 1
35. *Alchemilla mollis* x 3
36. *Dryopteris filix-mas* x 3
37. *Fatsia japonica* x 2
38. *Chelidonium majus* 'Flore Pleno' x 1

Vibrant Colours and Strong Forms

This is a garden of textures, deriving its impact from the range of edging materials used and the skilful choice of plants. To ensure that the plants complement rather than compete with each other, all but the very largest plants are in clumps of three or more, allowing the character of even the most delicate specimen to be clearly determined.

Pebble Beach
The pebble beach *(see pp. 80–81)* gives wildlife access to the water's edge, to be viewed undisturbed from the verandah.

Terraced Beds
On the "dry" side of the steps, terracing brings the plants up to form a screen between the verandah and the neighbouring garden.

❄❄❄

Matteuccia struthiopteris (shuttlecock fern)
Deciduous, rhizomatous fern that can be grown in normal soil or in moist ground. Dark brown, fertile innermost fronds stand erect in the centre, surrounded by lance-shaped, sterile fronds, 1–1.2m (3–4ft) in length, that spread outwards like the feathers of a shuttlecock. Propagate by division in autumn or winter. H 1m (3ft), S 45cm (18in).

TIMBER DECKING
Decking made from planks or preformed timber tiles *(see p. 130)* is best set above rather than level with the water surface, to prevent it becoming wet and allow rain to drain away.

Nymphaea 'Attraction'
Fully hardy with oval leaves that are light bronze when young, turning dark green in maturity. The cup-like, then star-shaped flowers have inner petals of a rich, deep garnet, and slightly lighter outer petals surrounding orange stamens. To propagate water lilies, *see pp. 162–163*. S 1.2–1.5m (4–5ft), water depth 37–90cm (15–36in).

Ligularia 'The Rocket'
Clump-forming herbaceous perennial with dark green leaves with deeply-cut, jagged edges, supported on dark stems. Narrow spikes of small, lemon-yellow flowers, also on dark stems, are produced in late summer. Prefers a site with deep, fertile soil, and a mulch around the base to help prevent moisture loss and wilting on bright, windy days. Propagate from seed or by division.
H 1.2–1.8m (4–6ft), S 1m (3ft).

Caltha palustris (marsh marigold, kingcup)
Deciduous, hardy perennial that grows freely alongside streams and ditches in the northern hemisphere. In spring it produces clusters of waxy, cup-shaped, bright golden-yellow flowers, 2.5cm (1in) across, held above smooth, deep green leaves. Propagate from seed or by division in spring or early autumn.
H 60cm (24in), S 45cm (18in), water depth to 15cm (6in).

MILLSTONE FOUNTAIN

RESERVOIR FEATURES pump water from a sunken or concealed container up through a decorative outlet such as a millstone or pile of cobbles, spilling and draining back into the reservoir *(see pp. 112–115)*. They are simple and effective water features for the smallest spaces, working well either as a tiny garden's main element or as an unexpected corner in a larger one. Here, in an area that is no larger than 2m (6ft) square, there is refreshment, sound, and movement. The simple informality is carefully crafted, using low-growing plants in the foreground that benefit from the misting effect of the fountain and the moisture-retentive "mulch" of cobbles. While the dry millstone on the left is real, the one forming the fountain is of textured fibreglass. Such features are easy to manoeuvre and install, and place less strain on the reservoir structure beneath; they are often available in kits, together with a suitable pump. The strength of the pump determines whether the water bubbles gently or spurts from its setting. Varying the depth of the water in the reservoir changes the volume and quality of the sound created.

A TRANQUIL CORNER
This carefully composed water feature does not require full sun; its charm lies in cool, restful greens and the contrast of the plants with the shapes and textures of the cobbles, millstones, and seat. The transition of colour from dry to wet cobbles highlights even further the beauty of natural materials, particularly when wet.

Composition in Green

Unity has been achieved in this small and subtle planting plan by using similarly-toned greens in a variety of shades. Darker colour in the background graduates to brighter foliage in the foreground, creating an inviting rather than oppressive atmosphere in this shady corner. Variety has been introduced by using plants with differently-textured foliage. There are no bright or showy flowers; instead, a simple and sparingly-used palette of white, pale yellow, and mauve ensures that attention is not distracted from the delicate leaf shapes and the way in which they associate with the rocks and stone features.

Dryopteris filix-mas (male fern)

Deciduous or semi-evergreen fern, usually pleasingly evenly and well-shaped, with upright, then elegantly arching mid-green fronds. Grows equally well either in moist or in well-drained but moisture-retentive soil, but prefers a shady site. Remove fronds as they fade. Propagate by division in autumn or winter. H 1.2m (4ft), S 1m (3ft).

Lonicera periclymenum
The scent of honeysuckle can be enjoyed from the seat.

Oriental Touch
Thriving in the shelter of the corner, a Japanese maple falls over the dry millstone.

Textured Foliage
The distinctive pinnate leaves of *Mahonia japonica* are shown off to their full potential in such a simple composition.

Damp Area
Moisture from the fountain increases the humidity to help ferns grow in the damp cobbles.

Linking Plants
Planting and pathway are beautifully brought together by the *Phalaris* in the foreground. A plant that needs keeping in bounds, it is controlled here between the reservoir beneath the cobbles and the path.

Brunnera macrophylla (Siberian bugloss)

Clump-forming, spring-flowering perennial which, planted in groups, makes good ground cover in a sheltered site. The delicate, star-shaped, bright blue flowers, on tall nodding stalks, are followed by heart-shaped, mid-green leaves. Propagate from seed in autumn or by division in spring or autumn. H 45cm (18in), S 60cm (2ft).

Key to Planting Plan

MOISTURE LOVERS
1 *Dryopteris filix-mas* x 1
2 *Brunnera macrophylla* x 3
3 *Phalaris arundinacea* var. *picta* x 4

OTHER PLANTS
4 *Mahonia japonica* x 1
5 *Iris* 'Wedgwood' x 4
6 *Lonicera periclymenum* 'Belgica' x 1
7 *Heuchera* 'Painted Lady' x 3
8 *Viburnum opulus* x 1
9 *Potentilla fruticosa* 'Abbotswood' x 1
10 *Potentilla fruticosa* 'Elizabeth' x 1
11 *Acer palmatum* var. *dissectum* 'Ornatum' x 2

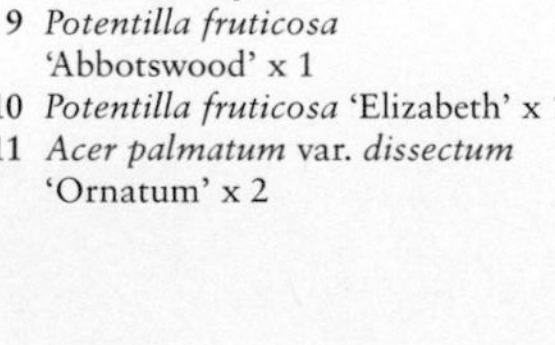

Planting Plan

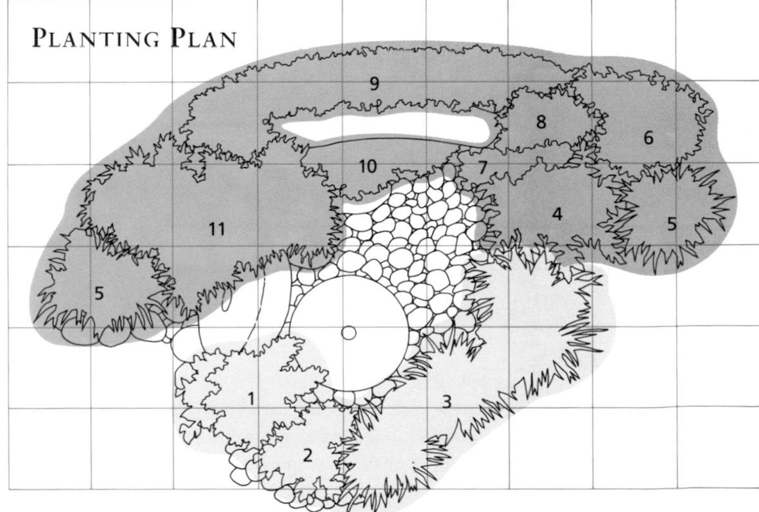

WILDLIFE POND WITH BOG GARDEN

NOT LONG AGO a completely open, windswept site, this coastal garden, with dry, sandy soil, now accommodates a sheltered, well-planted, informal pond surrounded by dense, vigorously growing, moisture-loving plants, making it a magnet for wild creatures from a wide surrounding area.

ENCOURAGING PLANT GROWTH

The plants around this pond are only in their second growing season, but so well planned was the feature to give plants good growing conditions that now, little space remains for new specimens. The main pool area has a soil layer placed on top of the flexible liner, supplemented by nutritious waste from several fish. Wide, shallow edges – more than half the pond is less than 30cm (12in) deep – allow aquatic, particularly marginal plants to spread. Around the edges, the flexible liner has been taken under the soil to form a broad band of moist ground; behind the pond, more wet pockets of ground have been created by lining holes with polythene. Both these and the shallow, clay-lined depression that forms a boggy pool beyond the main pond must be independently watered. A pebble beach, randomly placed boulders, and a small island ideally suit the needs and habits of birds, amphibians, and water-loving insects, setting up, with the fish and plants, a richly supplied food chain that keeps the water and its inhabitants in perfect ecological balance.

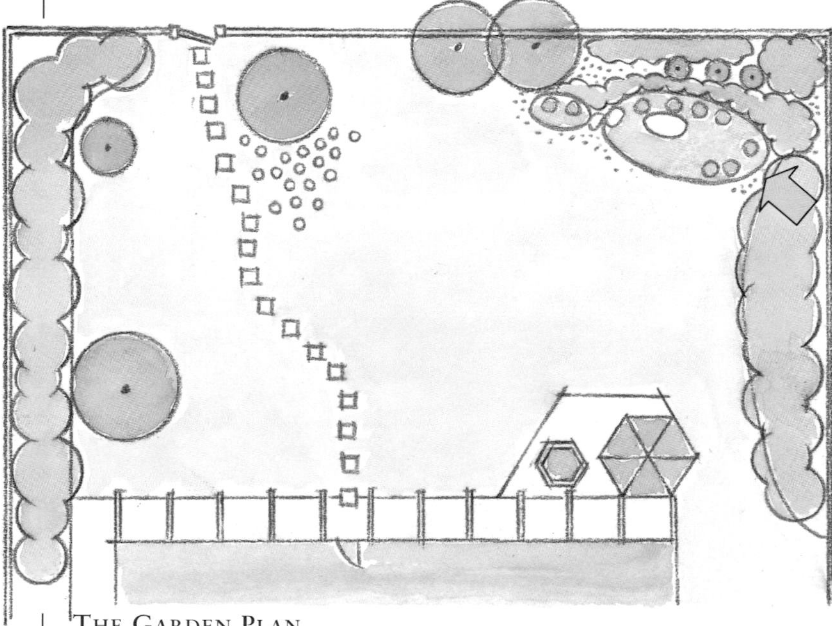

THE GARDEN PLAN
Most of this garden is open in plan to blend with the surrounding, gently undulating farm- and downland. On each side, and particularly around the pond (situated away from the house and main pathways to encourage shy creatures), a belt of trees and bamboos provides shelter from the damaging and, equally importantly, drying effects of sea winds.

Planting Plan for the Wildlife Pond

In order for a wildlife pond to be accessible to the maximum diversity of creatures, it is of primary importance to provide ample cover nearby. This will enable birds and animals to approach the water in safety. Here, the side of the pond seen across the lawn is relatively open, so that the feature can be viewed and appreciated, and cover is provided on the far side. Taller, closely spaced plants to the rear of the pond lead right up into the clumps of bamboos *(Fargesia)* and native trees, such as hawthorn *(Crataegus laevigata)*, that may be used as nesting sites. For other creatures, shelter underwater is important: the submerged stems of *Myriophyllum* and *Stratiotes* and, in the shallows, a host of marginal plants provide cover for fish and amphibians. Fringe lily leaves *(Nymphoides)* shade them from the sun – doubly important when water is shallow and heats up quickly.

Informal, Mixed Planting

In any water feature designed to attract wildlife, the style should be informal, and excessive tidiness avoided: rigorously removing plant and animal debris deprives creatures of food, shelter, and, for some, building materials. Allow plants to spread and mingle within reason (some lifting and dividing is essential to maintain their health). Here, while the planting is mixed, there are sufficient indigenous species to satisfy the dietary needs of a wide range of creatures. Common shrubs such as dogwoods *(Cornus)* and alder *(Alnus incana)* are pruned hard each year to keep them bushy. Wildflowers such as giant cowslips *(Primula florindae)* and water mint *(Mentha aquatica)* look appropriate and are often more attractive to insects than cultivated varieties, but there is no doubt that this scheme receives a real boost from the bright colours of selected lobelias. There are *Lythrum* cultivars, too, that will be far less invasive than common loosestrife can be, while just as appealing to bees.

Natural Stone Rounded sandstone boulders here blend in perfectly with the natural colour and texture of the garden's soil.

Ready for Occupation

This large water feature is a virtual metropolis for insects, birds, visiting animals, and aquatic creatures, with every facility for sheltering, feeding, and bathing provided. Randomly placed boulders accentuate the mound between the main pond and an independent, boggy pool that enables yet more marginal and moisture-loving plants to be grown. The island, an ideal refuge for wildlife, further increases the planting opportunities by extending the area of shallow-water space available.

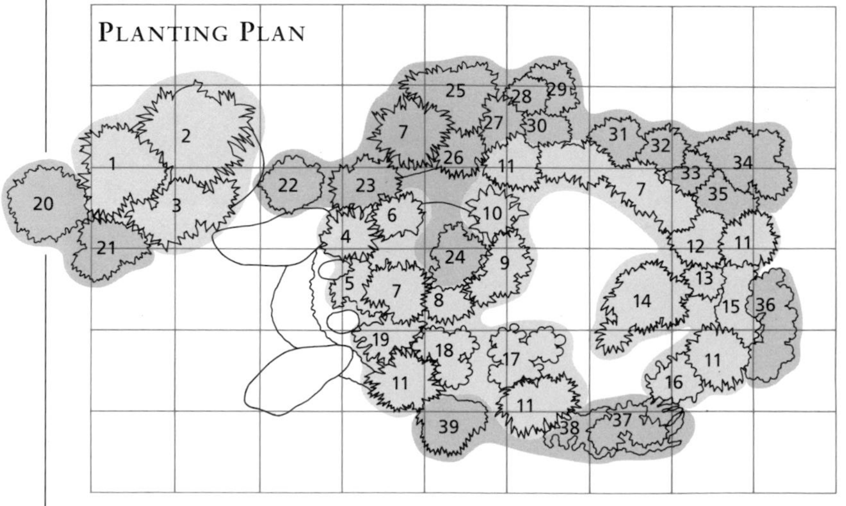

Key to Planting Plan

WATER PLANTS

1 *Schoenoplectus lacustris* subsp. *tabernaemontani* 'Zebrinus' x 3
2 *Schoenoplectus lacustris* subsp. *tabernaemontani* 'Albescens' x 3
3 *Pontederia cordata* x 7
4 *Alisma plantago-aquatica* x 2
5 *Mentha aquatica* x 3
6 *Lysichiton americanus* x 1
7 *Iris pseudacorus* x 9
8 *Juncus effusus* x 1
9 *Veronica beccabunga* x 5
10 *Sagittaria sagittifolia* x 1
11 *Cyperus longus* x 5
12 *Iris laevigata* x 3
13 *Caltha palustris* var. *palustris* x 1
14 *Stratiotes aloides* x 8
15 *Myriophyllum aquaticum* x 9
16 *Juncus effusus* 'Spiralis' x 1
17 *Nymphoides peltata* x 3
18 *Hydrocharis morsus-ranae* x 3
19 *Aponogeton distachyos* x 1

MOISTURE LOVERS

20 *Metasequoia glyptostroboides* x 1
21 *Carex elata* 'Aurea' x 3
22 *Trollius europaeus* x 1
23 *Gentiana asclepiadea* x 7
24 *Alnus incana* x 3
25 *Crocosmia* 'Lucifer' x 3
26 *Phalaris arundinacea* var. *picta* 'Feesey' x 1
27 *Deschampsia cespitosa* x 1
28 *Lobelia* 'Cinnabar Rose' x 6
29 *Petasites japonicus* x 1
30 *Liatris spicata* x 1
31 *Lobelia* x *gerardii* 'Vedrariensis' x 1
32 *Persicaria amplexicaulis* x 1
33 *Persicaria bistorta* 'Superba' x 1
34 *Lythrum salicaria* x 5
35 *Lobelia cardinalis* x 2
36 *Darmera peltata* x 3
37 *Primula florindae* x 3
38 *Lysimachia nummularia* 'Aurea' x 4
39 *Carex hachijoensis* 'Evergold' x 3

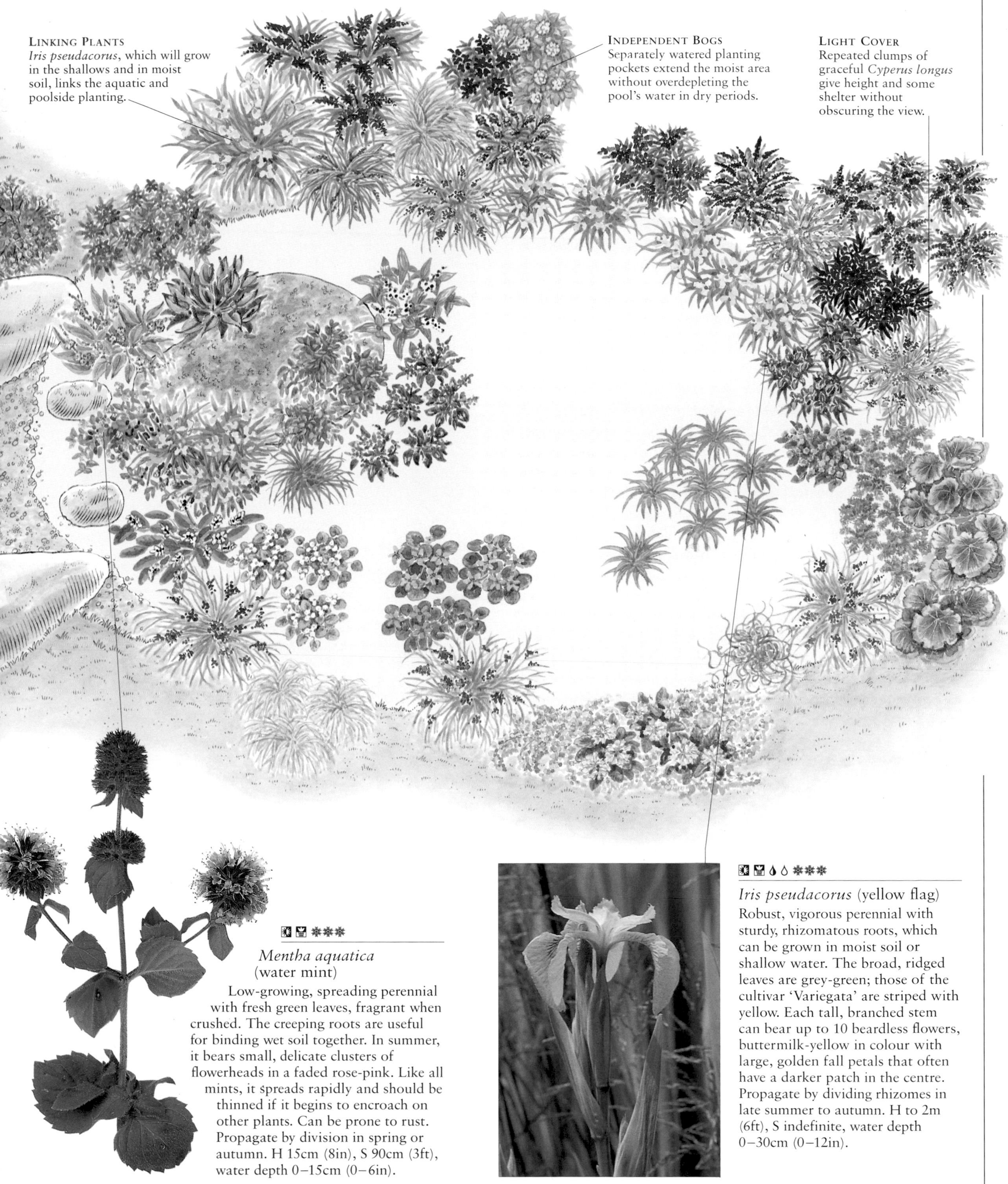

Mentha aquatica (water mint)

Low-growing, spreading perennial with fresh green leaves, fragrant when crushed. The creeping roots are useful for binding wet soil together. In summer, it bears small, delicate clusters of flowerheads in a faded rose-pink. Like all mints, it spreads rapidly and should be thinned if it begins to encroach on other plants. Can be prone to rust. Propagate by division in spring or autumn. H 15cm (8in), S 90cm (3ft), water depth 0–15cm (0–6in).

Iris pseudacorus (yellow flag)

Robust, vigorous perennial with sturdy, rhizomatous roots, which can be grown in moist soil or shallow water. The broad, ridged leaves are grey-green; those of the cultivar 'Variegata' are striped with yellow. Each tall, branched stem can bear up to 10 beardless flowers, buttermilk-yellow in colour with large, golden fall petals that often have a darker patch in the centre. Propagate by dividing rhizomes in late summer to autumn. H to 2m (6ft), S indefinite, water depth 0–30cm (0–12in).

STREAM FOR TOWN OR COUNTRY GARDEN

WITH A LITTLE INGENUITY, even the smallest plot can accommodate a stream surrounded by lush planting. This small back garden is given enormous impact by being entirely devoted to one well-designed water feature, rather than trying to incorporate a number of necessarily scaled-down elements.

STREAMSIDE EDGING AND PLANTING

Water bubbles up slowly among rocks on the left, flowing into a deeper area on the right, where a small submersible pump sends it back to the start again; the stream flows along, rather than down the watercourse. However, the garden does slope in the other direction, upwards away from the house. The well-mortared bank of irregularly shaped rocks in the foreground acts as a retaining wall for the stream, while on the far side, boulders and the roots of many plants consolidate a bank of rich, moist soil. Since the feature is generally viewed from one side, like a stage-set, the slope has been accentuated by planting low alpines in front, medium-height perennials in the middle area (on the far side of the stream), and to the rear, tall conifers and shrubs that also screen neighbouring houses. The stream is lined with butyl, and edged with a local red sandstone. Local stone, or reconstituted stone crafted to match it, usually complements the colours of local soil and housebricks.

THE GARDEN PLAN

This slow-moving stream can be observed at leisure from a paved patio or, on less clement days, from the sun room built onto the back of the house; the slight upward slope brings the stream, plants, and visiting wildlife directly into view from the comfort of window seats. A stone bridge gives access to the far side and also provides a different viewpoint.

PLANTING PLAN FOR THE STREAM

AS THIS FEATURE is mainly viewed from only one side, the planting plan has been conceived to create three distinct areas, layered to provide an amphitheatre of interest. In the foreground, planting is low level. With the exception of a planting pocket built to suit the moisture-loving *Juncus ensifolius*, a useful and attractive small, spreading rush, the soil is dry between the rocks: an excellent home for scrambling and creeping plants such as *Artemisia* and *Waldsteinia*. On the near margin of the stream itself, small plants have been chosen that will not obscure the view of the water lilies; although they dislike fast-moving water, they thrive in this very gentle current. On the far side of the stream, the planting becomes denser and more diverse, with a variety of marginal and moisture-loving perennials dominated by the large leaves of the umbrella plant, *Darmera peltata*, which forms long surface rhizomes that consolidate the soil, ideal for streamside planting.

A BACKGROUND OF EVERGREENS

At the back of the garden, conifers, bamboos, and evergreen shrubs form an informal screen and provide natural protection for the lush growth of the marginal and moisture-loving plants. They are a permanent backcloth for the changing display of the perennial plants, some themselves changing with the seasons: *Pinus sylvestris* 'Aurea' will begin to assume yellow tints in time to echo the bold clumps of Bowles' golden sedge *(Carex elata* 'Aurea'*)*, which lasts well into the autumn. Yellow is an excellent colour for bringing light into small enclosed gardens, and here there are splashes of yellow flowers or foliage to be seen throughout the year.

The darker greens of other shrubs and trees provide the perfect foil for the autumn's most striking display: the spectacular maroon tints taken on by the leaves of the *Darmera*.

INFORMAL BOUNDARIES
The softening effect of planting is well used here, giving the illusion of continuity to this mock stream, breaking up the hard edges of stonework and, at the rear, forming a natural boundary.

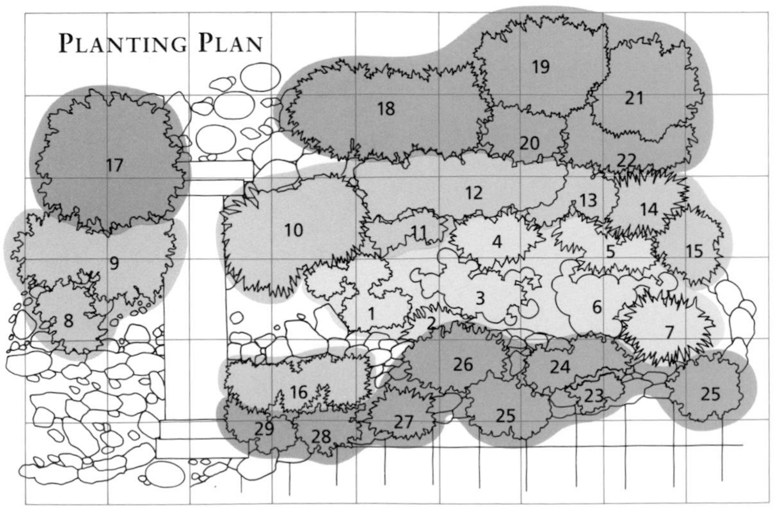

KEY TO PLANTING PLAN

WATER PLANTS
1 *Mentha aquatica* x 4
2 *Sagittaria sagittifolia* x 2
3 *Nymphaea* 'Escarboucle' x 2
4 *Menyanthes trifoliata* x 2
5 *Iris pseudacorus* 'Variegata' x 3
6 *Nymphaea* 'Gladstoneana' x 1
7 *Acorus calamus* 'Variegatus' x 1

MOISTURE LOVERS
8 *Polystichum setiferum* 'Divisilobum Densum' x 2
9 *Osmunda regalis* x 2
10 *Carex elata* 'Aurea' x 2
11 *Primula florindae* x 2
12 *Darmera peltata* x 5
13 *Mimulus luteus* x 3
14 *Phragmites australis* 'Variegatus' x 1
15 *Iris ensata* x 5
16 *Juncus ensifolius* x 6

OTHER PLANTS
17 *Metasequoia glyptostroboides* x 1
18 *Fargesia murieliae* x 3
19 *Griselinia littoralis* x 1
20 *Pinus sylvestris* 'Aurea' x 1
21 *Erica* x *veitchii* x 3
22 *Abies koreana* x 1
23 *Alchemilla mollis* x 2
24 *Erodium* x *variabile* 'Ken Aslet' x 1
25 *Waldsteinia ternata* x 2
26 *Artemisia frigida* x 1
27 *Persicaria affinis* x 2
28 *Hedera helix* 'Heise' x 2
29 *Thymus serpyllum* x 2

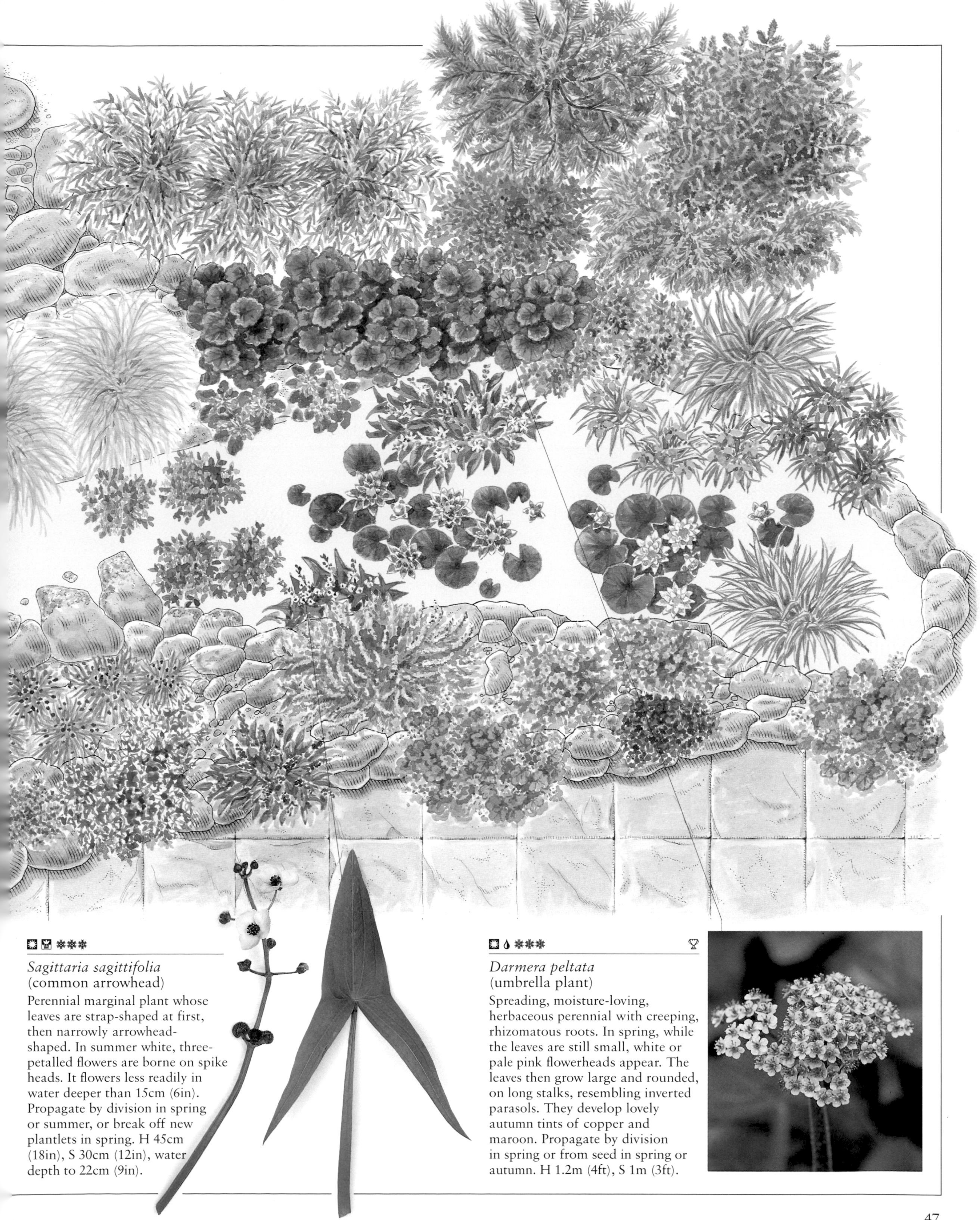

Sagittaria sagittifolia (common arrowhead)

Sagittaria sagittifolia
(common arrowhead)

Perennial marginal plant whose leaves are strap-shaped at first, then narrowly arrowhead-shaped. In summer white, three-petalled flowers are borne on spike heads. It flowers less readily in water deeper than 15cm (6in). Propagate by division in spring or summer, or break off new plantlets in spring. H 45cm (18in), S 30cm (12in), water depth to 22cm (9in).

Darmera peltata
(umbrella plant)

Spreading, moisture-loving, herbaceous perennial with creeping, rhizomatous roots. In spring, while the leaves are still small, white or pale pink flowerheads appear. The leaves then grow large and rounded, on long stalks, resembling inverted parasols. They develop lovely autumn tints of copper and maroon. Propagate by division in spring or from seed in spring or autumn. H 1.2m (4ft), S 1m (3ft).

Creating Water Features

Planning and Preparation

Choosing a Water Feature • Encouraging Wildlife • Siting • Excavation • Areas and Volumes • Construction Materials and Techniques • Pumps and Filters

Features with Still Water

Ponds with Flexible Liner • Beaches and Islands • Bog Gardens • Raised Pools Concrete Pools • Clay-lined Ponds Container Water Gardens

Features with Moving Water

Streams and Waterfalls Concrete Canals • Fountains Reservoir Features

Finishing Touches

Stepping Stones • Bridges • Lighting Edging • Timber Decking

Informal Stream *(left)*
The irregular arrangement of sandstone rocks and the careful but informal placing of plants gives a natural appearance to an artificially constructed watercourse.

PLANNING AND PREPARATION

CAREFUL PLANNING is the key to successful design and construction. Before making any decisions, it can be useful to make sketches in order to clarify your ideas. Visit specialist suppliers, builders' merchants, and aquatic centres: given information about your site and requirements, they may be able to offer advice on construction methods and materials that will save time and money.

CHOICE OF MATERIALS
In the right setting, even concrete can be attractive, and is one of the most versatile and economical of materials. Remember that setting times for foundations, floors, and walls must be incorporated when planning out construction schedules.

SITING AND DESIGN

The first major decision to be made is where to site your water feature. There are many factors to be taken into account *(see pp. 56–57)*, and drawing up a simple scale plan of your garden can be an invaluable exercise. You may discover that your preferred location is impractical, so be open to the possibility of alternative sites. Consider views both outside and from within the house, especially from favourite garden seats and armchairs.

ENCOURAGING WILDLIFE
Wildlife enthusiasts need to take into consideration the needs and preferences of birds, insects, and amphibians from the earliest planning stages (see pp. 54–55) *in order to provide an attractive and suitable environment.*

SURPRISING SITES
In small spaces, bold designs can be surprisingly effective. In this narrow, enclosed courtyard, the sophisticated raised pool has been styled to complement its urban surroundings.

SAFETY PRECAUTIONS
Bridges (see pp. 122–123) *add an extra dimension to a water garden, allowing access across water, and providing visual interest, but their safety must be considered; hand-rails need not be obtrusive, and can be softened by planting.*

A BOG GARDEN
A bog garden can adjoin a pond or, for plant enthusiasts who do not want to spend too much time on a pond's upkeep, can be a feature in its own right. They are cheap and easy to construct, and are an ideal way of growing moisture-loving plants where water conservation is of prime importance.

The design of the feature will depend very much on personal preference, but it should always be influenced by the site and its surroundings. You may not have the flexibility of incorporating water into a new garden plan, but with careful forethought, your feature will look naturally placed and as if it has always been an integral part of the overall garden design.

CONSTRUCTION AND MATERIALS

There are several methods of construction *(see pp. 64–69)* using a range of materials, each with advantages and disadvantages, so it is worth spending a little time thumbing through suppliers' catalogues. Compare the costs of liners and building materials, work out how long construction will take, and assess whether you are physically capable or skilled enough to carry out the work yourself and, if not, whether you are prepared to pay someone to do the job for you. Remember to take into account the practicalities of transporting and working with materials; concrete blocks and slabs, for example, are heavy, and large pieces of flexible liner are difficult to manoeuvre. If you decide to hire help or specialist machinery, think about whether, with an extra pair of hands or piece of equipment available, there are other jobs in the garden that could also be accomplished.

Skilled labour is of course expensive, and careful planning can save time and prevent costly errors. If taking on a challenging project yourself, it is worth having the name of a good builder to hand just in case you encounter unforeseen difficulties; struggling to complete the project yourself without the necessary skills may result in a feature that is never what you hoped it would be.

BRINGING ELECTRICITY TO WATER

The one area in which there is no substitute for professional expertise is the bringing of electricity to a pool, whether it be to power a pump *(see pp. 70–73)* or lighting. Even the installation of relatively risk-free, low-voltage equipment can be made easier and safer with advice on weatherproofing connections and routing buried cable. Only use equipment specially designed for garden and pool use, carefully follow the manufacturer's instructions, and, if necessary, call in a professional electrician to set up the system for you.

Choosing a Water Feature

Before making a choice, it is essential to consider which type of water feature will accommodate your needs and situation. The enormous variety of shapes, styles, and materials now available makes this easier, but remember to take into account both the practicalities involved and where your priorities lie. First, see how much space could be made available, then consider how much time and effort you are prepared to spare, both in building and maintenance. Choose a style that will blend in with the existing surroundings. Remember, too, that some construction methods and materials are more costly than others – this may rule out certain features.

The Right Pond for You

There are two basic styles of pond – formal and informal – and your choice will be influenced by the existing site. In formal design, where symmetry and geometric shapes are often strong elements, both the pond and its surrounds should be regular. A formal pond, for example, may look out of place in the middle of a lawn with sweeping curves of mixed border planting. Similarly, the popular kidney shape can look unsuitable in surroundings dominated by straight edges and formal planting. For a natural look, bog gardens *(see pp. 82–83)* or wildlife ponds *(see pp. 54–55)* are popular options.

Size and Shape of Feature

There is a recommended minimum size for still ponds: the surface area should ideally be no smaller than 4.5sq m (50sq ft), with a minimum depth of 0.5m (1½ft). This should reduce problems caused by green water, excessive temperature fluctuation, and inadequate water oxygenation. The larger the surface area, the deeper at least one area of the pond should be. If you only have a small space, consider alternative water features such as container gardens or wall fountains.

Square, circular, and rectangular ponds may be constructed with a concrete shell or preformed rigid liner; the latter also come in a range of small irregular shapes. Use flexible liner for larger irregular shapes, but keep the shape as simple as possible to make installation easier *(see pp. 66–67)*.

Formal Pond and Surrounds
This clearly defined, symmetrical pond would look out of place in an informal setting. Ambitious features such as this demand considerable resources both for construction and maintenance: the meticulously tended topiary here, for example, is a key element in the design.

Still or Moving Water

Still water is valued for its tranquillity and reflective qualities; the light it brings into an enclosed garden can transform its atmosphere. Still pools are ideal for viewing water lilies and ornamental fish, or, styled more informally, they can be a haven for wildlife *(see overleaf)*. To bring the sparkle of moving water

Access to the Water
These informal steps are attractive, but not everybody would find them easy to negotiate. Always try to incorporate one easy point of access to the water's edge.

Raised Pond
Raised ponds have definite safety advantages over sunken features, but the walls must be solidly constructed to withstand the pressure exerted by the water. A well-built, wide wall doubles up as a seating area, making it more comfortable and convenient to tend plants.

CHOOSING WATER FEATURES
Any number of factors can influence the choice of water feature. Those categorized below can all be constructed following the step-by-step sequences that appear later in this part of the book.

	Formal	Informal	Suitable for small garden	Sunken	Raised	Rectangular	Square	Circular	Irregular	Still water	Moving water	Inexpensive	Easy to install	Needs building skills	Easy to maintain	More vulnerable to low temperatures	Affected by soil condition	No areas of open water	Can be adapted for children	More suitable for wildlife	Suitable for creative planting	Suitable for fish
Simple pond with flexible liner *(pp. 76–79)*	●	●	●	●		●	●	●	●	●		●	●		●				●	●	●	●
Flexible liner pond with beach/island *(pp. 80–81)*		●	●	●					●	●		●	●		●				●	●	●	●
Flexible liner pond & stream *(pp. 98–103)*		●	●	●					●		●	●	●						●	●	●	●
Raised pool with flexible liner *(pp. 86–87)*	●		●		●	●	●	●		●				●	●	●			●		●	●
Independent bog garden *(pp. 82–83)*		●	●	●					●			●	●					●		●	●	
Rigid pond unit *(pp. 84–85)*	●	●	●	●	●	●	●	●	●	●		●	●		●				●		●	●
Rigid pond & stream units *(pp. 104–105)*		●	●	●					●		●	●	●		●				●		●	●
Raised pool using rigid unit *(pp. 88–89)*	●	●	●		●	●	●	●	●	●		●			●	●			●		●	●
Concrete-lined pool *(pp. 90–91)*	●		●	●		●	●			●				●					●		●	●
Concrete-lined pool & canal *(pp. 106–107)*	●		●	●		●	●				●			●		●			●		●	●
Clay-lined pond *(pp. 92–93)*		●		●					●	●					●		●			●	●	●
Container water garden *(pp. 94–95)*	●	●	●	●	●					●		●	●		●	●			●		●	
Cobblestone fountain *(pp. 112–113)*	●	●	●	●							●	●	●		●			●	●		●	
Wall feature *(pp. 116–117)*	●	●	●		●						●			●	●				●			

into a garden with no natural spring or stream it will be necessary to install a pump, and to bring electricity out into the garden *(see p. 72)*. However, the modern equipment now available makes pump installation relatively easy and, because splashing water contains more oxygen, moving water features can be much smaller than still ponds yet maintain a healthy water chemistry.

DIFFERENT CONSTRUCTION SKILLS

PLASTIC ART
Flexible liner allows you to create customized, irregular shapes, with scope to modify or extend designs in the future.

BUILDING SKILLS
Raised pools need well-built double walls.

DIY SKILLS
It is wisest not to attempt projects that involve bricklaying and symmetrical shapes and angles without some experience.

CONSTRUCTION METHODS

Building a water feature will be a satisfying and enjoyable task if you choose construction techniques *(see pp. 64–69)* that are comfortably within your capabilities. Flexible liners and preformed units are easy to install and maintain, but preformed units do limit you to the designs offered by the manufacturer. Laying concrete and bricks is not easy and requires some building experience to achieve an adequate result.

PERSONAL CONSIDERATIONS

The pond style will reflect the interests of the owner: the serious fish-keeper may well invest in a sophisticated filtration system *(see pp. 70–73)* in order to ensure that the water remains clear, whereas a pristine environment will not suit the purposes of the wildlife enthusiast. The design-oriented may see the feature as an opportunity to experiment with beautiful and unusual hard materials both in and around the water, while the plant enthusiast may see the water in a secondary role, as a canvas for widening the range of plants that can be grown in the garden. While following the guidelines relating to shape, size, and siting *(see pp. 56–57)* will ensure that the environment you create remains healthy and attractive, it is the basic choice of feature, and the way in which it is built and styled, that ensures that individual preferences and creative expression are realized to the full.

ENCOURAGING WILDLIFE

WATER WILL ALWAYS ATTRACT wildlife, be it birds, insects, amphibians, or mammals. The variety of wildlife will depend a little on the site and size of the water feature, but if you create a suitable environment, some creatures will be drawn to even the smallest pond. Careful planting is fundamental; plants should be chosen that not only sustain the water's ecosystem *(see pp. 136–137)*, but also provide cover and food. Native plants and flowers are usually more attractive to indigenous wildlife; natural streams and ponds in nearby countryside may suggest planting ideas (do not, however, take plants from the wild). In a successful wildlife pond, all plants and creatures play their parts in complex food chains; never use choice plants around a wildlife pond, nor stock it with costly decorative fish.

CONSTRUCTING A WILDLIFE POND

Natural or clay-lined ponds are ideal, but on a smaller scale, a well-planted pond with flexible liner can be a perfectly acceptable substitute. Make sure that the pond has plenty of variation in depth so that there are several different habitats that may support a wide range of plants and animals. The deep areas of the pond should be at least 45cm (18in), and preferably 90cm (36in), in depth. The sides of the pond should be gently sloping; both sunny areas and cool shade around the edges of the pond are important.

SMALL MARGINALS
Grade plants by size, from trees to small marginals, right down to the water's edge to provide continuous cover. Plants with mat-forming roots, such as water forget-me-not *(Myosotis scorpioides)*, spread well along the water's edge.

DIGITALIS PURPUREA
The flower spires of foxgloves *(Digitalis)* are magnets for bumble bees.

IRIS PSEUDACORUS

SAGITTARIA LATIFOLIA

FLOATING LEAVES
Deep-water aquatics provide vital shade, and large, flat leaves also make landing pads for insects. *Nymphoides peltata (here)* and *Nuphar* are less formal-looking alternatives to water lilies for naturalistic settings.

PERCHING PLATFORMS
Flat stones provide perching spots; birds also clean their beaks on the surface of such stones.

SCHOENOPLECTUS LACUSTRIS

NOOKS AND CRANNIES
Hollows among rocks will allow amphibians to shelter during the summer heat and hibernate in winter.

GRASSES AND SEDGES
Evergreen and semi-evergreen grasses and sedges such as *Carex* and *Schoenoplectus* provide cover at the edge of the water throughout the year. Many are preferred foods of the water vole, which, unlike the fierce water shrew, is vegetarian.

FOOD FOR FOWL
Duckweed *(Lemna trisulca)* and duck potato *(Sagittaria latifolia)* are so called because they are favourite food plants of ducks.

WATER QUALITY
Submerged plants keep the oxygen level sufficiently high to support insect larvae, such as those of the dragonfly, that live under pebbles on the bottom of the pond.

PEBBLE BEACH
A gentle slope ensures that amphibians, small mammals, and bathing birds can approach the water safely.

LAGAROSIPHON MAJOR
Submerged plants play a practical role, releasing oxygen directly into the water, and also shelter fish fry and other tiny creatures.

Further Information

- Wildlife Pond with Bog Garden – pp. 40–43
- Simple Ponds with Flexible Liner – pp. 76–79
- Clay-lined Ponds – pp. 92–93
- Beaches and Islands – pp. 80–81

SITING A WATER FEATURE

SITING CONSIDERATIONS SHOULD be fully explored when making any design and construction decisions. The majority of water plants need plenty of light, but siting is much more than finding the sunniest spot: it is the location of a feature where it instinctively feels right and where it can be enjoyed to the maximum. There are also many practical factors that must be taken into consideration. If you have a site in mind then with luck, having taken all factors into account, it will indeed prove to be the ideal location. If you have yet to decide, using a process of elimination to remove all unsuitable sites from the available area can be very helpful.

PRACTICAL CONSIDERATIONS

AREA AVAILABLE FOR SITING

First of all, you must establish the positions of any drains, pipes, and underground cables crossing the garden; on no account must you excavate over or near these. The lie of the land, the position of the water table, and the soil composition *(see* Drainage and Excavation, *pp. 58–59)* will give you an idea of the size of the job, in terms of excavation work, that construction on the proposed site will entail. Sloping sites, which can be exploited so well by streams and waterfalls, have their own design and building considerations. However, while the lowest point of a sloping garden presents itself as a natural site for a pond, it will make emptying the pond without a pump difficult. Low points or dips in the ground can also be frost pockets, and moreover may not be ideally placed for viewing.

REFLECTIVE POTENTIAL

Lay mirrors on the ground to see how much light the pond will reflect, and to avoid "doubling" any eyesores. Even a small expanse of water that reflects sky and plants can transform a garden.

CHECKING REFLECTIONS IN A MIRROR

SHADED AREAS AT DIFFERENT TIMES OF THE DAY

Identifying areas of full sunlight, partial shade, and dense shade during the day and early evening is important. A pond in full shade will be visually dull, without character or reflective movement; lacking adequate sunlight to penetrate the water and promote plant photosynthesis, it will also produce the kind of poor environmental balance that encourages algal growth. Partial shade can be acceptable: there are plants that tolerate these conditions, and dappled shade that produces contrasting patterns of light and dark can create effective mirror images on the water.

SOUTH-FACING GARDEN

PERMANENT SHADE
Do not site ponds where no sunlight will reach them during the day.

PARTIAL SHADE
Shade on part of the proposed pool or for part of the day need not rule out a site for a water garden. Dappled shade can also be attractive, as long as branches do not directly overhang the pool.

KEY TO DAILY SHADE PATTERN

Use string to mark out the areas that are shaded by planting and buildings in the morning, at noon, and in the afternoon.

- EARLY MORNING
- NOON
- EARLY EVENING

Consider whether you want to be able to see the feature from the house; this is particularly advisable in family gardens, so that you can keep an eye on children playing by the water.

Light and Shade

Choose a sheltered but open site that will afford the feature the maximum amount of sunlight. Avoid sun traps, however, or you will increase problems with water evaporation in summer; nor will fish be happy in baking heat. Although it may not be possible to find a spot completely free of shadows, the proximity of nearby tall plants and trees should be carefully considered: in addition to the shade they cast, falling leaves can become a problem. Site features as far as possible from trees with spreading root systems, such as poplars, which may damage foundations; from trees with toxic leaves and seeds, such as yew *(Taxus)* and laburnum; and from ornamental and fruiting *Prunus*, on which water-lily aphids overwinter.

For the best visual impact, try to locate the pond where the reflective qualities of the water can best be enjoyed. A mirror is an invaluable aid *(see facing page)*. Experiment with various positions by marking the outline of the proposed pool with string or hosepipe; study the direction and quality of light at different times of the day, and observe how well the pond can be seen from different vantage points.

Providing Shelter

Wind damages the soft, succulent stems of many bog plants, accelerates water evaporation, blows fountain spray out of the pool and, in some exposed sites, can result in the pond freezing over. Shelter can be provided by planting, or by erecting a trellis screen on the windward side of the pool. Alternatively, use a windbreak to reduce the speed of the wind before it reaches the plants. A hedge or a screen or fence with gaps *(see below right)* is a better windbreak than a solid structure, which simply deflects the wind to another part of the garden.

Finding the Ideal Site

Choosing the optimum location for a pond involves careful consideration of both aesthetic and practical factors.

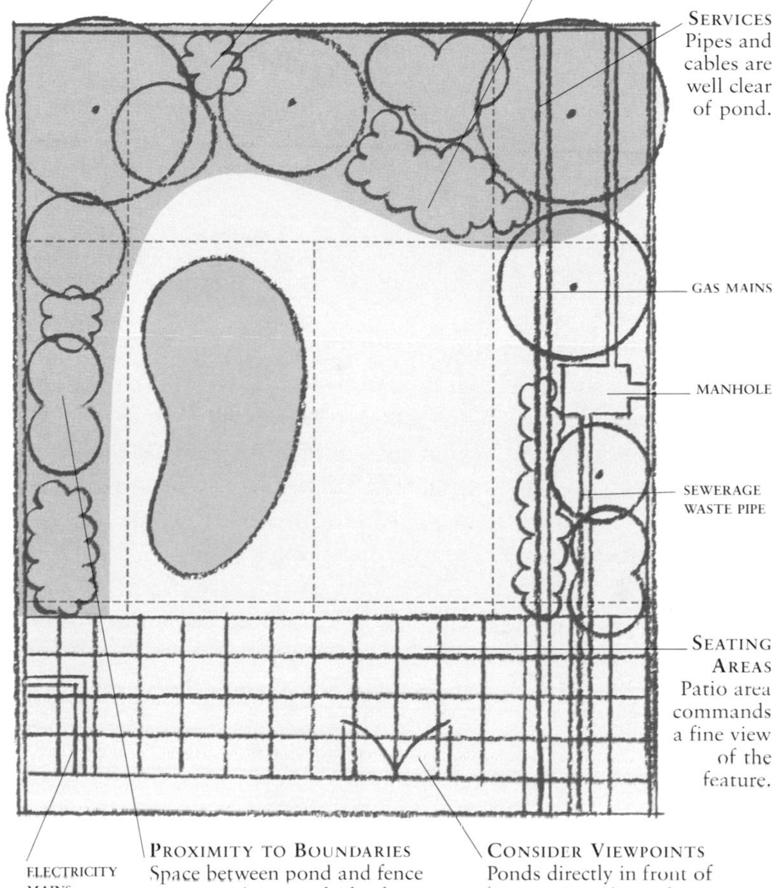

Access to Borders Pond does not restrict access to other areas of planting.

Area of Shade Pond is clear of shade cast by trees and overhanging branches.

Services Pipes and cables are well clear of pond.

Seating Areas Patio area commands a fine view of the feature.

Proximity to Boundaries Space between pond and fence accommodates poolside planting and allows for future additions such as a rockery or stream.

Consider Viewpoints Ponds directly in front of large or French windows can clutter and obstruct views beyond.

Viewing a Water Feature on a Sloping Site

Water features on sloping ground must either be cut into, or built up from, the slope *(see* Drainage and Excavation, *pp. 58–59)*; the method will depend on whether you wish to view the feature from further up, or from further down, the incline. If you are construcing a retaining wall that extends above ground level, site it on the side of the pond that is furthest away from the house, seating area, or other ideal viewpoint, otherwise it will obstruct the view of the water surface.

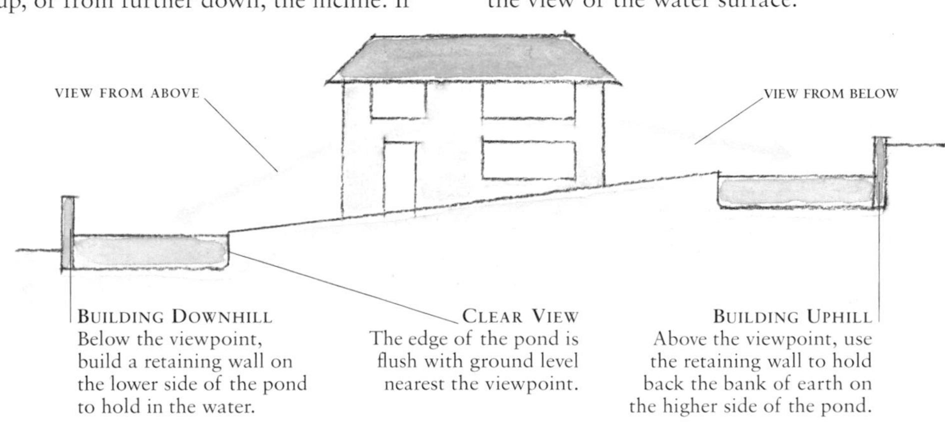

Building Downhill Below the viewpoint, build a retaining wall on the lower side of the pond to hold in the water.

Clear View The edge of the pond is flush with ground level nearest the viewpoint.

Building Uphill Above the viewpoint, use the retaining wall to hold back the bank of earth on the higher side of the pond.

Reducing Wind Speed

For maximum effect, a windbreak should be approximately 50 per cent permeable; the gaps in the structure serve to break up the air currents as they pass through.

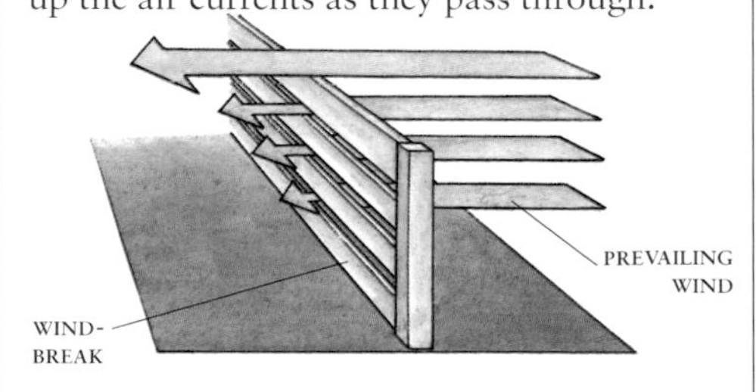

Further Information

- Choosing a Water Feature – pp. 52–53
- Excavation and Drainage – pp. 58–59
- Construction Techniques – pp. 64–69
- Soils and Containers – pp. 150–151

Excavation and Drainage

Even if your garden is reasonably well cultivated, you may never before have dug as deeply as you will to excavate a pond. You may therefore have little idea of the structure of the lower soil levels, and how easy they are to work with – for example, if a compacted or rocky layer exists that will entail extra labour or the hire of digging equipment. As soil can vary from one site to another, dig test holes to determine its structure and composition. Another important consideration is the position of the water table. More often than not this does not present a problem, but if it is high in your garden, temporary or permanent drainage may be needed.

Excavating a Site

If you do not have problems with wet ground *(see facing page)*, excavation is usually a reasonably simple, if laborious, task. Always stop if you feel any pain, and take breaks before, rather than when, you feel exhausted. If there is grass on the site, remove the turves and stack them upside down in an unobtrusive part of the garden; they will break down into a very good, fibrous loam planting medium. When excavating, first strip off the valuable topsoil to keep for planting areas. Place it separately from excavated subsoil. Use subsoil in the general landscaping of the feature, but always grade topsoil back over the subsoil when digging is complete. Dispose of excess subsoil, rather than dispersing it about the garden; it is of little use to plants.

Test Hole
Dig in the centre of the proposed site, assess the situation, and adapt construction depending on results.

High Water Table
With water collecting spontaneously at this level, drainage or perhaps a shallower, but semi-raised, pond should be considered.

Establishing Soil Drainage and the Water Table Level
Dig a hole 45cm (18in) deep and fill it with water. If all the water does not seep away, you have poor drainage or a high water table. Remove the water and dig 45cm (18in) deeper. If the hole begins to fill with water, the water table is high: its level can be gauged when the water stops rising.

Soil Composition

Sandy Soil | Cultivated Soil | Wet Moorland Soil

Soil Type
The appearance of soil will tell you a great deal about its structure. Dry, sandy soil is firm and drains well, while wet, spongy moorland soil has poor drainage. The upper levels of cultivated soil should be easy to dig.

Using Retaining Walls on Sloping Sites

Unless levelling off the site *(see below)* a retaining wall on at least one side will be necessary to stabilize ponds built on a sloping site. If the wall is to be visible, careful attention must be paid to achieving true horizontals, or the feature will always look askew.

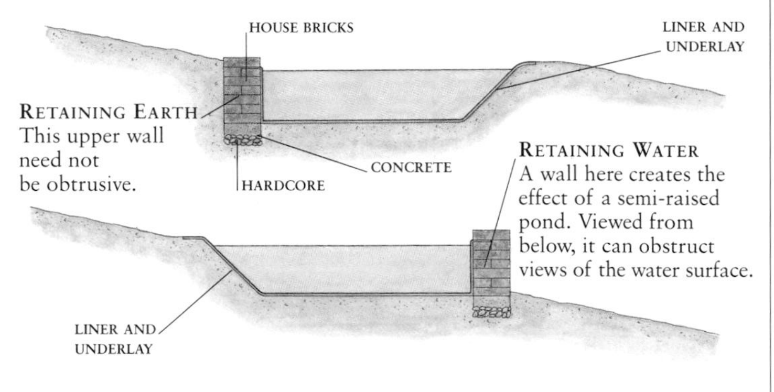

Retaining Earth
This upper wall need not be obtrusive.

Retaining Water
A wall here creates the effect of a semi-raised pond. Viewed from below, it can obstruct views of the water surface.

Sloping Ground
Plants with vigorous root systems will consolidate gently sloping earth banks.

Lower Slope
Build up the lower slope first with excess subsoil, and cover with topsoil.

Landscaping using Excavation Spoil
The "cut-and-fill" method is a simple landscaping technique for levelling a sloping site (right), *or for creating an earth bank using the soil excavated from a hole. It is essential, however, not to simply mound shovelled earth up as you dig to form the raised areas, or sterile subsoil will be brought to the surface, and the valuable topsoil buried where plant roots cannot reach it. Strip off the topsoil first and replace it once you have created the basic contours.*

Landscaping
Always build gently sloping banks that will blend naturally into the terrain.

Original Slope
Before excavation, the sloping ground would only have accommodated a very shallow pond.

Construction on Wet Ground

You may know, without digging a test hole, that your garden has a water table that is close to the surface, or that drainage is poor. Telltale signs include water pooling on lawns, or the presence of water-loving plants such as rushes, sedges, and mosses. A site on a high water table may seem ideal for the construction of a natural pond, but in practice the water table is rarely high enough for a satisfactorily full pond to be achieved, and a water-retentive liner is still needed. The problem then is that the water in the soil will exert upward and inward pressure on the pond shell, placing structural stress on non-flexible materials such as concrete, and causing flexible linings, such as butyl, to balloon or "hippo" upwards *(see below, top)*.

There are a number of ways of dealing with this. One is to avoid digging down by building a raised pond (for which firm foundations are vital on unstable wet ground) – or, if you want a sunken effect, to raise ground level artificially so that the pond does not dip below the level of the water table *(see left, centre)*. If the pond is not to resemble a volcano, however, it is essential to combine this with more general landscaping of the surrounding area.

The alternative is to install permanent drainage for the ground surrounding the pond. Trenches and pipes can vastly improve poor drainage; very few areas are so constantly rainy that a simple system cannot cope. But on a high water table, a pump will also be necessary *(see left, bottom)* so that water can be removed faster than it seeps back in again.

Even if you plan to build the pond so that it lies above the water table, when digging deeper to lay foundations, you may find that the accumulating water makes it extremely difficult to work. Dig out a small deep hole to act as a sump *(see above)* and, as water fills it, bail or pump it out. Make sure that the water is expelled in a place where it cannot seep back into the hole.

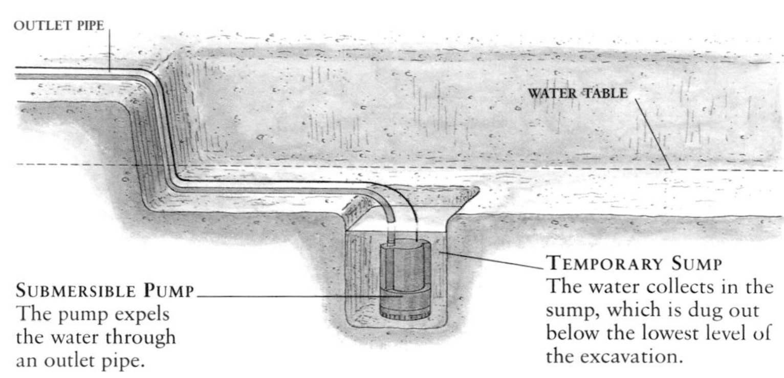

Temporary Drainage
A high water table leads to an accumulation of water in holes that makes further digging impracticable. To counteract this, dig a deeper hole to act as a sump; the sump will collect the water as digging continues. If necessary, use a pump with an outlet pipe to expel the water.

Laying Flexible Liner on a High Water Table

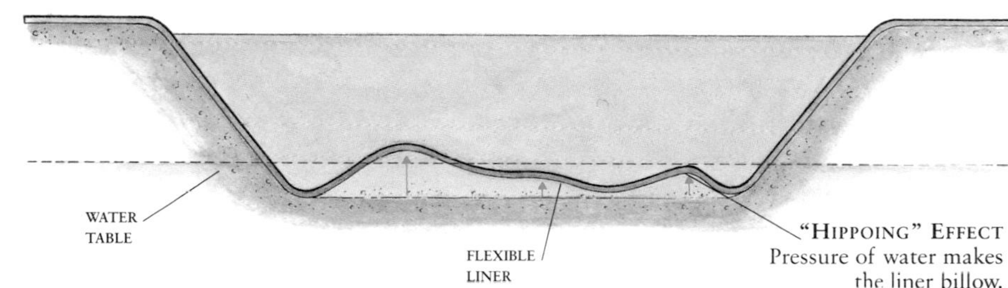

"Hippoing" Effect
If flexible liner is laid below the water table, the accumulation of water below the liner will exert pressure upwards, and so cause the liner to balloon up from the pool floor. With time, the sloping sides of the pond will slip down, causing further distortion.

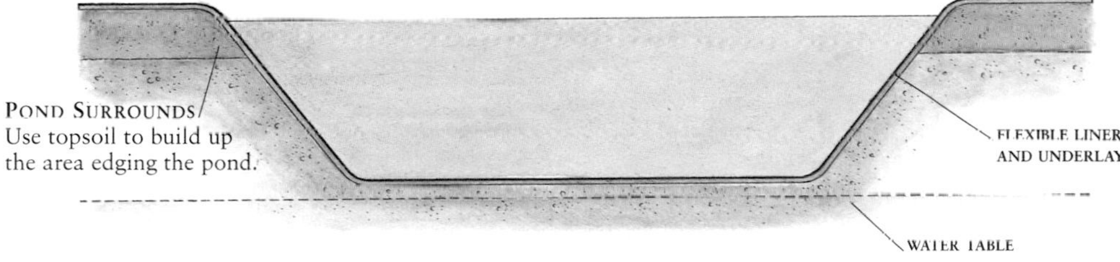

Building a Sunken Pond Above the Water Table
To keep the floor of the pond above the water table, build up the surrounding ground until an adequate depth can be achieved for the pond. Unless you are paving around the pond, you must use topsoil, bought in if necessary, or plants around the pool edges will not thrive.

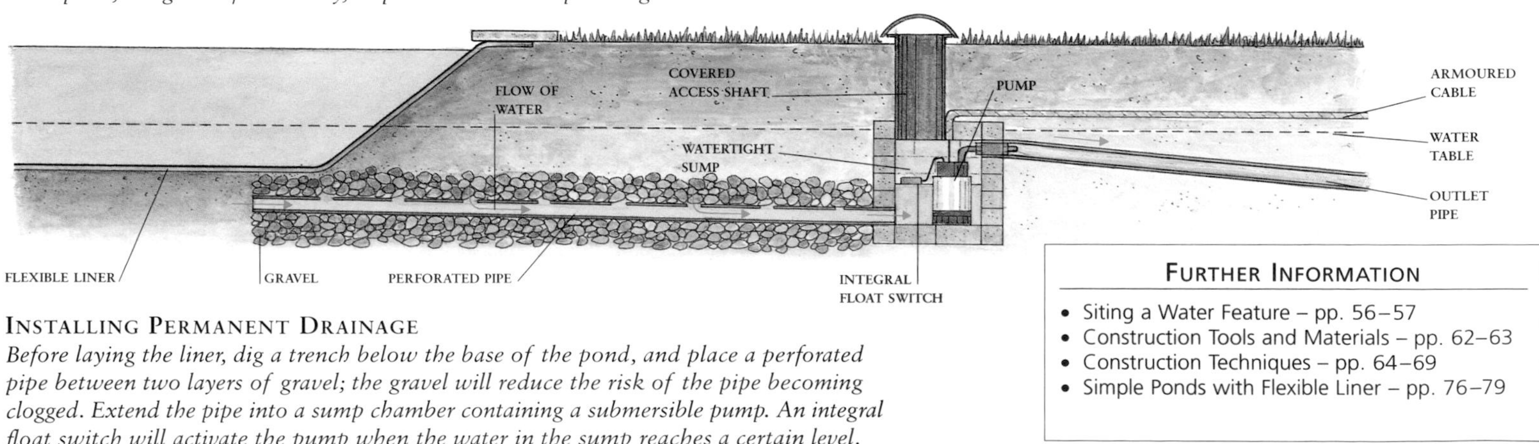

Installing Permanent Drainage
Before laying the liner, dig a trench below the base of the pond, and place a perforated pipe between two layers of gravel; the gravel will reduce the risk of the pipe becoming clogged. Extend the pipe into a sump chamber containing a submersible pump. An integral float switch will activate the pump when the water in the sump reaches a certain level.

Further Information

- Siting a Water Feature – pp. 56–57
- Construction Tools and Materials – pp. 62–63
- Construction Techniques – pp. 64–69
- Simple Ponds with Flexible Liner – pp. 76–79

MEASURING AREAS AND VOLUMES

FROM INITIAL PLANNING to the long-term care of a water feature, it will at times be necessary to know its dimensions, including the surface area of the excavation and of the water, and the volume of water it can contain. These statistics not only give a guideline to quantities, and thus costs, of construction materials (flexible liners, for example, are priced per square metre or foot), but are also used when choosing appropriate pumps and filters, and deciding the number of fish that a pond will house *(see p. 171)*, deciding the quantities of oxygenators necessary for a healthy environment *(see pp. 152–153)*, and the dosage rates of chemicals, if needed.

STILL WATER FEATURES

Formal pools in symmetrical shapes such as squares, circles, and triangles present the least difficulty in calculating dimensions, as they are easy to measure. Informal ponds can be more awkward. For simple, informal shapes such as the kidney shape, the surface area can be easily approximated, for most practical purposes, by drawing a rectangle around its outline, using the width at its widest point and the length of its longest axis. The surface area of this rectangle can be multiplied by the depth to obtain the pool's volume. For more complicated shapes that cannot be "squared off" so easily, divide the pool into sections, each with a regular shape such as a rectangle or semi-circle; their dimensions can be added together to give adequate approximate figures. When variations in depth occur, section the pool crosswise (as with the circular pool below). Remember that while marginal shelves make the volume of a pool smaller, they make the surface area of the hole bigger, and extra liner will need to be allowed for.

The various formulae for calculating volumes will give measurements in cubic feet or metres. To convert cubic feet to gallons, multiply the figure by 6.25. To convert cubic metres into litres, multiply the figure by 1,000.

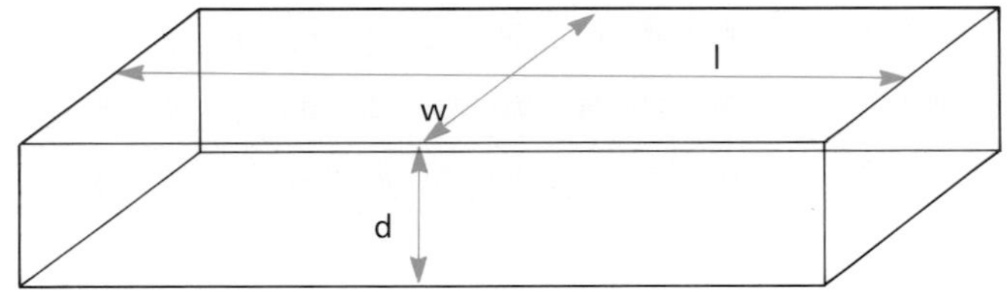

SQUARES AND RECTANGLES

It is easiest to calculate dimensions using measurements in metres or in decimal fractions of feet (e.g. 1.5ft for 18in). Multiply the length (l) of the pond by the width (w) to obtain the surface area. Multiply this figure by the depth (d) of the pool to establish its volume. For example, a pool 0.9m (3ft) wide by 1.2m (4ft) long has a surface area of 1.08sq m (12sq ft); with a depth of 0.45m (18in, or 1½ft), the pool's volume is 0.486cu m (18cu ft).

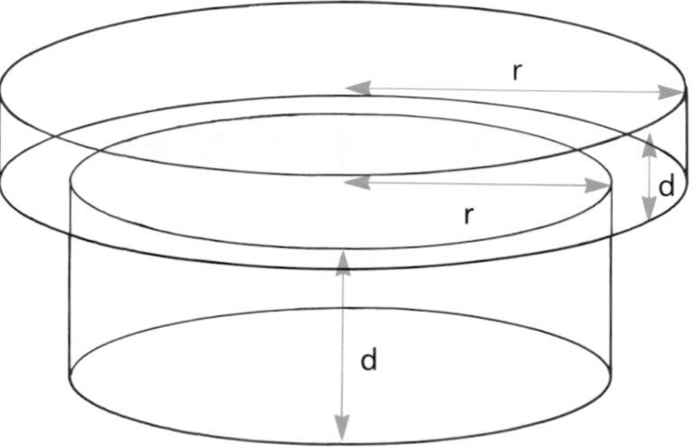

CIRCULAR SHAPES

Square the radius of the pool (r x r) and multiply this by the mathematical constant pi (π) – 3.14 – to obtain the surface area. To calculate the volume, multiply this figure by the depth (d). To calculate the volume of a circular pool with a marginal shelf, divide it transversely into two sections, as above, each with its own radius and depth, and add the volumes of the two sections together. To calculate the circumference of a circle, multiply the radius (r) by 3.14, then multiply this figure by 2.

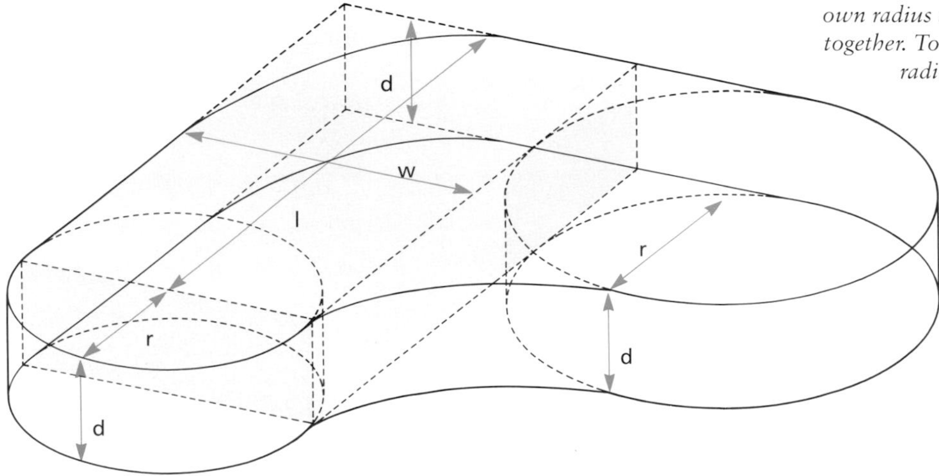

IRREGULAR SHAPES

For simple irregular shapes, use the maximum width, length, and depth to calculate surface area and volume as for a rectangle (above left). *For more complex shapes* (as right), *divide the pond into approximate square, rectangular, or circular or semicircular sections and calculate the surface area of each. Add the figures together to calculate the total surface area. Multiply this figure by the depth of the feature to obtain the volume.*

Moving Water Features

A waterfall or stream less than 60cm (2ft) in drop or length generally makes little practical difference to surface area or volume, and can be omitted from calculations, but longer streams and waterfalls should be added in. The height of the feature, from header pool or waterfall outlet to reservoir pool, is, however, always important: known as the "head", it is a factor in determining the power needed from a pump.

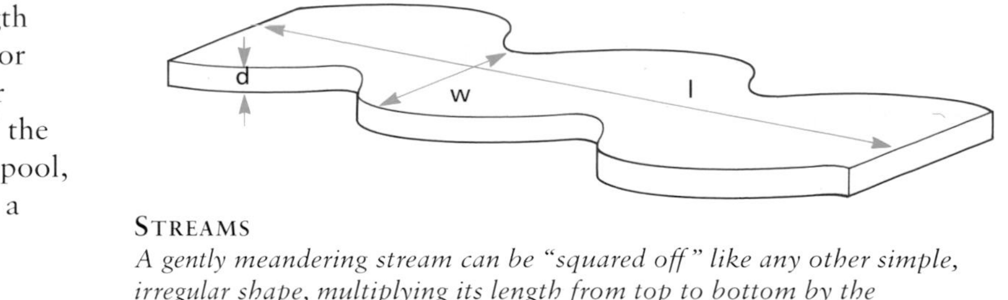

Streams

A gently meandering stream can be "squared off" like any other simple, irregular shape, multiplying its length from top to bottom by the approximate maximum width (average out measurements taken at several wide points) to obtain the surface area. Multiply this figure by the depth (including any layer of shingle or cobbles) to obtain the volume. The length of a widely meandering stream can be determined more accurately by following its curves with a tape measure, or draping string along its margin, then measuring the string.

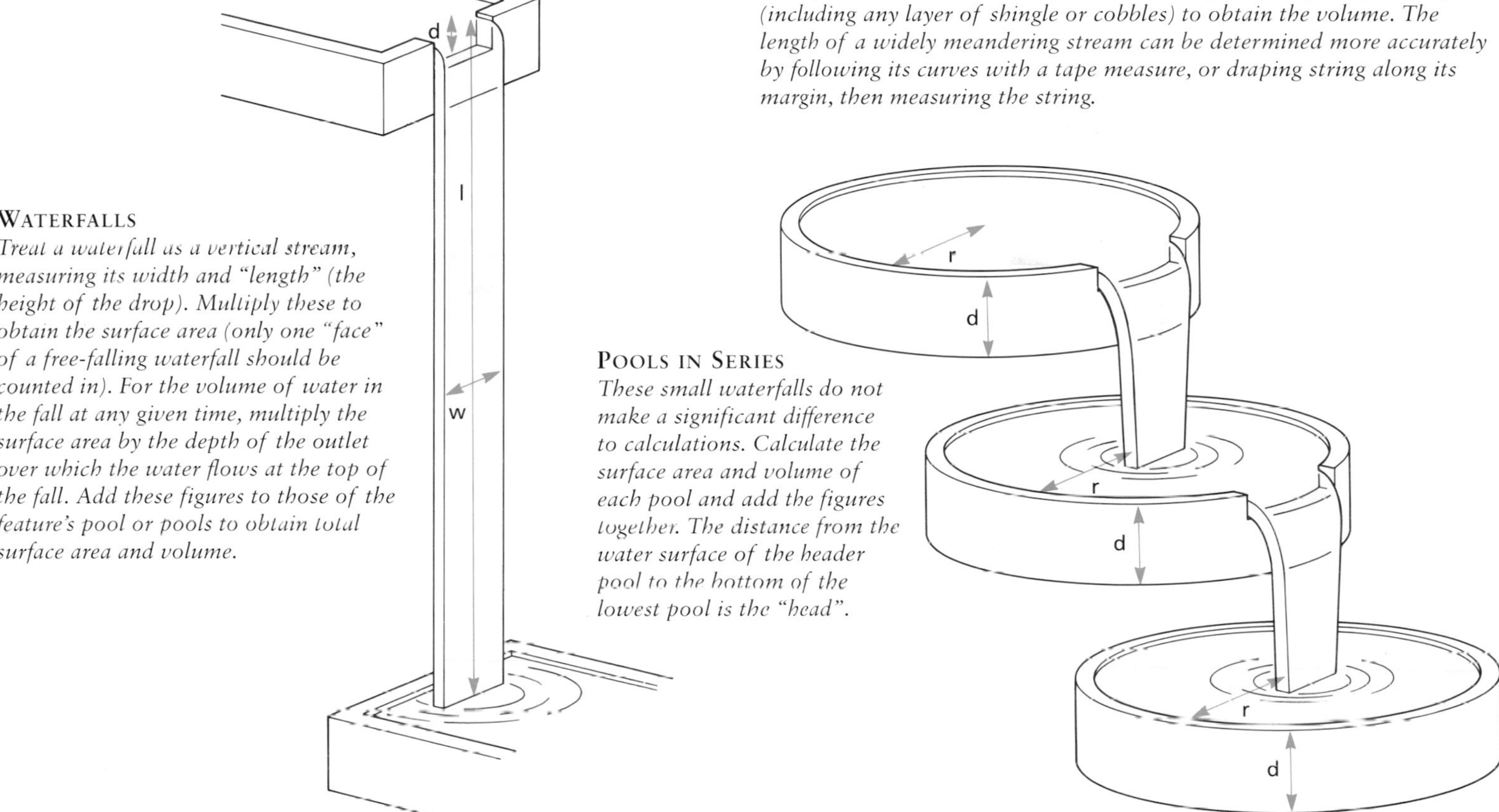

Waterfalls

Treat a waterfall as a vertical stream, measuring its width and "length" (the height of the drop). Multiply these to obtain the surface area (only one "face" of a free-falling waterfall should be counted in). For the volume of water in the fall at any given time, multiply the surface area by the depth of the outlet over which the water flows at the top of the fall. Add these figures to those of the feature's pool or pools to obtain total surface area and volume.

Pools in Series

These small waterfalls do not make a significant difference to calculations. Calculate the surface area and volume of each pool and add the figures together. The distance from the water surface of the header pool to the bottom of the lowest pool is the "head".

Construction Methods

A water feature with the same approximate surface area and volume, built in different styles, needs varying quantities of different materials; construction times can also vary. These five water features each have a surface area of 10sq m (96sq ft): as a rough guide, the formal pools could be 2.5m x 4m (8ft x 12ft) in width and length, and the informally shaped pools could be "squared off" to fit into a rectangle of these dimensions. Each has marginal shelf areas, and a volume of 4cu m (144cu ft): a water capacity of 4,000 litres (900 gals). To give some idea of the weight of water in the pools (and how strong the walls of the raised pool need to be), 1 litre of water weighs 1kg; 1 gallon weighs 10lb.

Guide to Requirements for Different Pool Styles

Style of pool	Digging time (with a helper)	Concrete, for foundations etc	Walling materials	Liner and underlay	Ready-to-mix mortar	Other materials	Coping stones/ edging
Raised oblong pool with double wall and flexible liner.	2 hours to dig foundations (but 20 hours' bricklaying)	50kg (110lb) cement, 1cu m (1cu yd) ballast	80 concrete blocks, 30 x 23cm (12 x 9in); 360 bricks, 8 x 30cm (3 x 12in)	5.2m x 3.9m (17ft x 13ft): 20.5sq m (221sq ft)	12 x 25kg (55lb) bags	–	20 coping stones, 60 x 30 cm (24 x 12in)
Oblong concrete pool lined with reinforced cement	10 hours, plus removal of spoil	1cu m (1cu yd) sand, 50kg (110lb) cement, 1cu m (1cu yd) aggregate	52 concrete blocks, 45 x 23cm (18 x 9in); 118 house bricks	–	6 x 25kg (55lb) bags	Reinforcing fibres for cement: 3 x 5kg (11lb) bags	20 coping stones, 60 x 60 cm (24 x 24in)
Informal pool with flexible liner and crazy-paving edge	10 hours, plus removal of spoil	1.5cu m (1½cu yd) sand, 50kg (110lb) cement, 0.5cu m (½cu yd) aggregate	–	5.5m x 4.3m (18ft x 14ft): 23.4sq m (252sq ft)	3 x 25kg (55lb) bags	–	12sq m (12sq yd) crazy paving
Pool as above, 30cm (1ft) less wide, with small rigid-unit stream	13 hours (inc. bedding in units on spoil-based mound)	1cu m (1cu yd) sand, 50kg (110lb) cement, 0.5cu m (½cu yd) aggregate	–	5.5m x 4.3m (18ft x 14ft): 23.4sq m (252sq ft)	2 x 25kg (55lb) bags	Two stream units, one header pool unit, sand for bedding in	10sq m (10 sq yd) crazy paving; 30 x 25kg (55lb) loose rocks
Wildlife pond edged with turf, planting and pebble beach	10 hours, plus removal of spoil	–	–	6m x 4.9m (20ft x 16ft): 29.4sq m (320sq ft) (for varied depths)	–	–	8 x 50kg (110lb) bags of cobbles for beach area

Construction Tools & Materials

The tools and materials necessary for building water features vary from project to project, although some, such as a spirit level, are essential for any construction task. Do-it-yourself enthusiasts may be familiar with many of the techniques used in the step-by-step projects featured in this section, and will have used the tools in other situations. It is important to choose the correct implement and materials for the appropriate stage of construction, and to use them with skill and care, in order to ensure a structurally sound feature. If in doubt, seek professional help; sometimes it is worth extra investment to obtain a good result.

Construction Tools

Using the appropriate tools for a job makes an appreciable difference to the ease with which the task can be accomplished, and in certain situations it is crucial to use the correct equipment. Consider borrowing or hiring tools that you might never or rarely need again. If buying, it is well worth investing, if you can, in good-quality tools: they are usually longer-lasting and more comfortable to use.

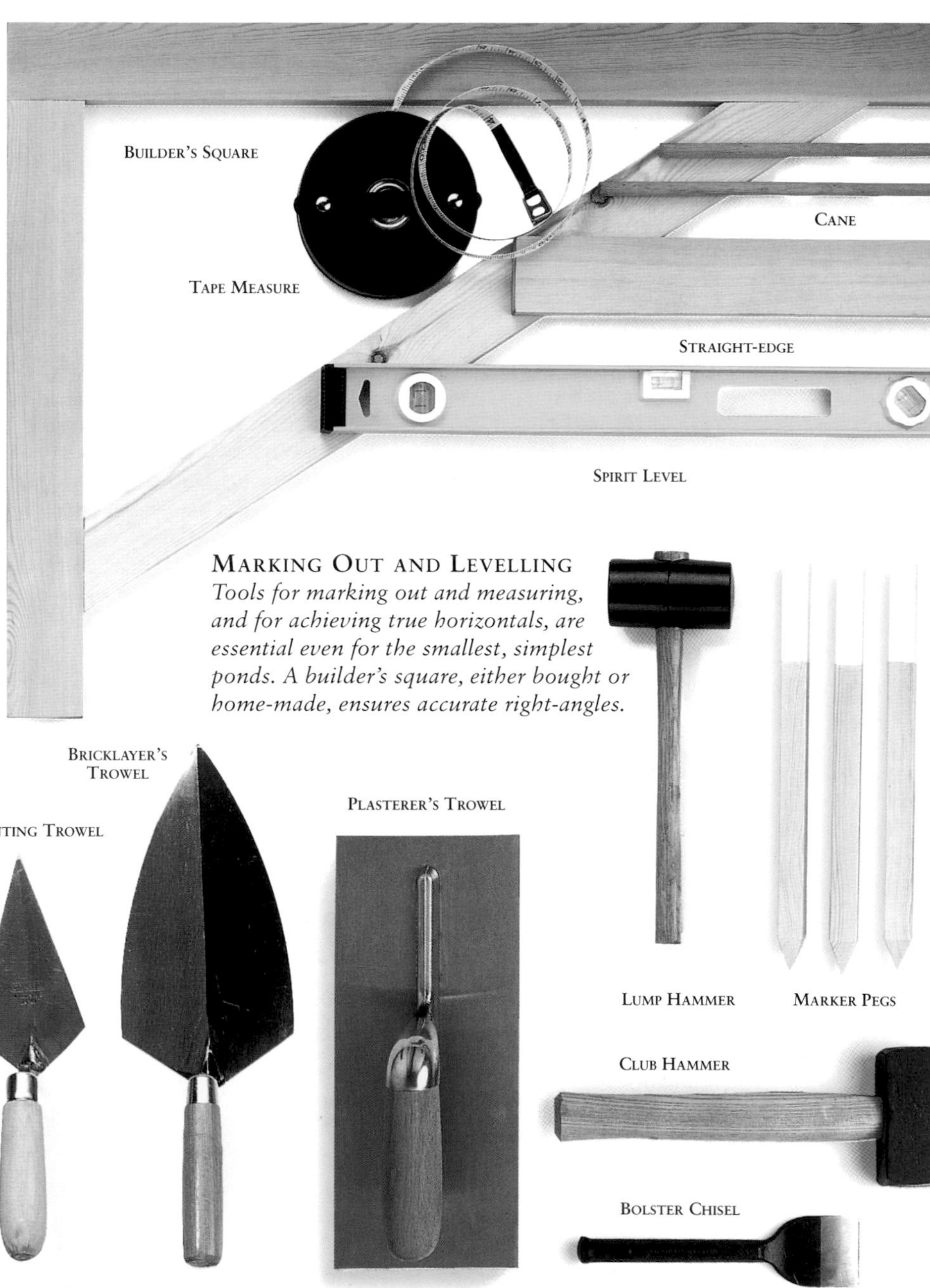

Marking Out and Levelling

Tools for marking out and measuring, and for achieving true horizontals, are essential even for the smallest, simplest ponds. A builder's square, either bought or home-made, ensures accurate right-angles.

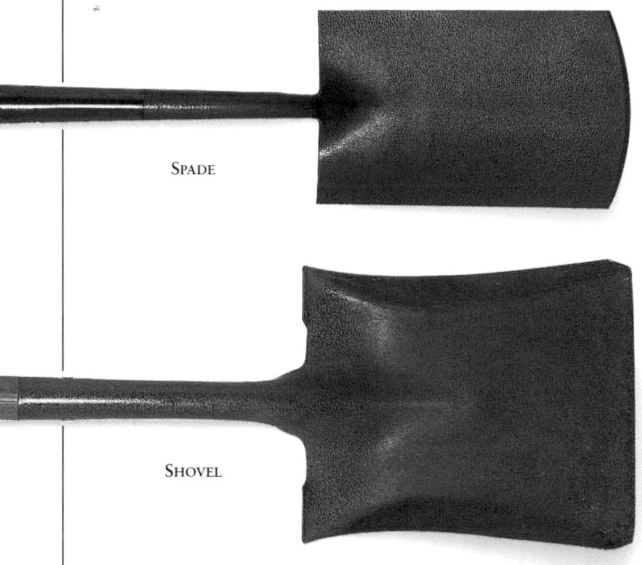

Digging Tools

Most gardeners will already own a good sharp-edged spade, but these generally have too small a blade to make large-scale excavation comfortable. Once the hole is big enough to stand in, use the spade to break earth up, then use a shovel, with its wide blade with incurved edges, to scoop the earth out of the hole.

Drilling Holes

A cordless drill is much more convenient, and safer, to work with outdoors. Always use the correct drill bits for wood or stonework.

Tools for Concrete, Cement, and Mortar

A bricklayer's trowel has a better shape than a garden trowel for handling wet building mixes. Much more skill is required to use pointing and plastering trowels: to create an acceptable finish you will need plenty of practice, since you must work quickly with fast-drying mixtures.

Cutting Bricks and Slabs

A hammer and chisel can be used to cut the odd brick or slab to fit a corner; however, if you have many pavers to cut into precise shapes, it is worth hiring an angle-grinder.

Materials for Construction

Unlike the decorative materials chosen for edging and other finishing touches, the basic materials used to build water features are often hidden from view. Most items will be available at any general builder's merchant. An aquatic centre will stock a range of pool liners and is also the best source for delivery hoses and other piping: because they specialize in water-feature construction, they will be able to tell you exactly what type of pipework you need to achieve the desired effect.

Standard Delivery Hose

Wide Delivery Hose

Lightweight Plastic Waste Pipe

Wide-gauge Copper Pipe

Narrow-gauge Copper Pipe

Wide-gauge Plastic Push-fit Pipe

Narrow-gauge Plastic Push-fit Pipe

Copper Elbow Joint

Compression Joint

Soldered T-bar

Soldered Elbow Joint

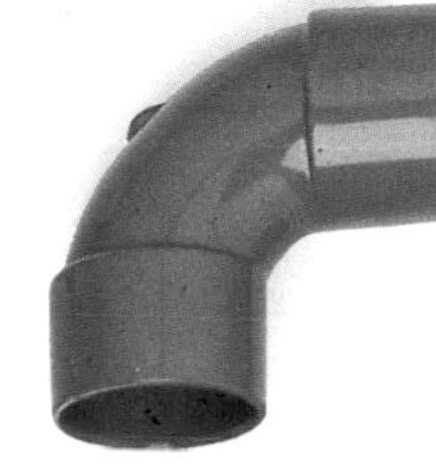

Plastic Elbow Joint

Pipework and Joints

Pipes conduct water and protect electricity cabling. If pipework has to be visible (for example, on a wall feature), copper piping is more attractive and will take on a weathered appearance. All flexible piping, even if reinforced, must have rigid elbow joints at sharp changes of direction, or the pipe will kink and restrict water flow.

House Brick

Concrete Block

Building Blocks

Common house or engineering bricks can be used to build everything from decorative walls to submerged plant plinths. Concrete blocks can be used to build concealed walling more quickly and economically.

Sharp Sand

Cement

Mortar

Mortar

Mortar is a mix that consists of cement, sharp sand, and water. It is available as a ready-made mix, but this is only economical where small quantities are used.

Lining Materials

Flexible liners are generally made of polythene, PVC, or butyl *(see p. 67)*. It is advisable to use some form of underlay to protect the liner, especially on stony sites. Polyester matting underlay will be available wherever liner is sold, and is not expensive. Clay-based bentomat *(see pp. 92–93)* is an attractive alternative to plastic liner – it is made entirely of natural materials and has an unobtrusive, textured matt finish.

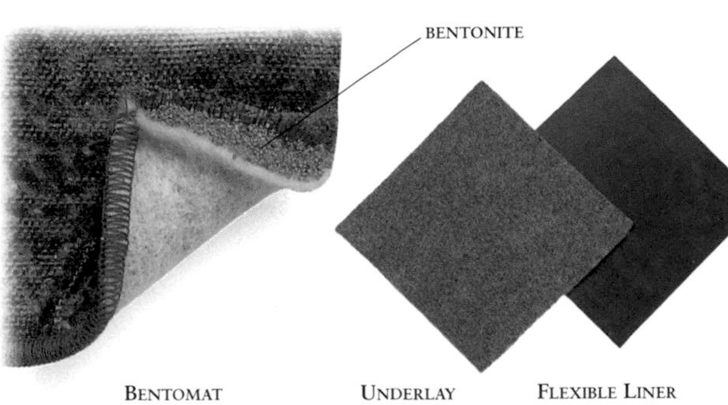

Bentomat

Underlay

Flexible Liner

Strengthening Additives

Grades of Ballast

Adding small stones and sand to cement creates concrete. The larger the size of stone, the stronger the concrete: for very solid foundations concrete is poured over compacted hardcore (rubble).

Reinforcing Fibre

This proprietary fibre, similar to glass fibre, makes a cement mix stronger and more flexible; a rendering of this mix on a concrete shell (see pp. 90–91) *forms a lining that is less susceptible to cracking caused by water pressure and small earth movements.*

Further Information

- Construction Techniques – pp. 64–69
- Pumps and Filters – pp. 70–73
- Edging Materials – pp. 126–129

CONSTRUCTION TECHNIQUES

SOME CONSTRUCTION METHODS are better suited to certain styles of water feature than others, and also to the type of job you are prepared to tackle. Rigid units such as preformed fibreglass pools *(see below)* are excellent choices for small to medium-sized, self-contained pools that are relatively quick and simple to install. For a freer hand with the size and shape of pool, plus the option of incorporating customized features such as islands and planting pockets, flexible liner *(see pp. 66–67)* is the obvious choice. With some basic building skills *(see pp. 68–69)*, formal and raised pools edged with brick, paving, and timber can be considered.

USING PREFORMED POOL UNITS

Installing a rigid container to hold water, whether a fibreglass pool unit or an improvised version such as a plastic bin, simply involves digging a hole of the correct size and shape to house it so that it is absolutely level, both for visual effect and to ensure that planting baskets sit securely on shelves or plinths. Small, evenly shaped units with only one depth level may be installed completely above ground level, but it is very difficult to give a larger unit with irregular contouring the support it needs unless the unit, or at least its deeper zone, is sunken into the ground.

DIGGING TIPS

- Place two polythene sheets beyond the hole's proposed edges: one for the valuable topsoil, the other for subsoil.
- Dig with a straight back and bended knees *(see left)* to minimize strain on your back.
- Once the hole is big enough, work from within it to avoid extra bending.
- You may find it easier to dig the hole down to the correct depth, then to enlarge it: chop at the sides with a sharp-edged spade, then shovel out the earth.
- Only shovel small quantities of soil at a time.
- If you are not accustomed to a lot of digging, wear gloves to prevent blistering; shoes with sturdy soles are also essential. Stop and rest as soon as you begin to feel tired, or if you feel pain of any kind.

STAGES OF CONSTRUCTION

Rigid units must be firmly supported and cushioned against sharp objects. Ensure that the base of the hole is firm, level, and free of sharp stones. Make the hole slightly wider than the unit so that you can backfill with ease. Part-filling the pool with water as you backfill will allow you to make adjustments so that the unit remains level as the weight of water settles it into position.

MARKING OUT Before digging, you may use canes to mark the perimeter of a unit that slopes inwards toward the base. Be very careful to avoid eye injury when digging close to canes.

FIRM SUPPORT Bed units into a firm layer of sand or sifted soil, free from sharp stones. Do not use sharp (builders') sand where plants are to grow.

MARGINAL SHELF Some trial and error is usually necessary to contour the hole for marginal shelves.

MARKING OUT

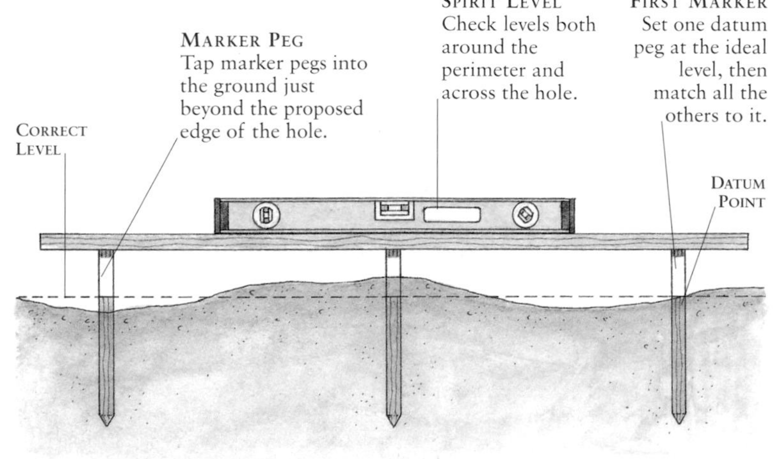

USING MARKER PEGS

Datum, or marker, pegs are used to obtain level, horizontal pool edges on uneven ground. Once the first datum point is established, use a spirit level to ensure that the marker level on all subsequent pegs corresponds to that on the datum peg, which should act as a reference point.

LEVELLING

USING A SPIRIT LEVEL AND STRAIGHT-EDGE *To check correct levels across a hole, or across distances wider than the length of a spirit level, use a straight-edge: a long, straight strip of wood on which the spirit level can be balanced. Check levels frequently, at every stage of construction.*

TYPES OF PREFORMED POND UNIT

In many ways preformed units make ideal ponds: they are easy both to install and clean. They are generally made of fibreglass or various plastics in a range of shapes and sizes, the maximum size being approximately 3.5m (12ft) across, and are available from most nurseries or garden centres. Fibreglass units are light, strong, and durable; they are recommended for semi-raised ponds. Plastic units tend to be cheaper, but may only last two or three years. Shallow, square or circular units make ideal small formal features; their bases can be disguised with gravel or pebbles. To accommodate plants and fish, however, a deeper unit, ideally with marginal shelves, is essential.

SIMPLE SHAPES The simpler the shape, the easier to install.

MARGINAL SHELF Shelf space is wide enough for planting baskets.

GREY COLOUR Neutral colours are the least obtrusive.

DEPTH Unit has a deep zone, essential for fish and for planted ponds.

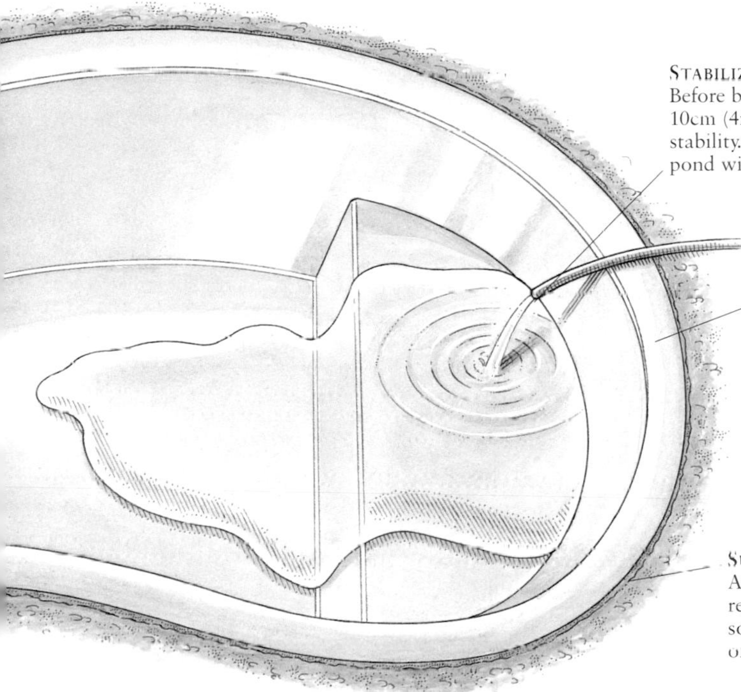

STABILIZING THE POOL Before backfilling, fill the pool with 10cm (4in) of water to increase its stability. Continue to slowly fill the pond with water as you backfill.

WIDE RIM The rim prevents soil from falling into the pond. It can be disguised with plants *(see right)* or with mortared-down slabs.

SUPPORTING THE LIP After backfilling, remember to press sand or soil firmly up under the lip of the unit to support it.

DISGUISING PREFORMED UNITS

SUNKEN POND
One disadvantage of preformed units is that their wide rims form an unnatural edge. Unless you are surrounding the pond with paving, planting is the best way to disguise and soften the rim. Use clump-forming plants, including some moisture-lovers to give a more natural waterside effect.

SEMI-RAISED POND
Semi-raised units must have a firm supporting wall of timber or mortared stones to remain secure. Backfill with rich, moisture-retentive soil and keep plants in it well watered.

BACKFILLING AND TAMPING

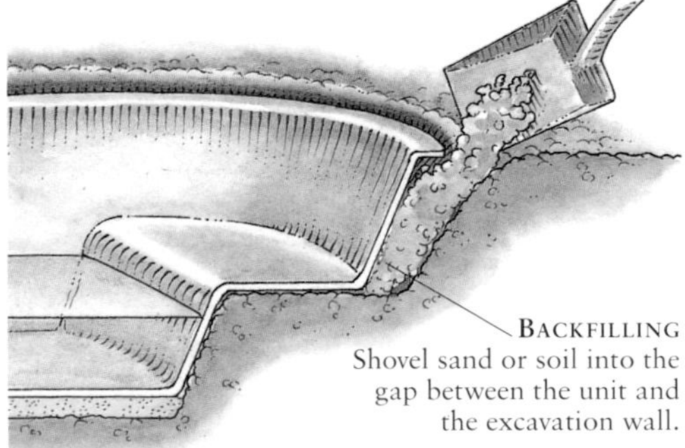

BACKFILLING Shovel sand or soil into the gap between the unit and the excavation wall.

1 MAKE THE EXCAVATION slightly wider and deeper than the unit so that you can backfill and tamp easily. Always shovel out or rake back spoil well clear of the hole so that it cannot slip back in. Shovel a small quantity of sand or sifted soil into the gap all around the unit.

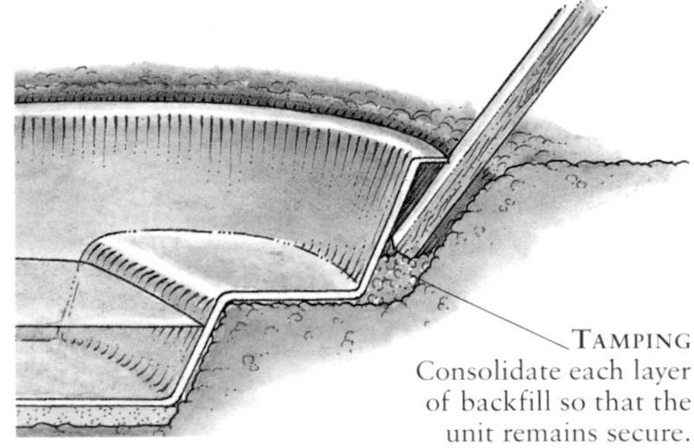

TAMPING Consolidate each layer of backfill so that the unit remains secure.

2 A SHORT LENGTH OF POST is an ideal tamping tool. Press the sand or soil down firmly all around the unit. Repeat the process, backfilling gradually around the sides. Do not tamp so hard that the unit is distorted: part-filling with water, and checking levels frequently, will help avoid this.

USING FLEXIBLE POND LINER

FLEXIBLE LINER IS THE MOST versatile material available to the water gardener. It can be used as waterproof lining for a porous shell – for example, a brick-built reservoir pool or an old half-barrel. An old, cracked concrete pond or rigid pool unit can be instantly "repaired" with a new lining. However, flexible liner comes into its own in the construction of informal ponds, allowing considerable freedom with the design of pools and streams, and the inclusion of a variety of additional features. Liner materials vary in price and quality. Cheap polythene can be adequate: high-density polythene is cheapest, but is of the poorest quality and should only be used in double thickness. It will deteriorate and crack under prolonged exposure to the ultraviolet rays in sunlight, and any exposed areas must be carefully concealed. Low-density polythene is of a slightly higher quality; it is stronger and fairly flexible. For a substantial, durable feature it is well worth investing in good-quality PVC or, at the top of the range, butyl *(see facing page)*. It will be far less prone to tearing, puncturing, and ultraviolet deterioration; top-grade PVCs and butyl usually carry at least a 10-year guarantee.

To avoid unnecessary expense, make a good estimate of the amount of liner you need *(see below left)*. Shortfalls can, fortunately, be remedied. Water pressure is usually sufficient to hold two overlapping sheets of liner together *(see pp. 100–101)*, or a thin layer of mortar can be used to "glue" down the overlap.

LINING AN EXCAVATION

You should ideally unroll liner prior to laying (see p. 76). *However, do not then drag it over the hole; you will disturb the underlay. Roll the liner up from both sides towards the middle, lift the roll into position across the centre of the hole and unroll carefully, without stretching it.*

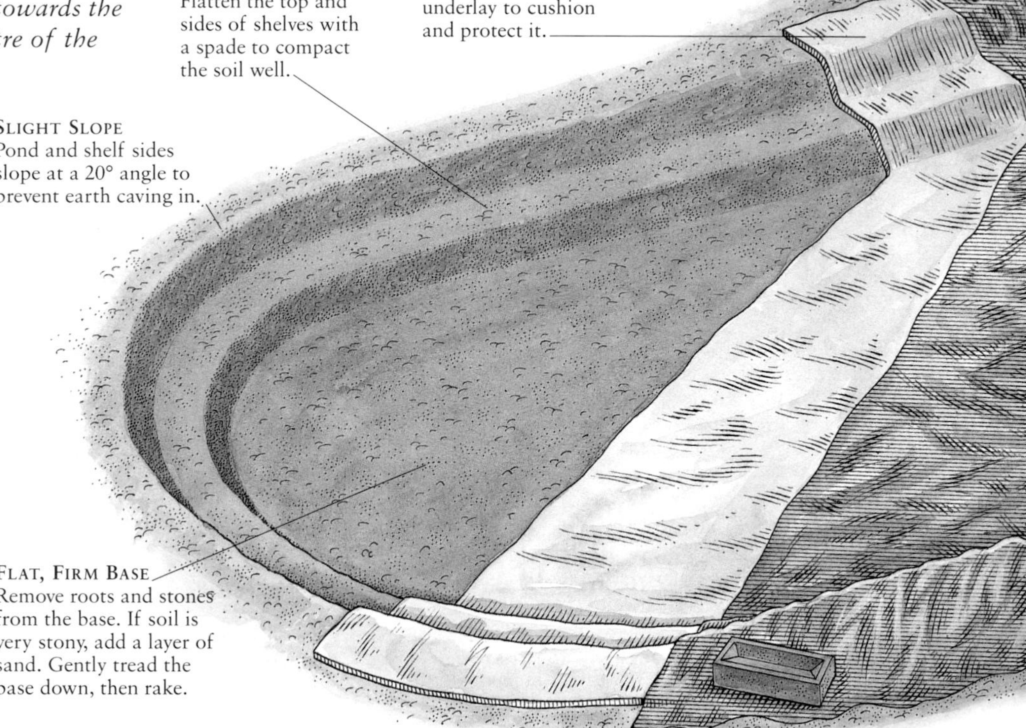

EXCAVATING THE POND

MARKING OUT AND DIGGING
String or hose, pegs, or sand are perfectly adequate for marking out an informal shape. Excavate the hole, angling the sides slightly inwards. Marginal shelves should be at least 30cm (12in) wide to accommodate planting baskets. If you are not incorporating a beach, you may wish to leave a sloping ramp on one side as an easy access or exit point for wildlife.

CALCULATING THE AMOUNT OF LINER

First determine the maximum length, width, and depth of the pond. The liner should measure the maximum width of the pond plus twice its depth, by the maximum length plus twice its depth. Add another 45cm (18in) to both width and length to allow for a flap overlapping the edge, in order to prevent leakage. If the pond sides are completely vertical, or for additional features such as an island *(see pp. 80–81)* or integral boggy area *(see pp. 82–83)*, extra liner will be necessary.

LAYING UNDERLAY

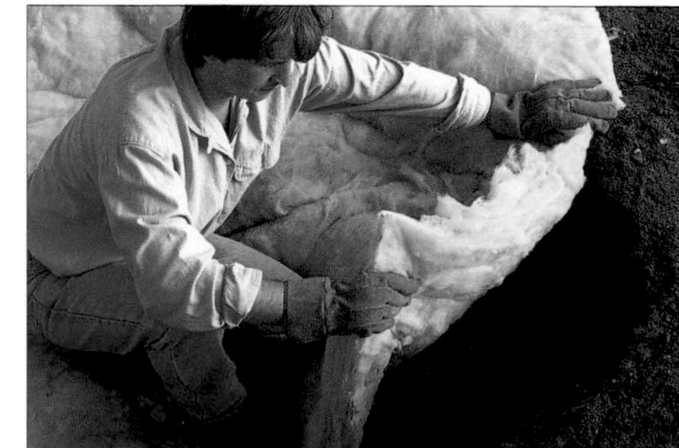

1 SPREAD THE UNDERLAY (here, fibreglass insulation material) over the base and sides of the excavation. Press the material firmly over and into the contours of the hole.

2 KEEPING THE UNDERLAY in position (try not to put your full weight on any marginal shelves) trim it neatly at, or slightly overlapping, ground level. Then unroll the liner over it.

Filling a Lined Pond

1 Using bricks as temporary weights, fill the pond slowly, gradually moving the bricks to allow the liner to settle down into the hole.

2 Only when the pond has been filled and the liner has ceased to move, trim off surplus material with scissors or a craft knife.

Smooth Finish
Gentle curving shapes are easy to line; pleat material at sharp angles.

Filling the Pond
Gently fill the pond, so that the water slowly presses and moulds the liner down into the contours of the hole.

Extra Liner
A generous margin will allow the liner to be taken up under soil or edging.

Pebble Beach
A gentle slope with a slight rim makes an ideal beach area.

Mortaring Stone on Liner

1 For a simple surround, mortar rounded or flat stones directly onto the liner. More formal paved edging requires foundations *(see p. 68)*.

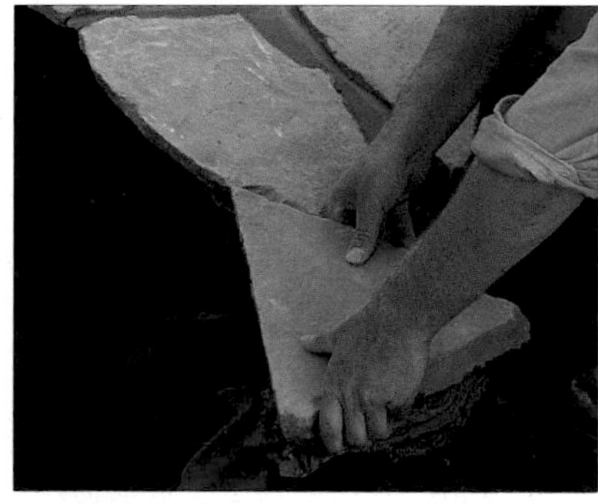

2 Flat slabs should overhang the pond by 5cm (2in) to disguise the liner. Do not drop mortar into the pond, or it will have to be emptied.

Grades of Liner and Underlay

The more expensive pond liners come in different weights and thicknesses, and the larger the area you wish to cover, the thicker the material should be. Black is the most unobtrusive colour, although others are sometimes available. If buying good-quality liner, always protect your investment by using underlay beneath it. There are some excellent products available that will prolong the liner's lifespan.

Underlay Material
Proprietary polyester matting underlay comes in rolls up to 2m (6ft) wide. Underlay can also be improvised, using insulation felts or even old synthetic carpet. Newspaper is sometimes recommended, but tends to disintegrate fast.

Carpet Polyester Matting

PVC Pond Liners *(below)*
PVC liner is becoming increasingly popular, as it has far greater flexibility than polythene. PVC comes in a number of grades, the thicker grades (0.5–1mm/ 0.02–0.04in) usually last longer, and should be sold with a guarantee. There is a more expensive, superior version in which nylon net is incorporated to give extra strength.

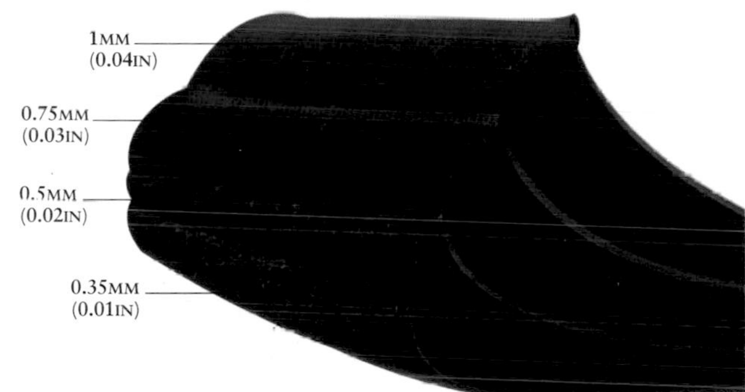

Grades of Butyl Liner *(below)*
The best lining material is butyl. Its 300 per cent elasticity allows it to be installed with fewer creases and folds than other types of liner, and it remains flexible even in cold weather. It is available in large sizes and has excellent resistance to ultraviolet light; it is also easy to repair (see p. 145). *The standard grade is 0.75mm (0.03in) thick, although it is available in other weights.*

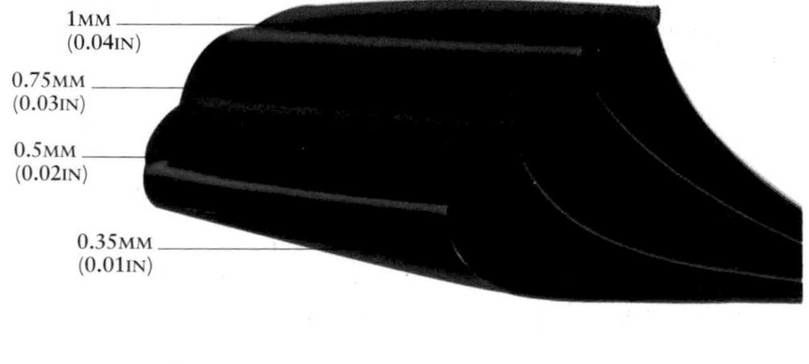

USING BUILDING MATERIALS

BETWEEN THE TWO EXTREMES of a simple hole lined with polythene and a raised brick-built pond with double walls lie a host of water-garden projects requiring some knowledge of basic building techniques. Structures that will be concealed, such as foundations, concrete-block shell walls, planting beds, and shelves must be well built in order to be durable, but they need not be perfectly finished. Flat paving and edging are not difficult to lay, provided that you work quickly and clean off excess mortar before it dries (dry mortar is almost impossible to remove). However, bricklaying and rendering are skilled tasks that must be done properly, or the finished product will be both visually and structurally poor, with no remedy but to have the job redone.

MARKING OUT STRAIGHT-SIDED SHAPES

USING A BUILDER'S SQUARE

It is essential that formal shapes are carefully marked out and checked regularly for accuracy during construction. Corners must be perfect right-angles, or walls and edging will not meet where they should: this can cause problems with both the shapes and quantities of blocks, bricks, and pavers.

LAYING A HARDCORE BASE

1 FOR SOLID FOUNDATIONS, spread a 10cm (4in) layer of hardcore over the base of the excavation before pouring in concrete.

2 HARDCORE CAN be compacted with a club hammer and block of wood, but if the base area is large, it is worth hiring a compactor. Its vibrating plate consolidates and flattens the hardcore, shaking smaller pieces into the spaces between larger stones.

CONSTRUCTING A STRAIGHT-SIDED POOL

Pools with straight edges and vertical sides are most effectively constructed using traditional building techniques and materials either beneath, or instead of, flexible pond liner. Firm foundations and solid walls are essential to prevent landslips around the edges of the pool; retaining walls of concrete blocks can be made watertight either with flexible liner (see pp. 78–79) *or, as here, with a rendering of cement made strong and flexible with special reinforcing fibres. With bricklaying skills, a low wall could be added around this pool to give a semi-raised effect.*

CONCRETE WALLING BLOCKS
These voids in blocks make them lighter to handle. Once in position they can be filled with concrete for extra strength.

CONCRETE INFILL
Use concrete to fill any space between walling blocks and the sides of an excavation. The mortar between the blocks must first be *completely* set.

VERTICAL-SIDED HOLES
Use a plumb-line to make walls as vertical and even as possible; small irregularities can be compensated for with a concrete infill.

HARDCORE AND CONCRETE FOUNDATION
A compacted layer of hardcore with concrete poured on top makes firm footings for walls and other structures such as stepping stones and bridge ends. For maximum stability, cover the entire base of a pool.

SAFETY PRECAUTIONS

- Even small bags of cement, mortar mix, and sand are heavy; great care should be taken in lifting them. Always bend from the knees, rather than bending your back. Be careful, also, to protect your back while digging *(see p. 64)*.
- Cement dust is an irritant: wear gloves when mixing mortar and concrete, avoid inhaling dust (wear a filter or cyclist's mask if possible), and never rub your eyes while working.
- String brightly coloured or fluorescent tape at waist height between canes around the hole when you leave it unattended.
- Never let children play alone near holes, tools, or materials.
- Make sure that any powered tools are fitted with a residual current device (RCD or circuit breaker).

LAYING CONCRETE

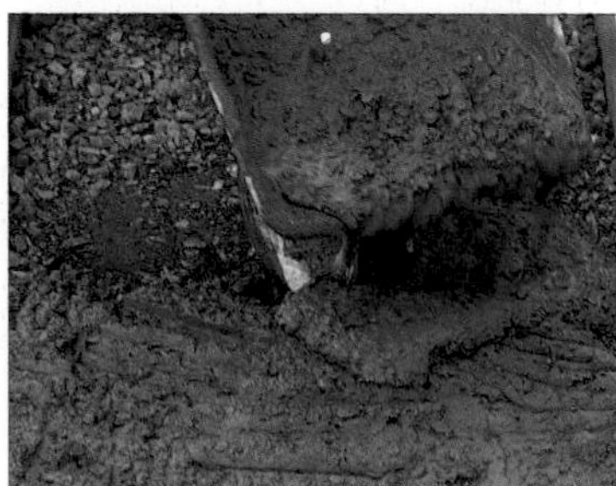

1 POUR LARGE QUANTITIES of concrete from a wheelbarrow. For even coverage, try to pour the mix in gently overlapping folds.

2 LEVEL AND FIRM the concrete, both cross- and lengthways, with a beam; rest a spirit level on the beam to check levels.

Simple Bricklaying

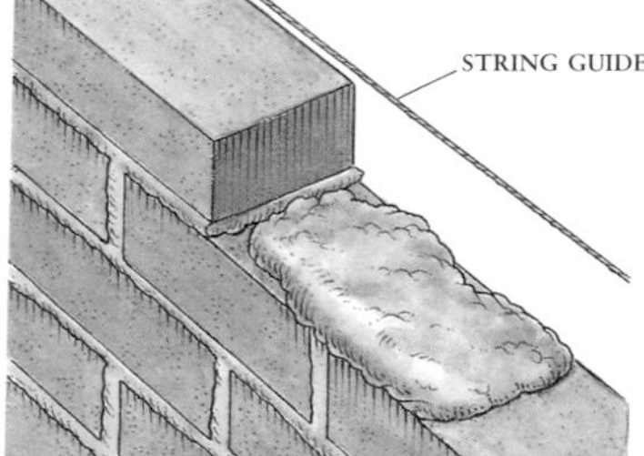

1 **Lay bricks**, frog downwards, in staggered rows (a "bond" pattern). Apply a layer of mortar where the next brick will be placed.

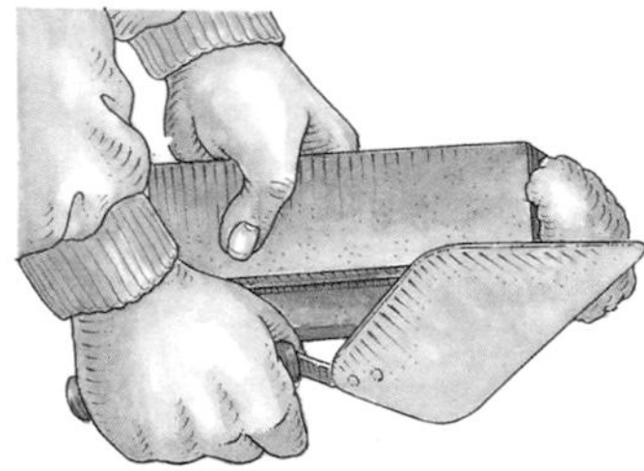

2 **"Butter" the end** of the next brick by drawing across it a trowel loaded with mortar. Do not overload the trowel.

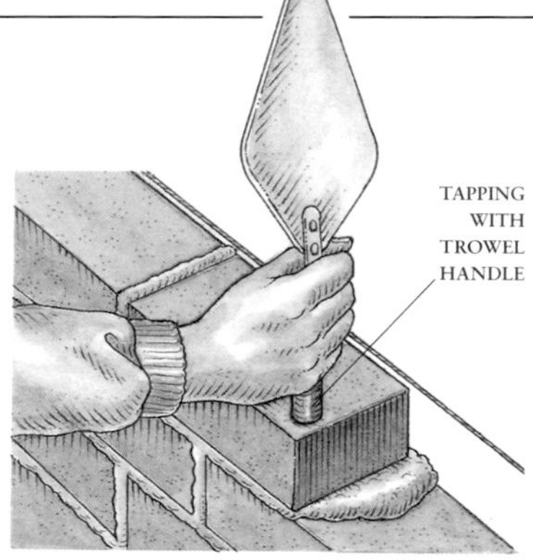

3 **Set the brick** down firmly and squarely. Working with the guide and, after every few bricks, a spirit level, tap the brick until level. Brush off surplus mortar with a wire brush.

Coping Stones
Bricks and pavers jutting over the pond edges must be securely mortared down for safety.

Adding Water
Never fill a cement-lined pool unless its surface has been sealed to lock in harmful chemicals. Or, fill the pool and add potasssium permanganate crystals, leave for a week to "cure" the cement, then empty and refill.

Surface Layer
A rendering of cement can be used on exterior walls as cladding, or to waterproof the interior of a pool.

Mortars and Concrete

Unless specific recipes are given, use a mix of 1 part cement to 3 parts sharp sand for bricklaying, or 5 parts sand for laying paving; for a general purpose concrete mix, use 1 part cement to 2½ parts sharp sand and 3½ parts aggregate.

- Before use, store ingredients in a dry place.
- Avoid frosty weather when laying concrete; the cold will cause it to disintegrate before fully hardened.
- Always mix dry ingredients well before adding water.
- Add the water to a well in the centre and fold the dry ingredients inwards.
- Add water very gradually to avoid an over-wet mix.
- Work as quickly as possible once mixes are made up.
- Colorants can be added to mortar for visual effects.

Working with Wet Concrete

A variety of items may need to be embedded into wet mortars and concretes before they set. Wall ties embedded at regular intervals will reinforce a double wall *(see pp. 86–87)*. Steel brackets can be fixed onto bolts sunk into wet concrete, to secure timber to a concrete base *(see pp. 122–123)*. Reinforcing wire can be sandwiched between layers of wet concrete *(see p. 91)*. Conduits for water overflows or for wiring can also be hidden between bricks or under coping *(see pp. 86–87)*.

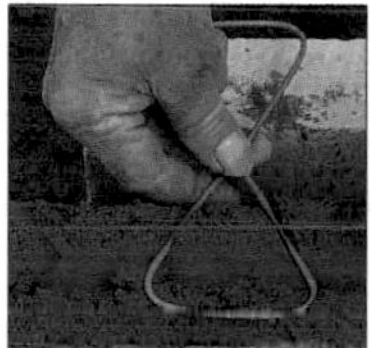

Wall Tie

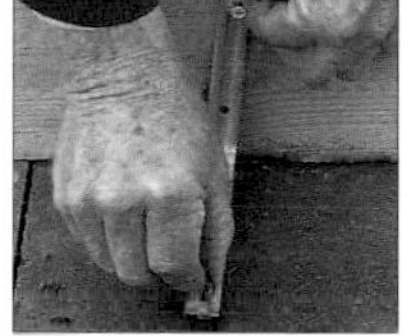

Bracket

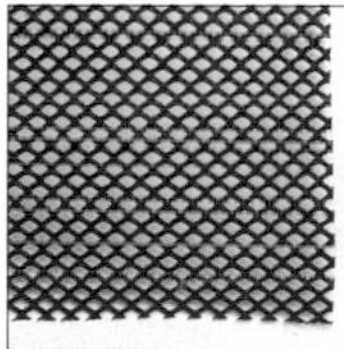

Wire Mesh

Overflow Pipe

Cutting Stone Slabs

1 **Place the slab** on a flat surface. Score a cutting groove on both sides and edges of the slab with the corner of a bolster chisel.

2 **Using the chisel** with a club hammer, carefully work along to deepen the scored line on both sides and at the edges of the slab.

3 **Balance the slab** on a length of timber. Align the groove with the edge of the wood and tap with a hammer handle until the slab splits.

Cutting Bricks

Score the cutting line with the edge of a bolster chisel, then chisel a 3mm (⅛in) deep groove along this line. Raise on to a piece of timber, and tap with the handle of a hammer.

PUMPS AND FILTERS

PUMPS ARE USED IN conjunction with water features in order to recirculate water. An electric motor draws the water in through an inlet to which a strainer is fitted to prevent the system being blocked by debris. Pressure pushes the water out through a pipe, which is attached to a waterfall, fountain, or filter. There are two types of pump – submersible and surface; submersible pumps run under water and high-voltage surface pumps are housed above ground. Pumps come in a wide range of models to suit every type of water feature. They fall into two main categories – pumps to run a fountain or waterfall and solids-handling pumps to work a filtration system.

TYPES OF PUMP

A pump is required to move water either within a feature (through a fountain or filter) or to travel around a watercourse. To operate the pump, electricity will need to be brought to the water *(see p. 72)*. Before choosing a pump, assess what you want it to do *(see* Points to Consider, *p. 72)* and consult a specialist supplier with your requirements.

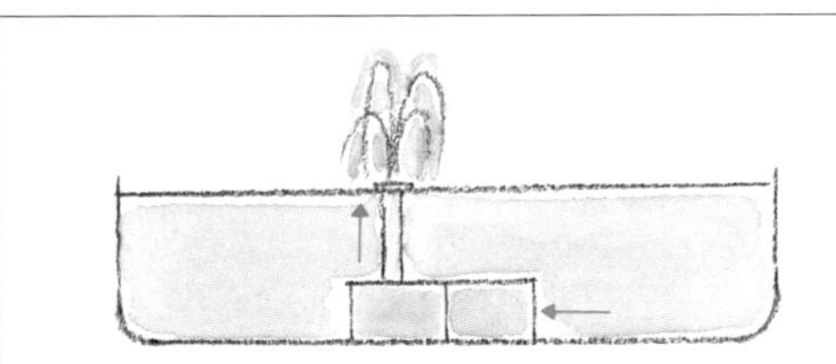

FOUNTAIN PUMP
A small fountain requires a submersible pump that has low output but high pressure. The pump may sit directly under, or away from, the fountain (see pp. 108–111).

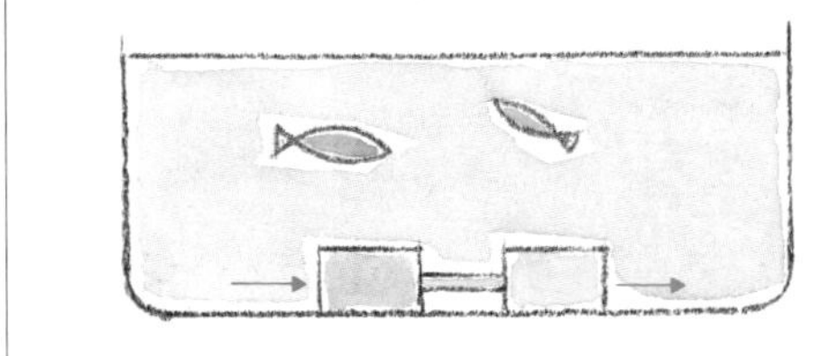

PUMP FOR FILTRATION SYSTEM
A pump is not always installed to produce visible water movement; it may also be used to push water through a filter. Heavily stocked fish ponds require this arrangement.

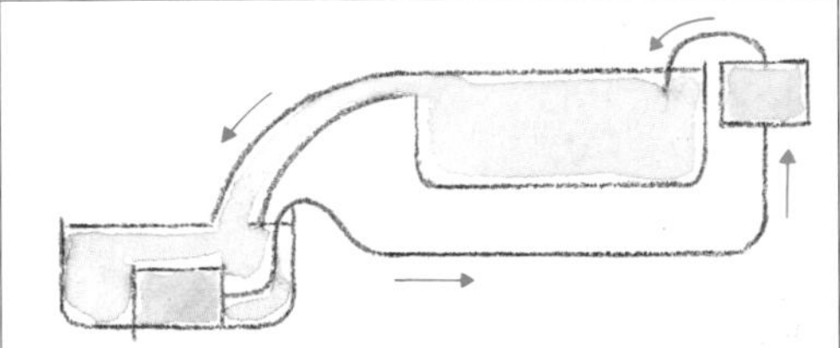

PUMP FOR WATERCOURSES
To move water any distance from a reservoir pool uphill to a header pool with waterfall requires a powerful pump with high output – in some cases, a surface pump.

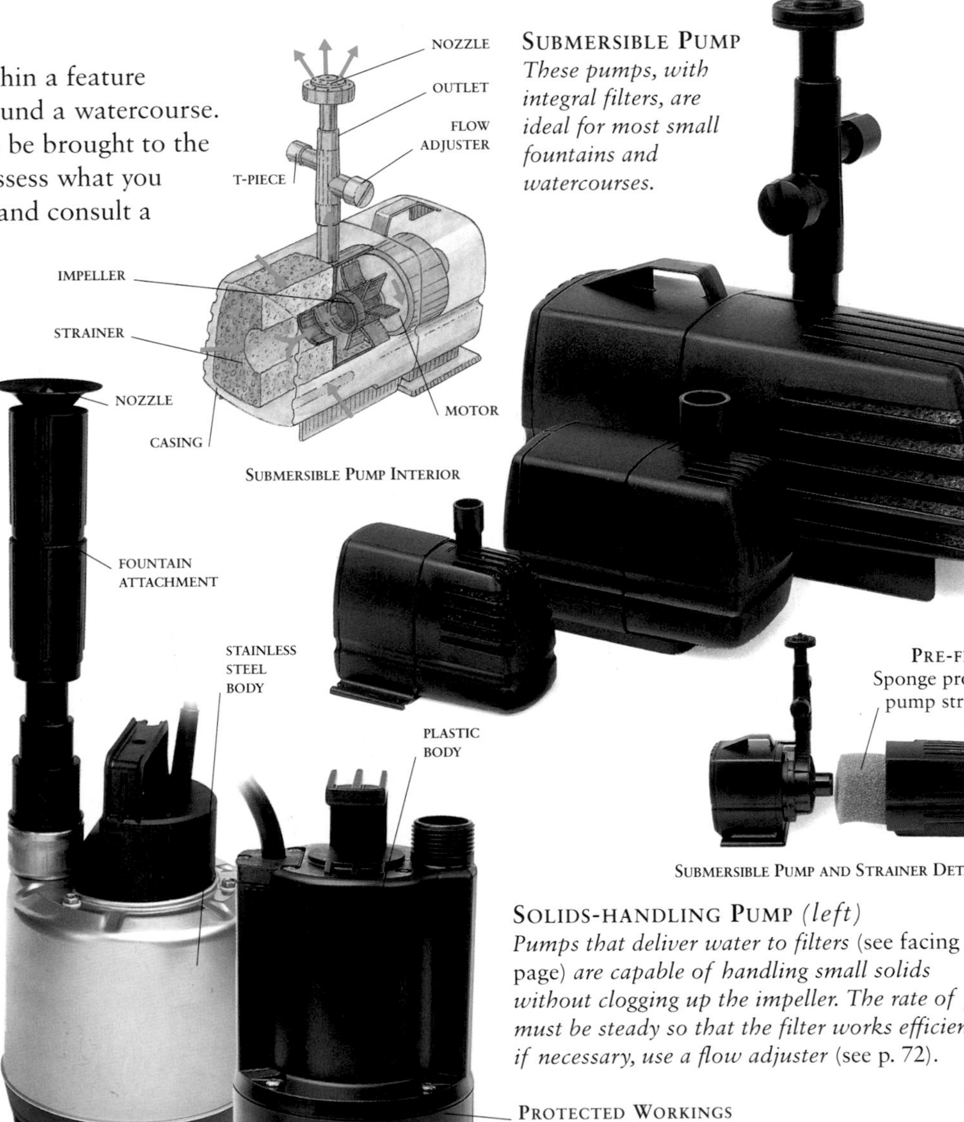

SUBMERSIBLE PUMP INTERIOR

SUBMERSIBLE PUMP
These pumps, with integral filters, are ideal for most small fountains and watercourses.

PRE-FILTER
Sponge protects pump strainer.

SUBMERSIBLE PUMP AND STRAINER DETACHED

SOLIDS-HANDLING PUMP *(left)*
Pumps that deliver water to filters (see facing page) *are capable of handling small solids without clogging up the impeller. The rate of flow must be steady so that the filter works efficiently; if necessary, use a flow adjuster* (see p. 72).

SURFACE PUMP *(right)*
The advantage of a powerful surface pump is that it has high output and is useful for operating large watercourses or a group of fountains. Surface pumps work from mains electricity and need to be housed in a chamber that is both dry and well-ventilated (see p. 73).

Filtration in the Pond

Pond water may be filtered either before it enters, or after it is expelled from, the pump *(right)*. There are two types of filtration materials – mechanical and biological. Mechanical filters simply strain out solid particles; they are effective as soon as the system is switched on and can be run intermittently. Biological filters use materials with very large, complex surface areas on which bacteria collect and flourish; these break down and purify waste products and ammonia gas.

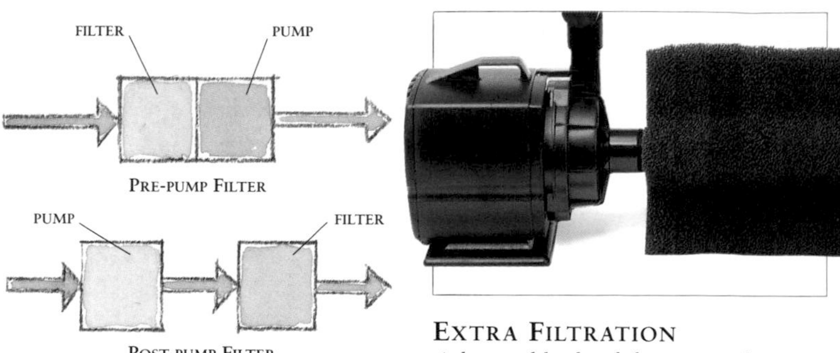

Extra Filtration
A larger block of foam may be pushed over the pump inlet of self-contained submersible pumps.

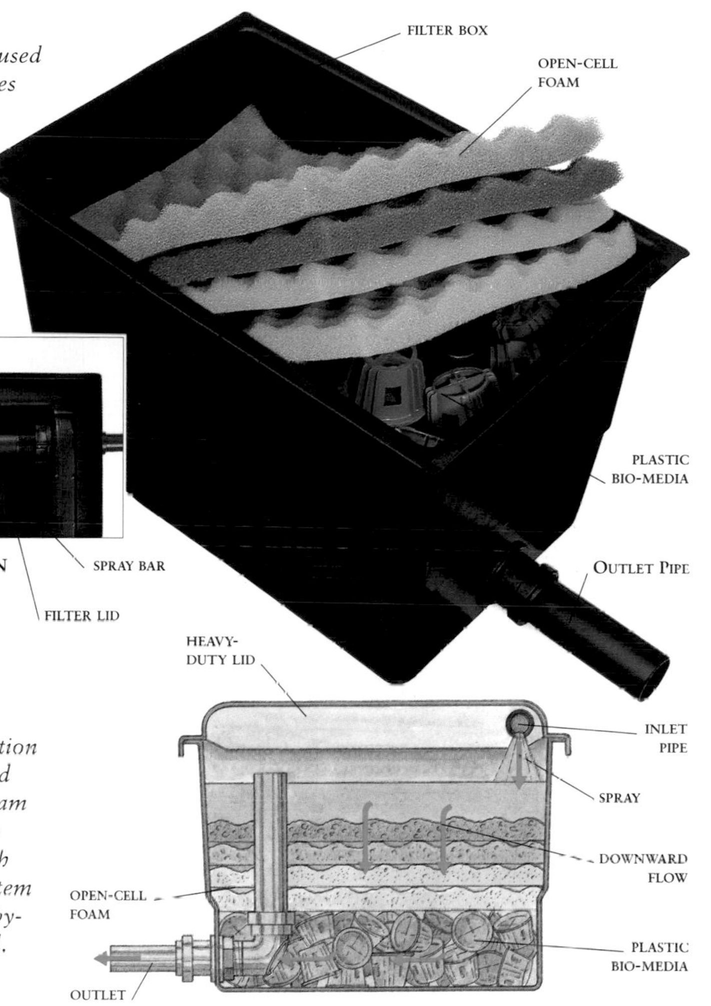

All-purpose Pond Filter
A filter chamber is normally housed outside the pond. A pump pushes the water through the filter's inlet pipe; it then passes through several layers of filter media. Once purified, the water returns to the pond via the outlet pipe.

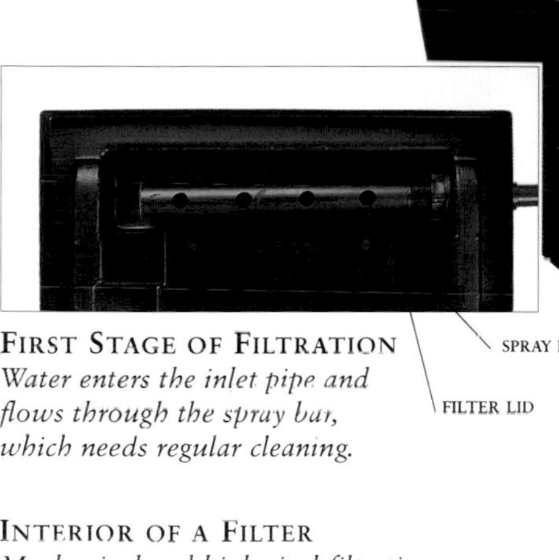

First Stage of Filtration
Water enters the inlet pipe and flows through the spray bar, which needs regular cleaning.

Interior of a Filter
Mechanical and biological filtration is combined in this popular pond filter. Fine layers of open-cell foam and plastic bio-media purify the water, which then passes through the outlet pipe. An overflow system is provided, so that the filter is by-passed when it becomes blocked. The foam sheets should then be removed for cleaning.

Other Filter Media

Brushes and Pads
Certain filters make use of brushes and pads arranged in the filter box, which catch any solids contained in the water before biological filtration.

Zeolites

Ring Media

Lignasite

Biological Filters
These materials are made of clays, glass, carbon granules, and other mineral compounds on which bacteria thrive.

Specialist Filter Systems

For crystal-clear water (for example, for a pond in which koi carp are to be displayed to best advantage), attach a UV filter and magnet to the existing system between the pump and filter. Ultraviolet radiation makes algae clump together, so that they may easily be strained out by the filter. The magnet is designed to prevent the build-up of minerals, on which algae thrive.

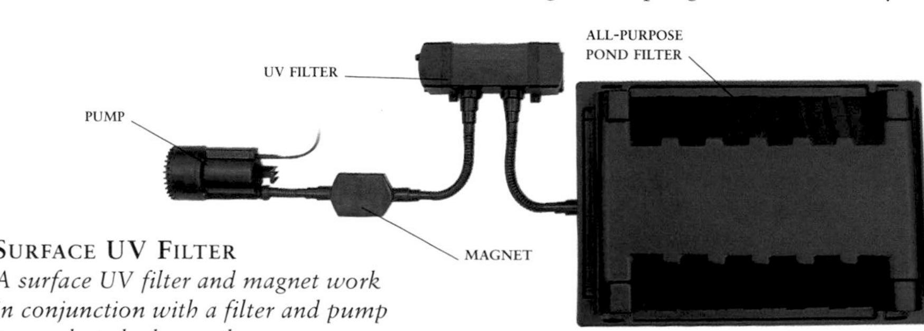

Surface UV Filter
A surface UV filter and magnet work in conjunction with a filter and pump to combat algal growth.

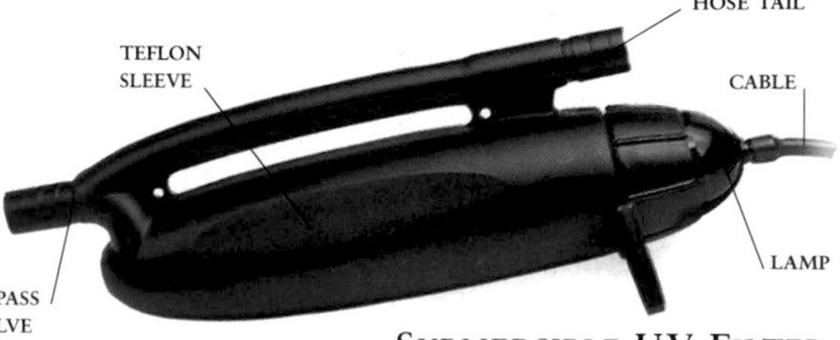

Submersible UV Filter
The newest low-voltage UV filters can be placed directly in a pond. They are small, economical, and durable, and have a high UV output.

Electricity and Water

All pumps are powered by electricity, either directly from the mains or passed through a transformer to produce a low-voltage current. Low-voltage pumps have a limited output and are only suitable for small waterfalls or a single fountain. A mains-voltage system, used for large watercourses, must not be run without a residual current device (RCD or circuit breaker), which makes electricity much safer to use in the garden. When buying a submersible pump, it should ideally have enough cable attached to extend on to dry land, to avoid having to connect cables underwater *(see* Positioning Pumps, *facing page).*

Safety Requirements

It is essential to have all cabling, connections, and fittings for mains voltage pumps installed by a qualified electrician. The system must be protected by a residual current device (RCD or circuit breaker), which will cut off the supply instantly in the event of a short-circuit or damage. Outdoors, only use switches, sockets, or cable connectors that are safety-approved for outdoor use. All cabling must be armoured or protected by a conduit, and should be attached with waterproof connectors, wherever possible above water level. Switch off all equipment before handling.

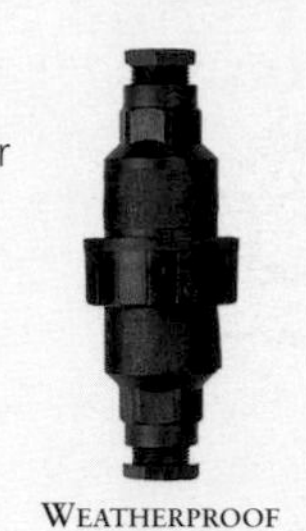

Weatherproof Connector

Low-voltage Electricity

A low-voltage system is used in conjunction with a transformer, and presents no danger from shock. The transformer should be sited indoors, close to the wall socket.

TRANSFORMER
CABLE
SMALL FOUNTAIN
WEATHERPROOF CONNECTOR
PATH
PLASTIC CONDUIT
PUMP

Mains Electricity

If a pump is connected directly to the mains, the cable must be armoured. It should be buried in rigid plastic pipe at least 60cm (2ft) underground.

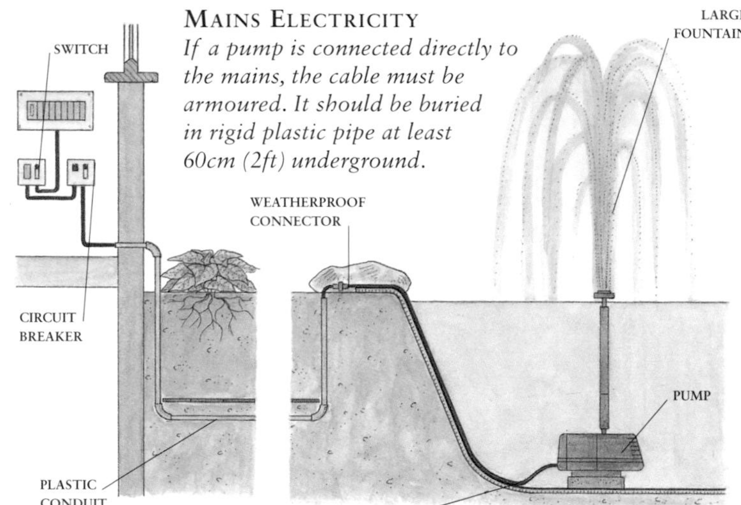

Pump Fittings and Connectors

Most submersible pumps come with a flow adjuster and a T-piece connector, which can easily be fitted between the pump's outlet and the delivery pipe. The T-piece makes it possible to send water in two directions, so that one pump can operate both a waterfall and a fountain. Two flow adjusters may be necessary to control each branch, as more water will go along the one that has the least resistance.

Standard Fittings

The T-piece and flow adjuster are secured to the delivery pipe with a hoseclip.

Points to Consider

When selecting a pump, it is advisable to seek help from a specialist supplier. You will need to be able to answer the following questions, where relevant:

- Is the pump required to operate a watercourse, fountain, or filter, or a combination of the three?
- What is the volume of the reservoir pool *(see pp. 60–61)*? The flow rate per hour should not exceed the pool's volume.
- For features where water runs downhill, what is the height of the header pool above the reservoir pool (known as the "head")?
- What is the width of any streams and spillways?
- What type of fountain spray is required?
- How high do you require the spray to be?

Delivery Pipes

Delivery pipes come in a range of sizes, and it is important to check that diameter and length are suitable for the pump. Delivery pipes are made of flexible plastic, and run directly from the pump to the delivery point: a filter, fountain, or header pool. Always check the dimensions of pump outlets before buying a delivery pipe, and always overestimate the length of pipe you will need.

Rough Guide to Flow Rate

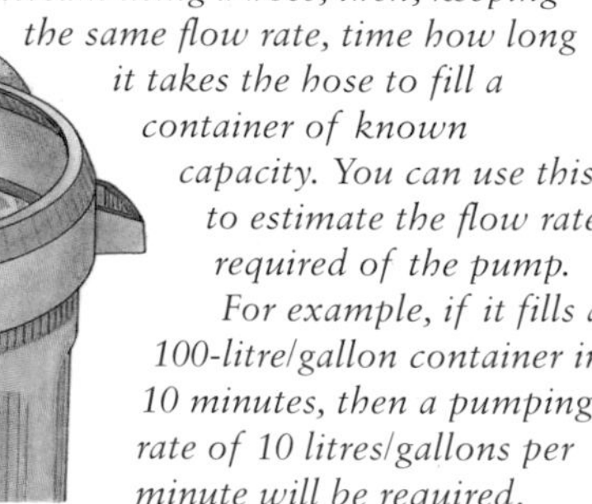

If you can achieve the desired flow of water over a fall or down a stream using a hose, then, keeping the same flow rate, time how long it takes the hose to fill a container of known capacity. You can use this to estimate the flow rate required of the pump. For example, if it fills a 100-litre/gallon container in 10 minutes, then a pumping rate of 10 litres/gallons per minute will be required.

Positioning Pumps and Filters

All submersible pumps should be placed on a plinth, easily made with bricks, in order to reduce the amount of sludge being drawn into the strainer. Surface pumps need some kind of housing in order to protect them from the elements and disguise their appearance. Submersible pumps operate silently and do not require priming. Modern surface pumps are also self-priming, but operate noisily. A well-built pump chamber will help cut down the noise, or if necessary the pump may be sited some distance from the water feature.

Submersible Pumps

The positioning of submersible pumps depends on whether a surface filter is being used. Without a surface filter, the general rule is to let the water take the shortest route between pump and outlet. The further the water has to travel through a pipe, the more it will be slowed down by friction, so to maximize use of a pump's power, delivery pipes should be as short as possible: site pumps directly below fountains or under waterfalls. However, if a surface filter is being used, the rules are reversed: the pump should be as far from where the filtered water enters the pond as possible, or pockets of water that are never drawn around the system, and hence never filtered, will develop.

Filter in Situ
Filters should be at the highest point of circulating features.

Positioning Filters

Surface filters need to be placed at the highest point in the circulation system. They can be disguised with rocks or planting, or they may be hidden under raised decking or behind walls, the filtered water returning via a culvert *(see p. 103)*. Where it is difficult to site a large filter on dry land, a submerged filter may be used that relies upon the pump's suction to draw water through the filtering media. Its drawback is that water circulation is uneven, which will cause beneficial bacteria to die.

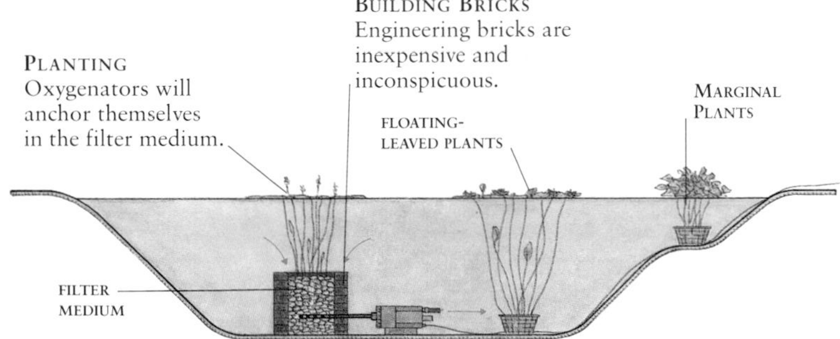

A Submerged Biological Filter
A submerged filter allows the pump to suck water through the filter media, rather than pushing it through, as in a surface filter. This example is simple and economical to build, using unobtrusive engineering bricks and a natural filtering medium (see p. 71), *rather than plastic. It may be disguised with shallow-rooting oxygenators that take nutrients up through their stems, not through their roots; these will happily anchor themselves in the upper layer of the filter material.*

Preventing Backflow

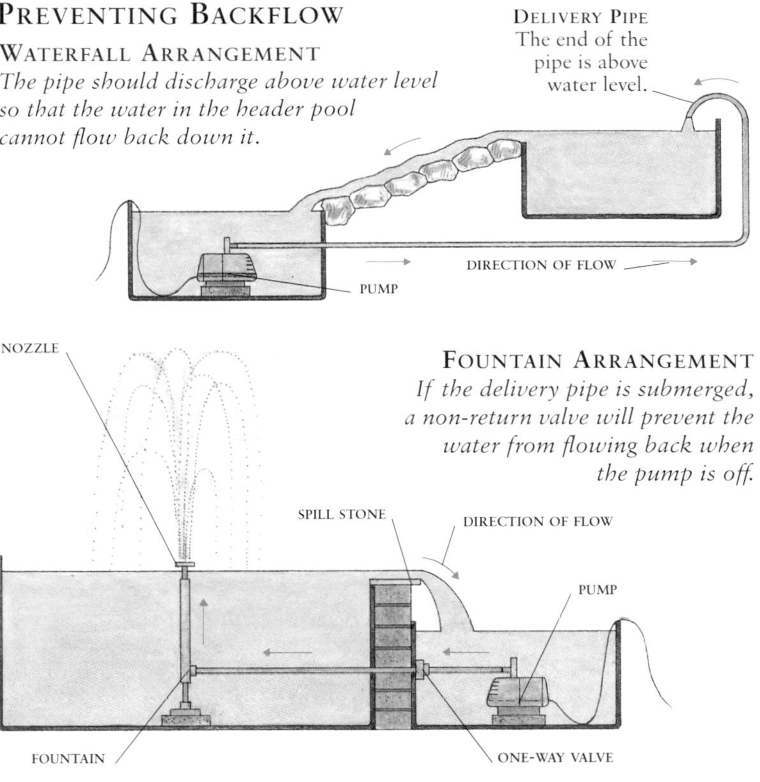

Waterfall Arrangement
The pipe should discharge above water level so that the water in the header pool cannot flow back down it.

Fountain Arrangement
If the delivery pipe is submerged, a non-return valve will prevent the water from flowing back when the pump is off.

Surface Pump Chamber

This small, watertight pump chamber has been installed directly beside a pond. The inlet pipe is not visible, having been mortared to the poolside wall and then painted with a proprietary sealant. The construction of the pump chamber must make provision for a ventilation brick, and for a large piece of rigid pipe to accommodate both the incoming electricity cable and the inlet pipe. As a precaution against flooding, there should be a drainage hole at the base of the chamber.

1 **Mark out the** outline of the chamber and lay trench foundations. Build brick walls four courses high, incorporating a ventilation brick and a conduit for the inlet pipe and cable.

2 **Thread the mains** electricity lead and inlet pipe through the conduit. Connect these to the surface pump, situated on a small paving slab inside the chamber.

3 **Fit a light,** painted timber lid over the chamber, which can be easily removed for pump adjustment. Paint the lid with preservative that is in keeping with its surrounds.

FEATURES WITH STILL WATER

STILL-WATER PONDS are ideal for any site, and provide a superb setting for a wide range of water plants – in particular water lilies, which dislike water movement. The pond may be formal or informal, raised or sunken, small or large, and can be built using a range of methods and materials. Additional interest can be created with a boggy area for moisture-loving plants, or with an island.

FORMAL POOLS

The main characteristics of formal pools are clearly defined edges and geometrical shapes; squares, rectangles, and circles are the most popular. The formal style gives an opportunity to use and display decorative edging material; a formal pond is also often associated with a paved area. Careful attention to measurements, angles, and levels is essential when constructing a formal shape. Water, of course, always finds its own horizontal level, and nothing is more revealing of uneven or sloping edges and paving than a still water surface.

REFLECTIVE SURFACE
Use the reflective surface of still water to mirror surrounding plants and the sky, bringing light into enclosed areas. Do not allow floating-leaved plants to spread too abundantly, or the effect will be lost.

PLANTING SOLUTIONS
This small informal feature, part pond, part bog garden, transforms what was a difficult planting area of dry semi-shade. The vigorous, paddle-like leaves of Lysichiton *and the brightly variegated irises are a welcome respite from the sombre background of rhododendrons, whose flower colours are picked out using candelabra primulas.*

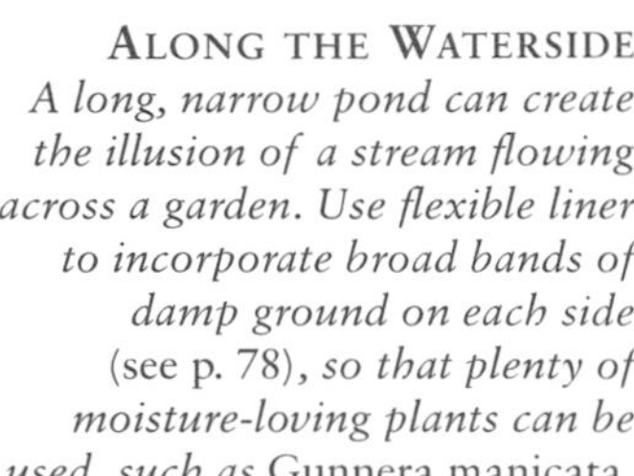

ALONG THE WATERSIDE
A long, narrow pond can create the illusion of a stream flowing across a garden. Use flexible liner to incorporate broad bands of damp ground on each side (see p. 78)*, so that plenty of moisture-loving plants can be used, such as* Gunnera manicata.

Formal, Semi-raised Pool
The still surface of this formal, partially raised pool provides an ideal contrast to the rich detail of the surrounding banks.

Sloping Bank
Do not simply heap up spoil from the excavation to create a bank sloping down to a pond. Instead, landscape the whole site, using good topsoil that will help plants grow vigorously, ensuring that their roots consolidate the sloping ground.

Concrete is in many circumstances the obvious choice for constructing formal pools, which require straight, solid sides. In the past, concrete mix was used to form a thick shell: a time-consuming task involving building expertise. Today, with the evolution of building materials, it is far easier to construct a simple shell of concrete blocks, and line this either with tough flexible material (for the range of liners, *see p. 67*) or with a thin skimming, or layer, of cement to which special reinforcing fibre has been added *(see pp. 90–91)*.

Informal Ponds

Informal ponds generally have curving edges. Although clay-lined ponds *(see pp. 92–93)* are the least artificial of all, the majority of gardeners will need to use a waterproof liner, whose edges should be carefully disguised. A kidney-shaped preformed unit *(see pp. 88–89)* can be made to look quite natural if plants are used to cover and soften its hard edge. However, flexible liner *(see pp. 76–79)* gives a great deal more freedom in constructing irregular shapes. It is best to keep the general outline simple: it is far easier to create inlets and promontories using rocks on top of the liner than to excavate and line a complicated shape. Islands *(see pp. 80–81)* may also be added on top of the liner, though incorporating these at the construction stage gives the option of creating either a "wet" or "dry" planting environment. An informal pond that has well-planted, shallow margins is particularly appealing to wildlife *(see pp. 54–55)*; formal ponds, with straight edges above the waterline and vertical sides, are less accessible.

An Appropriate Size

Still-water features can be built in any shape or size. In the examples illustrated on the following pages, each feature is given a specific size so that a practical guide to construction can be included. However, using simple calculations *(see pp. 60–61)*, the pond size and quantities of materials needed can be adapted to your requirements. Within the limits of site and the available budget, it is advisable to have as large a pond as possible: the smaller the volume of water, the more difficult it becomes to maintain a healthy ecosystem *(see pp. 136–137)*. Sufficient depth is particularly important; a large area of shallow water exposed to sunlight will suffer problems due to algal build-up that are extremely difficult to control *(see pp. 140–141)*.

Stocking and Maintenance

Knowing the volume and surface area of your pond will enable you to determine the quantity of plants *(see pp. 152–153)* and fish *(see p. 171)* that it can support. This is a useful guide for initial stocking; however, a pond is a dynamic world full of life which must be kept in harmony; regular attention to maintenance *(see pp. 140–141)* will keep major tasks to a minimum.

SIMPLE PONDS WITH FLEXIBLE LINER

FLEXIBLE LINER is the most versatile material to use in the construction of pond. When choosing a liner, however, do bear in mind that they vary considerably in their quality and durability *(see p. 67)*. Inexpensive polythene liners only have a life expectancy of three to five years if exposed to sunlight, while the more expensive PVC and butyl liners will last up to 50 years. When installing liner, make sure that no part of the material is left exposed above the waterline, as this will not only spoil the look of the finished feature, it will also leave an area of liner exposed to sunlight. This will cause cheaper brands to harden and crack, resulting in a drop in the level of water in the pond. To prevent the liner from being punctured by sharp objects such as stones or rocks, always use good quality underlay *(see pp. 66–67)*.

INFORMAL POND

LINING A SIMPLE POND WITH SHELF

CONSTRUCTION GUIDE

To build and line a 3m x 2.2m (10ft x 7ft) pond, you will need:

TOOLS
- Sand or string to mark out pond
- 10 pegs, one datum peg
- Lump hammer
- Spirit level
- Straight-edge
- Shovel, spade
- Rake

MATERIALS
- Soft sand or sifted soil: 0.5cu m (½cu yd)
- Underlay: 5m x 4m (15ft x 12ft)
- Flexible liner: 5m x 4m (15ft x 12ft)
- Bricks to hold liner temporarily in place

1 MARK THE OUTLINE of the pond *(see inset)*. Position a datum peg at the edge of the outline to indicate the proposed water level *(see p. 64)*. Position the remaining pegs regularly around the pond. Use a spirit level and a straight-edge to check that all the pegs are level.

USING FLEXIBLE LINER

Before buying flexible liner and underlay, calculate how much will be needed to line the pond *(see p. 66)*, including enough for a generous overlap. If possible, unroll the liner and lay it flat in the sun for at least half an hour. The heat will increase the liner's flexibility, and help to ease out any stiff creases. Roll it up again to make laying easier. When fitting liner into an irregularly shaped pond, do not strain it tightly over the contours of the excavation, as this will reduce its natural elasticity and make it more likely to be punctured by sharp objects such as stones or rocks.

2 REMOVE TURVES 5cm (2in) deep and 30cm (12in) wide from the edge of the pond, beyond the pegs. Retain the turves if a grass edging is planned. Excavate the entire area to a depth of 22cm (9in). After raking the surface, use sand to outline the proposed deep zone, leaving marginal shelf areas that are at least 30cm (12in) wide to accommodate plants.

3 EXCAVATE THE MARKED AREA to a depth of 37cm (15in). Rake the floor of the hole and remove any large or sharp stones. As an extra precaution against a sharp object piercing the underlay and liner, spread a 2.5cm (1in) layer of soft sand or sifted soil at the bottom of the excavation, where the water pressure will be strongest. Remove the pegs.

4 DRAPE THE UNDERLAY over the hole, then press firmly into the contours. Unroll the liner over the hole. Use bricks to hold the edges temporarily in place, and slowly fill the pond with water. The increasing weight of the water will settle the liner into the more difficult contours. Pleat any large creases as necessary. Adjust the bricks as the liner tautens.

5 **THE POND IS NOW READY** to be edged *(see pp. 126–129)*. For an informal grass edging, trim the liner to leave a 15cm (6in) overlap. Replace the turves removed earlier; firm them down, and water well. For a formal, sharp-edged grass surround – or if the edge will take heavy traffic – make provision at the planning stage to dig out and add a foundation *(see right)* as for a paved edge.

INFORMAL AND FORMAL EDGINGS WITH FOUNDATIONS

There is a wide range of edging materials and styles to choose from *(see pp. 126–131)*. For hard edging materials such as paving, or where earth may crumble under turf, foundations are advisable. This involves digging out a strip around the pond to a depth of 15–23cm (6–9in). The liner may be rolled over this outer shelf and the foundation laid on top of it *(below left)*; since it will be visible, choose attractive materials such as granite setts, mortaring together well to prevent water leakage. To hide a brick and concrete foundation *(below right)*, lay the liner on top of it.

GREENER GRASS
Until they are ready to be put in place, roll back the turves *(as shown)* or stack them grass to grass.

SETTS
To strengthen the area closest to the water – and to disguise the liner – place turves on setts mortared on to the liner. Once the mortar has set, backfill.

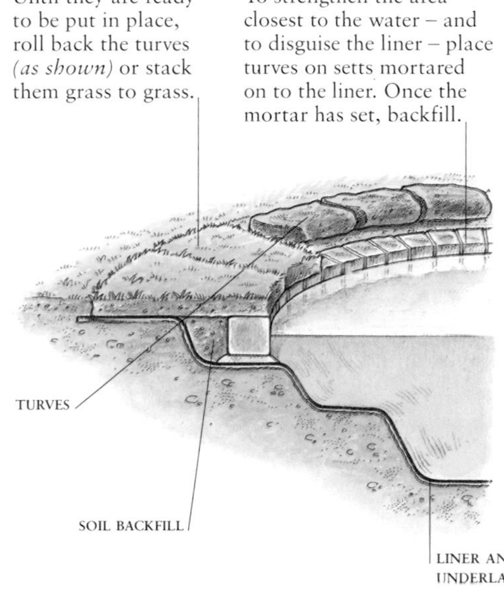

STABLE PAVING
Crazy paving should be carefully levelled, and laid flush with surrounding turf to prevent tripping and to ease mowing.

PERFECT DISGUISE
Sandwiching the liner and underlay between two layers of concrete serves to secure them and hide them from sight.

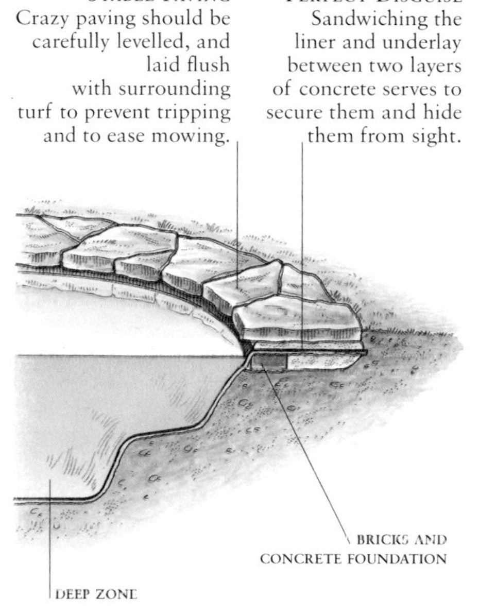

POND WITH CRAZY PAVING EDGE
Almost any artificially created pond can be transformed by strategic planting. Once the pond and its planted environs are established, it will be virtually impossible to distinguish it from a "natural" water feature. To make it easier for frogs and hedgehogs to climb out if they fall in, include at least one paving stone that slopes into the water. Overhanging paving stones provide fish with shade, and will help to disguise the liner by casting a shadow.

MULTI-PURPOSE FLEXIBLE LINERS

The use of flexible liner has become increasingly popular; it is now so widely available that there is a good case for completing all the necessary pond or stream excavations before buying the liner. By finishing the excavation first, last-minute variations can be made to the depth and shape of the feature without having to take into account the width and length of a liner bought at the planning stage. When the excavation is complete, view it from a distance, or from a window in the house; a fresh perspective might suggest any number of variations and allow you to judge the effect that a differently-shaped or enlarged water feature will have on the surroundings.

NATURAL EDGING
It is much easier to disguise the edges of flexible liner than it is to disguise the edges of rigid units or concrete pools. Here, large, rounded stones, along with marginal and moisture-loving plants, make a perfect disguise.

COMPLEX SHAPES

More complex, individualistic shapes designed to enhance particular surroundings are easier to create with flexible liner than with materials that require building skills. Liner is generally sold from rolls of various widths. One length of liner can be made to fit several shapes, including those that call for the feature to narrow to a waist. If the liner is much too large for a narrow section of pond or stream, and you do not intend to use the excess to create peripheral features the offcuts can be used elsewhere, taped together with proprietary waterproof tape or bonded together by specialist suppliers.

ADDING PLANTING FEATURES

One of the greatest advantages in using flexible liner is the variety of depths and edges that can be incorporated in one pond *(see below)*. By allowing adequate surplus liner around the sides of the pond above the waterline, it is quite simple to incorporate features such as integral planting beds, boggy areas, or a cobblestone or shingle beach *(see pp. 80–81)*. If the flexible liner is buried beneath the soil, even if above the water level, plants in the surrounding soil will draw moisture from the pond; this is known as the "wick effect". In small planting areas, this is useful for moisture-lovers, as they will take the

CREATING PLANTING ENVIRONMENTS WITH FLEXIBLE LINER
This pond was designed to include several planting environments (see pp. 148–149)*, each of which allows plants to grow without the need for containers. The main pond is deep enough to support submerged plants, the shallower pocket beside it, marginals. A combination of marginal and bog plants grow in the pondside pockets made with surplus liner.*

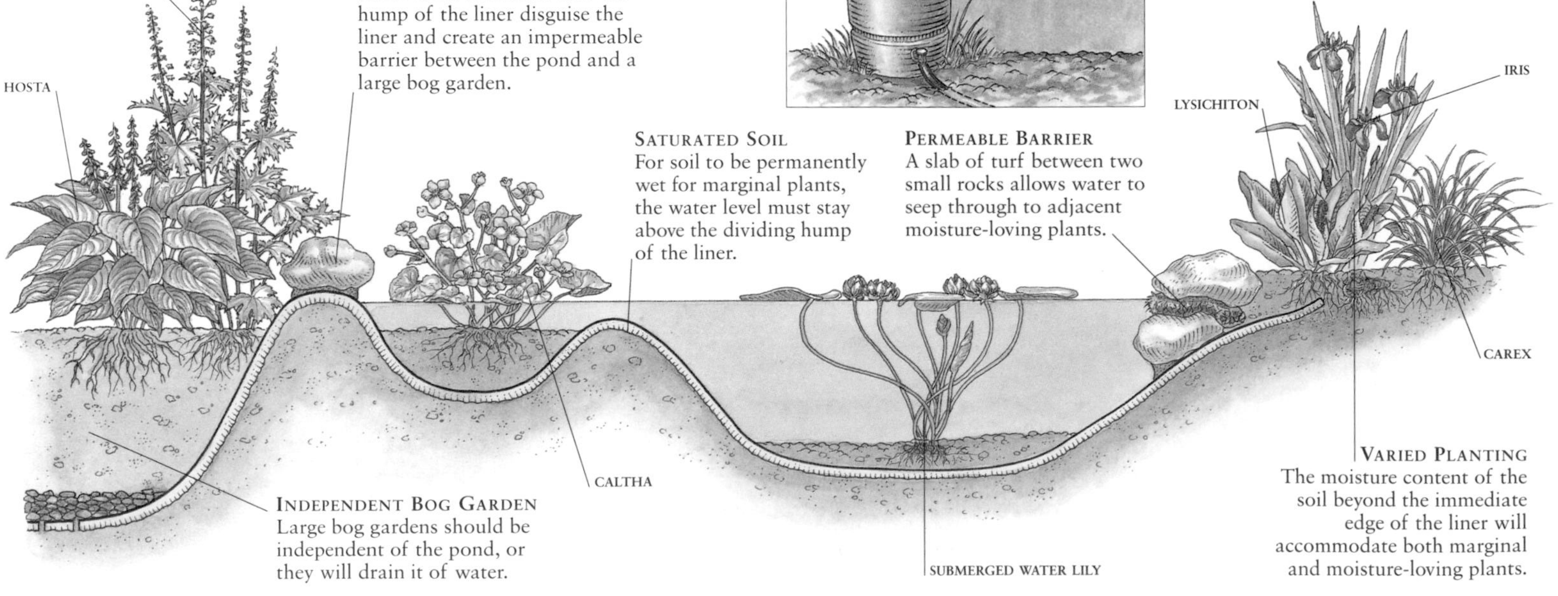

TOPPING UP
A rainwater butt equipped with a tap and buried hose leading into the pond is an ideal way to top up water lost through the "wick effect" of a large integral bog garden.

LIGULARIA

HOSTA

IMPERMEABLE BARRIER
Small rocks mortared onto the hump of the liner disguise the liner and create an impermeable barrier between the pond and a large bog garden.

SATURATED SOIL
For soil to be permanently wet for marginal plants, the water level must stay above the dividing hump of the liner.

PERMEABLE BARRIER
A slab of turf between two small rocks allows water to seep through to adjacent moisture-loving plants.

LYSICHITON

IRIS

CAREX

CALTHA

INDEPENDENT BOG GARDEN
Large bog gardens should be independent of the pond, or they will drain it of water.

SUBMERGED WATER LILY

VARIED PLANTING
The moisture content of the soil beyond the immediate edge of the liner will accommodate both marginal and moisture-loving plants.

water they need from the pond. If a large bog garden is not independent of the pond, however, the "wick effect" can quickly lower the level of water in the pond. To prevent this, the liner should come up out of the ground, or should have rocks or pavers mortared on to it to stop water from seeping out. Alternatively, install a topping-up system using a water butt *(see facing page).*

Lining Formal Shapes

Liners are often used to waterproof old, damaged concrete pools or containers that leak, such as old barrels. Always use top-grade butyl liner where there are sharp edges or corners to be covered; the cheaper PVC liners are liable to tear in these circumstances. Using top-grade liner in a large pool can, however, be expensive; it is more economical to use a rendering of cement mixed with reinforcing fibres over the shell of large, regularly-shaped formal pools *(see pp. 90–91).*

Waterproofing a Barrel

Old half-barrels make charming container water features, but they may leak. A lining of cheap polythene or PVC will make them watertight. Fold the liner neatly around the inside edges of the barrel, as shown here. Then wedge, and disguise, the liner under a small, thin wooden batten fixed to the inside top edge of the barrel with galvanized screws. Secure the batten as near as possible to the top of the barrel, so that the screws do not penetrate the liner, and are clear of the water. Then trim back the excess liner.

Lining a Barrel

Folding a Liner

Sharp curves in informal ponds, and the angles of corners in formal rectangular pools, will inevitably result in large creases having to be made in the liner. Careful folding of the liner can, however, make these folds look less conspicuous; the folds may also be disguised with coping stones or, in the case of informal ponds, stones mortared on to the liner *(see p. 67).* Once the pond is filled, the weight of water should hold the folds down; alternatively, pleated material can be secured with dabs of mortar. When making folds, ensure that there is ample liner at your disposal, so that the material does not have to be stretched too much, as the sheer weight of the water may cause it to split. Whatever the shape of the water feature, formal or informal, always complete the folding of the liner before releasing water into the pool; the weight of only a few gallons will make further manipulation of the liner very difficult.

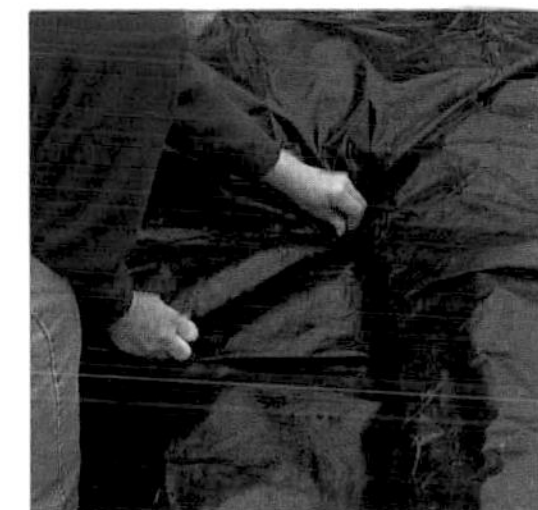

Making Folds
To create a neat corner fold, make a diagonal pleat in the liner. Hold the liner in place with bricks until the pressure of water can keep the fold in place.

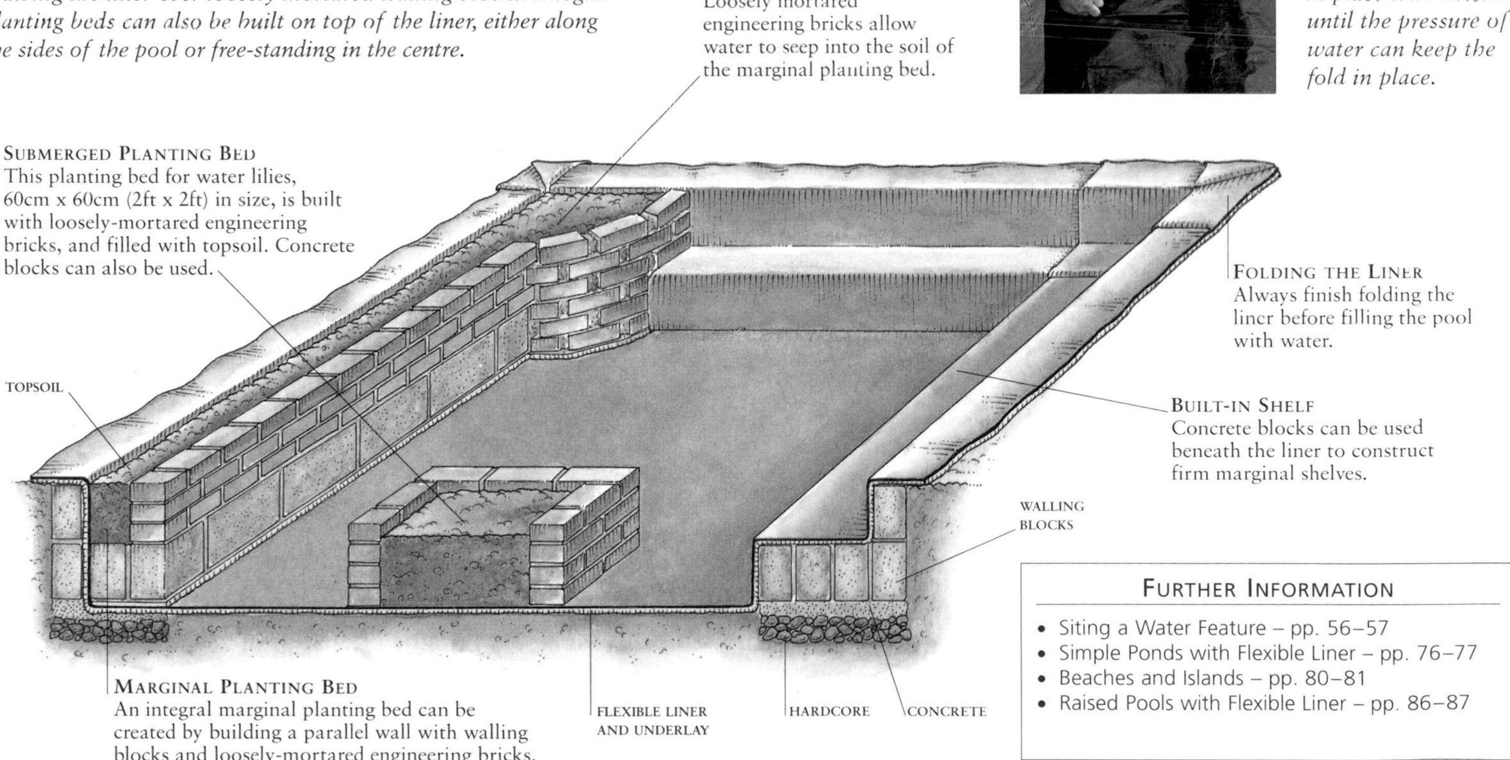

Flexible Liner in Formal Pool
This cross-section of a formal pool demonstrates how basic construction materials and flexible liner can be used to accommodate a variety of planting environments. A marginal shelf, suitable for containerized marginal plants, is created by drawing the liner over loosely mortared walling blocks. Integral planting beds can also be built on top of the liner, either along the sides of the pool or free-standing in the centre.

Further Information

- Siting a Water Feature – pp. 56–57
- Simple Ponds with Flexible Liner – pp. 76–77
- Beaches and Islands – pp. 80–81
- Raised Pools with Flexible Liner – pp. 86–87

BEACHES AND ISLANDS

MANY PONDS FAIL to attain their full potential as wildlife habitats *(see also pp. 54–55)* because their construction deters wild creatures, who will not approach water if they sense that it could trap them. Almost vertical side walls and large gaps between the water surface and overhanging coping stones or paved edges are common obstacles. A beach, gently sloping towards the water, is not only visually appealing, but will also allow access for a great variety of wildlife. It is better to make provision for islands at the design stage, although it is possible to install a "wet" island in an existing pond *(see facing page)*. Formal features tend not to have islands, but submerged formal beds can be built *(see pp. 78–79)* with retaining walls constructed from house bricks or walling blocks, and filled with topsoil.

COBBLES AND SHINGLE

MAKING A COBBLESTONE BEACH

Before positioning the underlay and liner, dig a shallow shelf sloping down to the water; the shelf should be 10–15cm (4–6in) deep at its lowest point and, to achieve a gentle, "natural" gradient, at least 60–90cm (2–3ft) wide. Draw the liner up over the prepared area. Build up a "lip" at the edge of the beach – as shown here – by mortaring cobblestones in place.

PLANTING POCKETS Soil between stones forms wet pockets for marginal plants.

COBBLESTONE FLOOR To protect the liner and underlay, use smooth, rounded cobblestones.

LINER EDGE Make sure the edge of the liner is drawn up well above the water level, and concealed with cobblestones.

NATURAL OUTCROPPINGS Protruding stones provide birds and other creatures with stepping stones, as well as with basking and resting places.

FLEXIBLE LINER AND UNDERLAY

RETAINING WALL Before the pond is filled, use mortar here to prevent the cobbles from slipping into deeper water.

SHINGLE BEACH

A simple, gently sloping shingle beach is an inexpensive, easy-to-install feature, which will be welcomed by small creatures attracted to the water's edge by the easily negotiable terrain. Only smooth, washed shingle should be used, as sharp stones could damage the liner. Press some shingle into a band of mortar along the beach's rim to stop the rest from slipping into deeper water.

CHOOSING COBBLESTONES

For the most natural effect, select cobblestones local to your area; imported "white" cobblestones can look artificial. Pebble-collecting is prohibited on many beaches, but if you are able to gather small stones, wash them thoroughly before introducing them into the pond; residual salt on the stones may damage pondlife.

GRADED PEBBLE BEACH

Pebbles, rounded cobbles, and larger stones make a natural-looking covering for a shallow beach, especially if in colours that match colours and textures of stones found naturally in the garden. Imitate nature by grading the stones, with the smallest nearest the water. The pebble floor will protect the liner from the claws of birds and animals, and from the damaging effects of ultraviolet light.

Constructing Islands

Islands should, ideally, be incorporated when the pond is built and, to ensure stability, should be at least 1.2m (4ft) across; anything smaller than this will constrain the number and variety of plants the island can accommodate, and as a result will not provide wildlife – primarily birds – with shelter, nesting sites, and protection from predators. The retaining walls can be constructed from sandbags, although polypropylene bags filled with rubble are longer lasting. Because an island will reduce the volume of water in a pond – thereby affecting the pond's ecosystem *(see pp. 136–137)* – the surface area of the water should be a minimum of four times the surface area of the island *(see pp. 60–61)*. The inclusion of both a "wet" and a "dry" island in one large pond will provide scope for a wide range of plants with differing moisture requirements.

Building a Wet Island in an Existing Pond

First, drain the pond water, then build up retaining walls with inward-sloping sandbags or polypropylene bags filled with rubble. Once the first three bags are in place, fill the centre with 24–30cm (10–12in) of rubble. Build up the walls and fill with topsoil. When they are within 10–15cm (4–6in) of the final water level, disguise them with two layers of inverted turves.

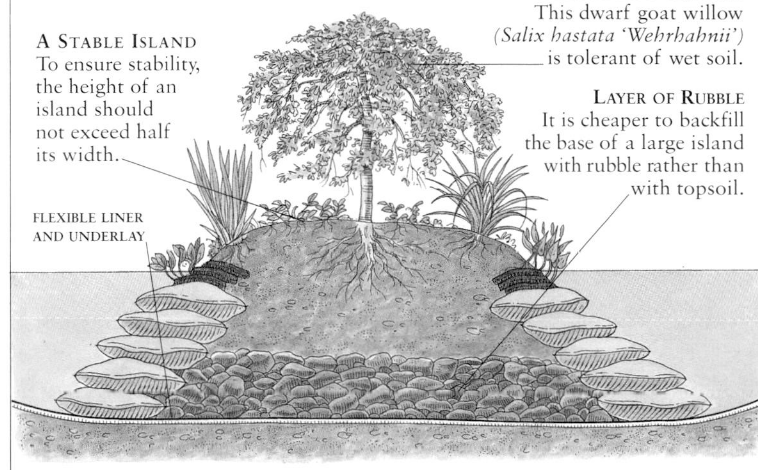

Making Dry Islands

Dry islands, which are designed to provide normal soil conditions, should be pre-planned, and constructed at the same time as the pond. In a flexible-liner pond, dig a moat around a flat-topped mound of earth that extends 10–15cm (4–6in) above the proposed waterline. Fit the liner over the contours of the mound; then, to expose the topsoil of the mound for planting, cut away the liner covering the top of the mound – above the waterline – and disguise the edges of the liner with topsoil or turves. Remember that it may be necessary to water plants on dry islands in dry conditions.

Making Wet Islands

To incorporate a shallow wet island in a pond at the design stage, leave a flat topped mound in the excavation that is at least 22cm (9in) lower than the proposed water level, covering the mound with the liner and underlay. Build up low walls around the edges of the mound with inverted turves *(see below, left)*, and fill with heavy soil, which will not easily disperse. To build a "wet" island in an existing pond, the pond should have a level bottom and a stable base *(see above)*. Marginal plants such as *Calla palustris* (bog arum) will thrive in wet island conditions.

Creating a Wet Island
Provided a flat-topped mound has been left under the liner to within 30cm (12in) of the final water level, a wet island is easy to build, with a wall of inverted turves retaining the topsoil. Once the edging of turves is in place, build up the centre of the island ready for planting.

Cross-section of a Wet and a Dry Island

The retaining walls of this shallow wet island (below, left) *are constructed with layers of inverted turves. To prevent the topsoil from dispersing before the spreading roots of the plants can consolidate it, heavy, clay-based soil should be used. The flexible liner on the dry island* (below, right) *extends above the waterline and is disguised and protected beneath two layers of turves.*

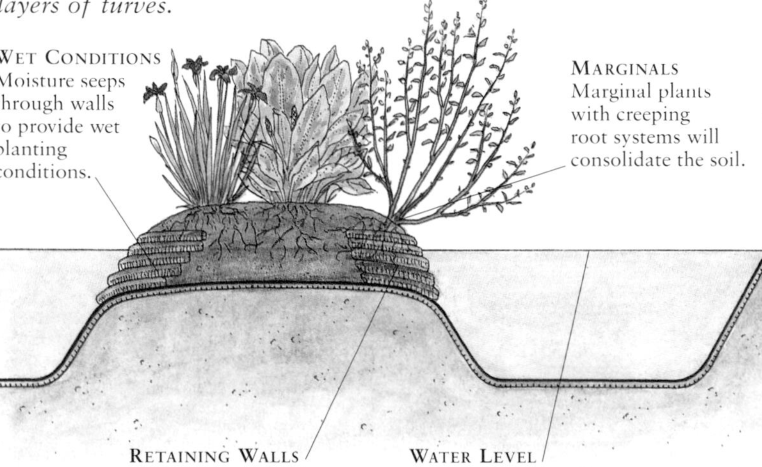

Further Information
- Encouraging Wildlife – pp. 54–55
- ConstructionTools and Materials – pp. 62–63
- Construction Techniques – pp. 64–69
- Simple Ponds with Flexible Liner – pp. 76–79

INDEPENDENT BOG GARDENS

BOG GARDENS MAY be incorporated into an existing water feature by extending the flexible liner. When a large bog area is linked to a pond, however, the "wick effect" of water moving from the pond to the bog *(see pp. 78–79)* invariably leads to a fall in the pond's water level, especially during summer. It is advisable, therefore, to create a separate bog garden that is independently supplied with water. A bog garden is one of the simplest, cheapest, and most water-efficient ways of creating an environment for those plants that demand a constant high-moisture content in the soil. Small boggy areas can be created anywhere, lined with polythene sheeting or feed sacks, and watered by hand; however, grouping plants together in an area that has an inbuilt irrigation system, as here, is less labour-intensive and generally looks better.

INDEPENDENT BOG GARDEN

CREATING A BOG GARDEN

CONSTRUCTION GUIDE

To create a round bog garden approximately 2.4m (8ft) across, you will need:

TOOLS
- Spade, rake, garden fork
- Knife or scissors
- Hacksaw, drill

MATERIALS
- Sand or string for marking out
- Heavy-duty polythene sheet: 3.5m x 3.5m (11ft x 11ft)
- Bricks or stones to hold liner down temporarily
- Pea shingle: 0.5cu m (½cu yd)
- Rigid plastic pipe: 2m (7ft) long, 2.5cm (1in) in diameter
- 2 elbow joints
- Short length of hose, jubilee clip, and hose connector with male/female lock

1 MARK OUT THE REQUIRED SHAPE with string or sand. Dig a hole approximately 60cm (2ft) deep, with sloping sides to minimize the crumbling of light soil. Keep the topsoil nearby on a polythene sheet for replacement. Rake the area and remove any large or sharp stones.

LINING AND DRAINING

As the lining used in a bog garden is covered with soil, and need not be completely watertight – in fact, it will have holes pierced in it – never use expensive pool liner; polythene sheeting will serve the purpose just as well. The holes are necessary to allow water in the soil to drain away, albeit very slowly, otherwise it will become stagnant and anaerobic (allowing harmful bacterial activity). Drainage is vital for the growth of many moisture-loving plants – as opposed to marginals – that will not survive in saturated soil. Drainage is aided by the layer of shingle, which also prevents the holes in the irrigation pipe from becoming blocked.

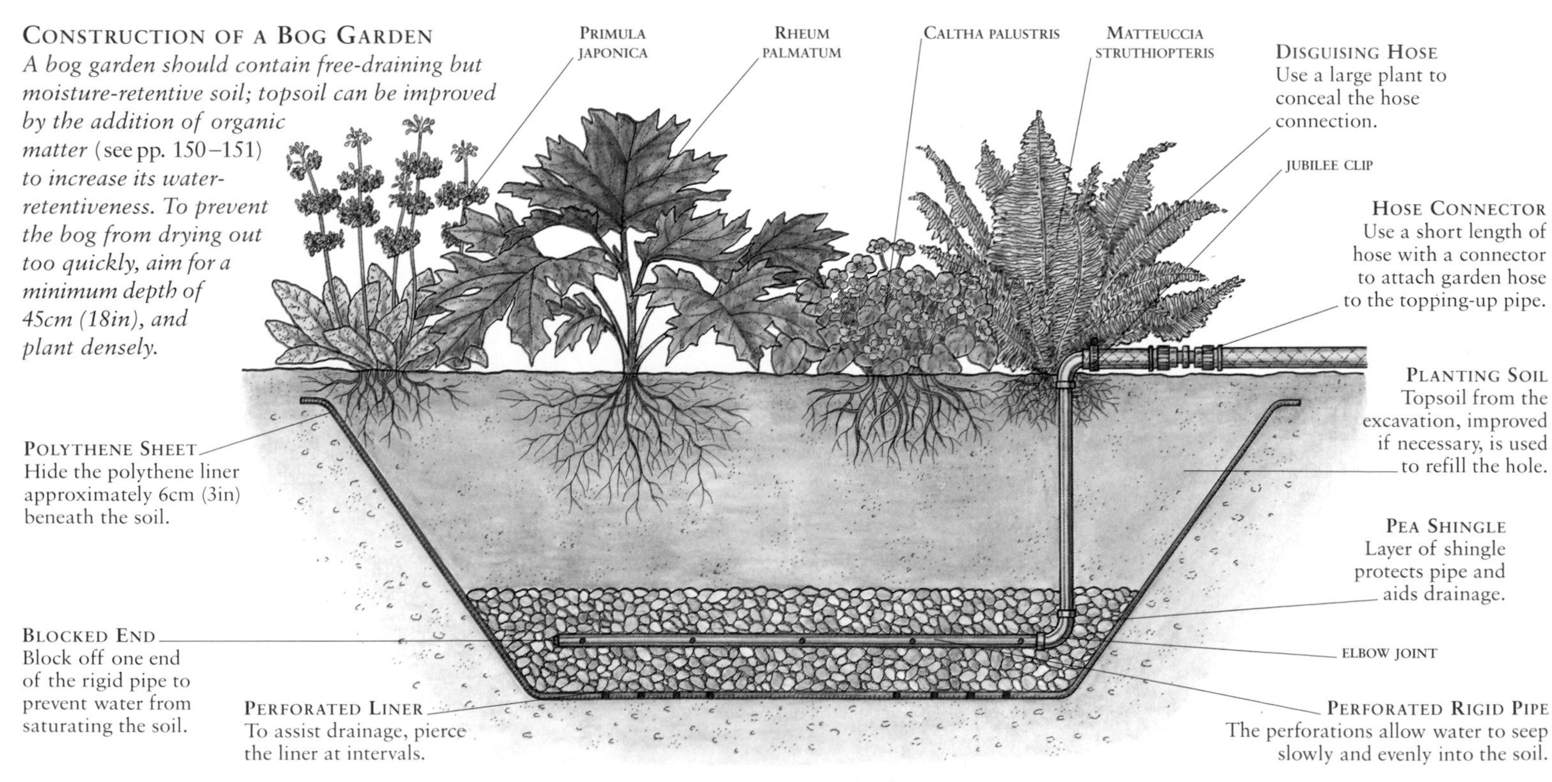

CONSTRUCTION OF A BOG GARDEN
A bog garden should contain free-draining but moisture-retentive soil; topsoil can be improved by the addition of organic matter (see pp. 150–151) *to increase its water-retentiveness. To prevent the bog from drying out too quickly, aim for a minimum depth of 45cm (18in), and plant densely.*

2 DRAPE THE LINING material over the excavation and press it into the contours. Put bricks or stones around the edges of the sheet to keep it in place while you walk on it. To make holes for drainage, pierce the liner at 1m (3ft) intervals with a garden fork.

3 SPREAD A 5CM (2IN) LAYER of pea shingle over the sheet. Then cut a 60cm (2ft) length off the rigid pipe. Drill holes along the longer section at 15cm (6in) intervals, then lay it across the base. Block one end and, at the other, use an elbow joint to join on the short pipe so that it extends vertically above ground level. Spread another 5cm (2in) layer of shingle over the pipe.

4 SHOVEL IN THE SOIL and firm it. Before the soil reaches the top of the excavation, trim off any surplus liner and hide the edges under a 7cm (3in) layer of soil. Remove the bricks and any excess soil. Attach the second elbow joint to the protruding pipe, creating a right-angle turn. Fit the short length of hose onto it with the jubilee clip, and attach the hosepipe connector.

PLANTED BOG GARDEN

Top up the bog garden whenever the soil surface is dry (this could be weekly in hot spells), adding water until the soil surface floods, to keep plants growing well. One of the advantages of a separate bog is that garden fertilizer can be used without the danger of substances seeping into the water of a pond and affecting its chemistry.

FURTHER INFORMATION

- Wildlife Pond with Bog Garden – pp. 40–43
- Simple Ponds with Flexible Liner – pp. 76–79
- Soils and Containers – pp. 150–151

Rigid Pool Units

Preformed rigid pool units are easy to install, and can be a good choice if a small water feature is required. Rigid units are particularly well suited to more formal gardens in which the surrounding area is to be paved – it is easier to disguise the smooth, often shiny edges of the unit with paving stones *(see p. 127)* rather than with plants. Many commercially available rigid units incorporate shelves designed to accommodate planting crates that fit into the contours of the unit. Units come in many sizes, styles, and colours; their smooth surfaces make them easy to clean. Although not difficult to install, the units do become very heavy when filled with water. If the site has not been properly prepared *(see also pp. 64–65)*, the build-up of water pressure can cause the unit to fracture as the earth settles under the weight of the water.

Rigid Unit in Position

Installing a Rigid Pool Unit

Construction Guide

To install a rigid pool unit with marginal shelves, you will need:

TOOLS
- Canes, string
- Spade, rake
- Straight-edge, spirit level
- Tamping tool
- Tape measure
- Hose

MATERIALS
- Rigid pool unit
- Walling blocks or bricks to support the unit temporarily
- Soft sand or sifted soil, enough to line the floor of the excavation to a depth of 5cm (2in)

1 If the unit chosen is completely symmetrical it can simply be turned upside down and its outline marked directly on to the ground. For irregular shapes, supporting the unit in exactly the right position, so that it can be marked around accurately, can be an awkward job, and is easier with a helper. You can temporarily support the unit on walling blocks or bricks *(see right)*. Once satisfied with the position of the unit, check that it is level with a spirit level, then mark out its shape by pushing canes into the ground around the perimeter. Lay a length of string around these canes to indicate the area to be excavated.

Buying Rigid Pool Units

- Since preformed units can be bought in a wide range of different sizes and shapes, shop around until you find one that ideally matches your requirements.
- Preformed pool units always look smaller after they have been installed and edged, so overestimate the size of unit that you require.
- If you want the pond to be a lasting feature, invest in a good-quality fibreglass unit; these are also easier to repair.
- If intending to stock with fish, check that the unit is of an adequate size and depth. Choose fish species that will be happy in a relatively small pond.
- Check that marginal shelves are wide enough to accommodate planting baskets securely.
- A non-abrasive bathroom cleaner applied with a soft cloth is ideal for cleaning pool units, but all traces of the cleaner must be rinsed away thoroughly.

2 Measure the depth of the unit from the lip to the marginal shelves, and dig a hole to this depth, 10cm (4in) wider than the unit all around. Place the unit (right way up) in the hole and press down gently. The mark left by the deep zone will act as a guide for further digging.

3 Excavate the deep area, checking depths by measuring down from the straight-edge *(as above)*. Make the hole 5cm (2in) deeper than the deep zone, and add a 5cm (2in) layer of levelled soft sand or sifted soil. Smooth and firm the sides and shelf areas of the hole, removing all stones.

4 LOWER THE UNIT into place and press it down gently so that the deep zone fits snugly into its hole and the unit is completely level. You may need to remove the unit and make adjustments several times until the unit is fully supported by the contours of the excavation.

5 TO INCREASE the stability of the pool, fill it with water to a depth of 10cm (4in), then start to backfill around the pool with soft sand or sifted soil *(see p. 65)*. Using the straight-edge and the spirit level, check regularly that the unit is absolutely level, then tamp down the backfilling of soft sand or sifted soil at intervals. Continue to add 10cm (4in) of water at a time, and to backfill and tamp around the unit. Once the unit is filled to within 5cm (2in) of its final depth, prepare the surrounding area for whichever edging material has been chosen *(see pp. 126–129)*. If paving stones are to overlap the rim of the pool, it is important to ensure that their weight is supported. You will need to add a foundation of hardcore topped with a thick layer of sand under the lip of the unit.

DISGUISING A RIGID POOL UNIT

This kidney-shaped pool is cleverly disguised, with paving that overlaps the water around the perimeter of the pond. Both the choice and positioning of plants growing outside the paving surround, such as the bearded iris in the foreground, enhance the informal aspects of the pond. However, plants such as these must be able to grow in normal dry soil, as no moisture will escape from the pool. If the pool has built-in marginal shelves, the plants growing in the planting baskets standing on the shelves will also help to disguise the rim of the unit.

FURTHER INFORMATION

- Measuring Areas and Volumes – pp. 60–61
- Semi-raised Rigid Pool Units – pp. 88–89
- Rigid Stream Units – pp. 104–105
- Edging Materials – pp. 126–129
- Timber Decking – pp. 130–131

RAISED POOLS WITH FLEXIBLE LINER

RAISED AND SEMI-RAISED pools make excellent focal points in formal or courtyard gardens, especially where their low surrounding walls can be used as casual seats from which to observe water plants and aquatic life at close quarters. Raised pools have distinct advantages: they need little excavation, are easier to empty by hand than sunken pools, are less likely to become cluttered with debris and, because their walls can be built to varying heights, they offer a fine design solution on sloping sites. On the other hand, raised pools are more costly than the sunken variety, take more time to build, and require bricklaying skills *(see pp. 68–69)*. They are also more prone to freezing over. A raised pool is often set within a paved area. In many cases, the shape of the pavers will suggest the shape of the pool, as with the hexagonal slabs below.

WALLING STONES

BUILDING A RAISED HEXAGONAL POOL

CONSTRUCTION GUIDE

To build this hexagonal pool, 60cm (2ft) high, and 2.8m (9ft 3in) between opposite corners, you will need:

TOOLS

- String, pegs, spade, shovel, plank, spirit level, straight-edge, bricklayer's trowel

MATERIALS

- For the concrete mix: 20mm (¾in) ballast: 0.5cu m (⅔cu yd), one 50kg (110lb) bag of cement
- 60 concrete blocks: 30cm x 21cm x 8cm (12in x 8in x 3in); 30 wall ties
- 380 decorative walling stones: 30cm x 8cm x 6cm (12in x 3in x 2½in)
- Ready-mix mortar: 9 x 40kg (88lb) bags
- Liner and underlay: 4.2m sq (14ft sq)
- Rigid overflow pipe: 28cm (11in) long, 2cm (¾in) in diameter
- 18 coping stones: 60cm x 25cm x 5cm (24in x 10½in x 2in)

REINFORCED WATERPROOF CABLE CONDUIT

1 HAVING MARKED OUT the perimeter of the pool with pegs and string, and installed any paved surround *(see p. 127)*, dig a trench 45cm (18in) wide and 20cm (8in) deep inside the perimeter. Insert datum pegs to establish a horizontal level about 2.5cm (1in) below ground or paving level, then pour in concrete, and tamp and level it with a straight plank.

CONSTRUCTION TIPS

Because of the pressure exerted by water, raised pools over 45cm (18in) high should be built with double walls. The foundation trench of this pool's walls is 45cm (18in) wide – twice the width of the 22cm (9in) double wall. The trench is filled with a concrete mix consisting of ballast (a mixture of sand and small stones) and cement, which should be allowed to dry for at least 48 hours before work on the walls begins. Ready-mixed mortar can be used for both walls. Wall ties, set 1m (3ft) apart, will consolidate the strength of the walls. Pavers and coping stones are often available in pre-cut halves. For advice on how to cut stone, see pp. 68–69.

2 WHEN THE CONCRETE IS DRY, build twin walls 5cm (2in) apart. Use two courses of concrete blocks for the inner wall, and the decorative walling stones for the outer wall. Work in from each corner; use a line and a spirit level regularly to check that the walls are level and vertical. Reinforce with wall ties 1m (3ft) apart *(see inset)*.

3 BUILD THE OUTER WALL to a height of 60cm (2ft), 15cm (6in) higher than the inner wall. Allow 24 hours for the mortar to dry. Drape the underlay and liner in the pool and up and over both walls, and smooth into position *(see pp. 76–77)*. Temporarily secure the overlap of liner on the inner and outer wall with bricks.

Walling Stones
Finish off the inner wall with two courses of decorative walling stones.

Cutting Bricks and Stones
For advice on how to cut bricks, walling stones, and coping stones, see pp. 68–69.

4 **To bring the walls level**, mortar two courses of walling stones on to the liner overlapping the top of the inner wall. The coping stones will sit across the two walls, so it is important to keep checking levels along the wall *and* across the gap.

5 **Mortar the coping stones** on to the inner wall and the overlapping liner on the outer wall. Below one stone, mortar in the plastic tube as an overflow pipe *(see below)*. Mortar in another one through which to thread electric cable, if desired. Check that the coping stones are level.

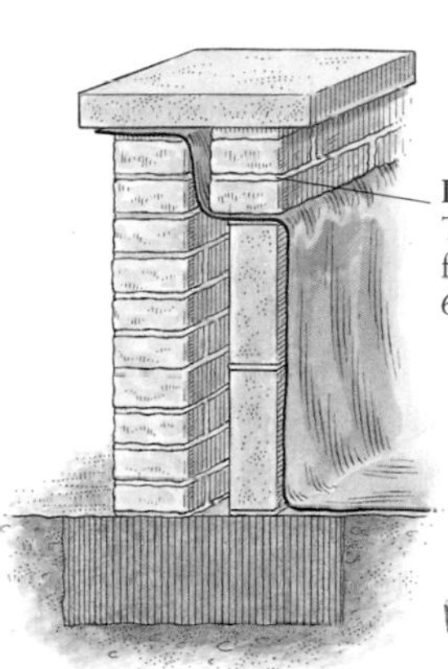

Ideal Height
The ideal height for a raised pool is 60–75cm (24–30in).

Section Through Double Wall
This section of a raised pool wall shows how the liner and underlay are hidden by mortaring them beneath the two final courses of decorative bricks on the inner wall.

Coping Stones
Overhanging coping stones provide shade and shelter for fish.

Overflow Pipe
An overflow pipe hidden beneath coping stones will prevent water from flooding over the sides of a pool after prolonged or heavy rainfall.

Ornamental Finish
For an attractive finish, use decorative walling stones for the outer wall.

Finished Pool with Planting
Although formal pools are not generally as densely planted as informal ponds, floating-leaved plants, irises, and tall grasses are often introduced. The floating leaves of water lilies (Nymphaea) *provide shade and shelter for fish, as well as checking the growth of algae by partly blocking out sunlight.*

Installing Electricity in a Raised Pool

If planning to include electrical features such as lighting *(see pp. 124–125)* or a fountain *(see pp. 108–109)*, install the wiring as the pool is being built. When installing electric cables for pumps, fountains, or lighting, safety precautions should be paramount *(see p. 72)*. Use only equipment specifically designed for outdoor or underwater use. All cabling attached to electrical equipment used in water comes ready-sealed. When cable is to be embedded in foundations, run under paving, or mortared between courses of bricks or beneath a coping stone, run it through a length of waterproof hose – as shown in Step 1 *(facing page)*.

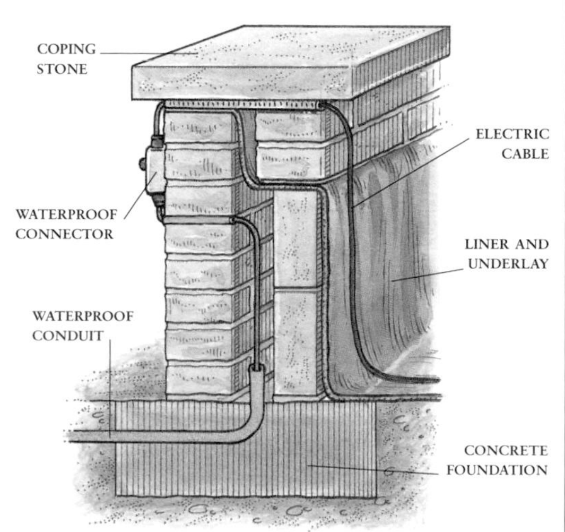

Further Information

- Choosing a Water Feature – pp. 52–53
- Siting a Water Feature – pp. 56–57
- Construction Tools and Materials – pp. 62–63
- Construction Techniques – pp. 64–69

SEMI-RAISED RIGID POOL UNITS

ALTHOUGH PREFORMED RIGID pool units are most commonly sunk in the ground (see pp. 84–85), they can also be used as semi-raised pools, provided the sides are given strong support. Although raised pools installed at ground level can make attractive features, they are prone to freeze during severe weather conditions. This problem is less likely to occur if the unit is partially buried in a shallow excavation, so that its deep zones are insulated by the surrounding earth. Materials such as log rolls, large rocks, decorative walling stones, or bricks make excellent pool surrounds. In addition to concealing the shiny outer surfaces of the raised unit, the surrounds can provide support for topsoil packed between them and the rigid mould; spreading plants grown here will soon cover the shiny lip of the pool.

FORMAL RAISED POOL

INSTALLING A SEMI-RAISED RIGID POOL UNIT

CONSTRUCTION GUIDE

To install a 2m (6ft) long, 45cm (18in) deep, 1m (3ft) wide rigid pool unit and log-roll edging, you will need:

TOOLS
- Rake, spade
- Spirit level, straight-edge
- Tamping tool
- Hammer, wire-cutters

MATERIALS
- Soft sand or sifted soil: enough to line the floor of the excavation and for backfilling
- 9 treated, pointed timber stakes: 45cm x 4cm (18in x 1½in)
- Log roll: 6m x 22cm (20ft x 9in)
- Twenty-four 5cm (2in) galvanized nails

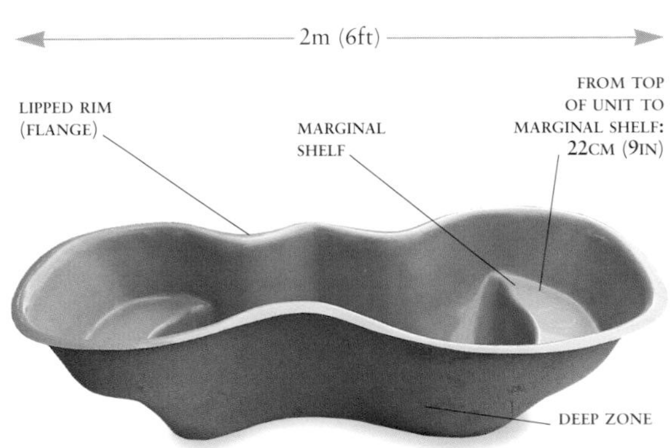

RIGID POOL UNIT
This preformed pool unit is of average size: 2m (6ft) long, 45cm (18in) deep, and 1m (3ft) at its widest point. It has two marginal shelves and is made of fibreglass, which has a life expectancy of at least 20 years. The pool's shiny surface makes it easy to clean.

1 WHEN A SITE has been chosen, clear the area of stones and organic debris and rake the surface of the area. To make a clearly visible imprint of the base of the unit, place it on the raked area and press down firmly. The impression left on the soil will show you where to dig.

CROSS-SECTION OF RIGID UNIT IN PLACE

The pool will look more pleasing if the unit is buried to the height of its marginal shelf, leaving only 22cm (9in) of the mould above the ground. Partial burying is also a fairly simple way to install preformed units on a sloping site, as only the upper part of the slope will need to be excavated to ensure that the unit is level.

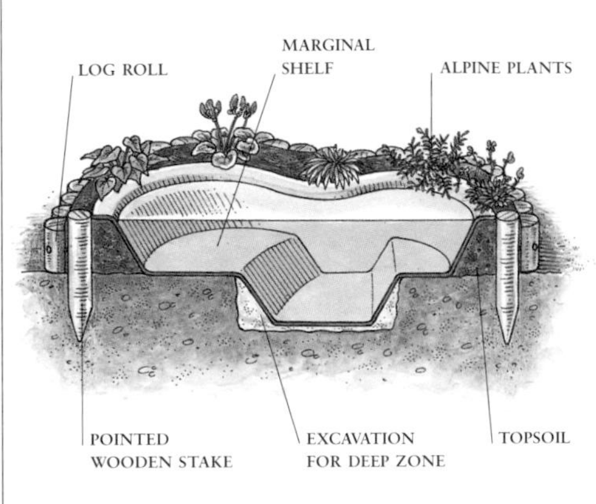

2 DIG A HOLE with slightly sloping sides, 5cm (2in) wider than the imprint left by the unit's base, and 5cm (2in) deeper than the deep zone of the unit. The extra depth allows for a layer of soft sand or sifted soil, the extra width for backfilling to support the unit sides.

3 PLACE THE UNIT in the hole and use the straight-edge and spirit level to check that it is level. If adjustments are necessary, remove the unit and add or remove sand beneath it. Begin backfilling around the sides (see p. 64) with soft sand or sifted soil.

4 PART-FILL THE UNIT WITH WATER to a depth of approximately 7–10cm (3–4in). This will stabilize the pool while the backfilling is being tamped. Use a hammer to drive the stakes into the ground around the perimeter of the unit at 1m (3ft) intervals. To ensure that the stakes firmly support the log roll, at least as much of the stake should be below as above ground. The tops of the stakes should be level with the lip of the unit, and with the top of the log roll when it is in place. The height of the log roll should equal the depth of the unit from the lip to the marginal shelf (here 22cm/9in).

5 UNROLL THE STRIP OF LOG EDGING and place it in position around the stakes. The logs are attached to each other with wire, so the roll is fairly flexible and should fit easily around the contours of the pool. If at any point the top of the log roll is found to be slightly higher than the rim of the unit and the tops of the stakes, dig a narrow trench and partially bury the base of the log roll. Since log rolls are sold in fixed lengths, you will need extra wire to join on another section if the edging comes up short. Use wire-cutters to cut the connecting wires if there is surplus log roll.

6 ONCE THE LOG ROLL has been wrapped around and cut to length, join the two ends with wire. Then use 5cm (2in) nails to fix the log rolls to the timber stakes already in place. For extra strength, use two nails, one at the top and one at the bottom of each stake. Keep the spirit level in place to ensure that the sides of the pool are not squeezed inwards as the log roll is nailed in place.

7 WITH THE LOG ROLL securely fixed, backfill the area between the logs and the unit with topsoil. Tamp the soil down firmly with a thin piece of timber. When compressed, the soil should be level with the rim of the unit. If soil spills into the unit, bale or siphon out the water, clean the unit's surface with a wet sponge, then refill to the correct depth.

ADDING PLANTS
Small plants in the free-draining topsoil between the log roll and the rigid unit will soon disguise and soften the shiny rim of the unit. Alpines such as Sempervivum *(houseleek),* Cyclamen, *and* Saxifraga *are ideal. Top-dress the soil with grit to conserve moisture and prevent soil dispersal.*

FURTHER INFORMATION

- Siting a Water Feature – pp. 56–57
- Construction Tools and Materials – pp. 62–63
- Construction Techniques – pp. 64–69
- Rigid Pool Units – pp. 84–85
- Edging Materials – pp. 126–127

SUNKEN CONCRETE POOLS

CONCRETE IS A strong and long-lasting material for formally shaped pools, made either with solid poured concrete or concrete blocks with a cement rendering *(as below)*. Pools made entirely with poured concrete can deteriorate in time, being prone to cracking in severe weather or if the surrounding earth moves. The thin layer of special, fibre-reinforced cement skimming used below dramatically reduces the risk of fracturing when the soil swells or shrinks. This method is equally successful for raised pools, although these require much more substantial and well-constructed double walls *(see* Raised Pools with Flexible Liner, *pp. 86–87)*. The safety of children should always be taken into consideration when choosing and siting a sunken pool, particularly one with straight sides and hard edges. If necessary, ring the pool with a fence.

SUNKEN CONCRETE POOL

CONSTRUCTING A SUNKEN CONCRETE POOL

CONSTRUCTION GUIDE

To build a 4m x 3m x 60cm (13ft x 10ft x 2ft) pool, you will need:

TOOLS

- Pegs, string, spade, shovel, tamping block, length of timber for levelling concrete, rake, plasterer's trowel, spirit level, straight-edge, paint-brush

MATERIALS

- Soft sand or sifted soil: 1cu m (1cu yd)
- Concrete mix – ballast: 1cu m (1cu yd); cement: one 50kg (110lb) bag
- Mortar – soft sand: 0.5cu m (½cu yd); cement: one 50kg (110lb) bag
- Cement rendering – sharp sand: 1cu m (1cu yd); cement: 2 50kg (110lb) bags; reinforcing fibres: 4 5kg (11lb) bags
- 64 concrete blocks: 45cm x 22cm x 10cm (18in x 9in x 4in); 128 house bricks; 128 brick-shaped pavers
- Proprietary waterproof sealant

1 MARK OUT and excavate a straight-sided hole 10cm (4in) deeper and 20cm (8in) wider all round than the intended size of the pool. Dig a trench 20cm (8in) wide around the inside of the excavation for poured concrete wall foundations. Presoak the trench; pour in, tamp, and level the wet concrete mix; then leave to dry.

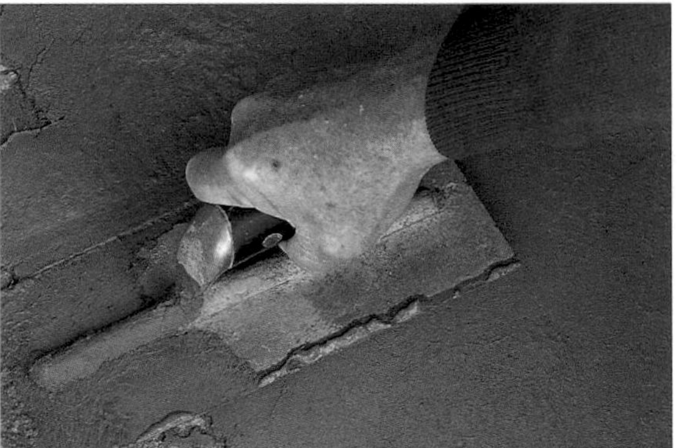

2 RAKE THE POOL'S BASE and remove any stones, then spread, rake level, and firm a 5cm (2in) layer of soft sand or sifted soil, level with the foundations. To make a firm, flexible base, use a plasterer's trowel to skim the sand with a 1cm (½in) layer of fibre-reinforced cement, overlapping the concrete of the foundations by 5cm (2in).

CROSS-SECTION, SUNKEN CONCRETE POOL

The walls of this pool are built on a concrete-filled trench, and consist of two courses of walling blocks and two courses of bricks topped with coping stones. The entire inner surface of the pool is lined with a 1cm (½in) layer of fibre-reinforced cement. Below the floor is a base layer of the cement mix on a firm layer of sand.

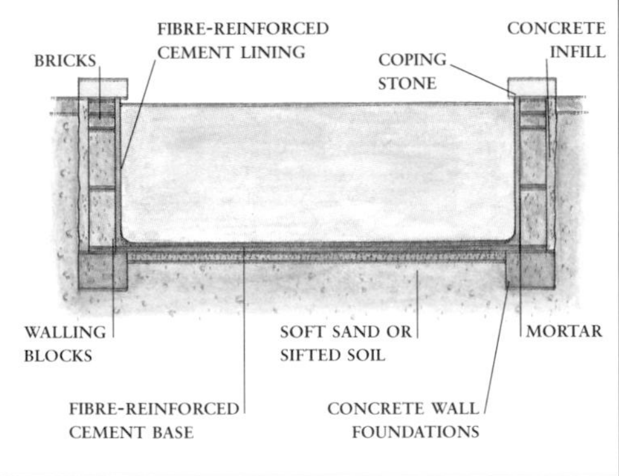

3 ALLOW AT LEAST 24 HOURS for the cement to dry, then mortar two courses of walling blocks on to the foundations in the trench. As you go along, fill the voids in the blocks with a stiffish concrete mix to give them additional strength. When the mortar has set, fill the space between the block wall and the surrounding soil with the same concrete mix *(see inset)*.

4 MORTAR TWO COURSES of house bricks on to the walling blocks *(see p. 69)*. Use a spirit level to check that each course is level, both vertically and horizontally. As you tap the bricks down with the trowel handle, scoop up the mortar that oozes out with the edge of the trowel. If this mortar is allowed to harden, you will be unable to achieve a smooth finish.

5 **ALLOW 48 HOURS** for the structure to harden, then, dampening each surface as you proceed, render the floor and the insides of the walls with a 1cm (½in) layer of fibre-reinforced cement. To give the corners additional strength, build up a chamfer where the base and side-walls meet.

6 **MORTAR THE COPING STONES** on to the side-walls so that there is a 5cm (2in) overlap on the inside of the pool; this will not only stop fish leaping out, it will also provide them with shade and shelter. The coping stones used here are brick-sized concrete paving blocks, laid side on.

7 **HAVING ALLOWED 48 HOURS** for drying, brush the inner surfaces of the pool to remove any fine debris. Then paint the whole inside with a proprietary waterproof sealant. This will prevent any impurities seeping from the cement rendering into the water *(see pp. 136–137)*.

TRADITIONAL CONCRETE-LINED POOL USING SHUTTERING

Without the use of a fibre-reinforced rendering, the construction of a concrete pool is a skilled, labour-intensive task, involving the construction of timber "shuttering". This forms a mould into which concrete is poured to create the side-walls. The base of the pool is formed by concrete poured over hardcore; flexible wire mesh, sandwiched between two layers of wet concrete, provides extra strength.

The wooden shuttering, erected inside the excavation and braced with timbers, is sprayed with water to stop the concrete sticking to the wood. Once wire mesh has been placed between the shuttering and the sides of the excavation, layers of concrete are poured in – and tamped – until the walls reach the required height. When the concrete is dry the shuttering is removed.

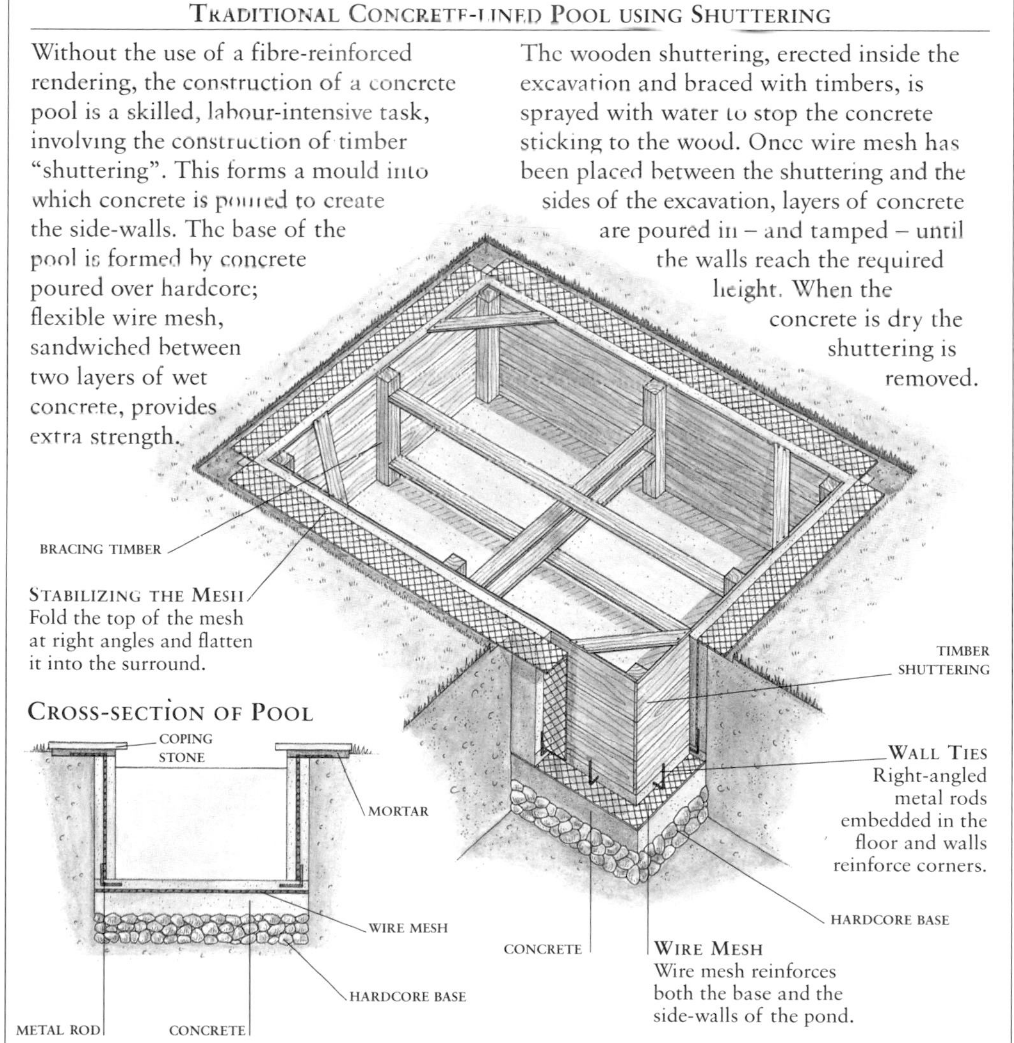

CONCRETE RESERVOIR POOL
This concrete pool serves as a reservoir for the water flowing down a shallow canal (see pp. 106–107). *The water, circulated by a pump housed in a chamber alongside the pool* (see p. 73), *passes through a surface filter installed at the top end of the canal.*

FURTHER INFORMATION

- Large Formal Pond – pp. 24–25
- Construction Tools and Materials – pp. 62–63
- Construction Techniques – pp. 64–69
- Raised Pools with Flexible Liner – pp. 86–87
- Concrete Canals – pp. 106–107

CLAY-LINED PONDS

IT IS RARE TO BE ABLE to construct a truly natural pond, but lining an informal pond with gently sloping sides with a layer of compacted clay gives a near-natural effect. If the existing soil is unsuitable, clay may be bought in. Local clay is usually available at a very modest price; importing clay from a distance, however, is expensive. An excellent alternative is sodium bentonite, a powdered clay, available from specialist suppliers, that swells into a water-resistant gel when mixed with water. Bentonite also comes in the much more convenient form of a mat – bentomat – that can be laid in much the same way as flexible pond liner. Clay linings should be always be completely covered with soil, which will both protect the clay and prevent it from drying out; the soil layer also forms a bed in which plants may spread informally.

NATURAL CLAY POND

USING NATURAL CLAY

If the existing soil is suitable *(see right)*, then, once the hole is excavated, its surface must be very well compacted to make it watertight. This can be done with booted feet, with a heavy wooden post, or with hired machinery. If the water table is high, a temporary sump *(see p. 59)* may be needed to drain away water as you dig and compact soil.

Clay-puddling simply involves lining a hole with a thick, well-compacted layer of clay. It is best to build up several thin layers, to at least 10cm (6in) thick on lighter soils. Excavate as for a pond with a flexible liner *(see pp. 76–77)*. Remove all sharp stones or roots, and dust the hole with soot; this deters tunnelling animals. Either plaster the clay on by hand or with a flat piece of wood, compacting it thoroughly. For large ponds, it is worth hiring a mechanical "sheep's foot" roller to do the job. While puddling, you must keep the clay wet. Dip your hands in water regularly as you work. As areas are puddled, either keep them moist with a sprinkler or cover temporarily with wet sacking. Then, add a 10cm (4in) layer of topsoil and fill the pond with water from a slowly trickling hose.

ASSESSING CLAY CONTENT IN SOIL

A site with soil that is sticky and pliable *(as below)* may be suitable for lining a pond. To test its suitability more accurately, place a small, sifted sample in a jar, adding water and a teaspoon of salt. Screw the lid on firmly and shake vigorously. Leave the jar undisturbed for at least two days (occasionally, it can take longer to obtain a satisfactory result), until the water has cleared and the soil particles have separated into individual layers of sand and clay. The sand will form the bottom layer, followed by a layer of clay, with organic matter floating on the surface. A suitable soil for puddling should have a clay content of approximately two-thirds.

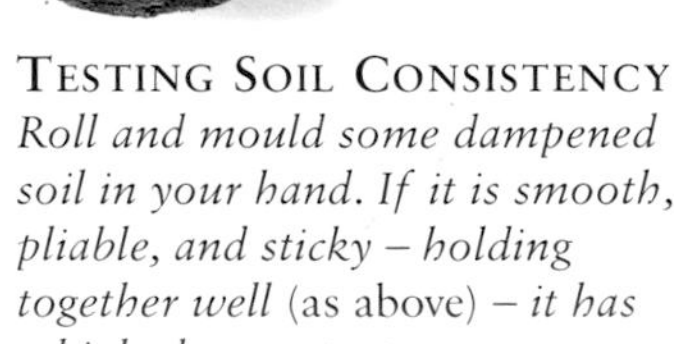

TESTING SOIL CONSISTENCY
Roll and mould some dampened soil in your hand. If it is smooth, pliable, and sticky – holding together well (as above) *– it has a high clay content.*

PROBLEM SOILS

HARDPAN
This is a virtually impermeable layer of compacted soil. Bearing in mind that clay ponds are generally large, it is advisable to hire a mechanical digger.

BLUE MOTTLING
Blue mottling on the soil surface indicates waterlogged soil. It is a good soil to puddle on, but temporary drainage will be needed while work proceeds (see p. 59).

CLAY-PUDDLED POND
All clay-lined ponds must be well filled, and scrupulously topped up, with water, so that the clay cannot dry out and crack. Deep-rooted and vigorous plants are best containerized, or they will penetrate the clay lining, making holes and causing problems if they need to be lifted and thinned. Do not plant trees or shrubs at the water's edge; their roots can penetrate the clay and cause water loss.

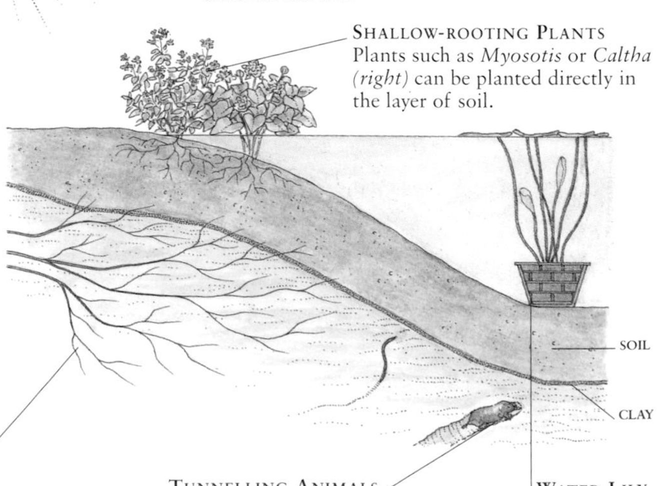

Waterproofing with Bentonite

Bentonite is a clay derived from fossilized volcanic ash and is sold in powdered crystal form or in the form of matting – bentomat – which, although heavy, is as easy to lay as flexible pond liner. In addition, unlike a clay lining, bentomat is not vulnerable to tunnelling animals and most plant roots, as the geotextile that forms the base layer is thick and impenetrable.

Laying Bentomat

On very light soils, or where several pieces of matting will overlap, additional waterproofing is advisable *(see below)*. Spread loose bentonite over the surface of the excavation, rotovate into the soil, and compact. Unroll the bentomat evenly over the excavation, as if laying a flexible liner. There should be as few wrinkles or creases as possible; if necessary, either make large, loose pleats or cut and overlap *(see right)* the matting. Cover the surface with a 30cm (12in) layer of topsoil. Slowly fill the pond with water – the moisture will soon penetrate the bentonite, causing it to swell and form an impermeable layer.

Bentonite Matting

Bentomat consists of bentonite granules sandwiched between two layers of geotextile. Bentomat is easy to handle and environmentally sound. It is ideal for lining large informal ponds, as pieces can be overlapped *(see below)* to cover an extensive area. Bentomat has a "right" and "wrong" side; always lay its non-woven side downwards.

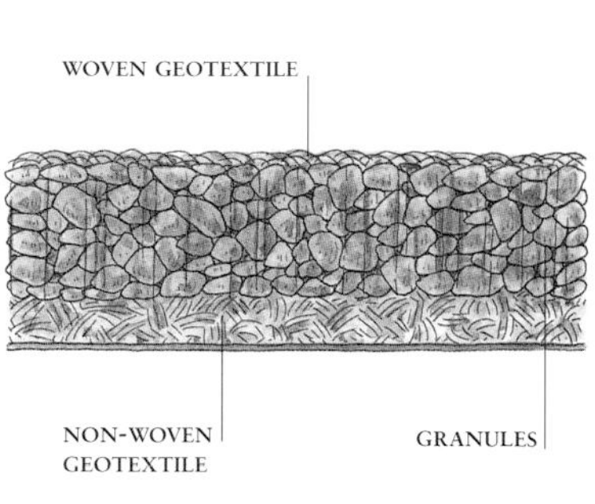

Joining Bentomat

To attach one piece of bentomat to another, spread a layer of bentonite granules on to the edge of the matting. Place the edge of the second piece over the granules, and press firmly. The granules will swell when wet, forming a watertight seal.

Planting a Bentomat-lined Pond

The sides of the excavation should not be steep – bentomat will sit more happily on a gentle slope, allowing plenty of informal marginal planting. You may wish, however, to containerize vigorous marginals and deep-water plants to make regular maintenance, lifting, and division easier. Tiles prevent the crates sinking into the soil, and roots escaping.

CAREX

CANDELABRA PRIMULA

ALISMA PLANTAGO-AQUATICA
Most non-invasive marginal plants need not be containerized.

CALTHA PALUSTRIS

EXTRA PRECAUTION
Fork or rotavate loose bentonite into the soil below for extra waterproofing; the granules will swell and form an extra impermeable layer.

LAGAROSIPHON MAJOR

TUNNEL-RESISTANT
Moles are unable to burrow through bentomat.

BENTONITE GRANULES

BENTOMAT

SOIL

CONTAINERIZED DEEP-WATER PLANT
Vigorous plants in deep zones, such as large water lilies, are easier to lift and divide if containerized.

HARD-WEARING
Tree roots cannot penetrate bentomat.

CONTAINERIZED MARGINAL
Typha, *Glyceria*, and certain other marginals with sharp roots should be confined in crates.

Laying Bentomat

Make sure that the hole is deep enough to accommodate both the required depth of water and the layer of topsoil that will cover the bentomat. Spread the bentomat over the base of the pond, extend it up the sides, and firm down with boots or, over large areas, a roller. Finally, cover with a layer of topsoil.

Further Information

- Excavation and Drainage – pp. 58–59
- Construction Tools and Materials – pp. 62–63
- Construction Techniques – pp. 64–69
- Simple Ponds with Flexible Liner – pp. 76–77

WATER GARDENS IN CONTAINERS

ALTHOUGH LIMITED IN SIZE, containers make water gardening possible in very small gardens and on patios, verandahs, and terraces. Even the most modest container, once planted, will quickly become a focal point, especially if it houses a small fountain. The addition of a couple of small fish transforms it into a fascinating feature for children. The only drawback container water gardens have is their susceptibility to rapid temperature changes and to the risk of freezing solid in prolonged periods of low temperature. This makes them unsuitable for fish or for tender plants, unless you are able to bring the container under cover in cold weather; an alternative is to sink the container into the ground so that only 10–15cm (4–6in) remains visible above ground; this insulates the contents to a degree.

SUNKEN BARREL

CHOICE OF CONTAINER

Almost any container, from barrels and decorative urns to sinks and home-made hypertufa troughs *(see facing page)*, can be used, as long as they are watertight. Earthenware pots should be glazed, and wooden barrels and tubs should be sealed; older, leaky barrels may also need a waterproof lining *(see p. 78)*. A plastic dustbin makes an ideal, inexpensive miniature water garden that can be sunk into the ground, or surrounded by other containers, to disguise its unattractive exterior. A group of container water gardens makes a striking arrangement, particularly if one of the larger containers is used to house a small pump and fountain. The humidifying effect of the circulating water will benefit surrounding plants, and keep the water fresh and sparkling; in containers without a fountain, oxygenating plants must always be included to keep the water clear. Apart from this one essential, planting can be as varied as space permits.

CONTAINER SHAPES

The most popular containers for miniature water gardens are barrels and glazed earthenware pots. To achieve the best effects, select containers with a wide neck, no narrower than 45–60cm (18–24in) across. The depth of the container need be no more than 38–45cm (15–18in).

WATERPROOFING A BARREL

Always clean tubs and barrels thoroughly. New ones will be watertight, but older ones may leak and require lining (see p. 79). *In order to protect the wood, and to ensure that any residues in the wood do not seep into the water, paint the insides of all wooden containers with a proprietary sealant.*

PLANTED BARREL

The plants in this barrel are in planting baskets, to prevent their roots from mingling. Marginal plants are placed on bricks or on empty up-turned baskets to bring them up to the correct planting depth.

Making a Hypertufa Trough

Construction Guide

To complete this step-by-step sequence, you will need:

TOOLS

- Paintbrush, spade, tamping tool, hammer, wide bolster chisel, wire brush

MATERIALS

- 2 wooden boxes made with cheap timber, one box 5–7cm (2–3in) bigger than the other
- Linseed oil
- Hypertufa mix: 2 parts peat substitute, 1 part coarse sand or grit, and 1 part cement made into a stiff mixture with water
- Wire netting: 2cm (¾in) mesh
- Plastic sheet, bricks or stones
- Proprietary liquid manure

1 **Coat the inside** of the larger wooden box, and the outside of the small box, with linseed oil *(see inset)* to stop the hypertufa from sticking. Line the base of the larger box with 2.5cm (1in) of hypertufa mix. Put reinforcing wire netting over this layer and around the sides of the box.

Covering a Glazed Sink

Thoroughly score the outside and rim with a tile- or glass-cutter, then coat with a bonding agent. Working from the bottom up, press hypertufa mix on to the sticky surface. To seal the plughole, use an ordinary drain plug, and cover with waterproof sealant.

2 **Add another layer** of hypertufa to the base, then put the smaller box on top of the base. Ensure that the netting between the sides of the two boxes is vertical, then fill the cavity between the boxes with hypertufa mix. To prevent air pockets from forming, keep tamping the mixture.

3 **Protect the trough** from sunlight, rain, and frost while the hypertufa sets. Do this by covering the top with plastic sheeting, securing it in place with bricks and stones. The hypertufa mix will form a strong shell if it is allowed to dry out slowly; a week or so should be sufficient.

4 **When the mix** has set, use a wide bolster chisel to gently prise the outer, then the inner box free of the hypertufa. For a more natural look, roughen the outside of the trough with a wire brush, then paint it with proprietary liquid manure to encourage moss and algae to grow.

Juncus effusus 'Spiralis'

Zantedeschia aethiopica 'Crowborough'

Equisetum hyemale

Veronica beccabunga

Acorus gramineus 'Variegatus'

Isolepis cernua

Planted Hypertufa Trough

Even in this small trough, a good mix of marginal plants, suited to the shallow water level, can be included. Always choose some, like the Isolepis *here, that will spill and trail down the sides of the trough, otherwise the plants will tend to look as if they are sharing a bath. On the trough's surface, algae and mosses will grow, encouraged by the peat in the hypertufa mix and the coating of liquid fertilizer.*

Further Information

- Container Gardens – pp. 26–27
- Construction Techniques – pp. 64–69
- Routine Plant Care – pp. 158–159

FEATURES WITH MOVING WATER

THE VISUAL EXCITEMENT and refreshing sound of moving water can enhance the smallest garden. Moving water is also beneficial to submerged life in creating additional oxygenation of the water. The range of pumps that is now available enables fountains, reservoir features, streams, and watercourses to be introduced in a wide variety of styles and sizes.

A MILLSTONE
This reservoir feature makes an attractive and compact fountain that is simple to install and easy to maintain. A small pump is housed in the reservoir, which is hidden underneath the fountain.

PLANNING AND INSTALLATION

Unless your garden encompasses a natural spring or stream, it will be necessary to create a feature in which the water is mechanically recirculated. While gravity will carry water down a watercourse and over falls and cascades, you will need a pump in order to drive the water back to its supposed "source". Distance, gradient, and volume of water will influence the strength of pump that you require *(see pp. 70–73)*.

SIMPLE SPILL STONE
Water trickles over moss-covered stones and then through boggy surrounds to give the impression of a woodland spring falling into a rocky hollow.

INFORMAL WATERCOURSE
This gentle slope with a cascading stream is enhanced by the use of flat-topped rocks along the sides. The immediate surrounds of the rock stream are clear of planting, allowing access to and over the water and creating the illusion of the stream having weathered the rocks through the years. The water itself is clear and inviting.

TIERED SPRAY
A fountain adds light, sound, and hypnotic movement. Fountains originated in hot climates, where the sunshine brought sparkle to the movement of the water. Fountains were also used to provide refreshment from the heat. Illuminating a fountain with artificial lighting can be spectacular, especially where the light source highlights fine droplets.

Only the largest features need a pump that cannot be hidden underwater. Today's submersible pumps are small and silent, making them unobtrusive. The delivery pipe can be buried until it reaches the source or header pool. This can then be styled to disguise the water outlet *(see pp. 102–103)*.

INFORMAL STREAMS AND WATERFALLS

A simple stream is created by digging a shallow trench, which may be lined either with flexible liner *(see pp. 98–99)* or rigid units *(see pp. 104–105)*. With more ambitious designs, a stream may meander into a series of pools and waterfalls *(see pp. 100–101)*. In informal settings, aim to make the watercourse as natural as possible by disguising the edges with plants or rocks. The speed of flow and appearance of cascades and falls can be adjusted by narrowing or widening the watercourse or by altering the pump's flow adjuster *(see pp. 70–73)*.

FORMAL CANALS AND FOUNTAINS

A formal watercourse consists of symmetrical lines and straight channels. Materials such as pavers are used for the edging *(see pp. 126–131)*. Canals *(see pp. 106–107)* may be installed in formal gardens, providing a refreshing focal point in hot, sunny situations. Fountains *(see pp. 108–111)* are good focal points and come in a multitude of styles and sizes. There is a wide variety of sprays to choose from, including tiered and plume sprays, and geysers; a geyser is ideal for hot or windy climates.

SMALL MOVING WATER FEATURES

Small water features *(see pp. 112–117)* can be accommodated in very little space. No pool is necessary to install a reservoir feature, such as a cobblestone fountain, or a wall feature, in which water falls from an ornamental spout into a basin below.

RECIRCULATING WATER SYSTEMS
The standard terms used below to describe the elements of a feature with recirculating water will help in the choice and purchase of materials.

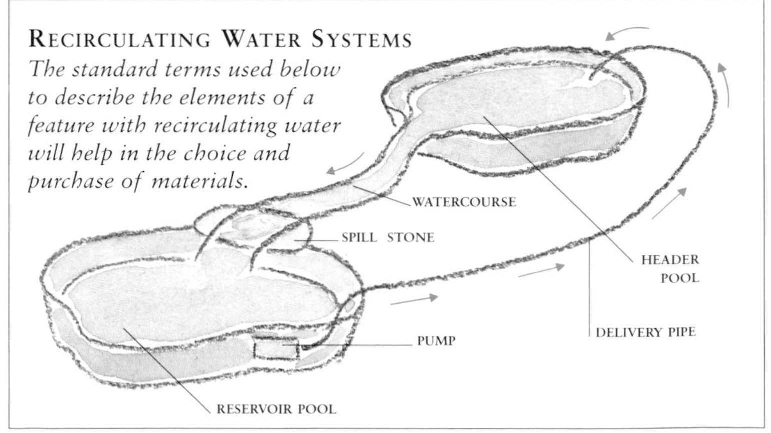

SIMPLE STREAMS WITH WATERFALLS

ANY GARDEN CAN incorporate a stream with waterfalls, provided that there is a slight change of level between the upper and lower pools. Even where the terrain has no natural incline, it is reasonably simple to create an artificial slope. In the example below, a rigid pool unit with a marginal shelf was already installed *(see pp. 84–85)*; using the rigid unit as a reservoir pool, a simple stream made with flexible liner was added in order to enhance the existing feature. The versatility of flexible liner makes it an obvious choice for the construction of informal streams. Lightweight liners made of butyl rubber or PVC are ideal for novices, because most mistakes can be rectified with some judicious tugging, packing, and filling. Rocks, pebbles, and planting will disguise the liner and protect it from the damaging effects of sunlight.

THE ORIGINAL SITE

CONSTRUCTING A STREAM

CONSTRUCTION GUIDE

To build this header pool and stream with waterfall into an existing pond, you will need:

TOOLS

- Marking pegs, string, spade, shovel, rake, trowel, watering can or hose, spirit level
- Submersible pump

MATERIALS

- Flexible liner and underlay: 4m x 2m (13ft x 6ft)
- 40 large rocks (including spill stones, foundation stones, and retaining wall stones) weighing approximately 20–50kg (55–110lb) each
- Ready-mixed mortar: 6 bags, each weighing 50kg (110lb)
- 4 x 40kg (88lb) bags of smaller rocks

1 MARK OUT THE PROPOSED course of the stream, and the outline of the header pool *(see p. 64)*. Working up from the existing pool, dig out a long trench, plus a backward-sloping header pool *(see illustration on facing page)*. Rake the areas to remove large or sharp stones.

2 PARTLY UNROLL THE flexible liner, and drape one end over the edge of the pool; make sure that the liner – although only partly unrolled – is correctly positioned over the excavation, and that there will be enough to overlap the sides of the stream once it has been pressed into the contours *(see pp. 76–79)*.

3 PLACE THE FOUNDATION stone on the marginal shelf in the pool; the stone should be hard up against the liner draped over the edge of the pool. If the foundation stone is not flat-bottomed, the pond will have to be drained and the stone mortared on to the base or marginal shelf.

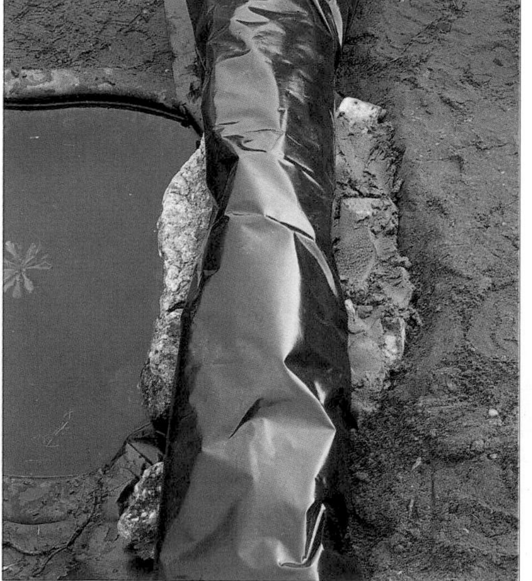

4 PACK STIFF MORTAR between the foundation stone and the overlapping liner, then roll up the liner again until it is lying over the foundation stone *(see above)*. To further increase the stability of the foundation stone, pack stiff mortar between the liner and the earth bank.

5 PARTLY UNROLL THE liner again. To make an unbroken fall of water into the pool below, place the spill stone on top of, and slightly overlapping, the foundation stone *(see pp. 102–103)*. Check the flow pattern with a watering can or a hose, then mortar the spill stone in position.

A STREAM IN PROFILE

A stream is essentially a series of elongated sections excavated on sloping ground and linked by waterfalls. The higher retaining rocks on either side of the spill stones ensure that water is funnelled over the fall.

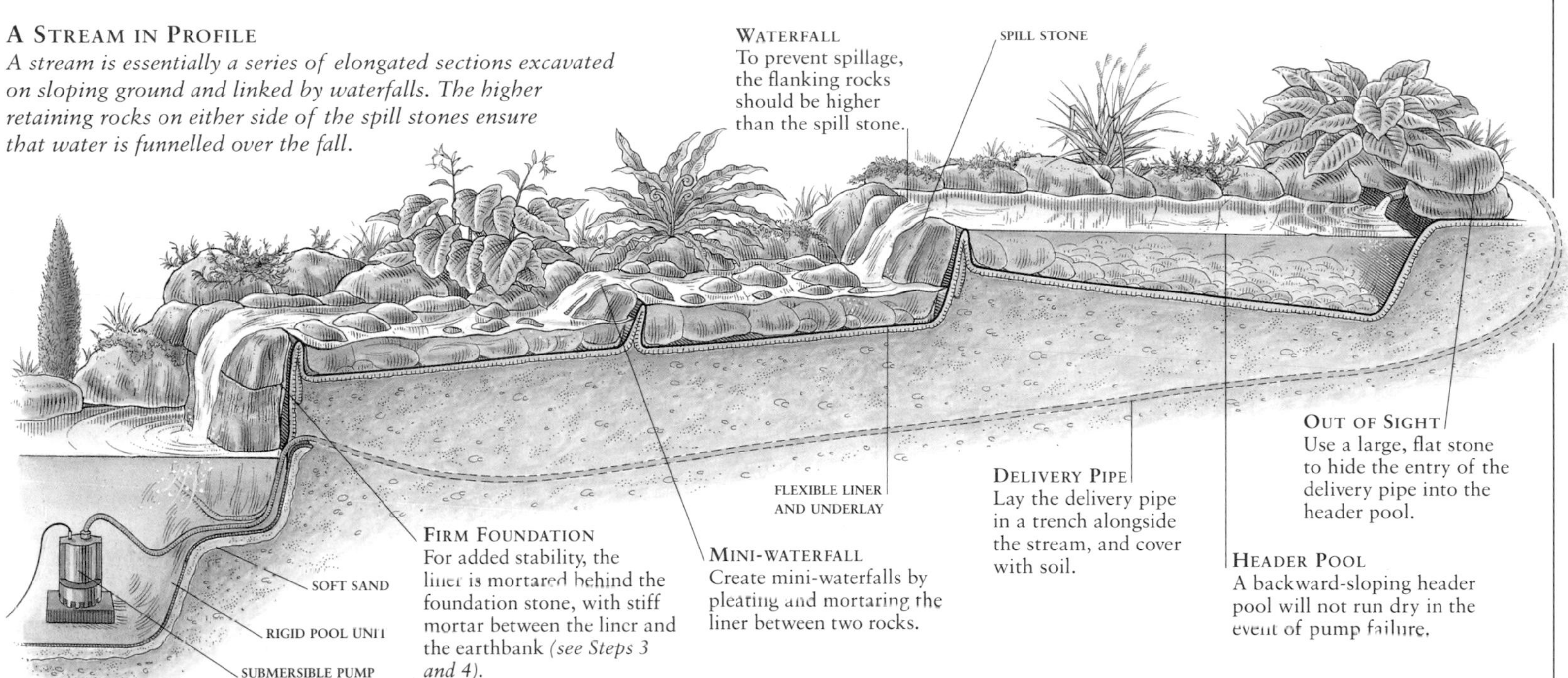

6 WHEN BUILDING UP the side walls, mortar the first layer of retaining rocks securely on to the liner before mortaring the others in place. To create a central channel for the flow of water over the waterfall, make sure that the rocks flanking the spill stone are higher than the spill stone itself.

7 CHECK THE water flow again with a watering can or a hose. To prevent the seepage of water, pull the liner level with the top of the spill stone, then pleat and mortar it behind the stone; now wedge and mortar another stone behind the pleated liner to keep it in place.

8 UNROLL THE LINER completely, and arrange large rocks along the outer edges of the stream and around the header pool, checking levels regularly with a spirit level. Mortar down another spill stone at the header pool's outlet *(see pp. 102–103)*.

9 LOWER A SUBMERSIBLE pump *(see pp. 70–73)* into the reservoir pool, and bury the delivery pipe, which will take the water up to the header pool, along the side of the stream. Use a large, flat stone to conceal the delivery pipe where it enters the header pool.

10 FOR ADDED AUTHENTICITY – and to hide the liner – place smaller rocks of mixed sizes and shapes on the floor of the stream. Planting in soil pockets between the rocks will soften the edging and emphasize the natural, informal design of the watercourse.

MORE IDEAS FOR STREAM CONSTRUCTION

ALTHOUGH THE BASIC PRINCIPLES of stream construction are quite straightforward, several factors should be considered if the stream is to be a complete success. If, for example, there are plans to create planting pockets, it is vital to ensure that the pump has sufficient output to maintain an adequate flow rate *(see pp. 70–73)*, and that the reservoir pool is big enough to supply both the header pool and the boggy soil. If the reservoir pool is too small, there will be a dramatic fall in the level of water as it circulates round the system. This will both endanger plants and water life and mar the visual appeal of the feature. It is therefore recommended that the surface area of the reservoir pool be approximately equal to or more than the total surface area *(see pp. 60–61)* of the rest of the water feature.

A STAIRCASE OF STONE
Although the principles of stream construction are always the same, the steeper the site of the stream, the more dramatic the effect. Using attractive spill stones for the falls will give the feature added charm.

WORKING WITH THE SITE CONTOURS

When determining the course of any informal stream, try to work with the natural contours of the site, especially when deciding the best place for any change of direction or drop in height. A gently meandering stream *(see below)* can be created by using a single broad strip of liner, and creating a curved channel for the water by mortaring rocks on to the liner. The outer areas can then be filled with soil to give the appearance of natural banks.

CREATING AREAS FOR STREAMSIDE PLANTING

In a wide, liner-covered trench, create a stream by mortaring on to the liner two rows of retaining rocks to act as a channel for the water. Fill the bordering areas with soil for streamside planting.

STREAMSIDE PLANTING
Line this area with rocks for drainage, then fill with topsoil.

LINER INSTALLATION
Smooth the liner into place, leaving a generous flap at the edges; these edges can later be hidden under soil.

DELIVERY PIPE
Conceal the pipe in a trench alongside the stream.

RETAINING WALL
Create the course of a stream by mortaring rocks on to the liner.

EXCAVATION
The streamside planting areas should be roughly the same depth as the stream: 15–30cm (6–12in).

RESERVOIR POOL
The reservoir pool should have enough capacity to supply the header pool and the streamside pockets.

SUBMERSIBLE PUMP
Ensure that the submersible pump has sufficient output to keep up an adequate flow rate *(see pp. 70–73)*.

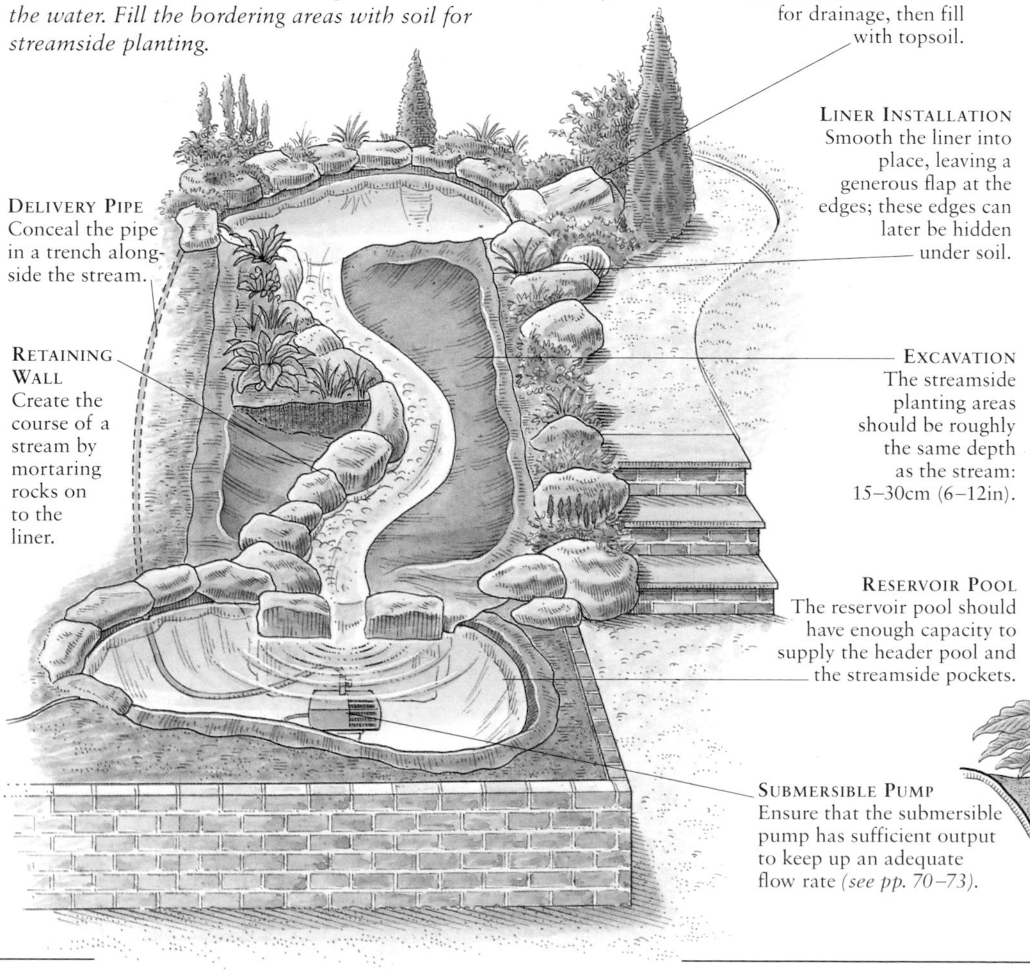

CROSS-SECTION, STREAMSIDE BEDS

Much of the attraction of a stream lies in the planting along its edges. Areas of boggy soil can be incorporated at the stream edges by creating elongated planting pockets that follow the contours of the watercourse. Once filled with soil, these pockets can be filled with plants such as *Parnassia palustris*, *Iris ensata*, and *Eriophorum angustifolium*, which thrive in saturated earth. Any plant that might be invasive should be confined to sunken planting baskets with a close weave. The retaining walls at the edges of the stream will help to prevent the planting soil from silting up the stream.

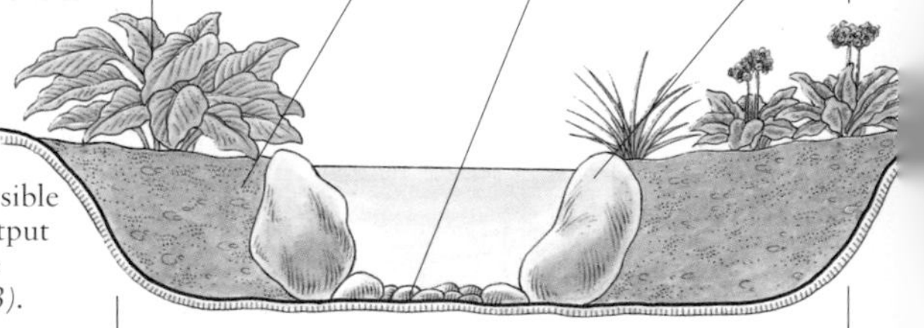

CARING FOR PLANTS
Never use ordinary garden fertilizer on marginal plants, as it will leak into the water.

PEBBLE FLOOR
To disguise the liner, place pebbles on the base.

SOIL

RETAINING ROCK

Extreme Changes of Direction

When constructing a stream of any kind, always work upwards from the reservoir pool. If a meandering watercourse is made with one piece of liner, the liner will have to be folded to incorporate changes of direction *(see pp. 66–67)*. If the stream is to include waterfalls and extreme changes of direction, however, separate pieces of liner may have to be used *(see below)*. Once the overall route has been marked out, decide where the waterfalls are to be sited, as the watercourse should narrow down to waists at these points. Where these narrow sections do occur, full use of the width of the liner can be made by incorporating adjacent planting beds.

In measuring for each length of liner, make allowances for an overlap at the end of each section. Measure the length between each waterfall, and the depth of the stream behind the waterfall at the downstream end where the liner will have to overlap another piece of liner *(see below)*. The liner should be long enough to extend above the waterline at the upstream end, where it will be overlapped by the next piece of liner. Once the liner is in position, the rocks that make up the retaining walls of the stream can be mortared on to it. The top of each waterfall spill stone should be high enough to retain at least 10–15cm (4–6in) of water in the stream behind it; this will prevent underwater creatures from being stranded when the pump is switched off. The edges of the stream can then be built up. The edges should be fairly level and at least 5cm (2in) higher than the top of the spill stone; this will ensure that the recirculating water is contained within the system rather than flooding over the sides.

Coping with Seasonal Evaporation

Even the most carefully constructed water feature may need topping up, particularly in warm months when evaporation from water surfaces, rocks, and boggy soil takes place. This loss can be replaced with water from a butt, or with tap water trickling from a garden hose *(see pp. 138–139)*. It is advisable to top up regularly, rather than leave it until the level is low enough to adversely affect fish and plants.

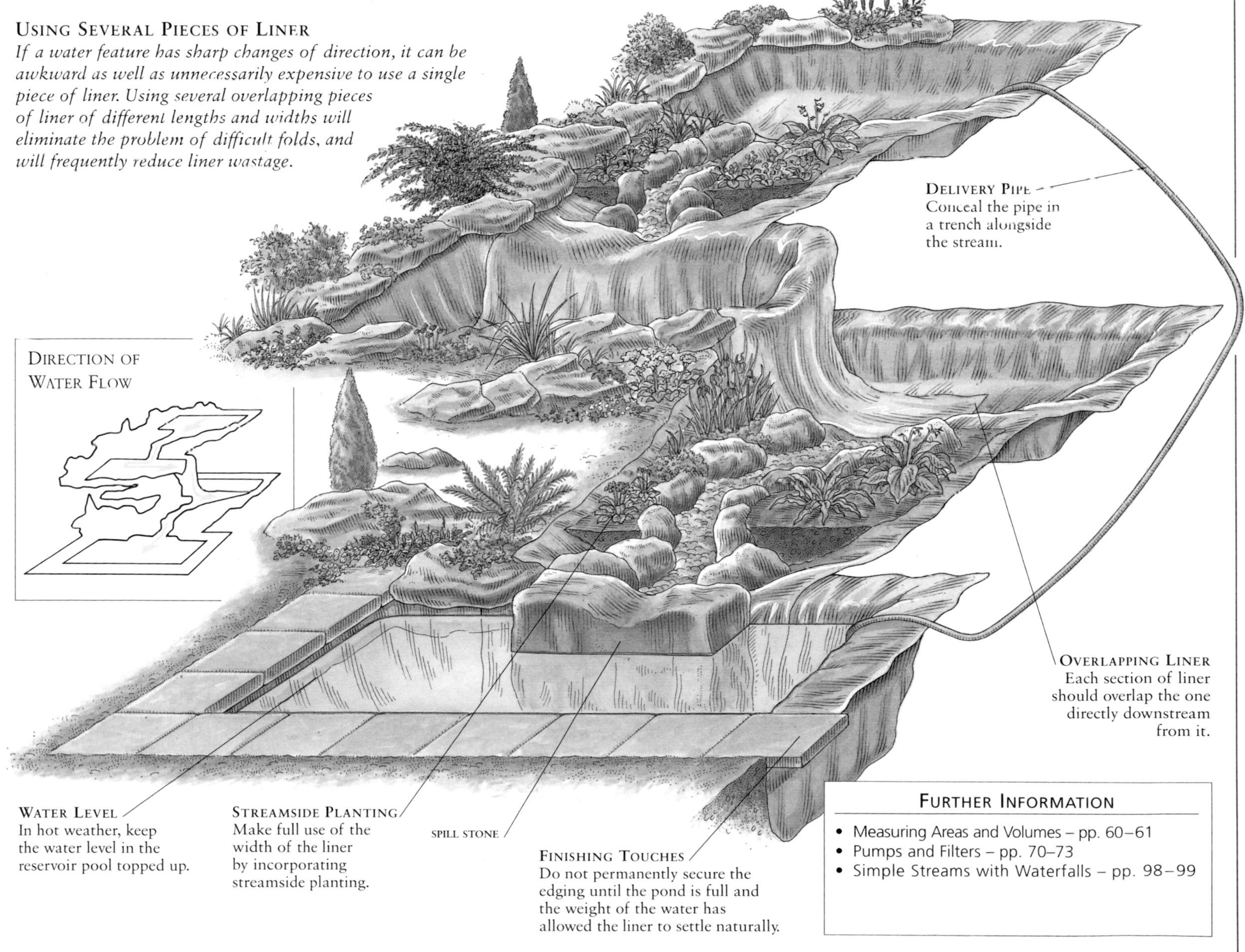

Using Several Pieces of Liner
If a water feature has sharp changes of direction, it can be awkward as well as unnecessarily expensive to use a single piece of liner. Using several overlapping pieces of liner of different lengths and widths will eliminate the problem of difficult folds, and will frequently reduce liner wastage.

Further Information

- Measuring Areas and Volumes – pp. 60–61
- Pumps and Filters – pp. 70–73
- Simple Streams with Waterfalls – pp. 98–99

HEADER POOLS AND SPILLWAYS

BOTH FORMAL AND INFORMAL watercourses usually terminate in a pond, in or near which the pump is housed. The pump draws the water from this reservoir pool, and sends it up to the head of the feature. At this point the delivery pipe fills a smaller reservoir of water, known as the "header pool", which brims over into the watercourse; this gives a much better effect than if the pipe simply discharges into the start of a channel. The header pool may be concealed, with water spilling out of a culvert, or styled to match the rest of the feature. The header pool, and any intermediate pools along a watercourse, should always be deep enough to retain water when the pump is off.

POSITIONING THE DELIVERY PIPE

Make sure that the end of the delivery pipe is above the water level of the header pool, so that it does not siphon water back as soon as the pump is turned off. If it is necessary to keep the end of the pipe under water, a non-return valve should be fitted at a convenient point in the delivery pipe to prevent siphon action *(see* Preventing backflow, *p. 73).*

INFORMAL STYLING

Informal header pools and streams are generally flanked by rocks of different sizes and shapes in order to retain surrounding soil and to direct the water along the watercourse. Use more rocks than are necessary; additional stones placed around the

INFORMAL STREAM WITH CHANGES OF LEVEL
The delivery pipe in the header pool is disguised with a pile of large stones and smaller pebbles to fill the gaps (see inset)*, and the flow adjusted so that water ripples out over the rocks. A natural effect is achieved when flat-topped stones are placed in the stream, providing shallow spills of water that are no more than 7–10cm (3–4in) high.*

CASCADING WATERFALL

INTERRUPTED FLOW
By using an uneven spill stone that is wider at the bottom than it is at the top, it is possible to create a cascading waterfall, rather than an unbroken curtain of water. It is also possible to create a cascade by using several rocks, each set back slightly from the one below, so that the water spills downwards in an uneven way.

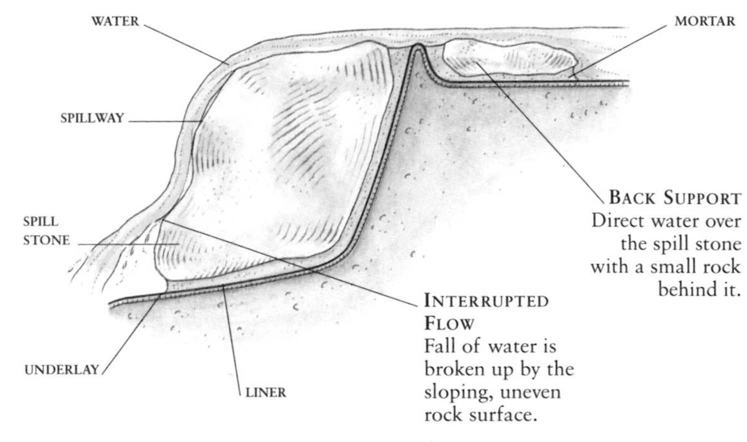

CURTAIN OF WATER

UNBROKEN FLOW
Here, the spill stone projects outwards over the fall to produce an unbroken curtain of water. A wide stone set only just below the water level, so that a broad film of brimming water is produced, is most attractive; few natural stones jut out in this way, so a foundation stone is usually used, with a flat stone mortared on top of and overhanging it.

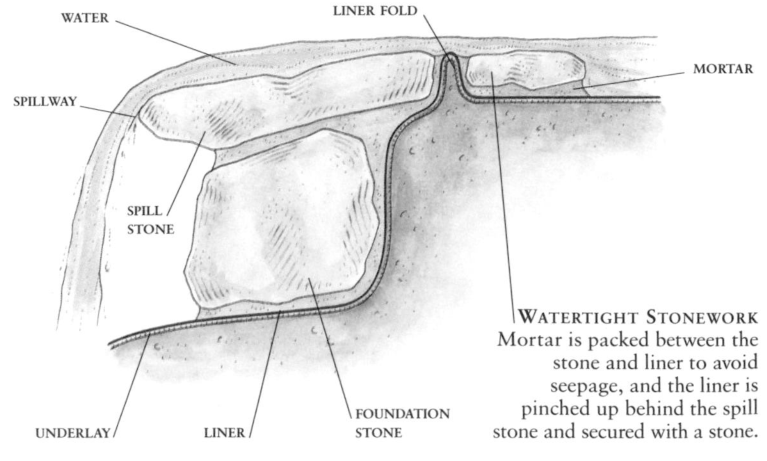

sides and upstream of the source will create a more natural effect, which planting will enhance. The shape and arrangement of stones at spill points will determine whether a free-falling curtain of water or cascading rivulets are achieved. For the latter, use a garden hose to judge the effect, and reposition stones as necessary before finally mortaring them down.

Formal Spillways

The simplest way of constructing a formal fall of water from a reservoir pool into a canal or another pool is to use a flat paver or tile as an overlapping spill stone: this method is ideal for a split-level pool *(see pp. 106–107)*, where water falls from one level to another over a common dividing wall. In order to construct the spillway, a gap is left in the last course of walling stone to take the flat spill stone. Any overlapping liner can be tucked under the spill stone. The stone must be precisely horizontal for the effect to be achieved: use a spirit level across both axes of the stone. The wall can be built up and around and over the spillway to form a formal culvert *(see below)*.

Large-scale Feature
Even when not in use, formal culverts can add a note of classical grandeur. Here, they have been integrated into a double stairway leading down to a broad pool. Remember that for water lilies to thrive in the vicinity of waterfalls, the flow must be little more than a gentle trickle.

Formal Culvert

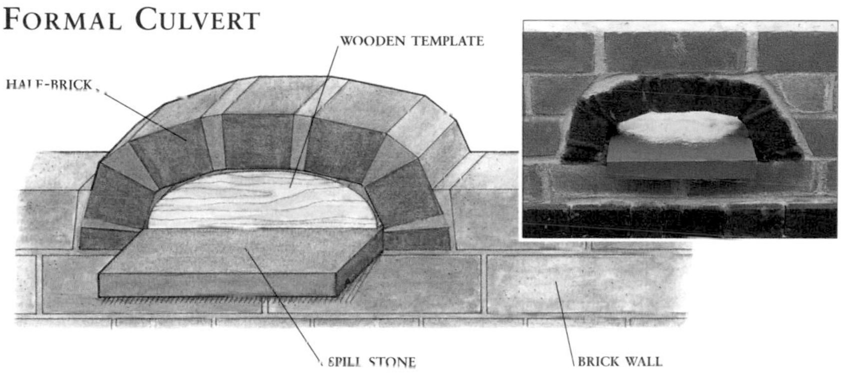

Constructing a Culvert in a Wall
Culverts allow water to flow out from concealed header pools that are ideal housings for filter boxes (see p. 73). *In order to construct a culvert, a wooden template is shaped to the internal measurements of the opening and laid on to the tile mortared on the course of bricks that will support the spillway. Bricks can then be cut and laid to form the arched shape within the next two courses. After about two days, when the mortar is completely hard, the template can be tapped out.*

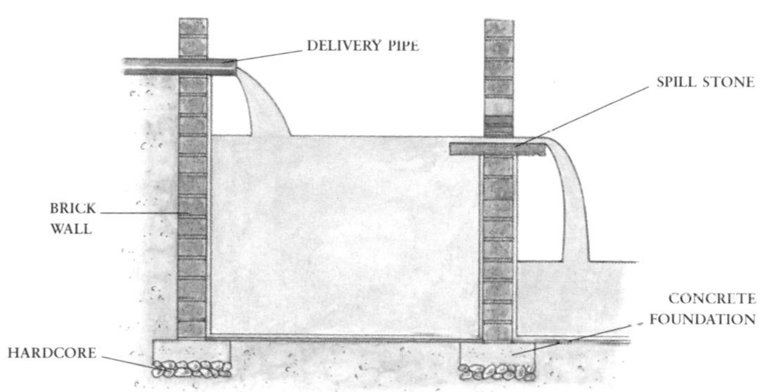

Formal Header Pool
Even if concealed, a header pool provides a more convincing flow of water than simply positioning the delivery pipe to discharge through a hole in a wall. Careful adjustment of the flow is necessary to ensure that water just brims over the spill stone. The pool's inlet pipe is at a higher level than the spillway to prevent siphoning back when the pump is turned off.

Recirculating Feature

Formal Spillways
In this formal feature, water falls from a raised reservoir through gaps in the top course of bricks: to interrupt the flow and create a splashing cascade, rather than a smooth fall, the wall has been built with bricks protruding at intervals. Rounded bricks provide gentle, smooth spillways in this series of coordinated shallow drops. The same type of brick has been used for all the surfaces – edging, spillways, and the base of the canal. Warm-toned terracotta, with plants softening the edges, prevents a severe effect.

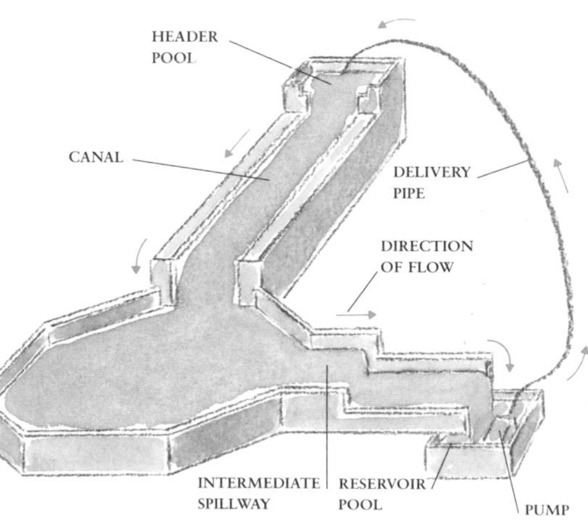

Concealed Plumbing
The reservoir pool can be concealed beneath a path, suggesting an ongoing system of canals rather than a small recirculating feature.

RIGID STREAM UNITS

MOST PREFORMED RIGID stream units provide a relatively easy way to create a stream and a series of waterfalls. Installing fibreglass rigid units is simpler, for example, than making a stream with flexible liner *(see pp. 98–103)*. Once units are purchased, hardly any other materials are necessary, although some extra rocks can help to blend the feature into its surroundings. Rigid units come in different sizes, materials, and finishes, such as pebbledash, textured rock, or grit. Most are made of fibreglass, which gives them resistance to damaging ultraviolet light. In addition to the bolted type *(see facing page)*, units also come in PVC and vacuum-formed plastic moulds, which are cheaper but have a limited life. A combination of units can include "connecting" units that link header pools, waterfalls, and miniature rock pools.

STREAM UNITS IN PLACE

INSTALLING FIBREGLASS RIGID STREAM UNITS

CONSTRUCTION GUIDE

To install these rigid stream units *(dimensions given below)* above an existing pond with a submersible pump, you will need:

TOOLS

- String and pegs
- Spade, shovel
- Spirit level, straight-edge
- Tamping block

MATERIALS

- Soft sand or sifted soil: 0.5cu m (½cu yd)
- 5m (15ft) delivery pipe with flow adjuster
- Topsoil, rocks, and plants

1 AFTER MARKING OUT THE SITE, work from the bottom up and dig a shallow trench with a slight backward slope. Bed the first unit on soft sand or sifted soil, its lip slightly overlapping the edge of the pond.

OVERLAPPING OUTLETS Each section's outlet should overlap the unit below it.

2 REPEAT THE PROCESS up to and including the header pool. The lip of each unit, including that of the header pool, should overhang the unit below it. Hide the delivery pipe in a 15cm (6in) trench alongside the stream.

3 FIRM IN THE UNITS with tamped soft sand or sifted soil, then add a layer of topsoil and some surrounding rocks. Use a flat rock to hide the delivery pipe entering the header pool, then turn on the pump to check the flow of water. Use the flow adjuster to achieve the desired effect.

WATERCOURSE CONSTRUCTED WITH RIGID STREAM UNITS

The addition of randomly placed rocks and plants is the key to making preformed units blend in with their surroundings. The layer of soft sand or sifted soil, and the free drainage afforded by the slope, make the site ideal for many alpines, which look well among rocks.

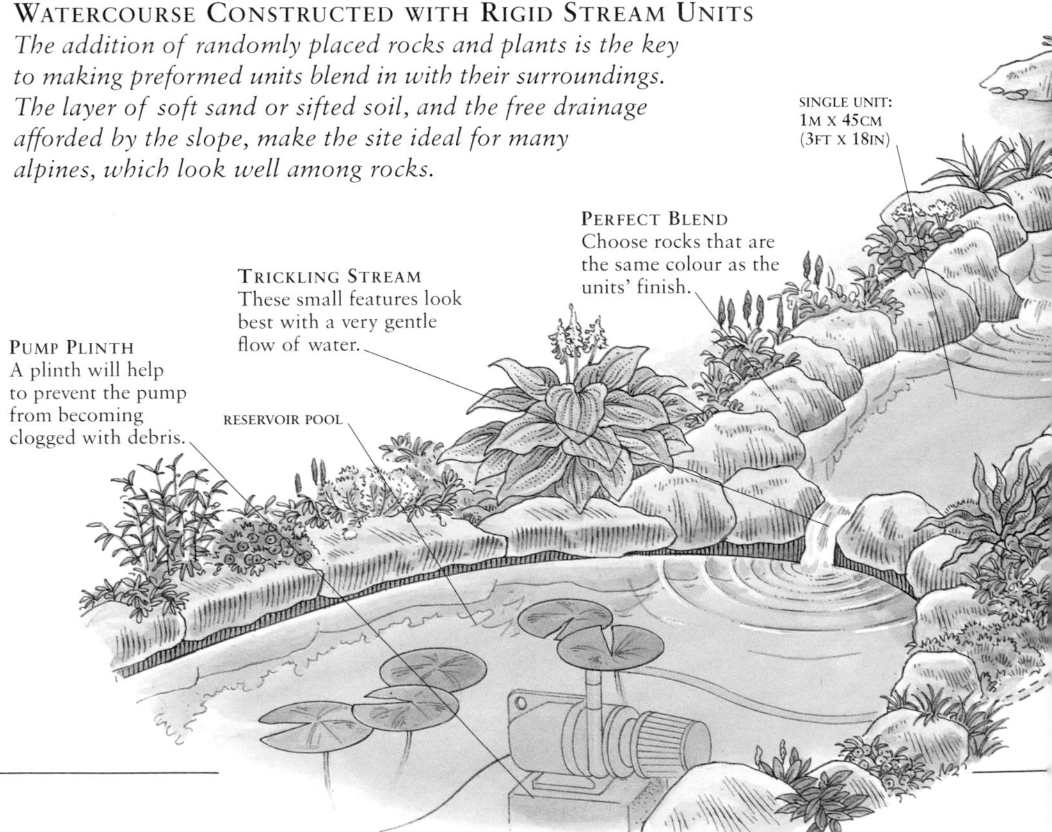

SINGLE UNIT: 1M X 45CM (3FT X 18IN)

PERFECT BLEND Choose rocks that are the same colour as the units' finish.

TRICKLING STREAM These small features look best with a very gentle flow of water.

PUMP PLINTH A plinth will help to prevent the pump from becoming clogged with debris.

RESERVOIR POOL

Installing Bolted Rigid Units

Bolted units in regular shapes are particularly suited to more formal gardens, and are often used to construct interlocking pools at different heights. To disguise the connecting plates, easy-to-install cladding with a variety of finishes is available. Once installed, the units make a more permanent feature than smaller and lighter preformed units, so be sure to create level and stable foundations for them. When excavating, always allow extra depth for a 5cm (2in) layer of sand, and check at each stage of installation that the units are perfectly level.

Durability and Permanence

Strong, interlocking and bolted rigid units are not only extremely stable, they are also much less prone to being damaged by soil subsidence. They are, however, a great deal heavier and sturdier than preformed fibreglass or plastic units, and are subsequently more difficult to install. It is advisable, therefore, to enlist the help of at least one other person when lifting, positioning, and backfilling around the units.

Due to their size and bulk, more skill will be required in disguising the hard edges of the units. Because they completely contain the water, no moisture will seep into the surrounding ground. A combination of quick-growing carpeting alpines, and small shrubs that tolerate the dry, well-drained soil along the perimeter of the stream, will help to integrate the feature into its surroundings. Alternatively, you may use flexible liner to make independent boggy areas *(see pp. 82–83)*.

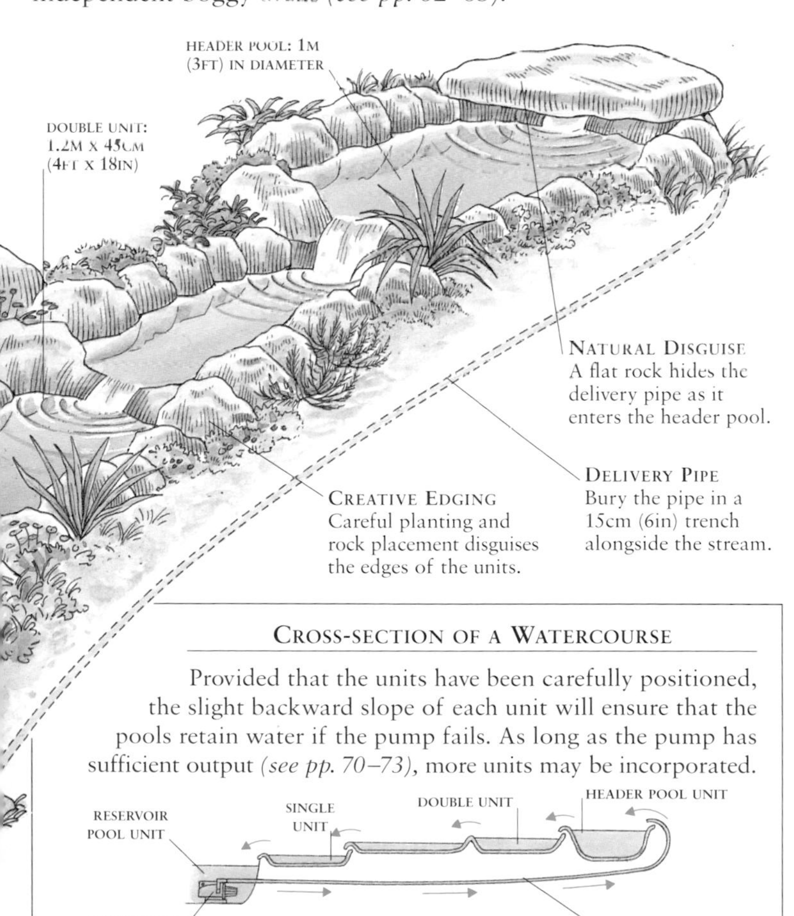

Natural Disguise A flat rock hides the delivery pipe as it enters the header pool.

Delivery Pipe Bury the pipe in a 15cm (6in) trench alongside the stream.

Creative Edging Careful planting and rock placement disguises the edges of the units.

Cross-section of a Watercourse

Provided that the units have been carefully positioned, the slight backward slope of each unit will ensure that the pools retain water if the pump fails. As long as the pump has sufficient output *(see pp. 70–73)*, more units may be incorporated.

RESERVOIR POOL UNIT
SINGLE UNIT
DOUBLE UNIT
HEADER POOL UNIT
SUBMERSIBLE PUMP
DELIVERY PIPE

Making a Watercourse with Bolted Rigid Units

1 **At the edge of** the pond, here made with flexible liner *(see pp. 76–79)*, dig out a platform for the first unit. Spread 5cm (2in) of soft sand or sifted soil over the base and check that it is level.

2 **Remove the unit**, bolt it to the plate forming the fall, and seal the joins with silicone sealant. Install the unit, making sure it is level. Backfill behind the plate when excavating the header pool.

3 **Line the base** of the header pool with soft sand or sifted soil. Bolt its unit to the top of the vertical plate and seal the joins. Check that the unit is level, then backfill around it.

4 **Install a submersible pump** in the reservoir pool. Connect one end of a delivery pipe to the pump, and bring it up to the header pool, burying it alongside the watercourse.

5 **Snap into place** the pebbledash cladding, then disguise the edges of the units by placing stones along the edges. Stones placed beneath the lip of the lowest unit will effectively camouflage the flexible liner used in the reservoir pool. Two large, flat stones will also disguise the entry and exit points of the delivery pipe.

Further Information

- Pumps and Filters – pp. 70–73
- Simple Ponds with Flexible Liner – pp. 76–79
- Simple Streams with Waterfalls – pp. 98–103
- Edging Materials – pp. 126–129

CONCRETE CANALS

STRAIGHT, SHALLOW CANALS of moving water, whether sunken, semi-raised, or completely raised, are ideally suited to flat terrain in formal settings *(see pp. 56–57)*. Canals can be of practical use – forming the boundary of a garden, or linking a formal garden to the more "natural" landscape around it – or they can be purely ornamental. The formal impact of a canal can be heightened by flanking it with symmetrical planting – perhaps of columnar evergreens or trained standards of bushes and trees. The canals themselves are best left free of plants. Bear in mind that the longer a concrete canal, the greater the risk of cracking caused by earth movements. The method shown here uses a skimming of strong but flexible reinforced cement to line the canal, greatly reducing the risk of such damage.

FORMAL CANAL

CANAL LINKED TO RESERVOIR POOL

This feature is enhanced by its clear water and by the fact that its workings are concealed. A filter is housed in the upper brick chamber with culvert (see p. 73), *while a surface pump sits in a ventilated chamber* (see pp. 102–103) *to the left of the lower cascade.*

REMOVABLE COVER

OVERFLOW PIPE

SURFACE FILTER Biological and UV surface filter housed inside brick structure.

CULVERT

DELIVERY PIPE Bury the delivery pipe in a trench under the paving.

CEMENT SKIMMING Cement mixed with reinforcing fibres makes a flexible lining for the canal.

WATERFALL An overhanging spill stone will accentuate the drop of the water.

PUMP CHAMBER Ventilated brick chamber with removable cover contains the surface pump.

SURFACE PUMP ON WOODEN PLINTH

BRICK PAVING SURROUND

DECORATIVE PAVERS Matching paving unites the edges of the reservoir pool and the canal.

CROSS-SECTION OF A FORMAL CANAL

The decorative pavers used as edging for this canal stand proud of the surrounding brick-paved area, giving the feature a semi-raised effect. To achieve the desired depth, only one course of bricks was used, and one course of decorative pavers. Skimming the floor and walls with a 1cm (½in) rendering of cement mixed with sharp sand and reinforcing fibres creates a waterproof lining for the canal that is more resistant to cracking than solid poured concrete.

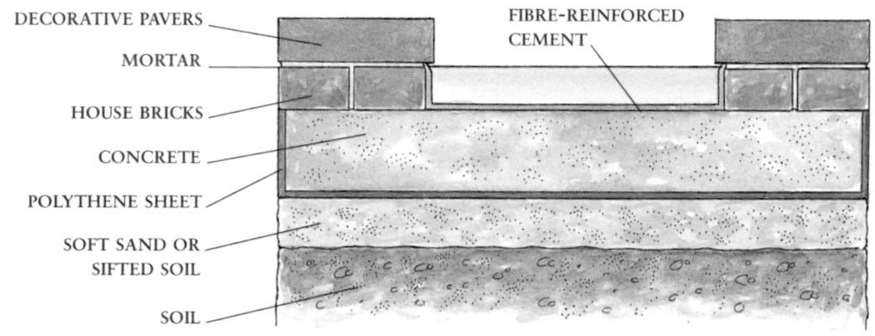

DECORATIVE PAVERS

FIBRE-REINFORCED CEMENT

MORTAR

HOUSE BRICKS

CONCRETE

POLYTHENE SHEET

SOFT SAND OR SIFTED SOIL

SOIL

Making a Concrete Canal

Construction Guide

To build the 2.5m (8ft) x 40cm (16in) concrete canal illustrated *(facing page)* you will need:

TOOLS

- Marking pegs, string, spade, straight-edge, spirit level, thin, straight plank, pointed trowel, plasterer's trowel

MATERIALS

- Soft sand: 0.5cu m (½cu yd)
- Heavy-duty polythene sheet: 2.5m (8ft) x 60cm (24in)
- Concrete: 35kg (77lb) cement; ⅔cu m (⅔cu yd) sand; 150kg (330lb) aggregate
- Mortar: 15kg (33lb) cement; ⅓cu m (⅓cu yd) sand
- Cement rendering: one 0.5kg (18oz) bag reinforcing fibres; 25kg (55lb) cement; 0.5cu m (½cu yd) sand
- 44 house bricks; 48 decorative pavers
- Proprietary water sealant

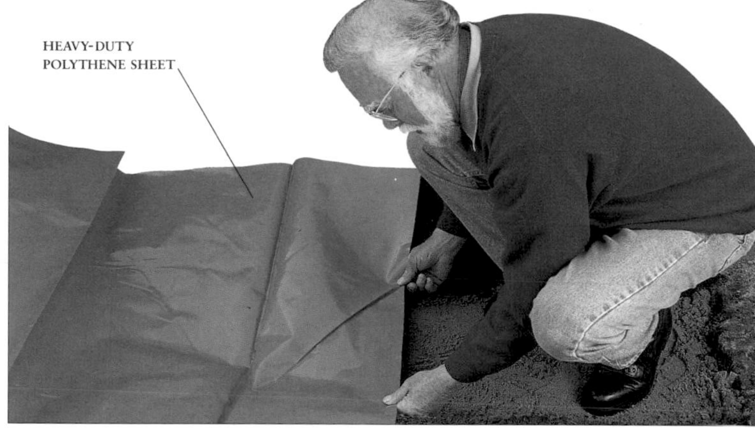

1 **Mark out the length and width** of the proposed canal. Excavate the area to a depth of 20cm (8in), which includes 5cm (2in) for a lining of soft sand. Rake the sand and check that the site is absolutely level, then line the floor and walls with the polythene sheet.

Circulating Water in Canals

Canals rely on pumps to push water along their length, and not on gradient; they must be built on level ground, or they will empty too rapidly. The delivery pipe from the pump can discharge into either a header pool or, as shown on the facing page, a concealed brick chamber, from which the water emerges via a formal conduit *(see pp. 102–103)*. An enclosed chamber can also be used to house a filter box *(see p. 73)*. It is important to make sure that the pump has sufficient output to maintain an unbroken fall, if desired, into a reservoir pool *(see pp. 70–73)*.

2 **Lay the foundation** by pouring a 5cm (2in) layer of concrete on to the polythene sheet, then firming and levelling it. Use a straight-edge and a spirit level to check that the sides of the excavation are at exactly the same height. Consolidate the foundation by tamping it down and levelling it with a straight plank.

3 **Allow two days** for the concrete to harden. Then construct the side-walls by first mortaring a course of house bricks *(see p. 69)* on to the foundation. Check regularly to ensure that the bricks are level. Mortar the decorative pavers at right-angles on top of the bricks. Move the string guide to help lay the pavers, overlapping the inside edge of the canal by 5cm (2in).

4 **Once the mortar has set,** use a plasterer's trowel to skim the floor and walls of the canal with the cement rendering mix containing the reinforcing fibres. This forms the canal's watertight lining, so ensure that coverage is complete, particularly up under the decorative pavers. When the skimming is completely dry, paint on a coat of proprietary water sealant to prevent harmful chemicals from seeping from the cement mix into the water and having an adverse effect on fish and plant life.

Canals Linking Reservoir Features

Canal in a Garden Setting
Formal canals need not be associated with paving to have impact. This arrangement of narrow, turf-edged canals linking three sunken reservoir pools, each with its own fountain, culminates in a recessed urn flanked by pergolas.

Further Information

- Siting Water Features – pp. 56–57
- Construction Tools and Materials – pp. 62–63
- Construction Techniques – pp. 64–69
- Pumps and Filters – pp. 70–73
- Concrete-lined Pools – pp. 90–91

FOUNTAINS

FOUNTAINS DATE BACK to antiquity, their use relying on ever more elaborate hydraulic technology and ornamental stonework until, in the 19th century, more natural trends in garden design emerged. In today's climate of eclectic and individualistic design, fountains can be installed in order to embellish all types of water garden, providing movement, sound, and refreshment in a range of styles. Fountains all work in the same way; the fountain head is connected to an electric pump, which drives water through the head, creating a spray. There are a range of fountain nozzles that will produce different spray patterns; the height of spray will depend on the power of the pump. In addition to their ornamental attraction, fountains also have practical value – in creating movement they increase the oxygen content of the water.

FOUNTAIN IN POSITION

INSTALLING FOUNTAINS

The simplest fountains discharge water from a vertical rigid pipe leading off a submersible pump, which sits on a plinth at the bottom of the pond. The pump may be disguised within an ornamental housing. For larger pools, it may be more convenient to site the pump close to the pool edge *(right)*, using a delivery hose to connect it to the fountain.

REMOTE PUMP INSTALLATION

If you wish the pump to be within easy reach for maintenance, install it at the edge of the pond. The pump can be concealed by extending the pond edging to include an overhanging paving stone.

FOUNTAIN JET
The pump need not be directly beneath the nozzle.

SIMPLE PUMP INSTALLATION

The easiest method of installing a fountain is to place a pump on a plinth in the centre of the pond, using a vertical discharge pipe with a fountain jet. Do not place certain plants too close – water lilies and free-floaters are disturbed by water movement.

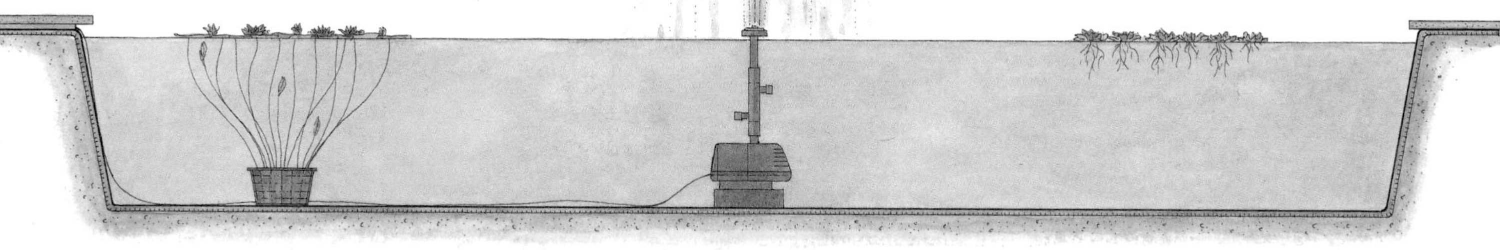

INSTALLING A PUMP IN A SMALL FOUNTAIN ORNAMENT

1 TO INSTALL A SUBMERSIBLE pump inside the base of an ornamental fountain, first remove the top section, place the pump inside, and thread the cable through one of the several openings. Then attach a short length of hose to the pump's outlet and secure with a hoseclip.

2 INSIDE THE ORNAMENTAL fountain there will be an integrated, rigid pipe. Using another hose clip, join this to the hose from the pump outlet. Then set the top half of the ornament securely onto the base and test the flow rate, altering by using the flow adjuster if necessary.

SAFETY PRECAUTIONS

A fountain may be connected to the domestic mains supply with a waterproof switch box at the poolside. Alternatively, a waterproof cable connector can be used, which in turn is connected to a standard switchbox inside. Except where the system is low-voltage, it should be protected by a residual current device (RCD or circuit breaker).

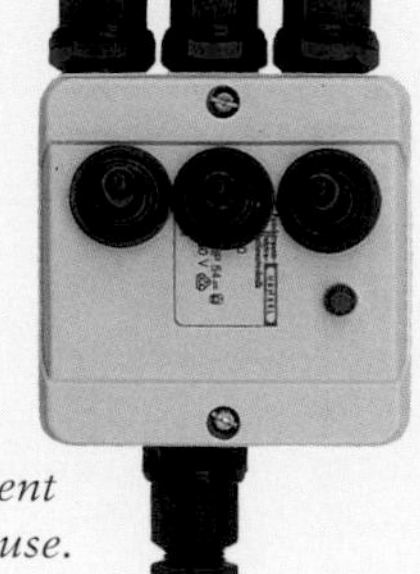

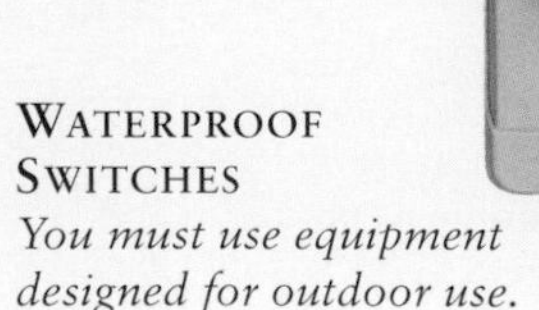

WATERPROOF SWITCHES
You must use equipment designed for outdoor use.

Spray Patterns

A standard fountain kit consists of a pump, a length of rigid pipe, and a fountain nozzle. The spray pattern is affected by the size and placing of holes in the nozzle. Standard nozzles may be connected directly to the pipe; use adaptors to connect more complicated nozzles. The flow adjuster controls the height and width of spray: for spray heights of up to 1.2m (4ft) use a low-voltage pump; to 2.2m (7ft), a mains submersible pump; over 2.2m (7ft), a mains surface pump.

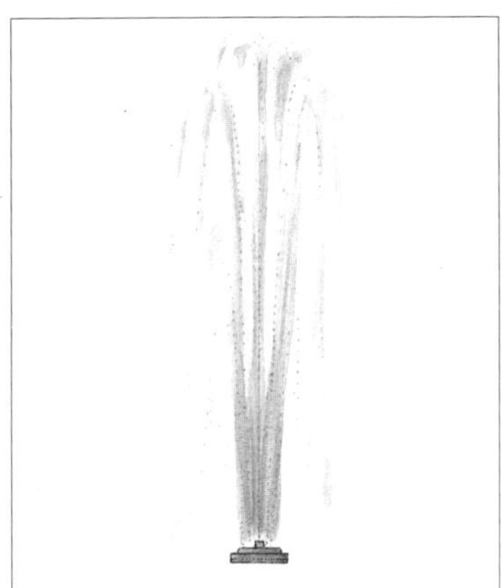

Single Spray
A single spray pattern can be accommodated in a small pool and can be achieved with a standard nozzle. The narrower the delivery pipe, the higher the spray will lift.

How a Fountain Works
The pump sucks water through an inlet pipe and pushes it out through the fountain's rigid pipe to a fitted jet, or to a remote jet via a delivery pipe (see p. 108).

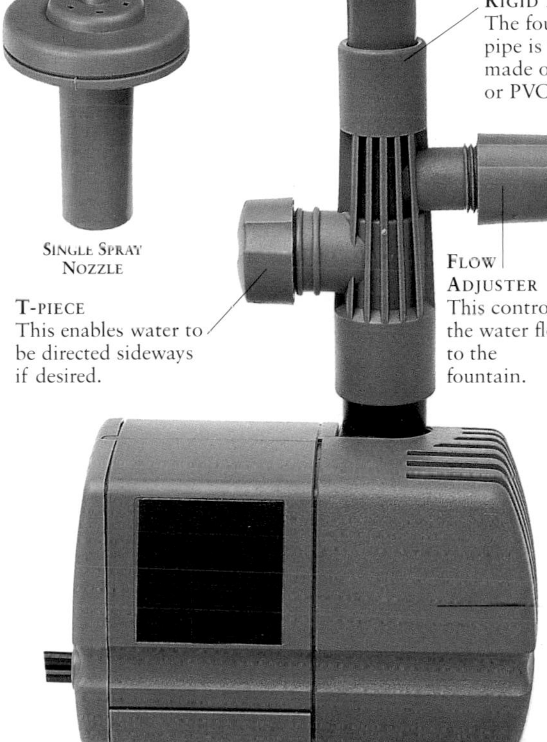

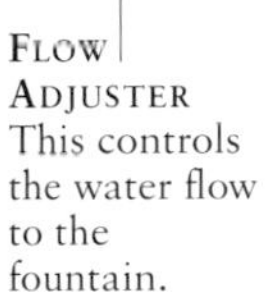

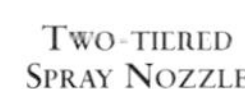

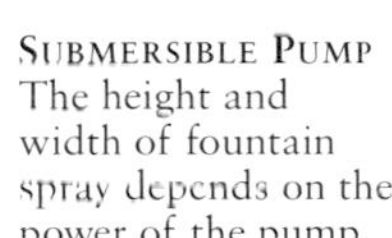

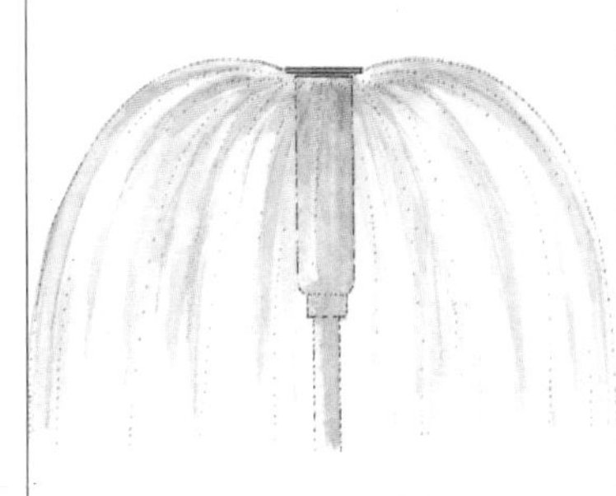

Bell Jet
A specially designed nozzle produces a thin, hemispherical film of water which causes little water-surface disturbance.

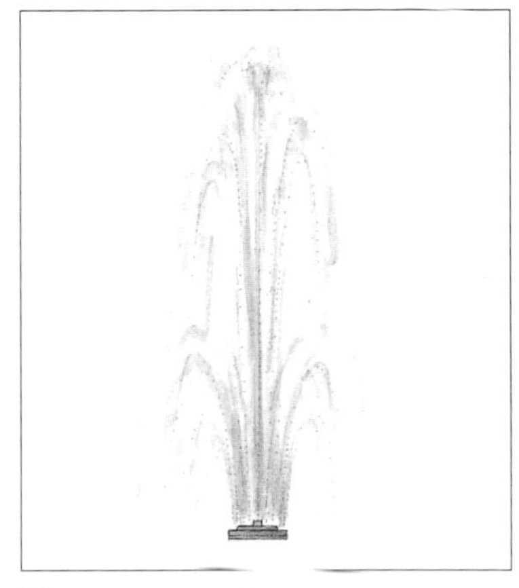

Two-tiered Spray
By altering the design arrangement and size of the holes in the nozzle of a single spray fountain, it is possible to produces a tiered effect.

Different Types of Fountain Spray Patterns

Simple Spray
This is the simplest and cheapest of all fountain sprays, and suits simple ponds better than the more elaborate types of spray such as a tiffany jet.

Surface Jet

Rotating Nozzle
To create a whirling effect, pressure from the pump forces the arms of the fountain jet to rotate in a way similar to that of a water sprinkler.

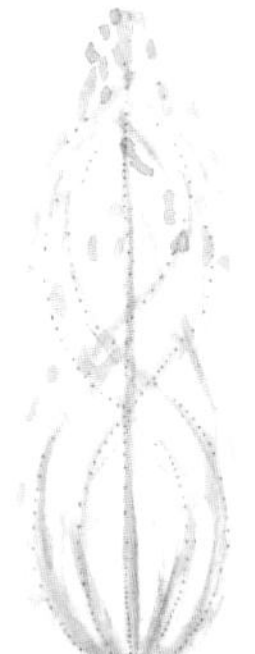

Whirling Spray

Tiered Effect
By arranging the position and size of the holes in the nozzle of a basic surface jet (see left)*, the spray will reach different heights and tiers.*

Three-tiered Spray

Double Domes
This combines the design of the bell jet fountain and a surface tiered jet to create the effect of a fountain within a fountain.

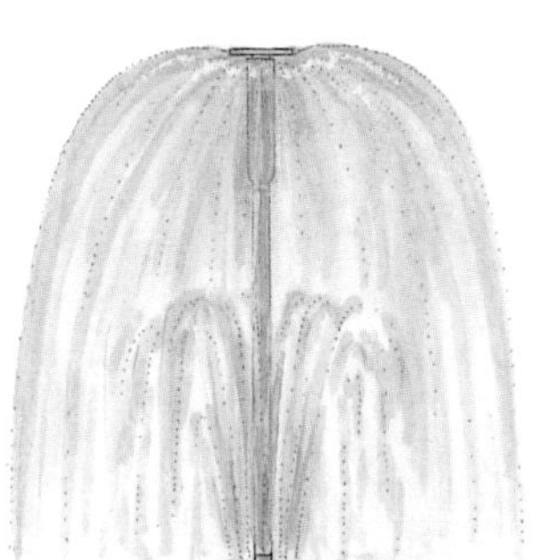

Tiffany Jet

Column of Water
This is a popular fountain for exposed, windy sites, where the dense foaming plume is less likely to be broken up by wind than fine spray.

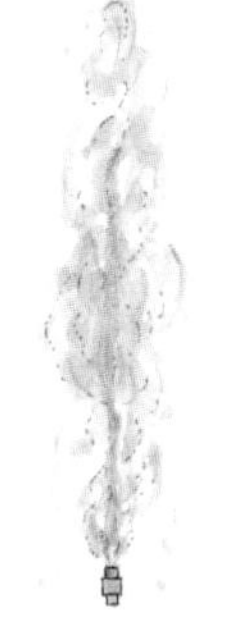

Geyser Fountain

CHOOSING FOUNTAIN STYLES

Perhaps more than any other feature, fountains can be used not only for their refreshing effects and inherent beauty, but also to influence the style and mood of water in the garden.

STYLES OF FOUNTAIN IN ISLAM

In Islamic gardens attention was focussed on the appreciation of water itself. The early technology of fountain design aimed to make minimal disturbance of the natural environment, making the garden a place of contemplation. Elsewhere, simple arching sprays used over long canals drew the eye towards beautiful examples of architecture without ornamental distraction.

FOUNTAINS IN MOGUL INDIA

Innovative fountain technology was taken a stage further in the gardens of Mogul India, where gardens were often associated with places of worship. Many of these gardens used fountain jets in retaining walls, forming chutes of sparkling water flowing into long formal pools beneath. Water pressure was harnessed from reservoirs in surrounding hills: the ample supply enabled water to animate every aspect of these exceptional gardens.

FOUNTAINS TO THE PRESENT

In the more formal approach to gardens in the Renaissance, fountains were sculptural, surrounded by symmetrical pools. As the naturalistic design movement gathered momentum during the 19th century, fountains became less widely used.

FINE, SINGLE SPRAY
An element of formality counterpoints an otherwise informal garden, where the circular outline of the pool lends itself to the fine single spray of a tall fountain. Its height is about equal to the pool's width – height should not exceed this in exposed sites.

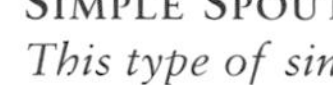

SIMPLE SPOUT
This type of single fountain spout works in both formal and informal settings. It is best suited to a formal design, as here, where a circular pool is surrounded by clear grass and tightly clipped, specimen yews. The spout is formed by a single jet that is wide enough to release a substantial column of water. This type of fountain must be absolutely vertical; any slight variation would ruin its effect.

FOUNTAIN ORNAMENT
This traditional fountain ornament is perfectly proportioned for this formal pool, edged with engineering half-bricks. The pool is sufficiently large for the turbulence created by the fountain to be limited to the central area, allowing water lilies to thrive nearer the edge. The pipework from the pump is hidden inside the base column and statue. The rate of flow is perfectly adjusted so that the water neither drifts, nor breaks up into small rivulets.

Moving water was more commonly featured in stream, grotto, and waterfall arrangements that convincingly mirrored nature, often with awesome arrangements of boulders.

In the present day, however, good garden design and water features are no longer the preserve of the wealthier classes, and are less dominated by prevailing fashions and trends. As a result, there is an enormous range of fountain equipment in "antique", international, and modern styles to complement any garden, be it large or small.

Spray Fountains

These fountains have their source close to or at water level, thus sending the water upwards, rather than falling from a receptacle, ornament, or orifice. Spray fountains are ideal for plant-oriented gardens where elaborate fountain ornaments would be lost to the surrounding detail in the planting.

Ornamental Fountains

There is a plethora of fountains manufactured in reconstituted stone or concrete, incuding small copies of the huge classical fountains found worldwide. For something more contemporary in style, modern fountains can be found, and it is worth seeking out examples from young, innovative designers working in this field. Good design and manufacture will allow ornamental fountains to be assembled with relative ease, requiring only a simple pump, as the pipework is built into the framework of the fountain. The main priority in their installation is ensuring that they are perfectly level and have a good foundation.

Circular Ring Fountain

How it Works

The pump is powerful enough to drive both the ring and a rose spray. The T-piece on the delivery pipe feeds the jets by a short piece of flexible pipe connected to an inlet spur on the underside of the ring. It is important to have individual control of both central spray and the ring by fitting separate flow adjusters (see p. 72).

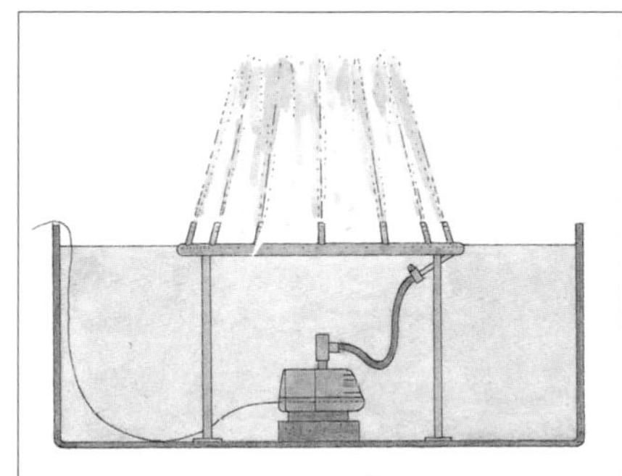

Mechanics of a Ring Fountain

Arching Spray Style of Fountain

Creating a Cascading Effect

How it Works

Pipework for the spray is fixed at the water surface along each side of the pool. The jets are placed just above water level and angled so that the spout of water forms an arch. To achieve the correct angle for the spouts, the pipe is fixed loosely and turned until the correct position is reached, when the pipe is tightened to the holding clamps. This rule can be applied with the jets turned downwards to form a cascade (see right).

Producing an Arched Spray

Reservoir Features

Because they are among the most uncomplicated and inexpensive ways to introduce the sound and sparkle of water into a garden, reservoir features such as the cobblestone fountain are ideal first-time construction projects. They require only a small pump and minimal maintenance, are very safe for family gardens, and can easily be integrated into both formal and informal settings. The surrounding area can be planted and styled to make the feature's size appropriate to the scale of the site. In the case of the cobblestone fountain, hanging the positioning of loose cobblestones close to, or overlapping, the nozzle of the fountain's delivery pipe provides ongoing opportunities to alter and refine the flow of water. An amber spotlight trained on the moving water *(see pp. 124–125)* will create the same relaxing effect as the gentle flickering of a fire.

Millstone Cobble Fountain

Making a Cobblestone Fountain

Construction Guide

To complete this step-by-step sequence, you will need:

TOOLS

- Tape measure, shovel, straight-edge, spirit level, rake, scissors, wire-cutters, tamping tool

MATERIALS

- Plastic dustbin
- Heavy-duty polythene sheet: 2m x 2m (6ft x 6ft)
- Submersible pump with filter *(see pp. 70–73)*
- Delivery pipe with flow adjuster
- Brick plinth
- Square of galvanized metal mesh, at least 10cm (4in) larger than the diameter of the dustbin
- Rigid plastic pipe to protect pump cable
- Cobblestones

1 Measure the depth and diameter – including the handles – of the dustbin, then dig a hole that is slightly wider and deeper than the bin. Place the bin – which will act as a reservoir pool – in the hole and use a straight-edge and a spirit level to make sure that it is level, with the rim flush with the ground.

2 Once the bin is in place, backfill the gap around its sides, tamping the soil down firmly. Rake the surrounding area to remove stones, then rake the soil up slightly away from the edges of the sunken bin to create a saucer-shaped depression with the bin at its centre. Remove any soil that has fallen into the bin.

3 Lay the polythene sheet over the prepared area and cut out a circle 5cm (2in) smaller in diameter than the dustbin. The purpose of the sheet is to collect the water being pumped out of the fountain, and allow it to drain back down the slight slope into the reservoir.

4 Connect the delivery pipe – complete with flow adjuster – to the pump outlet *(see pp. 70–73)*. Do not trim back the delivery pipe yet *(see Step 6)*. Lower the pump on to a brick plinth at the bottom of the bin; the plinth helps to prevent any debris from clogging up the pump.

5 CENTRE THE GALVANIZED mesh over the hole in the polythene, then use wire-cutters to cut a small hole in the middle, just wide enough for the delivery pipe. The cable linking the pump to the mains supply should be fed through rigid piping, which will be hidden under the cobbles.

6 TEST THE FLOW by filling the bin with enough water to cover the pump. Working from the edges inwards, start to arrange cobblestones over the mesh. If using a flexible delivery pipe, wedge it upright with cobblestones. Trim the pipe to length. Arrange just enough cobblestones around the feature to assess what the effect will be, then turn on the pump. If the flow needs to be adjusted, the cobblestones and the mesh will have to be removed. Once satisfied with the flow rate, fill the bin with water to a level approximately 5–8cm (2–3in) from the top.

7 ARRANGE MORE COBBLESTONES around the pipe until the desired effect is achieved. Once the area onto which water falls is established, trim surplus polythene and bury the edges under soil – or, to allow future enlargement of the feature, fold or roll up the polythene before burying.

STYLING THE FEATURE

This fountain is the centrepiece of a minimalist, low-maintenance planting scheme. A permeable membrane, which allows water through but prevents weeds from growing, has been laid over the surrounding soil. Cut small crosses in this material and fold back each corner to make planting holes. Once the plants are in place, spread shingle evenly over the membrane.

OTHER RESERVOIR FEATURES

THE SIMPLE PRINCIPLE of recirculating water demonstrated by the cobblestone fountain *(see pp. 112–113)* can be exploited with a variety of decorative outlets, including urns, bamboo cane, and old cast-iron water pumps. The sound and movement of the water can be controlled and enhanced by increasing or decreasing the flow from the pump.

All the following features have the advantage of minimal maintenance. The growth of algae in most reservoir features is reduced because sunlight makes little contact with the water surface *(see pp. 136–137)*. Any open reservoirs may be covered with fine mesh to prevent debris from falling into the water. If mesh is used, it is important to ensure that it is strong enough to support any ornament. To compensate for the loss of water by evaporation, top up reservoirs in hot weather.

BUBBLING URNS

The psychological effect of the sound of gentle running water has a major impact upon how a garden is perceived. One of the most calming sights and sounds is of a brimming urn that softly overflows, with the water sparkling in the sunshine and highlighting the rich colours of a terracotta or ceramic pot. Urns can either be supported on timbers over a sunken reservoir, or raised above ground on supporting plinths. Raised urns will be less dominated by surrounding plants and foliage.

MILLSTONES AND HAND PUMPS

A millstone with water rippling over its surface into a reservoir below makes another restful water feature. The hole in the middle of the millstone may have to be widened to accommodate a small delivery pipe from a pump housed in a reservoir below the stone. Genuine millstones can be difficult to obtain and are very heavy. You can, however, buy fibreglass millstones that have sharp sand dusted over and glued to the surface, giving a natural finish. They may be sold complete with a pump as an easy-to-build fountain kit.

MILLSTONE FOUNTAIN
The simplicity of a millstone fountain overflowing into a cobblestone surround is enhanced by a planting of iris, trollius, and bugle.

Cast-iron hand pumps make a feature that produces louder splashing sounds than those of urns and millstones. The hand pump can be free-standing over a sunken reservoir or set in or next to a barrel filled with water, in which case it will not require a sunken reservoir. As with all features requiring electricity, it is important to protect the cable leading from the pump to the mains. As a safety precaution, always use a contact circuit-breaker at the mains supply *(see p. 72)*.

CAST-IRON ORNAMENTS
Cast-iron hand pumps make delightful reservoir features. Here, the spout releasing water is almost hidden by an abundance of flowers and foliage. The pump is not above, but next to, its reservoir pool. Whether raised or sunken, it is advisable to cover reservoirs with fine wire mesh to prevent debris from falling in. If possible, submersible pumps should be placed on a plinth at the bottom of the reservoir pool; this helps to stop the pump from becoming clogged up. With most ornaments, it is possible to hide the delivery pipe inside the feature.

The Japanese Tsukubai

Recirculating water is also used to create many of the symbolic or functional features frequently seen in Japanese gardens. The Japanese use a variety of containers, such as troughs or hollowed-out rocks, to collect water to honour their tea ceremonies and to support other rituals of purification. One of the most popular of these is the *tsukubai*, a low stone basin that is continually refilled with water. This was traditionally used for handwashing before entering the tea-house. In order to make the visitor stoop in humility to use the vessel, it was also traditional for its height to be no more than 20–30cm (8–12in).

Water reaches the stone basin through a bamboo cane spout that conceals, or is attached to, the delivery pipe from the pump housed in the reservoir below. Having been filled with water, the basin gently overflows from one point only. The overflowing water trickles over cobbles and falls into the reservoir, which is protected from encroaching debris by wire mesh covered with stones. The mesh must be strong enough to support the weight of the cobbles. Polythene sheeting surrounding the feature ensures that any water seepage will be directed back into the reservoir. To complete the feature, appropriate plants such as evergreen grasses and ferns can be added.

The Shishi Odoshi

Another feature using bamboo cane as a water outlet is known as the *shishi odoshi* ("deer scarer"). This was developed by Japanese farmers to ward off wild animals with an intermittent clicking noise, caused when a hinged length of bamboo cane strikes a stone. The shishi odoshi works on the same principle as the tsukubai. Water from a sunken reservoir is pumped up through a delivery pipe that is concealed within a vertical "post" of hollowed-out bamboo. The delivery pipe is connected to a thinner, hollowed-out bamboo spout set near the top of the post, through which the water runs out.

Approximately halfway up the fixed post a hole is cut, into which another length of bamboo is set to pivot on an axle *(see below)*. This piece of bamboo is hollowed out only as far as its first node or joint, so that the opposite, and heavier, end falls under its own weight to strike a stone positioned beneath it. The hollow, lighter end lies beneath the spout to receive water pouring from it. The weight of the water accumulating in the hollowed section of the pipe eventually overbalances the pipe, the water runs out, the pipe swings back up, and the far end strikes the stone as it falls.

Styling Japanese Water Features

Water, foliage, and stone are the main elements in Oriental-style gardens. To achieve a subtle balance between the existing landscape and the newly planned elements, water features like the tsukubai and shishi odoshi should be integrated with great care. With the exception of evergreen azaleas, flowering plants do not play a major role in the overall scheme of a Japanese garden; plants such as bamboos and Japanese maples are chosen for their ornamental stems and leaf interest.

Japanese Water Features

The tsukubai *(below)* is a popular Oriental water garden accessory. As with the shishi odoshi *(see right)*, the tsukubai makes striking use of natural materials such as bamboo and rocks to create a simple and subtle feature that is in complete harmony with its surroundings.

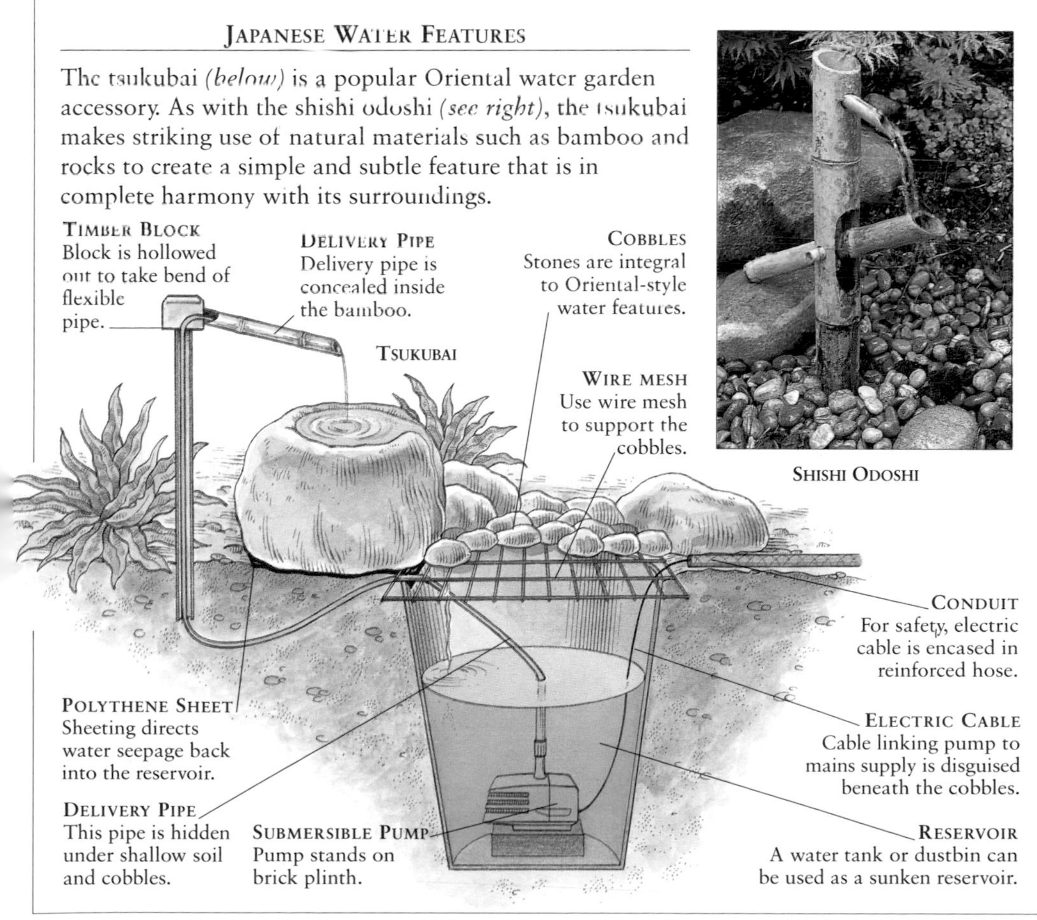

Shishi Odoshi

A Brimming Urn

This urn, with water moving gently over its surface, is a most restful water feature. The weight of the urn is supported on lengths of timber over a sunken reservoir. A rigid delivery pipe is fed through the bottom of the urn.

Further Information

- Pumps and Filters – pp. 70–73
- Reservoir Features – pp. 112–113
- Lighting Water Features – pp. 124–125
- A Balanced Ecosystem – pp. 136–137

WALL FOUNTAINS

WALL FOUNTAINS BRING water to patios, courtyards, conservatories, and small, enclosed gardens – anywhere, in fact, where there is insufficient room for a full-scale pool. Stone masks and other decorative forms are popular as outlets: antique stone features are expensive, but new terracotta and convincingly textured plastic and fibreglass versions are not, and being lighter, do not need such a strong supporting wall. The water falls into a reservoir pool, which may take various forms: a small, brick-built tank, an old sink or cistern disguised with plants, or a decorative stone bowl. The pump may be submerged in the pool, or in a chamber to the side of it; a small, low-voltage pump is easily powerful enough for most wall features. Also available are preformed, easy-to-install kits, with built-in pump and reservoir pool.

ORNAMENTAL MASK

INSTALLING A MASK FOUNTAIN OUTLET

CONSTRUCTION GUIDE

To install a mask on a brick wall approx. 1.2m (4ft) above a reservoir pool, you will need:

TOOLS
- Electric drill with 2cm (¾in) masonry bit
- Mortaring trowel
- Screwdriver
- Hacksaw

MATERIALS
- Small submersible pump
- 1.2m (4ft) length of 2cm (¾in) copper piping
- Two 2cm (¾in) elbow joints
- Three 2cm (¾in) hose clips
- 2m (6ft) length of 2cm (¾in) flexible plastic delivery pipe
- Small quantity of mortar mix

1 AT THE HEIGHT where the mouth will be (outlets usually look best just below eye level), drill a hole between bricks. Drill a second hole about 1.2m (4ft) below it where the pipe will come back through the wall to enter the reservoir pool.

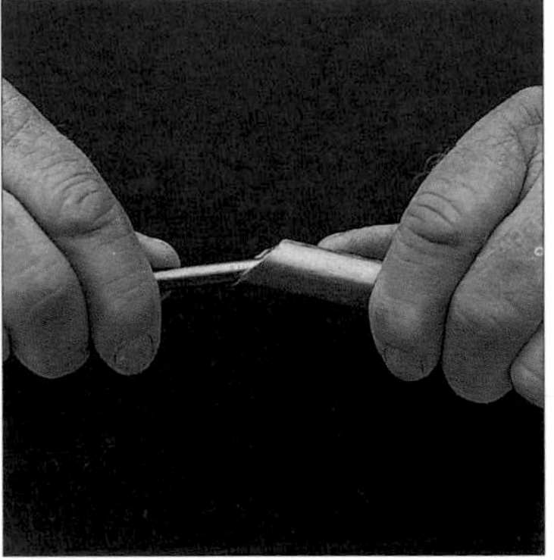

2 CUT LENGTHS of copper pipe for the two holes, the lower one 5cm (2in) longer than the width of the wall, the upper one 5cm (2in) longer than the width of the wall and the mask; angle the end of this pipe and smooth its edges with a screwdriver.

3 THREAD THE PIPES through the holes in the wall. The burred end of the pipe at the front of the wall should fit into the mouth of the mask. The protruding end of the pipe at the back of the wall will be attached to the delivery pipe.

4 WHERE THE COPPER pipes appear behind the wall, attach an elbow joint (the upper one turning down and the lower one up) and another 20cm (8in) length of copper pipe. Clip flexible delivery pipe between them.

5 MIX THE MORTAR into a stiffish paste. Wet the back of the mask so that the mortar will stick more effectively to its surface. When spreading the mortar, do not cover the area around the mouth opening. Also leave the edges of the mask clear, so that mortar will not escape when the mask is pressed against the wall.

6 SLIDE THE MASK over the copper pipe, and press it firmly against the wall. Wipe away spilt mortar. While waiting for the mortar to dry (this can take up to 36 hours), install and connect the pump, using flexible delivery pipe to run from the pump's outlet to the lower protruding end of copper pipe, securing with a hose clip.

WATER FLOW
The flow of water issuing from the mouth of the mask should be strong enough to allow the water to spout into the centre of the reservoir pool without splashing over the sides. If the force of the water is too strong, turn down the flow adjuster on the outlet of the pump (see pp. 72). *Depending on the distance between the spout and the reservoir pool, there will inevitably be a degree of splashing against the brickwork. This will encourage the growth of mosses and algae which will, in time, make the feature look attractively weathered.*

TIERED FOUNTAIN
The delivery pipe, which feeds into the back of the upper triangle of this tiered wall fountain, is hidden behind the trellis supporting a variety of climbing plants. This feature works with the merest trickle of water; short lengths of chain have been added to create links of water between the tiers.

WALL FOUNTAIN WITH SPILL BASIN

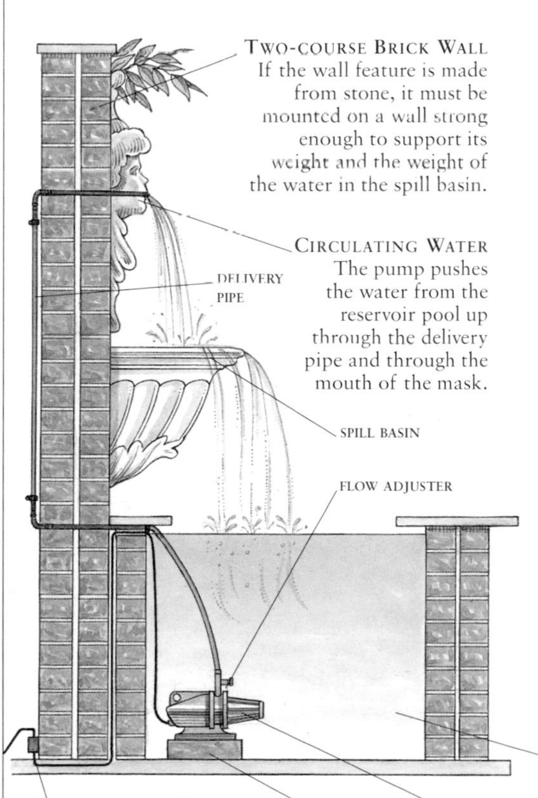

TWO-COURSE BRICK WALL
If the wall feature is made from stone, it must be mounted on a wall strong enough to support its weight and the weight of the water in the spill basin.

CIRCULATING WATER
The pump pushes the water from the reservoir pool up through the delivery pipe and through the mouth of the mask.

PREFORMED WALL FOUNTAIN
To consolidate the visual appeal of this type of wall feature, it is important to disguise the pipes used in its installation. One way is to fit, and mortar, the pipe into a channel chiselled into the wall. Another way is to camouflage the pipe with climbing plants, such as ivy and Virginia creeper, which will complement the bricks and stonework.

SPILL BASIN WITH INTEGRAL T-BLOCK

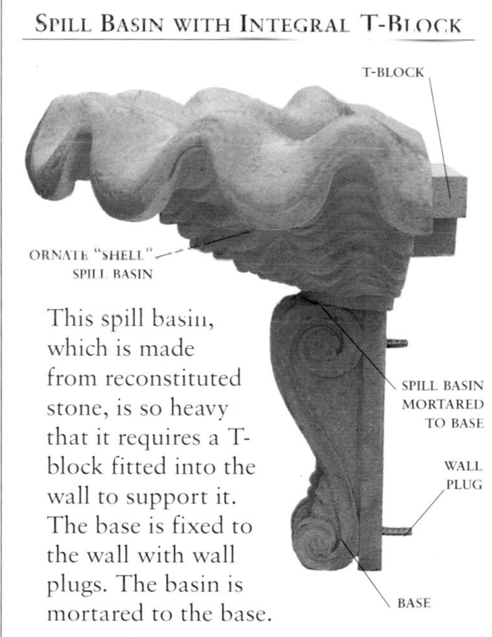

This spill basin, which is made from reconstituted stone, is so heavy that it requires a T-block fitted into the wall to support it. The base is fixed to the wall with wall plugs. The basin is mortared to the base.

FURTHER INFORMATION

- Pumps and Filters – pp. 70–73
- Fountains – pp. 108–111
- Reservoir Features – pp. 112–115

Finishing Touches

Extra features that enhance the look of a pond can also be functional: bridges and stepping stones, for example, add interest and provide access across a pond. Lighting brings a magical quality to a garden and allows one to see it at night. Edging materials such as paving and timber decking not only strengthen pond edges but add enormously to their aesthetic appeal.

Stone Statuette
The focal point of this feature is the stone statuette positioned in the centre of the pond. A stone table towards the back of the garden continues the use of ornament, and informal planting complements the figure's naturalistic pose. Planting in the pond is restrained, leaving clear areas of water so that the figure's reflection can be seen.

Stepping Stones and Bridges

Stepping stones are popular additions to informal ponds and streams, but can also be incorporated in a formal pool, using the same, or complementary, materials as the edging for a unified effect. Stepping stones require a firm foundation and, if necessary, should be set on stone or brick piers *(see p. 122)*. They should be considered carefully in sites where children play regularly – a large, flat boulder at the poolside may be more appropriate. Avoid crumbly or porous stone, even if well out of the water, as it encourages the growth of algae and moss.

Informal Stepping Stones
The ornamental use of rocks and stones is an important element in Oriental-style gardens. Beyond the huge boulder in the foreground, lily-pads echo the natural placement of stepping stones.

Formal Stepping Stones
Timber tiles on piers form a pathway over a large pond, their clean lines flattered by the neat definition of Pontederia *foliage. The timber is in good condition, the surface having been regularly scoured with a wire brush to ensure that it is free of slippery mosses and algae.*

Lighting a Water Garden
Here, powerful lighting brings boulders, stones, and leaf shapes into focus, contrasting with the darkness of the water. The pond can also be approached in safety.

Informal Timber Bridge
This simple, wooden bridge comprises two parallel railway sleepers. Bridges can be used to divide as well as cross the water. To protect them from predators, young fish, tadpoles, and any other small creatures are here separated from the main pool by a submerged barrier of fine mesh underneath the bridge, retaining them in the smaller pool area behind.

A bridge *(see pp. 122–123)* may serve a functional purpose, allowing access from one side of a pond or stream to the other, as well as adding visual interest to a water garden. In order to ensure that a bridge is completely safe, the construction must be sturdy and its surface non-slip; if necessary, firm handrails should be installed. There are a number of building materials with which a bridge can be constructed, including traditional stone, timber, concrete, steel, and iron. To a certain extent, the material used will be determined by both the style of garden and the available budget. If the sides of the bank are soft, foundations will be necessary to stabilize the bridge.

External and Submersible Lighting

Carefully positioned lighting *(see pp. 124–125)* can transform a feature; illuminating a water garden also enables people to use the area at night. A water garden can be lit with both surface and underwater lights. Surface lighting accentuates pool surroundings; underwater lighting is ideal for fountains or waterfalls. All lighting should be well concealed so that the source is not visible. It is essential that lighting is installed correctly, since the combination of electricity and water can be extremely dangerous. Installing an efficient lighting system requires expert advice – if you have any doubts it is advisable to employ a qualified electrician to set up the system. Mains electricity is necessary for powerful lighting; a wide range of low-voltage lighting is also available and requires a transformer to modify the mains current.

Edging Materials

Edging *(see pp. 126–131)* provides a means of blending a water feature with its surroundings; in many cases it also has a practical function, consolidating a feature and preventing soil subsidence. Decoration is provided by choice of materials – even cement can be enlivened by mosaic tiles or shells. Edging materials for formal ponds include bricks, timber, tiles, and slabs, and these surfaces need regular cleaning and maintenance to remain non-slip *(see pp. 140–141)*. Formal edging may either echo or contrast with the surroundings in both colour and texture. Informal edging should provide as natural a finish as possible – materials include shingle, pebbles, turf, and timber.

STEPPING STONES

STEPPING STONES LEAD the eye from one part of the garden to another, and offer an irresistible invitation to cross water (which must be borne in mind in gardens used by small children). They also make it possible to tend plants in the centre of a pond. Consider carefully both the size and placing of stepping stones at the design stage; to install them later may entail draining the water feature. Each stone should be at least 45cm (18in) square, and the gaps between stones no wider than 38–45cm (15–18in). If in doubt as to how many stones to use, it is better to err on the side of too many. The crisp outlines of paving slabs particularly suit formal ponds; they will, however, need strong supporting piers, installed as the pool is being built. Large, rounded or flat-topped boulders, irregularly placed, suit more informal ponds.

FORMAL STEPPING STONES

BUILDING FORMAL STEPPING STONES

CONSTRUCTION GUIDE

To build each of these stepping stones with pier, you will need:

TOOLS
- Spirit level
- Shovel
- Pointing trowel and mortar board
- Wire brush to clean up mortar droppings

MATERIALS
- 32 water-resistant bricks
- Ready-mix mortar: 20kg (44lb)
- One 60cm x 60cm (2ft x 2ft) paving stone

1 IN THIS CONCRETE-LINED POOL, the piers can be built directly on to the pool floor *(for flexible-liner ponds, see box, below right)*. For a small slab, 60cm (2ft) square, in water no deeper than 60cm (2ft), make a slender pier using courses of four bricks butted at right angles to each other; this will eliminate the need to cut bricks, and allow the slab to conceal the pier by overhanging it slightly. Lay the first course of bricks on to a mortar base 1cm (½in) thick. Press the bricks down firmly until a little mortar is squeezed out. Use a spirit level to make sure that this first course of bricks is absolutely level.

FORMAL MATERIALS

For safety, when building stepping stones on piers, make the piers tall enough to allow the stepping stone to sit at least 5cm (2in) above the water surface, to keep it dry. If using concrete slabs, choose those with a non-slip, textured surface. Square paving stones are used mainly in formal schemes that have square or rectangular outlines. Disc shapes are particularly attractive in water gardens, echoing the shape of water-lily leaves. Irregularly-shaped concrete paving stones are manufactured in pleasant colours for use in more informal schemes. Make sure that each stone is big enough to stand on comfortably.

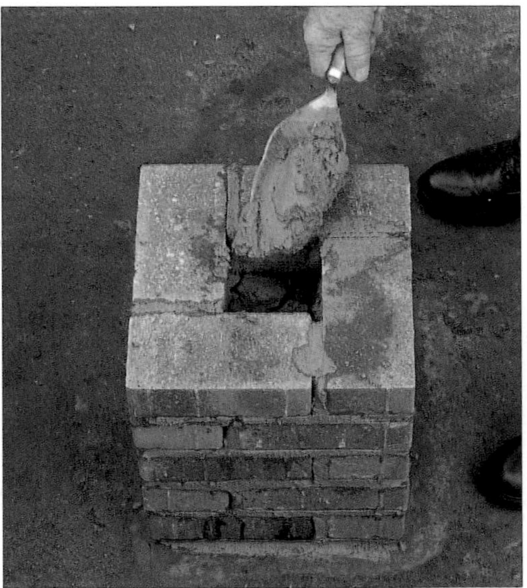

2 LAY THE REMAINING bricks in seven more courses, alternating the direction in which the bricks run. Use a spirit level to check that each course is level. Retaining enough mortar for a 1cm (½in) layer on top of the pier, pile any surplus into the centre for additional strength.

3 SPREAD THE REMAINING mortar over the top course of bricks, and position the paving stone squarely over the bricks. Tap it down evenly onto the soft mortar *(see p. 69)*, checking that it is absolutely level. Leave to dry for at least two days before filling the pool.

FORMAL PIER WITH FOUNDATION

Piers installed in pools or bog gardens that have a flexible liner will need a solid base to make them stable. Pour concrete into an excavation lined with hardcore. Make sure that the surface of the concrete is absolutely level. When the concrete is dry, lay the liner and underlay, then mortar the first course of bricks on to the liner.

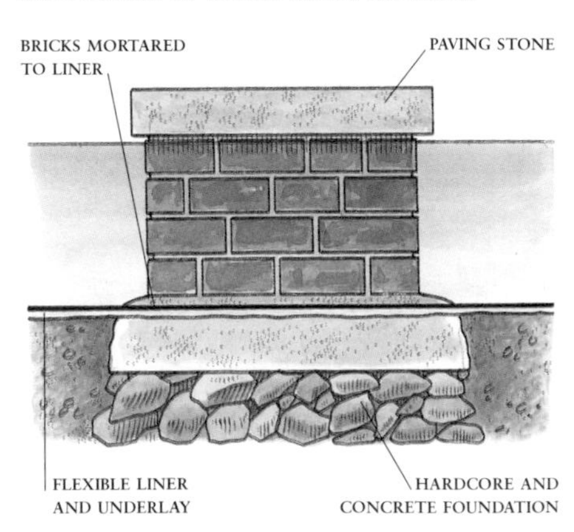

INFORMAL STEPPING STONES

Flat stones and sections of timber make perfect stepping stones in shallow water, and are by far the safest option in family gardens. Rounded boulders suit the Oriental style, and look particularly good in slightly deeper water in which they can be partially submerged. The top of a waterfall is an excellent point at which to introduce a few stepping stones that will give a view of the clear, still water of the header pool as well as the more turbulent water falling over the spill stone.

It is important to select hard-wearing, non-porous stone such as granite or millstone grit. Softer stones, in particular limestone and certain sandstones, will crumble in time, and are notorious for attracting slippery algae. While softwood will eventually rot, sections of round, hardwood tree trunks are likely to last for several years. Treat timber rounds with a fish- and plant-friendly wood preservative at least once a year.

SAFETY PRECAUTIONS

It is imperative that informal stepping stones do not slide or wobble underfoot. In shallow water, flat stones or timber rounds can be mortared directly to pool bases. Irregular boulders must be either sunken well into the floor of a natural or clay-lined pond, or, in flexible-liner or concrete ponds, mortared onto a concrete base *(see below right)*. Staple chicken wire over timber rounds to give a more secure footing, and clean all stepping stones regularly with a stiff brush to remove slime and algae.

TIMBER STEPPING STONES
Irregularly placed rounds of hardwood can be used to make an attractive and unusual ford over shallow water. These sections, about 15cm (6in) thick and 50–60cm (20–24in) in diameter, have been mortared directly onto flexible liner, which is hidden under a layer of shingle.

FORMING A LINK
Large, flat or gently rounded boulders make "natural" stepping stones which can provide a link between different parts of a pond or stream, or make a short cut across the corner of a pond, as above, where the mass of the boulder also provides continuity between the broad timber deck and the cobbles at the poolside. Clean algae off stones regularly with a stiff brush.

STABILIZING BOULDERS

Unless the size, shape, or weight of a boulder precludes movement, it will need a foundation to make it stable and safe to step on. Make a concrete "nest" that approximates the contours of the bottom of the boulder. Allow the concrete to dry for a day, then mortar the boulder onto it. Extra layers of underlay can be used under the concrete to protect the liner.

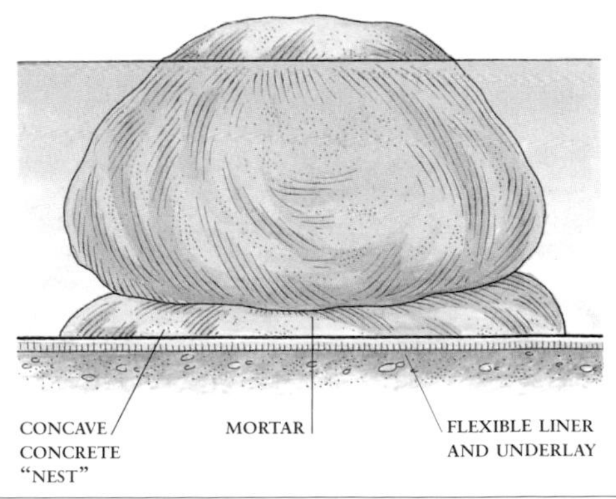

FURTHER INFORMATION

- Courtyard Pool – pp. 32–33
- Siting Water Features – pp. 56–57
- Construction Tools and Materials – pp. 62–63
- Construction Techniques – pp. 64–69

BRIDGES

BRIDGES, LIKE PONDS and streams, can be as simple or as ornamental as the setting suggests. Although ready-made bridges are available in a range of materials, such as iron and steel, they can be expensive: a simple timber bridge *(see below)* is both easy and economical to build, and can be up to 2.5m (8ft) wide without requiring a central pier or support. A bridge should be functional as well as decorative; bridges installed solely for visual effect can look contrived, and may actually spoil the feature they are meant to enhance. If possible, design and build a bridge at the same time as you install a pond or a watercourse. The pond or stream can be "waisted" to create a narrower width to span with the bridge: if its ends are surrounded with plants, the bridge will make the water appear wider than it really is.

BRIDGE IN POSITION

SIMPLE TIMBER BRIDGE

CONSTRUCTION GUIDE

To build this 2.5m x 60cm (8ft x 2ft) bridge, you will need:

TOOLS

- Spade, shovel, straight-edge, spirit level, screwdriver, drill

MATERIALS

- 8 rough pieces of 10cm x 5cm (4in x 2in) timber: four 60cm (2ft) long, four 1.2m (4ft) long
- Ready-mixed concrete: two 50kg (110lb) bags
- 2 treated timber joists: 2.4m x 15cm x 5cm (8ft x 6in x 2in)
- Four 12cm (5in) galvanized brackets with 8 galvanized 5cm (2in) bolts and nuts
- 15 treated cross-planks: 60cm x 15cm x 2.5cm (2ft x 6in x 1in)
- 68 countersunk 5cm (2in) 8-gauge screws

1 TO MAKE MOULDS for semi-raised concrete block foundations at the bridge's ends, dig two holes 2m (6ft) apart on either side of the water, 1.2m (4ft) x 20cm (8in) x 10cm (4in) deep. Surround the holes with the rough timbers to make two rectangular forms *(right)*, and hold them in place with bricks. Shovel in concrete, using a spirit level and a long straight-edge to make sure the two foundation blocks are level with each other.

FIRM FOUNDATIONS
Foundations should be built at least 22cm (9in) from the water's edge so that sloping poolsides do not affect their stability.

2 BEFORE THE CONCRETE DRIES, set the two joists 45cm (20in) apart, hold the brackets against them, and mark through the holes to show where to put the bolts. Embed these in the concrete, screw end protruding by 2.5cm (1in). Bolt the brackets on to the concrete when dry.

3 REMOVE THE foundation moulds, and screw the joists to the brackets. Draw up and secure any liner under the bridge. Lay all the cross-planks over the joists, 1cm (½in) apart to allow expansion when wet. Fix each end plank first, and stretch string between them as a position guide for the rest.

CONSTRUCTION OF A TIMBER BRIDGE

The construction techniques used for this bridge are well within the capabilities of the amateur. A well-made bridge of stout, good-quality timber, with firm foundations at each end, will be solid and long-lasting. For safety, make any steps leading up to bridge ends firm and conspicuous, or build earth or timber ramps.

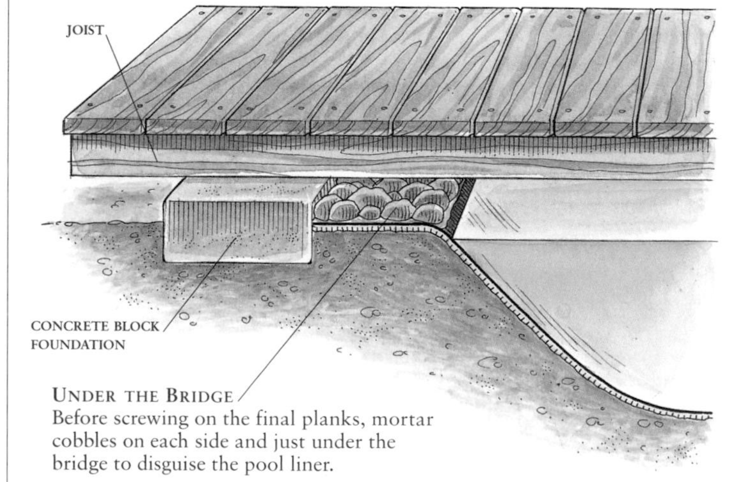

UNDER THE BRIDGE
Before screwing on the final planks, mortar cobbles on each side and just under the bridge to disguise the pool liner.

Serving a Purpose

To make them practical and safe, bridges should be at least 60cm (2ft) wide; wider, if it is necessary to cross them with garden equipment such as lawn mowers or wheelbarrows. Always ensure that paths and paving are absolutely flush with the ends of the bridge to avoid tripping. In addition to providing a path across water, bridges offer excellent viewpoints from which to watch fish, or simply enjoy the reflection of light and colour on the surface of the water; adding a handrail will make pausing on the bridge more inviting and comfortable.

Handrails

Like the bridge itself, rails should blend as naturally as possible into the surroundings. Thin, over-ornate handrails usually tend to clutter an otherwise restful scene, and moreover may be unsafe: handrails should always be strong enough to bear the weight of an adult leaning against them. A height of at least 1m (3ft) is essential if a bridge is very narrow or traverses particularly deep water, and if the bridge is to be used by young children, it is as well to cover the space between the rails with wire netting.

Try to merge the ends of the rails into planting, rather than coming to an abrupt, vertical stop. The vertical uprights of a bridge can be extended upwards and joined over the top to form a frame, so that the bridge resembles a tunnel. The impact can be dramatically increased by festooning the uprights and top rails with climbing plants such as wisteria and clematis.

Safety

For safety reasons, the maximum span of an unsupported bridge should be 2.5m (8ft). Wider bridges need additional supporting piers or posts (minimum size 10cm x 10cm/4in x 4in). Either build brick piers like those used to support stepping stones *(see p. 120)*, or drive supporting posts deep into the floor of the pond – this will involve hiring a pile-driving machine.

Any materials used for walking on should have a textured rather than a varnished or glazed finish. To ensure a safe, non-slip surface on a wooden bridge, firmly nail in place a covering of fine wire mesh *(see p. 140)*, and prevent the growth of moss or algae by regularly scrubbing with water to remove dirt.

Arched Bridges
Arched bridges built from scratch demand very skilled construction techniques. They can, however, be bought ready-made. Choose one with a gentle gradient; a handrail is also recommended. Ask for advice on installation: a good supplier will tell you what foundations are necessary.

Although bridges made from timber are the simplest and often the most successful, they have a shorter lifespan (10–15 years), and require more maintenance, than those made from concrete, stone, or metal: rotting wood will become weak and slippery. Treat timbers with a wood preservative at least once a year, and scrub all exposed areas with a wire brush at least twice a year to prevent the build-up of slippery algae. Be sure to check that the wood preservative will not affect plants and fish.

Finally, remember that the temptation to, not only cross, but also dangle feet and hands from a bridge is often more than young children can resist. A flat bridge set low down over shallow water is the safest, but it is advisable nevertheless to supervise children as they play.

Timber Bridge
This zig-zag timber bridge over shallow water is not used to cross the pond, but to tend the plants in the centre with ease. A brick pier supports the central section where the timbers meet. The plants softening the sides of the bridge give added emphasis to the rustic simplicity of the timber.

Further Information

- Construction Tools and Materials – pp. 62–63
- Construction Techniques – pp. 64–69
- Stepping Stones – pp. 120–121
- Timber Decking – pp. 130–131

LIGHTING WATER FEATURES

LIGHTING NOT ONLY extends the hours of viewing pleasure, it also brings a new dimension to the appeal of a water garden. When darkness falls, textures and contrasts dulled by sunlight are newly defined, greatly enhancing the appearance of plants and ornaments. Surface lighting will sharpen any image, and can be more effective when it does not shine directly on the water. Underwater lighting, though, produces the most atmospheric results, illuminating fish, plants, and features such as fountains and waterfalls. For safety, durability, and strength of illumination, use good quality, purpose-made equipment. If a pump *(see pp. 70–73)* is already in place, the main work and expense of bringing electricity to the feature will already have been incurred, but even if you are adding lighting to an existing system, professional advice is advisable.

UNDERLIT FOUNTAIN

TYPES OF INSTALLATION

Lighting a large area or feature usually demands high-voltage mains lighting. (Do not light up the whole of a fish pond, as this might disturb the fish.) Only a qualified electrician should install high-voltage systems *(see p. 72)*. A residual current device (circuit breaker) is essential, and high-voltage electric cable must be armoured and protected below ground *(see box, below right)*. However, an inexpensive low-voltage system, which reduces the mains current through a transformer, is powerful enough to light a group of plants or a small pool with a small fountain. Low-voltage systems come in simple kit form *(see facing page)*, often sold complete with pump and attachments. For any system, it is preferable to site switches indoors; switches outside must be encased in a safety-approved waterproof switch box *(see p. 108)*.

GAUGING THE EFFECT

Restraint and subtle placing are the keys to successful lighting. Experiment with underlighting by using a powerful torch, or a spotlight on a long lead (*never* place this in water). Do not let lights shine directly on water; indirect lighting turns the surface into a dark mirror, reflecting plants and ornaments.

TRANSFORMING A FEATURE
A low spotlight creates a sense of drama and mystery, throwing shadows over the water, foliage, and rocks in this pond. Subdued downlighters in the background serve to illuminate pathways beyond the pond.

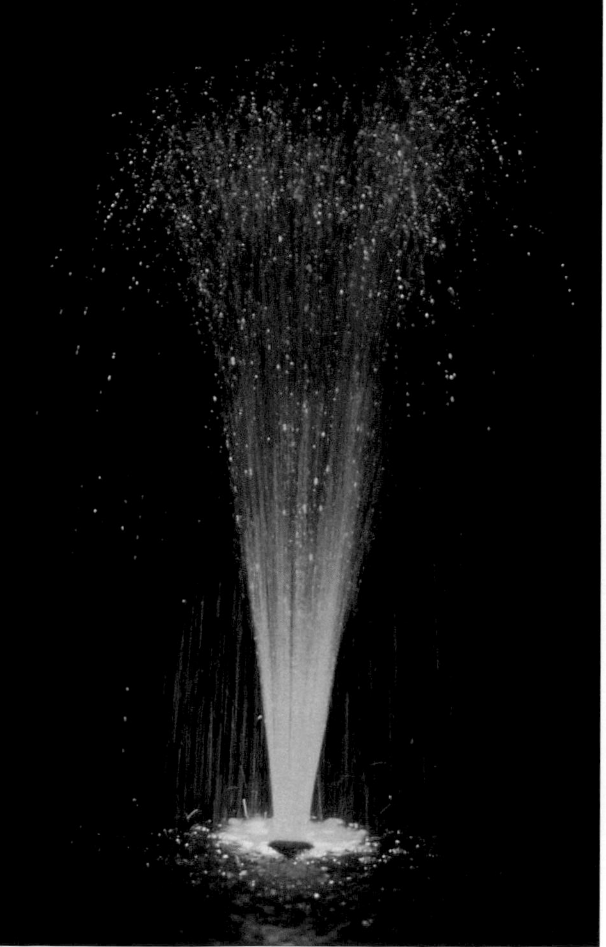

UNDERLIGHTING A FOUNTAIN
Use a high-intensity submersible light to illuminate water gushing from a fountain. Ensure that the beam is pointing upwards into the spray – this will create the illusion that the light is "moving" with the water.

SAFETY PRECAUTIONS

For high-intensity lighting, use only equipment specifically designed for outdoor or underwater use. Ask a qualified electrician to connect the equipment to the mains supply. Always include a residual current device (RCD or circuit breaker); this effectively cuts off power within 30 milliseconds of a problem occurring. Never use outdoors any lights or electrical equipment designed for indoor use. The sealed cable leading from the light must be connected to the mains supply cable with a waterproof connector located near the pool – most ready-to-use systems come complete with snap-connect and push-connect connections. The cable between the connector and the mains socket must be armoured. Bury this cable at least 45cm (18in) underground. For extra safety, place roofing tiles over the cable, then put bright warning tapes on the tiles before filling the trench *(see also* Pumps and Filters, *pp. 70–73)*. There is little danger of serious electric shock from a low-voltage system, provided that it is properly installed.

ARMOURED CABLE

Choosing and Positioning Lighting Equipment

Choose subdued colours for bulbs, lenses, and the casings of the lights; shiny stainless steel or bright white casings can be obtrusive in daylight. If possible, conceal equipment and casings behind rocks or plants. External or underwater spotlights trained on a specific area are the simplest forms of lighting. A spotlight behind a waterfall or cascade can be dramatic; underlighting a fountain *(see facing page)* is also very effective. Ensure that the beam is pointing upwards into the spray to create the illusion that the light is travelling in the same direction as the spurting water. Floating lights *(right)* add an informal note of unpredictability, and they may also be submerged to reveal the underwater world usually hidden by the glare of day.

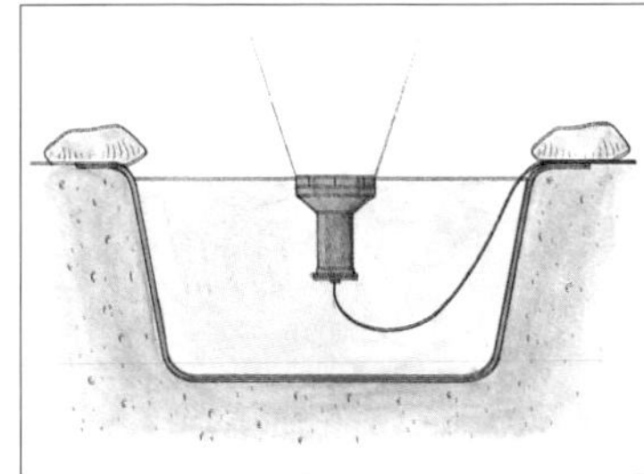

Floating Spotlight
Most of the lights sold in kit form can be detached from the fountain to be used as either floating or submerged illumination. To submerge, place a heavy object on the flying lead to anchor the light in position.

Transformer

A transformer greatly reduces the voltage of an alternating current, making it safe in the event of cabling and equipment beyond it being damaged. Transformers should be installed indoors so that only low-voltage cable is used in the garden.

LOW-VOLTAGE CABLE
MAINS CABLE
PUSH-CONNECTOR FOR LOW-VOLTAGE LEAD
TRANSFORMER IN SEALED CASING

Pump and Lights in Kit Form
The lights in this kit need not be attached to the pump. Low-voltage cables from the pump and each light are joined in a waterproof connector box outside the water, from which one cable runs to a transformer.

How it Works
The three evenly spaced lights around the fountain nozzle provide even uplighting for the spray, impossible to achieve with a single lamp. For a more diffuse effect, the lamps may float loosely.

Lit Cobble Fountain
Small, bubbling fountains can be illuminated by an angled spotlight at ground level that, with suitable connectors, can use the same low-voltage power source as the small pump. Choose a lens whose colour will complement the colour of the stones. Disguise the casing with plants, or position it within a collection of cobblestones.

Bulbs and Lenses

Tungsten bulbs, such as those used in the home, are the most popular low-voltage bulbs for lighting water gardens. If a more intense light is required, halogen bulbs are ideal, as they provide more light for the same wattage. As technology evolves, new techniques involving laser lighting and fibre optics will become more common. Although lenses are available in a variety of colours, white is the most popular and is usually the most effective. Avoid using too many different-coloured lights.

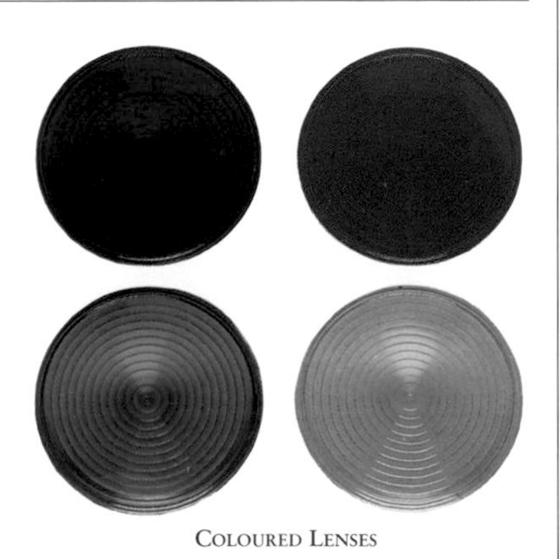

Coloured Lenses

WROUGHT IRON CANDLE HOLDER
HANDLE
GLASS CASING

Portable Candle Holder
The simplest way to light small areas is with candles in windproof casings; this holder has a tall ground spike so that it can be moved around. Citronella-scented candles will also discourage gnats, which congregate by water.

Further Information

- Siting a Water Feature – pp. 56–57
- Construction Techniques – pp. 64–69
- Pumps and Filters – pp. 70–73

Edging Materials

Edging is vital to the durability of water features, consolidating poolsides to give a firm footing and also disguising pond linings. It also contributes greatly to the visual impact of the feature. Always consider the edging you will use from the earliest planning stages, so that it will suit the style both of the water feature and of existing garden materials. The more adventurous range of colours and textures now available means that even the most traditional or inexpensive materials can, with imaginative use, give a completely fresh look.

Edging with Natural Stones and Rocks

Informal Stone
Sandstone of varying sizes creates a natural-looking edge to this pond, echoed by a stepping stone path to the beach.

Informal ponds and streams can be enhanced by the placing of natural rocks or stones around the edges. Large retailers supply a wide range of stone types. Local stone is generally the least expensive, and will merge most effectively with its surroundings. The two most common types of stone available are limestone and sandstone, both of which come in a variety of colours.

Rocks and stones should be placed as naturally as possible around an informal pond; where stones have clearly defined strata lines, aligning these *(see below and facing page)* will create the illusion that the rocks are naturally outcropping the water. Use loose, small pieces of stone to fill any gaps. To create extra cushioning, place offcuts of underlay on top of the liner.

Rounded, sea-washed pebbles and cobblestones make good informal edging. Pebbles are especially effective when wet, as the water brings out their natural colours. Where pebbles are likely to slip, press them into a layer of mortar. Gravel and shingle beaches *(see pp. 80–81)* also complement informal ponds, and provide an excellent textural contrast to the water.

Informal Stone Edging
Rocks, pebbles, and shingle create an informal transition from dry ground to water. The materials are easy to place, and come in a variety of colours and sizes, making it possible to choose an edging material that will match existing materials. If used to disguise a liner, first lay underlay on top of the liner in order to prevent it from tearing.

Red Gravel

Shingle

Grey Gravel

Slate Chippings

Pebbles and Cobbles

Granite

Laying Rocks and Stones

An Informally-laid Beach
The rocks and stones that edge this pond gradually decrease in size as they get closer to the water, creating a natural effect. Rocks and stones have been placed at the edge of the liner in order to secure and disguise it. The gradual slope provides an informal finish and invites wildlife to approach the water.

Mortared Absorbent Rock
Position absorbent rocks so that the strata lines run along the sides, and are invisible from above (as left). *A gently overlapping diagonal arrangement enhances the weathered appearance.*

Mortared Non-absorbent Rock
Most non-absorbent rocks, such as granite, have cleavage planes rather than strata lines; try to make these appear broadly parallel. They look better angled more acutely than softer stones.

USING ROCKS WITH STRATA LINES ON SLOPES

As when edging on the flat with these rocks (see facing page), *make sure the strata lines are visible not from above but from the side, as in nature, when using them to edge a sloping stream. After positioning the first rock, make sure that the strata lines of each successive rock are parallel, and that the angle at which each rock is set is the same; this may involve burying some of the stone, but will give a better effect.*

SLATE SLABS

Dark, wet slate is a good foil for cascading water. Position it so that any natural veining runs parallel with the water flow.

INFORMAL ROCK WALLS

Where rock walls are built up as internal edges to hide liner, use flattish stones mortared together for stability. Disguise the mortar at the front with small pebbles wedged in to create a "dry stone" effect.

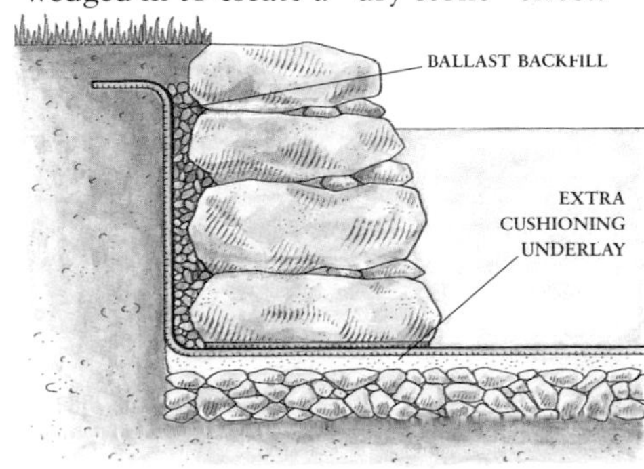

FORMAL EDGING AND PAVING

FORMAL PAVING

Bricks and paving slabs have been combined to produce an effective edge to this formal stream; the bricks also echo the wall and arch.

Bricks, slabs, setts, and pavers are available in many different materials, colours, and textures. Using small paving units such as setts or bricks in formal situations requires great care to ensure that lines and right angles remain constant. Large paving slabs are easier to lay regularly, but their sheer weight makes them difficult to handle. Concrete is the most cost-effective material to use and is also extremely hard-wearing, although not particularly decorative. Concrete pavers are simple to lay; just place them side by side and spread dry mortar over the surface. Alternatives to costly natural stone slabs are granite or clay setts, clay pavers, or terracotta tiles. Always lay bricks, slabs, setts, or tiles on a levelled hardcore base *(see p. 68)* with mortar on top for a firm finish; if necessary, fill the joints with bedding mortar.

TYPES OF BRICK

Be sure to use weatherproof bricks as edging, such as those shown below. Different colours are available that can be used singly or together. When using bricks with "frogs" – hollows – lay the the brick with the frog facing downwards.

PATTERNS IN BRICK

Brick edging can be extended to form a broad surround or terrace, which will be enhanced by laying the bricks in patterns *(see below)*. A simple theme is often more effective than an over-ornate one – a complicated design may lessen the overall impact of the feature. Do not let the cut edges of bricks show at the water's edge, as they do not make an attractive finish.

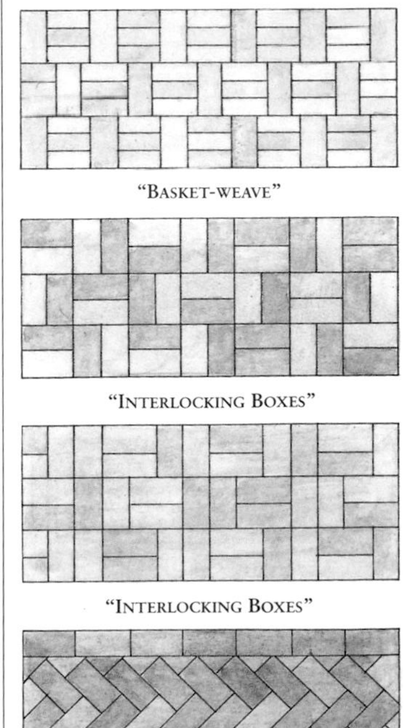

LAYING BRICKS AS A POOL SURROUND

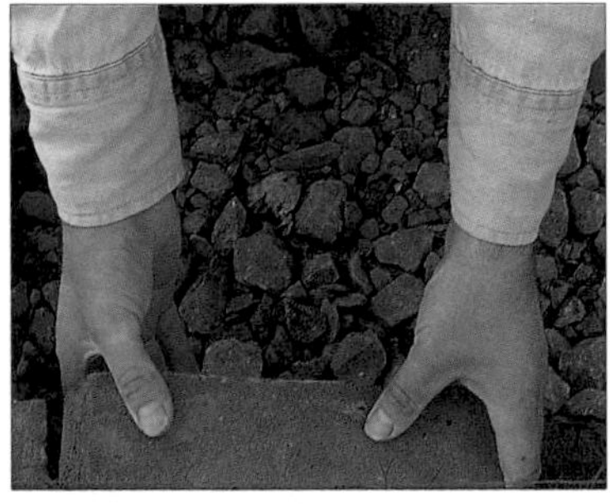

1 EXCAVATE THE SURROUNDS of the pool, allowing for a 10cm (4in) layer of hardcore and 2.5cm (1in) of mortar. Lay the perimeter bricks first, using string and pegs to ensure that they are level.

2 HAVING MORTARED the perimeter bricks, bed the remaining bricks on to a layer of mortar, spacing them evenly. Using a spirit level and straight-edge, tap down until the bricks are level.

3 SPREAD A LAYER of dry mortar over the surface and brush it between the joints. Use a watering can to sprinkle the bricks with water in order to set the mortar. Brush over the surface thoroughly.

LAYING CRAZY PAVING

CRAZY PAVING MATERIALS
Sandstone is particularly suitable for crazy paving, as it breaks up easily into flat, thin pieces. More random shapes must be carefully positioned for a level surface.

1 USE DATUM PEGS or string when marking out to establish a horizontal level. Spread a layer of hardcore and compact. Lay the edging pieces first, with their straight edges facing outwards.

2 FILL IN THE rest of the area with large slabs infilled with smaller ones. Check that all the stones are level. To adjust the height, tap with a club hammer over a wood block.

3 FILL THE JOINTS with almost dry mortar; alternatively, brush in sand. To achieve a good finish, use a trowel to bevel mortar so that any surface water will drain away.

USING SQUARE SLABS

RIVEN SLABS

NATURAL FINISH
The range of reconstituted stone slabs now available provides far more convincing substitutes for natural stone than previously. Even cement slabs are now textured and coloured to be more compatible with the existing landscape.

GRANITE SETTS

WATERTIGHT EDGE
In order to disguise the liner, lay it under two widths of granite setts and wedge the edge upright with a paving slab. Trim the liner level with the top of the paving slab and infill with mortar between the slab and the setts.

RECONSTITUTED STONE

TEXTURED RED CEMENT

BLEND OF MATERIALS
Concrete setts form the edge of this pool, and are surrounded by larger, traditional paving stones that have a riven, non-slip finish. The dark colour of the concrete contrasts with the light paving slabs; both blend well with the water.

MAKING CURVED EDGES FOR FORMAL PONDS

SHAPED BLOCKS

CONCRETE BLOCKS
In addition to being inexpensive, moulded concrete blocks are versatile, coming in a wide range of shapes and sizes. These setts are convincingly textured and have been produced in a "keyed" shape that makes them ideal for curved pond edges.

USING SMALL SETTS
The smaller the blocks, the easier it is to fit them closely around curving edges. The gaps are then filled with mortar (see p. 126).

SOFT AND HARD TEXTURES
Square slabs arranged in a circular pattern inevitably leave key-shaped gaps. These can be turned to advantage as planting spaces.

FORMAL EDGING
The labour and expense that hand-cut "keyed" slabs involve can be avoided by buying pavers specially shaped for circular pond edges.

Using Timber to Edge a Pond

Timber Edging
Treated timber sleepers create completely watertight edging for this spillway. Timber also creates a discreet finish.

Timber edging is a popular choice for both formal and informal pools, and combines particularly well with turf. Hardwood or treated softwood planks may be arranged horizontally, and strips of log roll vertically *(see pp. 88–89)*. Timber edging can also be extended to create a decking seating area or patio *(see pp. 130–131)*. Old railway sleepers make very durable edges, but are usually too heavy to use on top of the walls of raised pools. When exposed to water, wood tends to warp and rot, and should be treated with a preservative. To ensure that harmful chemicals do not seep into the water and harm wildlife, a proprietary sealant should always be applied. Make sure that all wood is held firmly in place, whether nailed to a timber support or fixed to a wall or a concrete foundation *(see below)*.

Decking Tiles

Timber Edgings
Due to its versatility and natural look, wood has become very popular as an edging material. Decking-style tiles and planks that overlap the edge of the water can hide unsightly liner and provide partial shade and shelter for fish. Log rolls, easy to install, can enhance the simplest pond. Railway sleepers are hard-wearing, but heavy to handle – do not attempt to install a sleeper single-handed.

Log Roll

Timber Sleeper

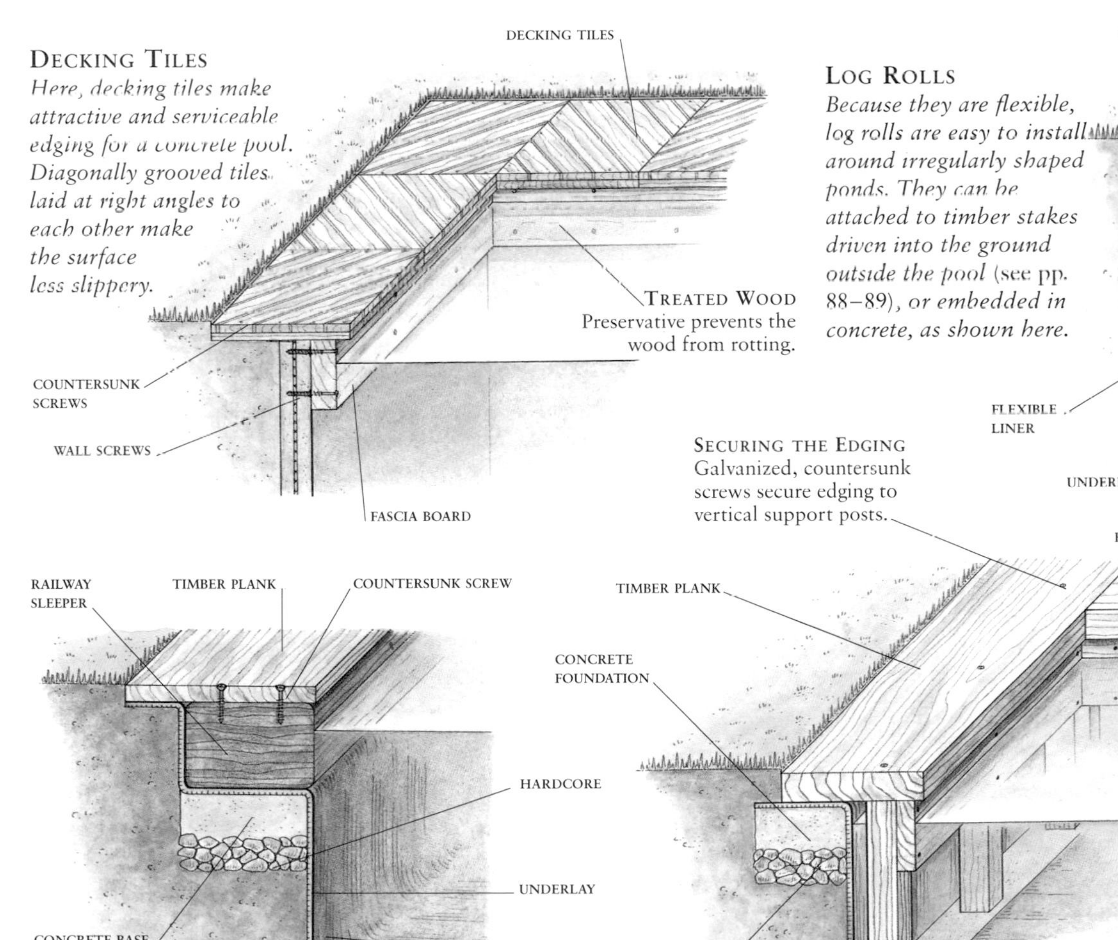

Decking Tiles
Here, decking tiles make attractive and serviceable edging for a concrete pool. Diagonally grooved tiles laid at right angles to each other make the surface less slippery.

Treated Wood
Preservative prevents the wood from rotting.

Log Rolls
Because they are flexible, log rolls are easy to install around irregularly shaped ponds. They can be attached to timber stakes driven into the ground outside the pool (see pp. 88–89), or embedded in concrete, as shown here.

Securing the Edging
Galvanized, countersunk screws secure edging to vertical support posts.

Timber Planks
These treated timber planks border a regularly shaped pool constructed with flexible liner. Use countersunk screws to attach the plank to vertical support timbers, which are set into concrete at 22cm (9in) intervals. Use thin wooden planks as fascia boards to disguise the supports.

Timber Railway Sleepers
To stabilize a sleeper, install it on a concrete foundation. Use countersunk screws to fix a timber plank over the sleeper in order to make an even surface for walking on.

Further Information

- Construction Tools and Materials – pp. 62–63
- Construction Techniques – pp. 64–69
- Semi-raised Rigid Pool Units – pp. 80–81
- Timber Decking – pp. 130–131

TIMBER DECKING

ONE OF THE many advantages of using timber decking as edging is that it is easier to overlap the edge of the water with wood – thus providing a platform to view and feed fish from – than with paving or other hard-edged material. Decking not only makes an ideal edging, it can also be designed to form a seating area at the waterside, or a jetty extending well over the edge of the water. Wooden decking tiles with a diagonal pattern are particularly attractive when laid at right angles to each other. If possible, use long-lasting hardwood, but if cheaper wood is used, ensure that it is treated with a preservative that will not adversely affect plants, fish, or wildlife. As with bridges and stepping stones *(see pp. 120–123)*, the safety aspects of timber decking should be carefully considered, especially if young children are likely to play on it.

WATERSIDE TIMBER DECKING

LAYING DECKING AT THE WATERSIDE

CONSTRUCTION GUIDE

To build a 3m x 2m (10ft x 6ft) timber deck with jetty, you will need:

TOOLS
- Spade, straight-edge, spirit level, tape measure, saw, screwdriver, hammer

MATERIALS
- 10 timber uprights: 8cm sq (3in sq); 10 steel supports; 40 proprietary wall bolts 5cm (2in); galvanized nails: ½ kilo (1lb) 75mm (3in); 250 5cm (2in) 8-gauge screws
- Ready-mixed concrete: 8 bags 25kg (55lb), hardcore: 1cu m (1cu yd), sand: 1cu m (1cu yd); 8–10 house bricks
- 10cm x 5cm (4in x 2in) bearers: two at 3m (10ft) long, two at 2m (6ft) long
- 10cm x 5cm (4in x 2in) joists: five at 3m (10ft) long, two at 2m (6ft) long, five at 1m (3ft) long
- 28 decking tiles: 50cm sq (20in sq)
- Battens, fascia boards

1 TIMBER UPRIGHTS in steel supports bolted on to concrete foundations provide the firmest underpinning for a framework of bearers and joists. Lay foundations – consisting of 10cm (4in) of concrete above the same depth of hardcore – in holes measuring 30cm x 30cm (1ft x 1ft) at the ends of each bearer, at 1.2m (4ft) intervals. Allow 48 hours for the concrete to harden, then place steel supports on the concrete, and mark the four bolt positions. Then drill four corresponding holes and insert and tighten four 5cm (2in) proprietary wall bolts into the foundations. Use a straight-edge and a spirit level to make sure that the timber uprights are level, then nail the bearers, wider side down, on the uprights.

ALTERNATIVE FOUNDATION

Bed the bearers on firm soil in excavated channels containing hardcore covered with a 5cm (2in) layer of sand. If necessary, use bricks to adjust the height of the bearers.

2 SKEW-NAIL THE three middle joists – 45cm (18in) apart – to the bearers. If joists have to be joined, make a 5cm (2in) horizontal cut and a 10cm (4in) vertical cut at one end of each joist, and half-lap them at the point where they cross the bearer. Finally, nail the two end joists in place.

3 FOR ADDITIONAL SUPPORT, wedge bricks underneath bearers where they are crossed by joists. Check levels along and across joists as you do so, so that you can make adjustments to height where necessary by varying the depth of the depressions you scrape out for the bricks.

4 USE EIGHT 5cm (2in) screws to fasten each grooved, non-slip decking tile to the joists. To achieve a chequerboard effect, as well as to reduce further the chance of slipping, position the tiles so that the diagonal treads are at right angles to each other.

5 If using flexible liner and underlay, pull these materials up over the top of the joists, and secure them well above the waterline with timber battens nailed horizonally behind the joist *(see also illustration below, left)*. This step should be completed before screwing in place the decking tiles that overlap the edges of the structure.

6 Once the overlapping wooden tiles are in place, screw on a timber fascia board to hide the liner and the rough wood of the bearers from side-view. If desired, the fascia board can be wide enough to extend down to the waterline. Where the edge of the pond meets the decking, mortar on to the liner – well below the waterline – a row of retaining cobblestones, then add smaller pebbles.

Construction of Decking with Jetty

To incorporate this small jetty over water, two of the bearers should be 1m (3ft) longer than the others. To support the ends of the bearers, bolt steel supports with timber uprights (see Step 1, left) *on to brick plinths* (see pp. 120–121). *The positioning of three 85cm (34in) joists will ensure a firm base on which to screw the last four decking tiles: nail the first joist where the jetty joins the main structure, the next 45cm (18in) away and, to provide for a 5cm (2in) tile overhang at the end of the jetty, position the last joist 40cm (16in) away. Then nail in place the two 1m (3ft) long end joists on either side of the jetty* (see illustration, right).

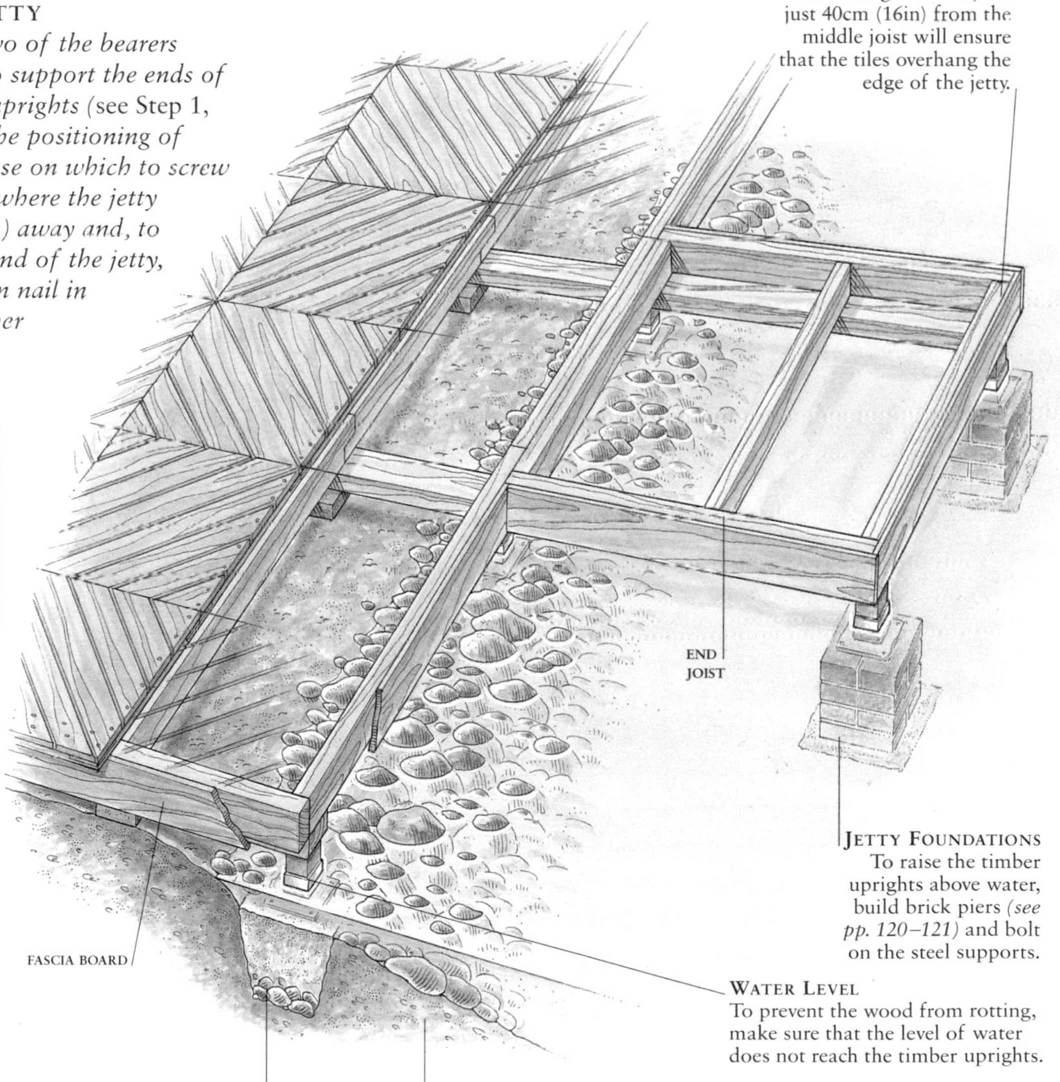

Overhanging Tiles
Positioning this last joist just 40cm (16in) from the middle joist will ensure that the tiles overhang the edge of the jetty.

END JOIST

Jetty Foundations
To raise the timber uprights above water, build brick piers *(see pp. 120–121)* and bolt on the steel supports.

Water Level
To prevent the wood from rotting, make sure that the level of water does not reach the timber uprights.

FASCIA BOARD

Sunken Foundations
For firm underpinning, line the excavation with hardcore before filling with concrete.

SUBSOIL

Securing the Liner

Decking that forms a right angle over the water creates the illusion that water laps up to and beneath the decking. Where the liner has to fit around a sharp corner, it should be carefully pulled and pleated *(see pp. 78–79)* before being secured with battens, and hidden from side-view by timber fascia boards.

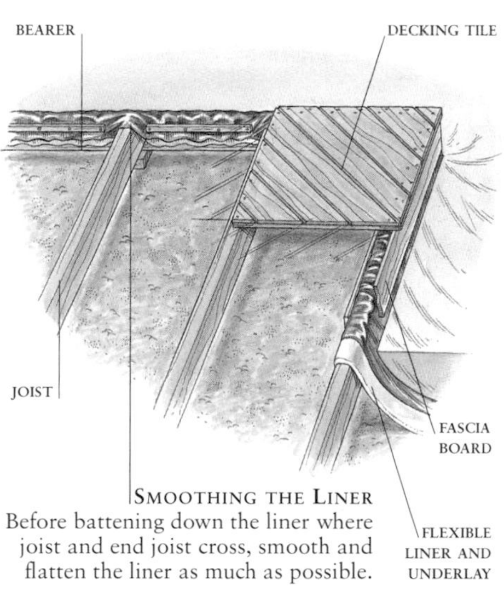

Smoothing the Liner
Before battening down the liner where joist and end joist cross, smooth and flatten the liner as much as possible.

Further Information

- Construction Techniques – pp. 64–69
- Simple Ponds with Flexible Liner – pp. 76–79

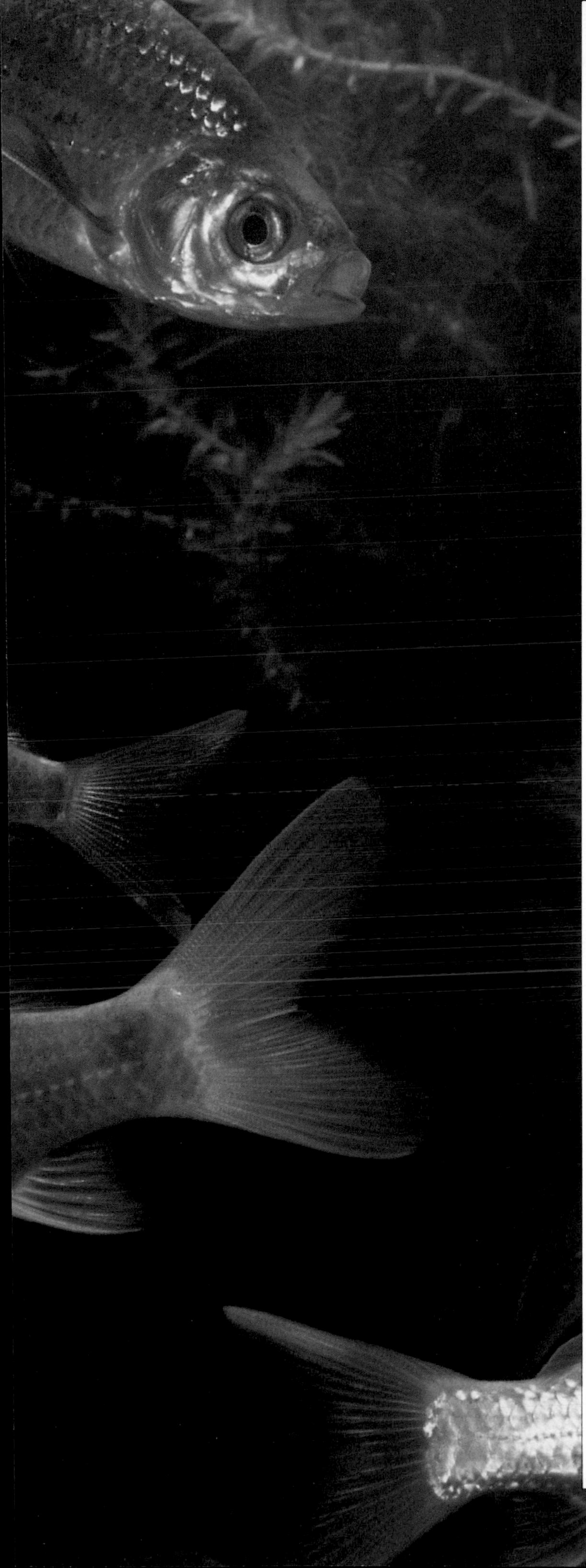

Stocking & Maintenance

Maintaining a Healthy Pond
A Balanced Ecosystem • Seasonal Changes • Routine Tasks for Pond Health
Pond Cleaning • Pond Repairs
Plants for Water Gardens
Planting Environments • Soils and Containers • Planning Planting Schemes
Buying Plants • Planting Techniques
Routine Plant Care • Division and Propagation • Plant Pests and Diseases
Fish for Water Features
Fish Species and their Requirements
Buying and Introducing Fish • Routine Fish Care • Fish Pests and Diseases

Ornamental Fish *(left)*
Goldfish are among the most popular fish for ponds and have been kept in captivity longer than any other fish. They are hardy and easily cared for, and come in a wide variety of decorative types.

MAINTAINING A HEALTHY POND

PROVIDED THAT A POND has been well sited, designed, and built, and that care is taken to ensure a healthy balance when stocking with plants *(see pp. 152–153)* and fish *(see pp. 170–171)*, it should not be difficult to tend. Major emptying and cleaning of a water feature *(see pp. 142–144)* is certainly neither necessary nor advisable, in the majority of cases, for at least four or five years.

CREATING A HEALTHY POND

The planning, construction, and stocking of a pond are crucial to the ecological balance, or ecosystem *(see pp. 136–137),* that exists within it. The well-being of plant and animal life depends upon many factors, including light levels, water temperature, and the proportions of the various gases dissolved in the pond's water. Appropriate functional planting *(see pp. 152–153)* will help initially to achieve a natural balance and clear water.

CLEAR WATER
The condition of this cascading waterfall is very satisfactory; the water is extremely clear, with no sign of algal growth, allowing the decorative pebbles to be seen. The bubbles show how the splashing is increasing the oxygen content of the water.

THE POND IN WINTER
In cold climates, precautions must be taken to ensure that ice does not completely cover the water surface. Not only does a solid sheet of ice exert pressure on the pond edges, it also traps waste gases that may build up in the water and harm fish and other animal life.

SUMMER REFRESHMENT
A well-kept feature needs little attention in the summer months, allowing time for relaxation and enjoyment of the water. In prolonged hot weather, be aware of the need for topping up, particularly if a fountain is increasing the rate of evaporation.

Green Water
Small, free-floating plants such as duckweed multiply extremely rapidly, and may soon choke a pond. Although useful additions to a new pond, providing temporary shade and shelter, they should be rigorously controlled as the pond becomes established. Overhanging trees and shrubs should be avoided, if possible, when siting a pond, or they will, as here, shed leaves into the water. If not removed, these will eventually sink and decompose.

Routine maintenance *(see pp. 140–141)* is necessary to ensure that the water remains healthy – in particular, the regular thinning of plants so that the pond does not become blocked up. While all water features benefit, from time to time, from a major clean-up, it is vital not to do this too often. Each time a pond is emptied and refilled, it can take anything up to two years for a balanced ecosystem to re-establish itself.

Water Features Through the Year

The structure of water features and their surrounds should be inspected regularly throughout the year, but other tasks become appropriate only in various seasons. In winter, fish become dormant at the bottom of the pool. Water plants are largely herbaceous, dying back in winter and remaining dormant until regrowth begins in the spring. Pond life is best therefore left undisturbed, unless freezing weather is forecast. Then, there are a number of measures that can be taken to protect the pond and its inhabitants *(see p. 139)*.

When the pond starts up into life again in spring, plants and fish should be checked for health, and any restocking done so that the feature looks its best for summer. Prolonged spells of hot weather can damage pond life – the pond should be topped up regularly *(see p. 138)* to combat water loss caused by evaporation. Remember that over the years, debris accumulating at the bottom of a pond will gradually make it more shallow, leaving fish with no cool, deep water in which to escape the heat. The removal of this layer of sludge is one of the principal reasons for emptying and cleaning a pond.

Moving Water Features

Equipment such as pumps and filters needs additional, careful maintenance if it is to function well. However, such equipment does have other advantages where pond maintenance is concerned. It is much easier to drain a pond that has a pump in place and, with an electricity supply already present, a small pond heater can be added with ease in cold weather.

Structural Repairs

Pond repairs may become urgently necessary if a large leak develops, but more often small underwater punctures and cracks go unnoticed until a pond is drained for cleaning. Most of the materials used to line ponds can be repaired quite satisfactorily *(see p. 145)*. However, attention must also always be paid, year-round, to the condition of any structures above water, such as timber edging, bridges, or stepping stones; if not kept in good condition, they are a threat to safety.

A Balanced Ecosystem

The ecosystem of a pond involves the interaction of a number of factors – water, gases, minerals, sunshine, plants, and creatures. In every pond, a balance must be found between clinically clean water that offers no hospitality to submerged and amphibious creatures, and a murky, crowded environment that begins to stifle life. The health of a pond is affected by its size and shape, the acidity or alkalinity (pH level) of the water, the amount of surface area exposed to the air and to the sun, the type of plants used, and the presence of pond life. If the ecological balance is disrupted, algae will spread, and the water quality will deteriorate rapidly.

Life in the Water

Most ponds must initially be filled with tapwater, which is generally alkaline and may contain additives. It is advisable to let the pond settle for a week or so and become more hospitable to life before stocking with plants or fish. Wherever possible, use rainwater for topping up, although it can be acidic.

The water capacity of the feature can also affect a pond's health. The larger the pond, the more likely it is that a balanced ecosystem, in which many varied life forms interact, will develop naturally. The deeper the water, the less likely it is that water temperatures will fluctuate and disturb the ecosystem.

Exchange of Gases

Healthy water contains enough oxygen to support life. Fish and other aquatic creatures consume oxygen and produce carbon dioxide. Submerged plants absorb carbon dioxide and release oxygen into the water in a process called photosynthesis, which is activated by sunlight. However, the action of sunlight on mineral salts also causes algae to spread; these microscopic plants can rapidly deplete the water of oxygen, harming wildlife. As the water becomes murky with algal growth, plants starved of light will also begin to decay. Dead and decomposing plant and animal matter release poisonous methane into the water, further endangering life. It is essential, therefore, to partly shade a pond with floating-leaved plants to prevent too much sunlight reaching the water; also, ensure that oxygenating plants *(see pp. 148–149)*, which compete with algae for nutrients, are present.

A Healthy Pond
Water quality is a good indicator of pond health. This pond's clear, bright water and healthy planting indicate that it has been well tended. The water is free of algae – due in part to the shade provided by both water lilies and marginal plants, and in part to oxygenating plants that have absorbed the nutrients on which algae thrive.

Guidelines for a Balanced Ecology

The following tips will help to create and maintain a healthy ecosystem:

- Site pond in the optimum position *(see pp. 56–57)*
- Ensure that at least part of the pond has a minimum water depth of 45cm (18in)
- Use floating plants and water lilies to shade about half the pond *(see p. 152)*
- Add oxygenating plants *(see p. 152)*
- Do not overcrowd with plants or fish
- Do not overfeed fish *(see pp. 172–173)*
- To boost oxygen levels, install a fountain *(see pp. 108–115)*
- Regularly check pH levels *(see p. 151)*
- Carry out seasonal tasks on time

An Unhealthy Pond
The appearance of this pond indicates neglect. Due to the lack of floating or oxygenating plants, algae have been allowed to spread over much of the water surface. No sunlight is able to penetrate the water, causing a further fall in the level of oxygen. Evaporation has also occurred – evident in the drastic drop in the water level. A layer of scum suggests that the water is also polluted, which may have been caused by a number of factors (see facing page)*. Due to these unhealthy conditions, the plants have not been able to survive.*

Natural Pond Cycle

In a healthy pond, plants and animals coexist within an efficient and interconnected food chain. The process involves the interaction of bacteria, plants, herbivores, and carnivores with inorganic matter. The water level may be affected by the pH level, which should be tested regularly (see p. 151)*: tapwater is high in acids; rainwater tends to be more alkaline. All pondlife will suffer if the water quality is poor.*

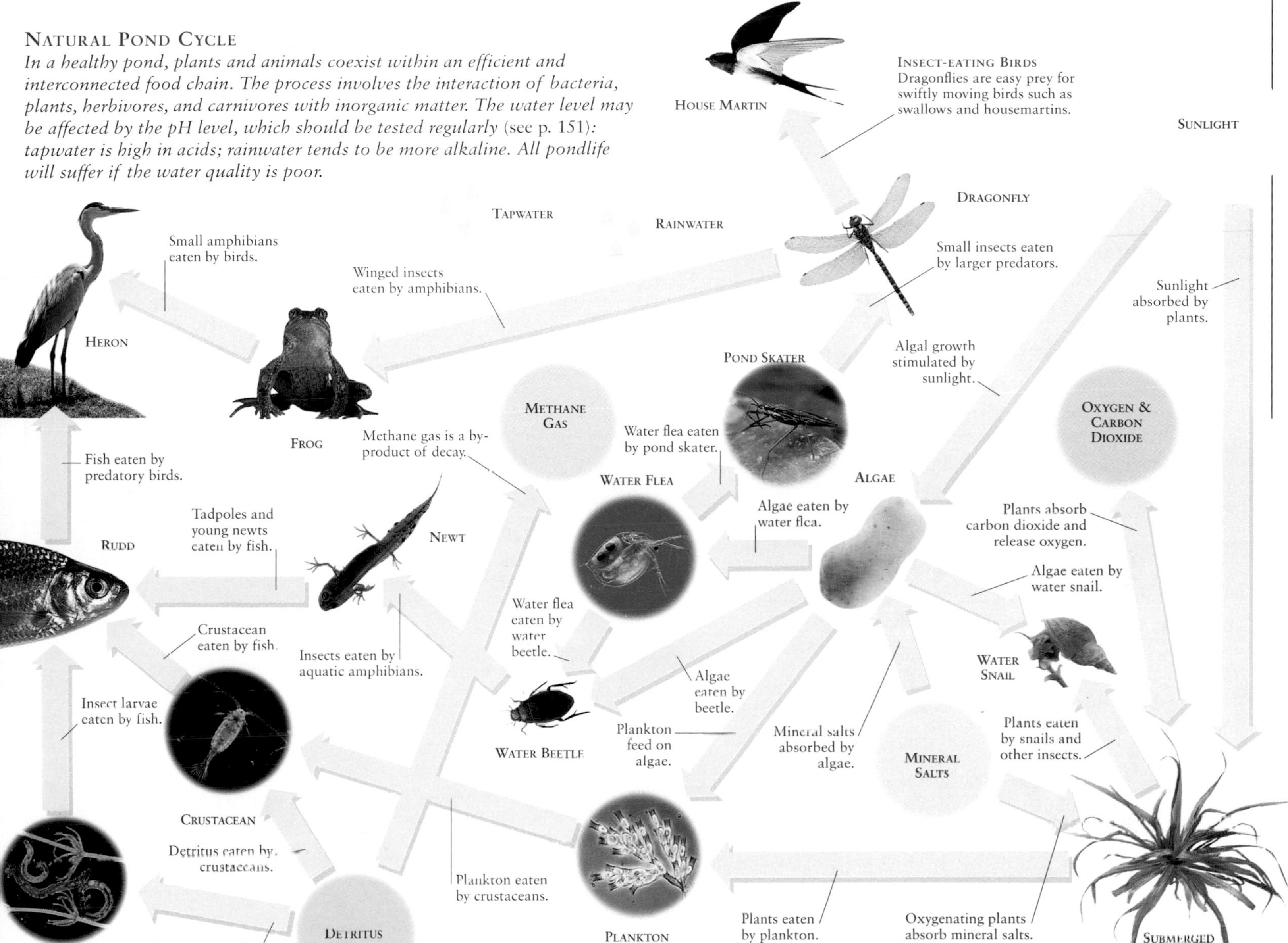

Feeding and Waste

Most ponds support a complex food chain. Bacteria, snails, and worms feed on organic debris; they are then eaten by water beetles and dragonfly larvae, which in turn are eaten by fish and frogs. In all but large wildlife ponds, fish may need additional feeding. The plants feed on nutrients such as mineral salts dissolved in the water: they will, however, benefit from slow-release plant fertilizers *(see p. 150)* from time to time.

Maintaining a Balanced Ecosystem

Regular maintenance is necessary *(see pp. 140–141)*, but avoid emptying the pond too often. Do not overstock with plants – their dying leaves will create much decomposing matter that releases methane. A surplus of fish will deplete the pond of oxygen; overfeeding will leave surplus food to rot. If the water freezes over, make sure that there is an ice-free area so that waste gases can escape *(see p. 139)*. Avoid using pesticides and do not use ordinary fertilizers on water plants. Finally, test the water pH regularly *(see p. 151)* – an imbalance can harm pond life.

Poor Water Quality

	Symptoms	Possible Causes
PH OUT OF BALANCE	• Fish more prone to disease • Plant growth diminished • Biological filters less effective	• Tapwater, lime seeping from cement or decorative limestone (high alkalinity) • Rainwater, decomposing plants or fish waste, nitrites building up (high acidity)
LOW OXYGEN LEVEL	• Fish gasp for breath at pond surface • Fish start to die with no symptoms of disease • Water blackens or becomes malodorous	• Too many floating plants or fish • Decomposing organic waste • Prolonged hot weather • Excessive algal growth
POLLUTION	• Dead fish • Discoloration of water • Yellowing of plants • Numerous bubbles (particularly noticeable under ice)	• Build-up of methane • Build-up of nitrites and ammonia • Run-off from local farmland using nitrogenous fertilizers • Overfeeding fish

SEASONAL CHANGES

IN MILD WEATHER CONDITIONS, routine attention and, when necessary, pond cleaning *(see pp. 142–145)* will maintain a healthy and attractive water environment. However, when weather becomes severe – long, hot summers and bitter winters – special care must be taken to ensure that both the structure and the plant and animal inhabitants of a pond are not harmed. In climates or sites that are regularly subject to extreme weather, careful siting and design and appropriate choice of plant and fish species are necessary preventive measures, but in temperate climates, there are many practical tips that will protect a pond from occasional fluctuations.

HOT, DRY WEATHER

Long periods of hot sun with little rain will cause the water level to drop through evaporation. If the pond is not topped up, this will result in warmer water, which will encourage the growth of algae and reduce the level of oxygen *(see p. 136)*. Lack of oxygen may be manifested by distressed fish gulping for air, while the deterioration in water quality will make plants more susceptible to pests and diseases *(see pp. 164–165)*. There may also be structural problems – a severe drop in water depth will expose flexible liner to sunlight, for example, which will eventually cause less expensive brands to crack.

MAINTAINING A POND IN HOT WEATHER

If using tap water, top up with a slowly trickling hose – mains water may contain higher concentrations of additives in summer and should be added slowly. If algal growth becomes excessive, you may need to use an algicide. Oxygen levels can be increased by creating water movement; either spray the surface with a garden hose or, better still, install a small, bubbling fountain. If necessary, transfer fish to a temporary cool tank and move plants to lower depths, or shade them.

DESIGNS FOR HOT, DRY GARDENS

An informal pond with shallow margins and a large surface area is particularly vulnerable to water loss. In hot, sunny sites, it is worthwhile considering a more formal design, with a deeper pool that has overhanging edges to further minimize water loss through evaporation.

DECORATIVE CANAL
Canals originated in cultures with hot climates, such as those of ancient Egypt, Persia, and Rome. With their small surface area, they conserve water extremely efficiently.

SEVERE HOT-WEATHER PRECAUTIONS

During prolonged spells of hot, dry weather, there are a number of ways in which to protect fish and plants, and to improve the condition of a pond. Remember when building a fish pond that a deep area of cool water to which they may retreat is essential.

EMERGENCY MEASURES
To rapidly oxygenate and cool water if fish are in distress, use a hose with a fine spray nozzle.

FLEXIBLE LINER
When the water level drops the liner is exposed to sunlight, which may in time cause it to crack.

TOPPING UP
Top up the pond with a slowly trickling hose to minimize disruption to the water ecology.

UV CLARIFIER
Where algal spread is a continual problem, consider adding a UV clarifier *(see p. 71)*.

PERMANENT RELIEF
A low-bubble fountain oxygenates water while minimizing evaporation.

WARNING SIGNAL
Turn on a fountain or hose if fish rise to the surface and gulp for air.

Overwintering a Pond

If severe winter weather is anticipated, every precaution should be taken to protect the pond and its wildlife. A sheet of ice puts an enormous strain on a pond's structure, and can seriously affect water quality. Check the pond daily, and take every advance measure possible to protect the plants and fish.

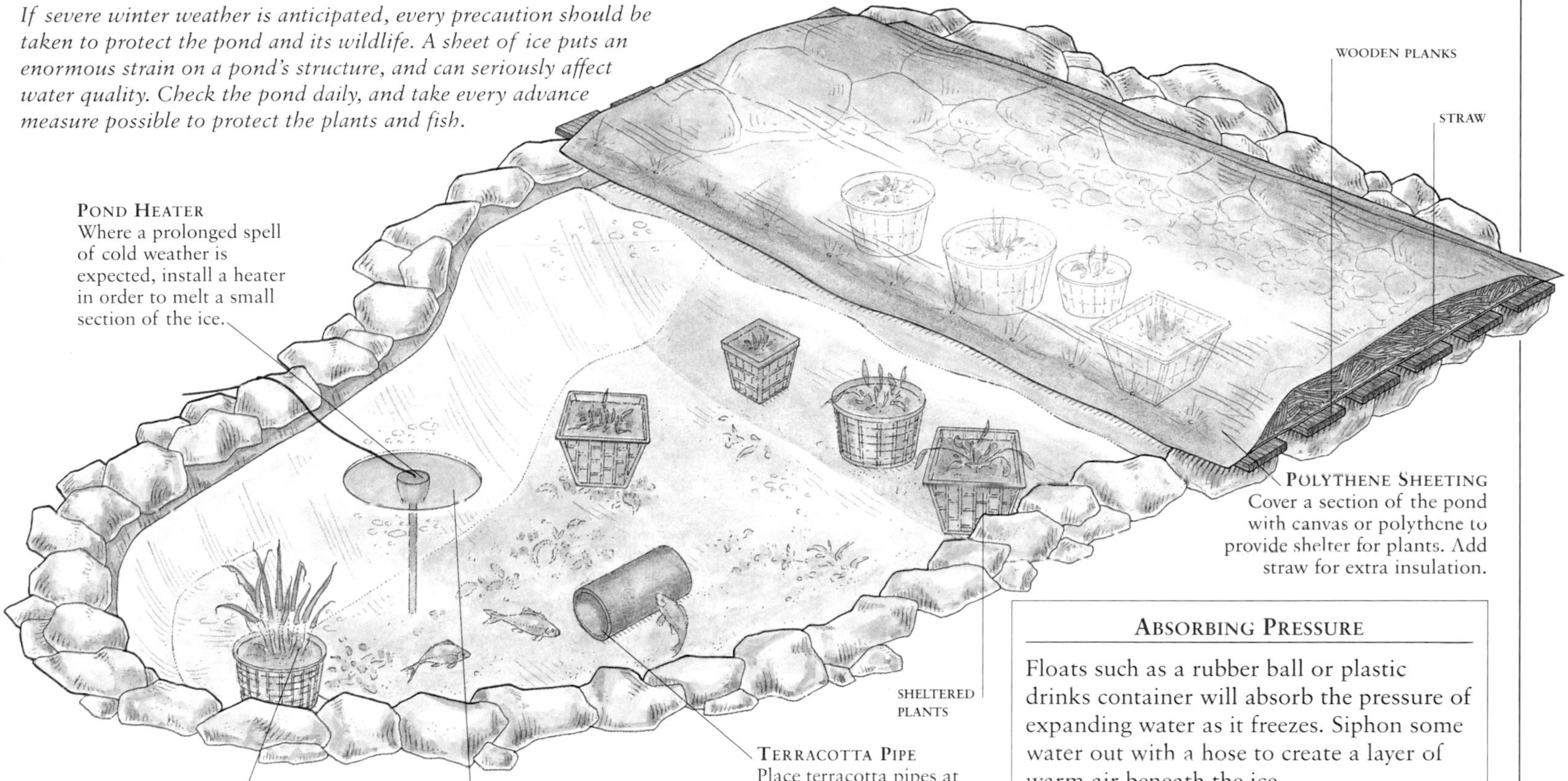

WOODEN PLANKS

STRAW

Pond Heater
Where a prolonged spell of cold weather is expected, install a heater in order to melt a small section of the ice.

Polythene Sheeting
Cover a section of the pond with canvas or polythene to provide shelter for plants. Add straw for extra insulation.

SHELTERED PLANTS

Terracotta Pipe
Place terracotta pipes at the bottom of the pond to provide fish with hides from hungry predators.

Dormant Plants
Fully hardy deep-water plants lie dormant and protected at the bottom of the pond during the winter months.

Poisonous Gases
An open area in the ice will allow poisonous gases such as methane to escape.

Absorbing Pressure

Floats such as a rubber ball or plastic drinks container will absorb the pressure of expanding water as it freezes. Siphon some water out with a hose to create a layer of warm air beneath the ice.

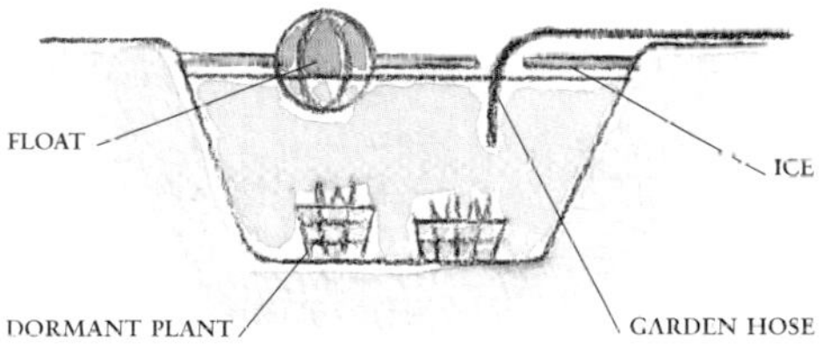

FLOAT

ICE

DORMANT PLANT

GARDEN HOSE

Freezing Weather

In temperate climates, it is extremely unlikely that a water feature of adequate depth will freeze solid, but when the surface of the water freezes, the ice expands, placing great pressure on the sides of a pond. Flexible-liner ponds resist this pressure better than concrete, particularly if the sides are slightly sloping. When building with concrete, reinforcing fibres will give flexibility and strength *(see pp. 90–91)*. Where walls are vertical and made of bricks, a polystyrene layer that will compact under pressure *(see right)* is invaluable. Place floating objects on the water surface before the pond freezes, so that some of the expansion is absorbed.

Poisonous Gases

When ice seals a pond, the exchange of gases is prevented. By removing snow from the surface, light can enter the pond and oxygen levels will increase. However, methane released by decomposing organic matter becomes trapped under the ice, and a hole must be created to allow it to escape. If the pond contains fish, never smash the ice: the vibrations will shock and may kill them. Always melt the ice gently – use a pond heater or stand a pan of boiling water on the ice. When the ice is broken, siphoning off a small quantity of water creates an insulating layer of warmer air beneath the ice that will protect pond life.

Insulating a Pond

Raised ponds are particularly vulnerable to freezing air temperatures. Polystyrene, in sheet or granular form, can be used both for its insulating effects and to absorb ice pressure, protecting the pond's structure.

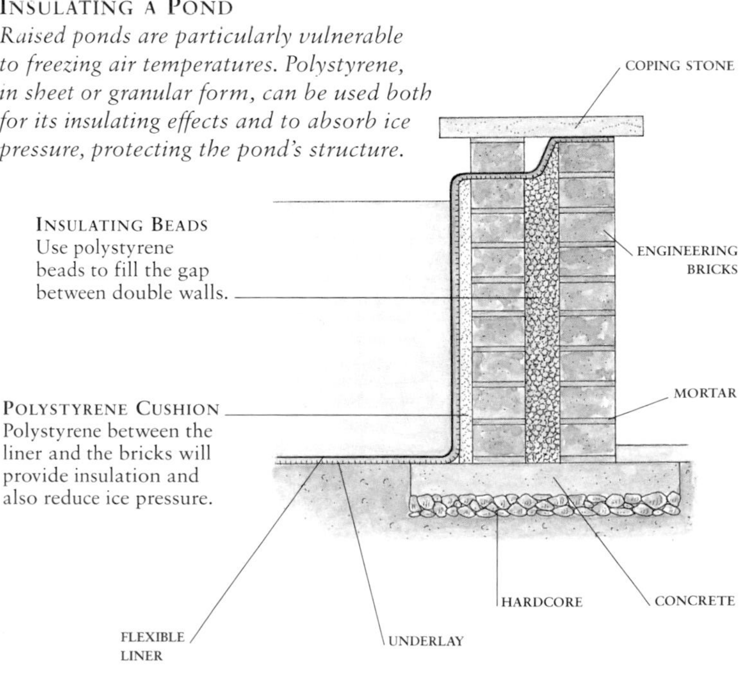

Insulating Beads
Use polystyrene beads to fill the gap between double walls.

Polystyrene Cushion
Polystyrene between the liner and the bricks will provide insulation and also reduce ice pressure.

Routine Tasks for Pond Health

PROVIDED THAT A POND is well constructed and sensibly stocked, it should not be too difficult to care for and maintain. It is important to ensure that the water is at the correct level at all times; insufficient depth will cause temperature fluctuations, which will affect the water quality and consequently the well-being of plants and fish. Structural damage to the pond may occur – lining materials are especially vulnerable in extreme weather conditions *(see pp. 138–139)* – and may necessitate repair work *(see p. 145)*. Any surrounding structures such as paving and bridges should be checked regularly; this is especially important for reasons of safety.

Maintaining a Water Feature

Regular Cleaning
With a formal feature such as this, any neglect in the maintenance of water clarity, plants, gravel, and surrounds will be apparent.

Pond care involves maintaining every component of a water feature, and this includes both the plants and wildlife within the pond, the quality of the water, and all surrounding surfaces and structures.

Structural Care

Any structures incorporated by and over the water, such as bridges, stepping stones, and timber decking, should be checked regularly for structural damage. A screw missing on the handrail of a bridge, for example, could be potentially dangerous. Ensure that supporting foundations are sound; check also for rusting ironwork, and make sure that brickwork does not need repointing, especially after a period of heavy frost.

Any surfaces should be regularly cleaned. Timber should be treated with preservatives once a year, and any wooden or stone surfaces scoured with a wire brush in order to remove moss or lichen. A slippery surface could be extremely dangerous – if necessary, cover the surface with fine wire mesh *(see below)*.

Water Level
During periods of hot weather when water evaporation is likely to occur, keep the pond regularly topped up from a slowly trickling hose (see inset). *Failure to do this will allow the water level to drop, as is evident here in the water marks on the stepping stones. If the water level remains low for too long a period, pond life will suffer, and flexible liner may crack.*

A Natural Water Balance

Pond water is host to a community of microscopic organisms that are part of the water's ecology *(see pp. 136–137)*. In early spring, as the water warms up and receives higher levels of sunlight, it becomes rich in minerals; phytoplankton (free-floating algae) feed on these minerals, and their presence causes the water to turn green and cloudy. This is only a temporary condition, indicating that the microscopic pond life is re-emerging, having lain dormant during winter. Algae play an

Safety and General Care

Timber Decking
Timber decking complements water well. It may be used in any climate, provided that it has been treated with a wood preservative. Bear in mind that all wooden surfaces need regular maintenance, even in hot, dry climates. Check surface areas for any splits or cracks at least once a year, and ensure that no screws or brackets have rusted. Wooden surfaces require regular cleaning with a scouring brush, especially in damp climates. Chicken wire tacked to the decking (see inset) *will provide an unobtrusive, non-slip surface.*

Securing and Cleaning Stones
Any stones used as stepping stones must be completely stable and, if necessary, secured with mortar (see pp. 68–69). *Surfaces should also be scoured regularly with a wire brush, to ensure that they are non-slip and free of algae.*

SEASONAL TASKS FOR POND CARE

Spring	Summer	Autumn	Winter
• Clean out the pond, if necessary *(see pp. 142–144).* • Carry out any repair work *(see p. 145).* • Clean off algae from surrounding paving, decking, or stepping stones. • Remove water heater for storage. • Reinstall pumps, filters, and lights. • Check the water chemistry with a proprietary test kit *(see p. 151)* and, if necessary, treat water with a pH adjuster. • Check plants for signs of disease and treat as necessary *(see p. 164).*	• Check water chemistry with a proprietary test kit *(see p. 151).* • Clean the pump's strainer to ensure that it remains unclogged. Do this once a week *(see below).* • Control algae with a proprietary algicide. • Remove blanketweed regularly *(see below).* • Add barley straw in nets to combat blanketweed (the type of bacteria attracted to the straw feed on algae). • Keep the water free from decaying foliage *(see pp. 158–159).* • Check the water level weekly, and top up if necessary *(see p.138).* • Protect fish by netting off predators such as great diving beetles *(see p. 174).* • If herons are preying on fish, fence the pond or cover with proprietary netting. • Keep any fountains on all night in sultry weather *(see p. 138).*	• Secure a net over the pond to collect falling leaves and debris *(see p. 159).* • Keep the water clear of dying foliage *(see pp. 158–159).* • Cut down foliage of marginal plants *(see pp. 158–159).* • Cut back excess growth of submerged oxygenators *(see pp. 158–159).*	• Install a pond heater *(see p. 139).* • If not being used, remove, clean, and store pumps, filters, and lights. • If the pump is still operating, add extra bricks to its plinth to raise it nearer to the surface of the water. • Remove any dead leaves from water. • Place a floating object on the water to stop the water from freezing *(see p. 139).* • Remove snow from ice sheets, if necessary, to allow light to enter *(see p. 139).*

important role in forming the first link in the food chain. As they use up nutrients and other creatures devour them, the algae will slowly diminish, leaving the pondwater clear.

Maintaining Clear Water

Functional planting *(see pp. 152–153)* and regular care should maintain clear water, but a long period of hot weather could disrupt the ecological balance, encouraging algal growth *(see pp. 136–137)*, particularly of blanketweed. For quick results, proprietary algicides are available, but be sure to follow the instructions carefully. For a long-term solution, a biological pond filter and a UV clarifier with a magnetic descaler *(see p. 71)* is appropriate.

Decomposing plant tissue will cloud or even blacken the pond, polluting the water with toxic by-products, and creating an unhealthy environment for fish. By regularly thinning and cutting back plants *(see pp. 160–161)* – especially in late summer when plants are beginning to die back – this potential problem may be averted. During autumn, place a net over the pond to catch the accumulation of fallen leaves before they enter the water *(see p. 159)*. To prevent water evaporation in long periods of hot weather *(see p. 138)*, keep the pond topped up with a slowly trickling hose. Bear in mind, also, that freezing conditions can damage a concrete pond, and precautions may need to be taken *(see p. 139)*.

Cleaning Accessories

Pump Maintenance

Clean the pump and strainer as recommended by the manufacturer; this may be as often as once a week during summer. Pumps should also be stripped and serviced once a year.

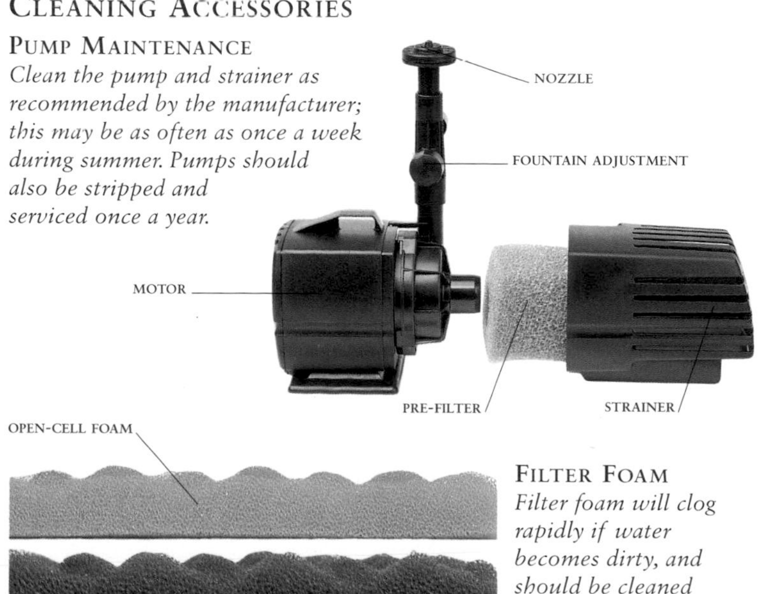

Filter Foam

Filter foam will clog rapidly if water becomes dirty, and should be cleaned twice a month.

Removing Excess Plant Growth

Blanketweed

Blanketweed, a mat of filamentous algae, should be removed regularly. To do this, rest a long stick on the water surface, turn gently, and pull out the strands of blanketweed that wrap around the stick.

Ornamental Planting

Ensure that no more than half of the pond surface is covered with floating-leaved plants. If the plants become invasive, thin them to allow sunlight to enter.

Cleaning out a Pond

Every pond needs periodic emptying and cleaning, the frequency depending on its size. Small ponds require attention every four to five years, while large ponds may need cleaning less frequently. The process involves emptying the pond of water and its inhabitants in order to remove the layer of decomposing debris lying on the bottom of the pond, which mainly consists of rotting leaves; there may also be dead creatures. The clean-out also provides an opportunity for dividing established clumps of deep-water plants, such as water lilies, which may have become overgrown. While the pond is empty of water, examine its structure for cracks or punctures. Late spring is the best time to clean out a pond, allowing time for plants and wildlife to recover and re-establish over the summer. If you have large or expensive fish, it is worthwhile seeking advice from a specialist supplier on temporary holding facilities that will keep them safe and stress-free.

How to Empty your Pond

You Will Need

TOOLS
- Pump or length of flexible tubing to siphon water
- Garden hose
- Several plastic buckets
- Dustpan
- Soft broom or brush

MATERIALS
- Rubber boots or waders, with cleated rather than studded soles
- Old newspapers
- For fish, a paddling pool or large holding container, e.g. plastic dustbin
- Large, soft fish net
- Net or towel for covering fish

An Untended Pond
When a pond becomes overgrown, it is advisable to carry out a major clean-up. This will provide the opportunity to control the plants' growth by dividing or thinning where necessary.

1 If the pond has a submersible pump, you can drain the pond by disconnecting the delivery pipe and connecting a hose in its place: otherwise, start to siphon away the water. If the pond contains fish, remove just enough water at first to make it easier to catch them. Fill a holding container for fish with pond water.

2 Remove containerized plants from the margins of the pond; integral planting beds need not be disturbed, unless plants need dividing. Wrap planting crates in wet newspaper and place in a shady area. Water the plants and wet the newspaper every few hours.

Containerized Plants
Remove any aquatic plants that are in containers.

3 Catch as many fish as are visible with a net and bowl *(see facing page)* and place them in the holding container in the shade. Remove containerized deep-water plants and water lilies, wrap the containers in wet newspaper, and place them with the marginals. Remove floating plants and oxygenators, retaining a few bunches of each in a bucket of water.

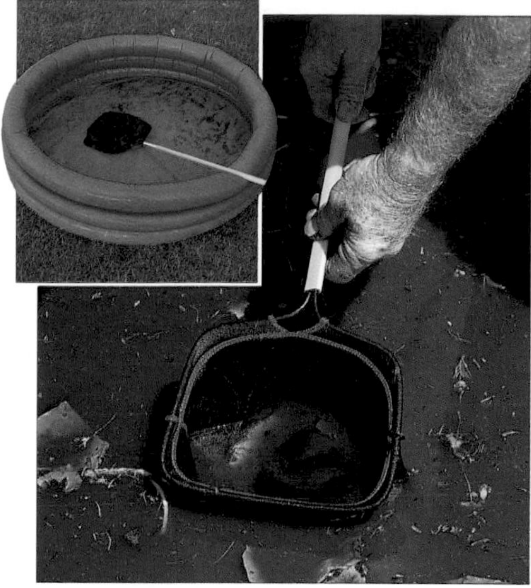

4 REMOVE ANY DECAYING plant matter that may be concealing more fish. Trawl the net through the water to catch any remaining fish. Place them in the holding container *(see inset)* and cover with a net or wet towel. Switch off the pump and remove it.

5 USE A PLASTIC BUCKET to remove the remaining water. Check the bucket for any beneficial creatures, such as frogs, and place them in the holding container. The water may be used on adjacent borders – do not pour it down a drain, as it will clog the silt traps.

6 SCOOP UP THE MUD with a dustpan. Take care not to score the surface of any lining material. Reserve a small amount of mud and water in a bucket to help reacclimatize the fish when releasing them into the clean pond. The remaining mud can be added to compost.

7 WITH THE POND now empty of fish, plants, and most of the mud, add a little water and brush away any remaining algae, mud, or plant debris. Then bail or siphon out the dirty water. Inspect the surface of the lining for damage and carry out repairs, if necessary *(see p. 145)*.

8 PARTIALLY REFILL THE POND to a depth that will allow you to stand in the water in rubber boots or waders. Unwrap the water lilies and other deep-water plants. Divide them *(see pp. 160–161)* and trim them in order to remove any damaged stems and foliage.

9 SUBMERGE THE WATER PLANTS in the deeper areas of the pond. Any new, small plants should initially be placed on stacks of bricks *(see p. 157)*. Position ornamental plants such as water lilies first, then add oxygenating and submerged plants.

(Continued overleaf.)

10 ONCE THE DEEP-WATER plants have been installed, add the bucket full of reserved mud and original water *(see p. 143)*. This will help fish and any other pond life resting in the holding container to re-establish themselves quickly when put back in the pond.

11 BEFORE TRANSFERRING THE FISH from the bucket into the pond, examine them carefully. Check that they have not been damaged in any way, and look for signs of fungal growth or other disorders *(see pp. 174–175)*. Then reintroduce them to the pond.

12 UNWRAP THE MARGINALS, and divide or thin them *(see pp. 160–161)*, if necessary. Then replace them in their planting baskets on the marginal shelves. Having done this, you can then refill the pond to its correct level. Reconnect and position the pump.

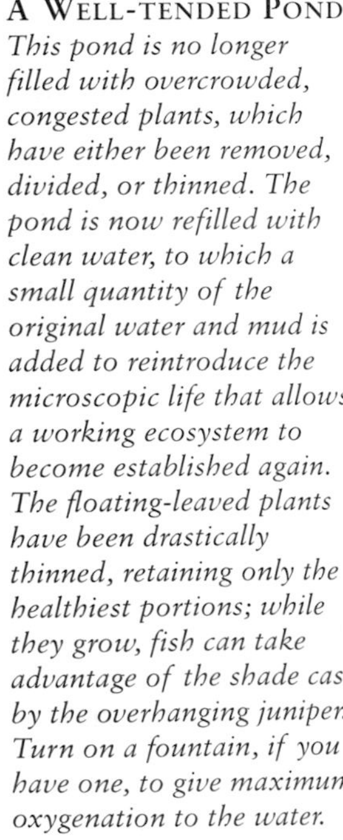

A WELL-TENDED POND
This pond is no longer filled with overcrowded, congested plants, which have either been removed, divided, or thinned. The pond is now refilled with clean water, to which a small quantity of the original water and mud is added to reintroduce the microscopic life that allows a working ecosystem to become established again. The floating-leaved plants have been drastically thinned, retaining only the healthiest portions; while they grow, fish can take advantage of the shade cast by the overhanging juniper. Turn on a fountain, if you have one, to give maximum oxygenation to the water.

Pond Repairs

Pond cleaning provides an ideal opportunity to inspect pond linings for structural damage, because a pond must be empty in order to effect repairs. Large holes or cracks are usually obvious, because the water drops to their level. Minimal damage, however, will cause only very slow seepage, and may be hard to locate. Damage may be accidental or caused by extreme weather conditions *(see pp. 138–139)*. Inexpensive flexible and rigid liners are more likely to develop cracks than good-quality ones. Reinforced concrete pools *(see pp. 90–91)* are extremely resilient, but ordinary concrete will deteriorate within a few years.

Repairing Flexible Liners

The simplest way to repair butyl or PVC liners is with double-sided, adhesive PVC tape *(see right)*, which can be obtained from suppliers of aquatic goods. It is probably not worthwhile repairing an inexpensive polythene liner. Before carrying out repair work, it is important to clean the surrounding area thoroughly with a scrubbing brush and water. Having completed the repair work, wait at least 12 hours before refilling the pond.

Repairing Preformed Rigid Units

If a preformed rigid unit is not level, or if the ground underneath and the backfilling around it has not been thoroughly consolidated, the unit is likely to crack eventually under the weight of the water. This applies particularly to cheaper plastic units. The crack can be repaired with a motor repair kit containing fibreglass matting. Firstly, roughen the surrounding area with coarse sandpaper and clean it with water. Allow the area to dry, and apply a patch of fibreglass matting that is one-and-a-half times larger than the damaged area. Wait 24 hours for the compound to set. Check that the ground around the unit is well compacted.

Repairing Concrete Ponds

It is possible to repair cracks and fractures in concrete ponds, although this is not a long-term solution. Firstly, clean the damaged area thoroughly with a scrubbing brush and water, and allow it to dry; then fill the crack with mortar. If there is any likelihood of rain, cover the area with a sheet of polythene. Then apply a waterproof sealant and allow at least 24 hours for the compound to dry.

If a concrete pond is irreparable, lining the shell with butyl and underlay will prevent the pond from leaking. (Although expensive, butyl is the most suitable type of lining material for a concrete pond, as it is less likely to be damaged by rough edges than PVC or polythene.) Lay the liner and underlay over the shell *(see also pp. 78–79)*, allowing for an overlap of about 10cm (4in); bury the edges of the liner in the surrounding earth. If the pond is surrounded by edging, trim the liner and mortar it to the paving at the point where it meets the edge of the pond.

Repairing a Flexible Liner

1 Allow the damaged area to dry, and clean with a soft cloth, dampened with alcohol.

2 Place double-sided adhesive tape over the puncture and allow two minutes for it to become "tacky".

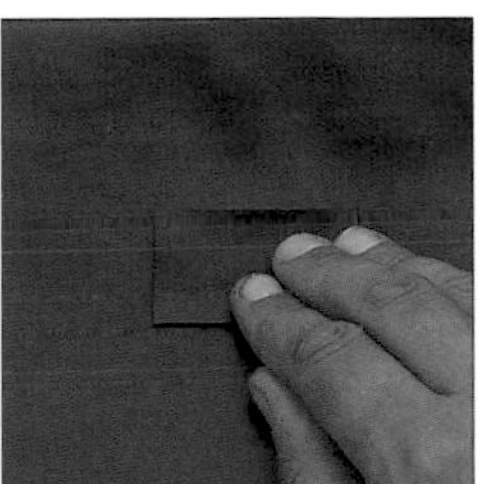

3 Cut a patch from a spare piece of liner and press firmly onto the tape, ensuring that the edges are flat.

Repairing Cracks in Concrete

1 To mend a fine crack, first use a thin stone chisel and a club hammer to widen the gap, tapping very gently.

2 Clean off dust and debris by brushing vigorously in the crack and surrounding area with a stiff wire brush.

3 Using a small pointed trowel, fill the crack with mortar. Allow at least two days for the mortar to dry.

4 Brush the mortar with a proprietary pool-sealing compound. This will prevent toxins from leaking into the water.

PLANTS FOR WATER GARDENS

FOR GARDENERS, the chief excitement of creating water features is the opportunity they provide to use a new range of plants that need special growing conditions, and to grow and display more commonly seen garden plants in a new and attractive environment. The pleasure of watching the birds, insects, and other wildlife attracted by the water and its planting is a valuable bonus.

PLANTING NEW WATER FEATURES

Of all the specialist plant groups, water plants are among the easiest to grow successfully. Given the correct planting site and healthy water conditions, they will thrive with a vigour that is extremely satisfying. Provided that initial stocking is done with care, the majority of water features will look respectably furnished by the end of the first growing season, and positively well established by the end of the second.

UNDERWATER PLANTS
Submerged plants play an important role in water health and, seen waving under the surface, heighten the effect of a natural pond. The roots and partially submerged leaves of Stratiotes aloides, *the water soldier, provide food and shelter for wildlife dwelling below the water surface.*

FLOATING LEAVES
Water lilies not only have superb ornamental value, but also perform a functional role: the floating lily-pads shade the water, helping to restrain the growth of algae.

INFORMAL PLANTING
To create an informal effect, allow plants to spread and mingle. Marginal beds permit grasses, reeds, and sedges to grow freely within the limitations of the site. Free-floating plants form changing patterns on the water, moving gently with winds and water currents. They multiply readily and, like vigorous marginals, need regular thinning.

EXOTIC DISPLAY
If climatic conditions do not allow tropical plants to be used outdoors year-round, they can be used in exotic container displays. Here, the pink of Nymphaea *'Emily Grant Hutchison' contrasts strikingly with pea-green* Pistia stratiotes *(water lettuce).*

FORMAL PLANTING
The restrained use of well-tended plants both in and around the pool enhances a formal setting. A raised pool always gives a formal effect, and makes plant care easier too. Here, the planting softens without subduing the impact of the elegant stonework and a surrounding parterre of formally shaped clipped hedging and topiary.

ESTABLISHED WATER PLANTINGS

The fact that plants in and around water grow with such vigour does mean that, as plantings mature, care must be taken to ensure that plants do not become crowded, with both soil and water space becoming congested and unhealthy. The free circulation of water or air around and within plants is important; a stagnant environment encourages the growth of fungal spores and other harmful organisms. In addition, more dominant specimens will stifle smaller plants, and upset the balance between different plant types that is so crucial to pond health. In warmer climates, or where water features are sited under glass, particular care must be taken that plants which remain evergreen do not take over, because of the head start they have over herbaceous plants that must regrow each spring.

THE RANGE AVAILABLE

Although the range of plants that grow in water is limited compared to that available when stocking a border, the choice is always increasing, particularly as more non-native plants are developed for sale. Even if you are restricted by climate to the hardiest of natives, there will be options for choice. Water hawthorn *(Aponogeton distachyos)*, for example, is a charming alternative to water lilies; moreover, it flowers earlier than most *Nymphaea*, and will often produce a second flush of flowers in the autumn, when the water-lily season is over.

When it comes to choosing moisture-lovers for pond surroundings, the range is wide enough for any taste, and includes not only traditional favourites such as hostas, iris, and primulas, but increasing numbers of new cultivars (not always fully hardy) of plants such as lobelia and mimulus.

Most general garden centres now have a small section devoted to water plants, though you may find a wider choice of well-grown plants at specialist nurseries and aquatic centres. Remember that it is in many cases illegal to collect plants from the wild, and in all cases most inadvisable. Even though some very common, unendangered species of submerged plants ("pond weed") can often be found in natural ponds on farms or common land, they may carry blanketweed, pests, and diseases, all of which will have a detrimental effect on a garden pond and its plant and animal inhabitants.

Planting Environments

Plants used in and around water features may be divided into two broad groups: those that will survive with their roots under water or in permanently saturated soil, and those that enjoy a high moisture content in soil that must, nevertheless, have some drainage, creating air pockets within the soil structure. In the first category – the truly aquatic plants – fall certain types of plant that are essential to a healthy pond: those that have submerged foliage, and those that have floating leaves. These must be added to any new pond. Plants for moist soil around the water's edge are used largely for ornamental effect, or to create wildlife habitats.

Submerged Plants

Plants that have underwater leaves play a vital role in aquatic ecosystems. These plants usually have fine, feathery foliage to provide a large leaf surface area, which compensates for the reduction in light levels below water (they will tolerate a maximum depth of 90cm/3ft in full sun). The oxygen released from their leaves as a by-product of photosynthesis (the process by which plants gain energy) passes directly into the water. The water is then able to support other life forms, and a healthy ecosystem develops, from which the plants also benefit.

Submerged plants also absorb minerals dissolved in the water, competing with algae and suppressing their growth. Their roots play a much less significant role in absorbing nutrients, and tend to be shallow, frequently acting as little more than light anchors. There is equipment available that will carry out the purely functional role of submerged plants; however, plants have other advantages; apart from their attractively textured foliage, they are essential for wildlife ponds, providing cover in which creatures may shelter and breed. They grow rapidly, but can be controlled very simply by removing handfuls of surplus stems.

Well-balanced Planting
Here, sensitive planting has produced a lush setting that is dense without being too crowded. Deep-water aquatics play a functional role, while moisture-loving plants such as astilbes create a soft edge to the pond, and the clump of Iris sibirica *provides colour.*

Deep-water Aquatics

Water lilies are by far the most popular plants among those that root in deep water. While their roots and tough, flexible stems are submerged, their leaves and flowers must be above water,

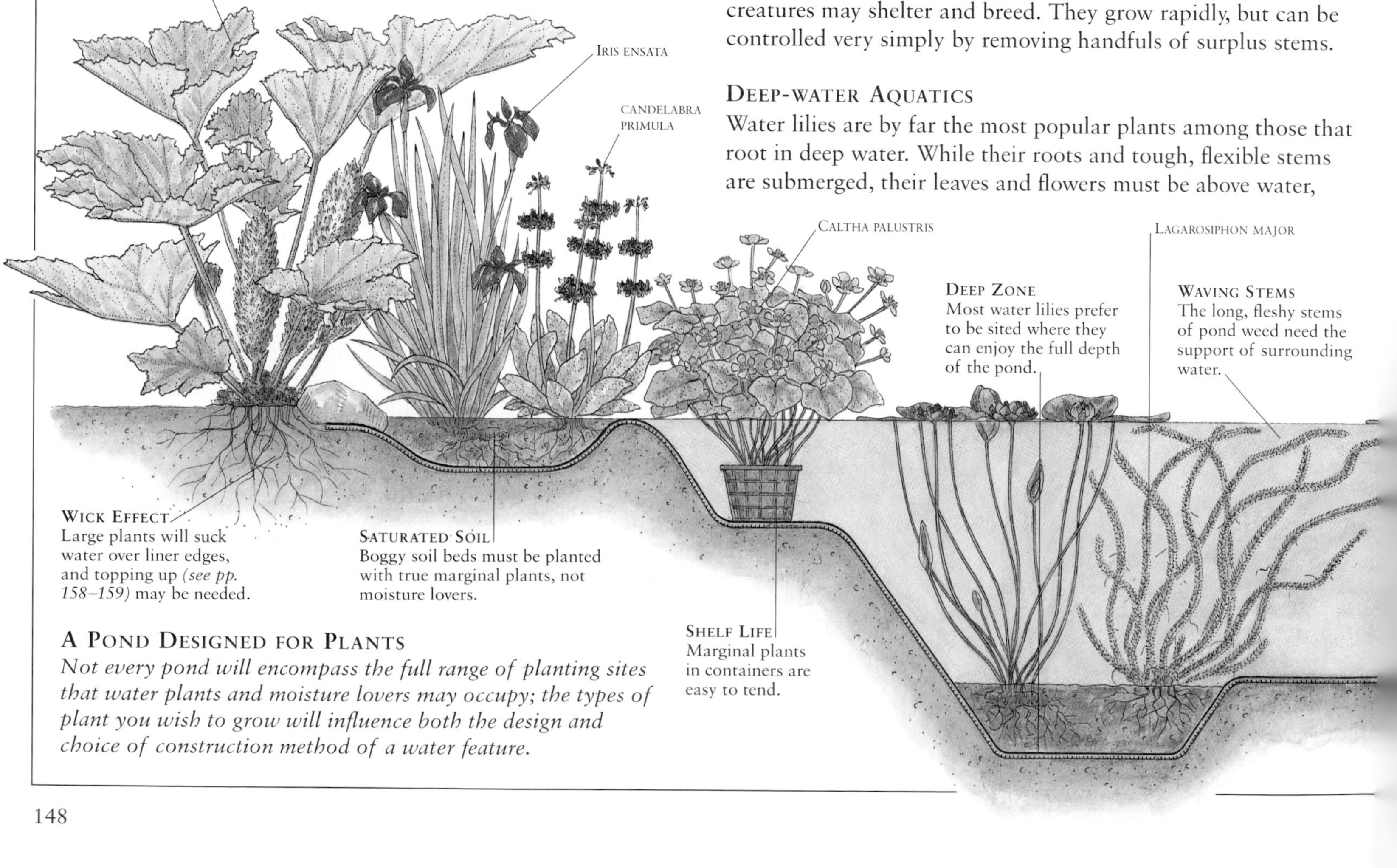

Gunnera manicata

Iris ensata

Candelabra primula

Caltha palustris

Lagarosiphon major

Deep Zone
Most water lilies prefer to be sited where they can enjoy the full depth of the pond.

Waving Stems
The long, fleshy stems of pond weed need the support of surrounding water.

Wick Effect
Large plants will suck water over liner edges, and topping up *(see pp. 158–159)* may be needed.

Saturated Soil
Boggy soil beds must be planted with true marginal plants, not moisture lovers.

Shelf Life
Marginal plants in containers are easy to tend.

A Pond Designed for Plants
Not every pond will encompass the full range of planting sites that water plants and moisture lovers may occupy; the types of plant you wish to grow will influence both the design and choice of construction method of a water feature.

usually floating on the surface. They must be given a planting depth suitable for their size and vigour so that leaf and flower stalks can reach the surface, otherwise the plant will drown. A number of water lilies, such as the vigorous *Nymphaea alba*, thrive in water that is up to 3m (10ft) deep. Those more suited to medium-sized pools generally prefer a depth of 45–60cm (1½–2ft). In all but large informal ponds, the growth of deep-water plants needs to be controlled, by root restriction, regular division or, in small ponds, a combination of both.

Free-floating Plants

These plants absorb all their nourishment from the water, through fine roots which hang suspended from leaf-clusters or rosettes that float on the water surface. They perform the same function as rooted plants with floating foliage, and many that are semi-submerged also play an oxygenating role. If chosen correctly for the prevailing climate, they need virtually no attention, with the important exception that their sometimes invasive vigour and spread will need regular control. Surplus plants can simply be scooped off the water with a rake or net.

Marginal Plants

Warm shallows and waterlogged soil at the edges of informal ponds can be populated with a variety of plants that thrive with their roots in depths of water up to 15–22cm (6–9in). Submerged plants, most free-floating plants, and some floating-leaved plants, including dwarf water lilies, will thrive in shallow water, but marginal plants are more commonly chosen for the vertical interest they bring to the edges of the pool, holding their foliage and leaves well above water.

Although they do not contribute to the balance of the water chemistry, marginal plants contribute to a pond's ecosystem, providing an excellent refuge for wildlife, especially aquatic insect life *(see pp. 54–55)*; they are also a key ornamental element in most planting schemes. Many marginal plants are vigorous growers; using planting baskets helps restrict growth and protects the pond structure (in particular, flexible liner) from certain species, including *Typha latifolia* and *Glyceria maxima*, which have sharp, penetrating roots.

Functional Plants

Submerged Oxygenator
Submerged pond weeds such as Myriophyllum aquaticum *support the ecosystem by releasing oxygen directly into the water. They also compete with algae for minerals.*

Floating-leaved Plants
Water lilies are the most popular aquatics for the deep, central areas of a pond. In addition to their ornamental value, their floating foliage provides essential shade.

Moisture-loving Plants

The range of moisture-lovers includes not only traditional waterside species but also a broad range of plants, such as hostas and astilbes, that may be used in any bed or border that contains well-watered, water-retentive soil. It must be remembered that moisture-loving plants differ from marginals in needing oxygen at their roots; the majority will not tolerate waterlogged, boggy areas. However, with some drainage provided *(see pp. 58–59)*, they bring welcome variety to pond surrounds, and play an important role in blending water features into the more general garden planting scheme.

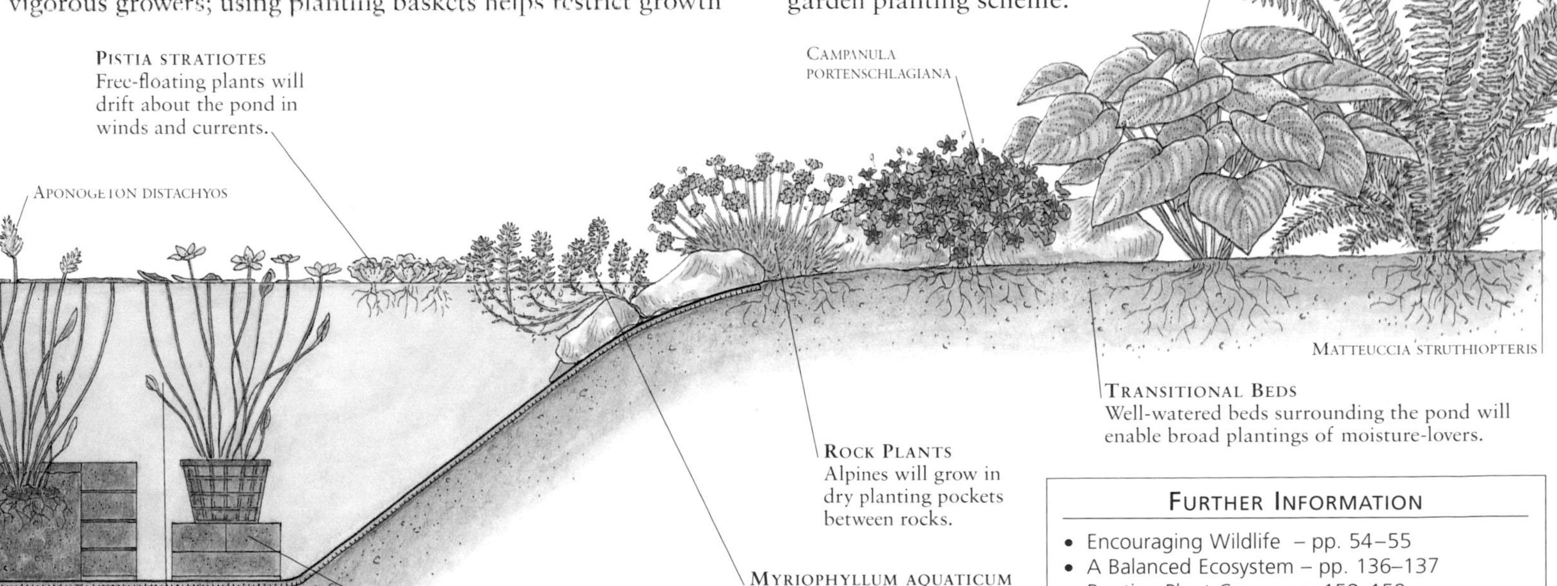

Further Information

- Encouraging Wildlife – pp. 54–55
- A Balanced Ecosystem – pp. 136–137
- Routine Plant Care – pp. 158–159
- Plant Catalogue – pp. 176–207

SOILS AND CONTAINERS

MOST WATER PLANTS are tolerant of a wide range of soil types; it is the quality and the acidity or alkalinity – the pH balance – of the water that is chiefly important. Unlike many other types of plant, water plants do not require a medium rich in nutrients, which will encourage algal growth. Growing mediums must be of a certain texture, but if garden soil is unsuitable, it can be improved; alternatively, there are proprietary aquatic composts that can be purchased. Within the pond, planting baskets or crates are also ideal, not only restricting growth in smaller ponds, but also making it easy to lift, divide, and move plants.

PLANTING MEDIUMS

Ordinary garden topsoil may be used both in integral planting beds and in planting crates, provided that it is of good quality and suitable structure. In a well-cultivated garden the topsoil, rich in organic matter, will have a consistency that is firm yet porous; too light a soil will dissipate in the water and will not allow plants to develop a sound root system, while a very heavy soil will compact and stifle the roots.

SOIL CONTENT

Soil is generally classified according to its clay, silt, and sand content; it can be tested *(see right)* to discover what proportion of each it contains. Most garden plants enjoy a soil that is not dominated by any one constituent, contains a good proportion of humus, and has a clay content, generally, of between eight and 25 per cent. Soil for water plants ideally needs to be heavier, and clay should be added to sandy and silty soils.

SOIL NUTRIENTS

Soil taken from a garden that grows healthy plants will help most water plants off to a good start. Never add proprietary fertilizers on planting, nor take soil from a bed that has recently been dressed with fertilizers; the feed will dissolve into the water and provide nourishment for unwanted algae. Concentrated fertilizers in small ponds may also severely disrupt the water chemistry and can be toxic to fish. As soon as microscopic life develops in a new pond, a food chain is set in motion *(see pp. 136–137)* that will give plants supplementary nourishment. As plants mature, soil renewal when dividing *(see pp. 160–161)* or a supplement, in spring, of slow-release fertilizer will replenish nutrient levels. Good aquatic composts usually contain slow-release fertilizers in their mix.

ORGANIC MATTER
A layer of organic matter floats on the surface.

CLAY
Clay is the last type of soil to settle.

SAND
Sand forms the bottom layer.

SOIL COMPOSITION
Take a small quantity of soil and dry it thoroughly, so that it is crumbly and can be rubbed easily through the fingers. Half-fill a watertight container with water and add the soil. Place a lid on the jar, shake firmly, and leave for three to five days, after which time there will be three individual layers consisting of sand, clay, and organic matter. A suitable soil for water plants should have a layer of clay twice as deep as the sand.

SOIL STRUCTURE AND COMPOSITION

CROSS-SECTION THROUGH SOIL
From the surface downwards, left: topsoil contains the nutrients plants need; its composition varies (right) *according to the locality. Subsoil has little or no nutritional value, and increasingly consists of compacted stony matter, sand, or solid clay.*

SAND
Sand is dry, light, and free-draining.

SILT
Silt is reasonably moisture-retentive, but easily becomes compacted.

CLAY
This heavy soil is slow-draining.

GARDEN SOILS
The drainage of different soil compositions varies.

SOIL FOR MOISTURE-LOVING PLANTS

In planting areas around ponds and in bog gardens, the key quality of the soil is its moisture-retentiveness. With too free a drainage, water will pass through too quickly and evaporation from the soil surface is also increased. Aquatic composts are ideal, but in large beds it is more economical to improve garden soil. Again, clay should be added to light, gritty soils, and with all soils, work in a good proportion of well-rotted organic matter before planting, adding more in subsequent years. Provided that fertilizers cannot leach out into pond water and upset the water chemistry, moisture-loving plants may be given supplementary feeds.

IMPROVING SOIL STRUCTURE
Using a fork, dig in organic matter such as compost to improve the structure of the soil.

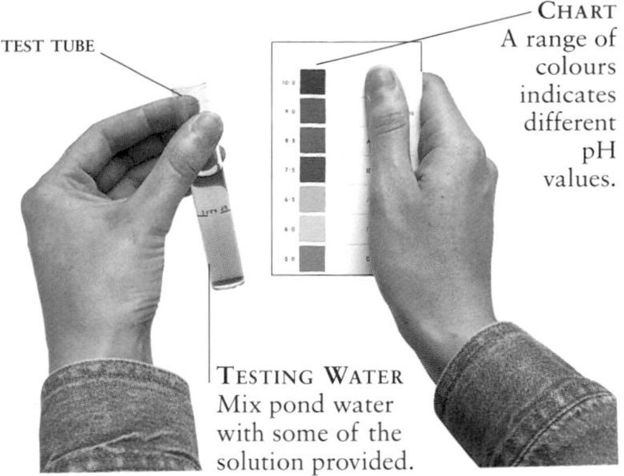

TESTING THE PH
Simple pH kits can be used to check the acidity or alkalinity of soil and, importantly for aquatic plants, pond water. Mix with some of the solution included in the kit. Then check the colour of the liquid against the chart in order to find the pH level.

TEST TUBE

CHART
A range of colours indicates different pH values.

TESTING WATER
Mix pond water with some of the solution provided.

PLANTING CONTAINERS

While the effect is never quite as natural as that of plants growing and mingling in a soil layer, growing water plants in containers has many advantages, especially in small and formal ponds. Water lilies, deep-water plants, and marginal plants can be planted in baskets to prevent them from growing too large; containerized plants rarely achieve more than half their maximum spread when growing freely. Also, plants may need lifting and dividing at different times; if growing together in soil beds, their roots will soon become entangled, making it difficult to avoid damaging them. Planting containers make it possible to deal with plants separately.

BASKETS AND CRATES

Plastic planting baskets and crates are readily available in various sizes and shapes. Aquatic centres stocking preformed rigid pool units usually have a range of crates specially tailored to fit the contours of these pools and their marginal shelves. Containers have open-lattice sides in order to allow water and gases to reach the soil. Planting baskets with wide-meshed sides will need to be lined with hessian or polypropylene, otherwise soil will fall out before the plant's roots have a chance to grow and bind it together. The piece of material used to line the basket needs to be approximately twice the size of the basket. Fine-mesh containers, however, do not require lining.

Always choose a size of basket appropriate to the size of the plant; if the basket is too small, the plant will become top-heavy and may topple over. With taller marginals it may be necessary to anchor the basket *(see p. 157)* with a brick placed in the bottom, or by adding pebbles on top of the soil. When established plants grow too large for their containers, in most average-sized ponds it is usually preferable to divide the plant *(see pp. 160–161)* and only replant the healthiest portion into the same basket, discarding the older, less vigorous parts, rather than to move the whole plant into bigger quarters.

TOP-DRESSING THE SOIL
Always top-dress the soil with pea shingle or grit in order to prevent it spilling out into the water.

OTHER CONTAINERS

Although planting crates are not expensive to buy, other containers may be improvised. Submerged plants may be grown in ordinary plastic plant pots, since they take their nourishment directly from the water; the roots merely act as an anchor. However, deep-water plants and marginals must have containers with openwork sides, in order to permit the free percolation of water and gases around their roots. The shallow type of plastic laundry basket, for example, will house a large, vigorous water lily, although it would be far too large for less invasive plants or, at first, for young lilies. Integral planting beds within ponds *(see pp. 78–79)* may also be constructed with bricks, mortared loosely to hold the structure together, yet allowing water to pass through the walls into the soil.

AQUATIC PLANTING CONTAINERS

ROUND CONTAINER

SHAPED CONTAINER

LARGE, SQUARE CONTAINER

WIDE-MESH CONTAINERS
The wider mesh-sided baskets allow the maximum level of gases to exchange through the sides between water and plant roots. They do, however, also let out soil and will require some form of permeable lining. These containers come in a range of shapes and sizes.

LARGE, ROUND CONTAINER

LINING A CONTAINER
Make sure that there is a sufficient overlap of hessian to prevent soil escaping.

HESSIAN LINING
Traditional and effective, hessian is an ideal cheap lining for wide-mesh containers, allowing gases and water through without letting the soil or aquatic compost spill out.

ROUND CONTAINER

SQUARE CONTAINER

IRREGULARLY SHAPED CONTAINER

FINE-MESH CONTAINERS
Newer plastic containers with fine-mesh sides do not need to be lined, since soil will be unable to fall through the fine holes.

Planning Planting Schemes

Deciding which plants to choose for a water garden may at first seem a little daunting; there are, however, some fundamental rules to follow, which should make choosing easier. The first priority is to provide an adequate number of functional plants in order to establish a well-balanced pond as quickly as possible. It is important to achieve the correct numbers and balance of these plants, avoiding understocking or overcrowding. Ornamental planting may be more flexible, depending to a large degree on personal taste, but it is important to consider flowering seasons to provide variety and create a long period of interest.

Essential Plants

In order to develop and maintain a healthy environment within a pond, it is vital to have some submerged plants and floating-leaved plants, whose role is to filter and oxygenate the water and, by competing successfully for sunlight and nutrients, to minimize algal growth in the water. Floating leaves will help to reduce the inevitable greening of the water with algae that occurs in high light conditions when the pool has inadequate surface cover. It occurs temporarily both in new ponds and each spring, before other plants have a chance to grow, but once they do, a balance is restored and the water clears.

To help this process, a third to half of the pond's surface should be covered by the leaves of free-floating and deep-water plants. In established ponds, water lilies are especially important, since they are among the first plants to spread their leaves in spring. However, they and other deep-water plants take time to establish. Free-floating plants are especially useful in the early establishment of a new pool, or in prolonged hot, sunny weather. *Azolla filiculoides*, for example, spreads rapidly and will provide enough cover within three months in a small pond. Its growth will soon need to be strictly controlled, however. In features with limited surface areas you may wish, once water lilies and other deep-water plants have grown, to remove the floaters in favour of the more permanent ornamental plants.

Stocking Levels for New Ponds

Pond size	Oxygenating plants	Temporary cover	Water lilies
Small 2.5m x 2m (8ft x 6ft)	15 bunches	6 free-floaters	1 water lily
Small to medium 4m x 2.5m (12ft x 8ft)	30 bunches	9 free-floaters	2 water lilies
Medium 5m x 2.75m (15ft x 9ft)	45 bunches	9–12 free-floaters	3 water lilies
Medium to large 6m x 4m (20ft x 12ft)	60 bunches	12–15 free floaters	4 water lilies
Large 10m x 5m (30ft x 15ft)	75 bunches	20–30 free-floaters	5 water lilies

Submerged plants, such as *Lagarosiphon* and *Myriophyllum*, also play an essential role. Not only do they compete with algae for nutrients, they also release oxygen into the water, enabling it to support life. In a new pond, it is vital to add enough plants *(see above)* to provide an adequate density of submerged foliage.

Other Practical Considerations

Once functional plants have been chosen, the design and surroundings of the individual feature may be considered in more detail. Certain plants, notably water lilies, do not tolerate

Plants for Initial Stocking

Oxygenating Weed
An adequate quantity of submerged plants such as Lagarosiphon major *should be added to new ponds, so that their leaves may begin to produce oxygen that will aerate the water and enable a healthy ecosystem to develop.*

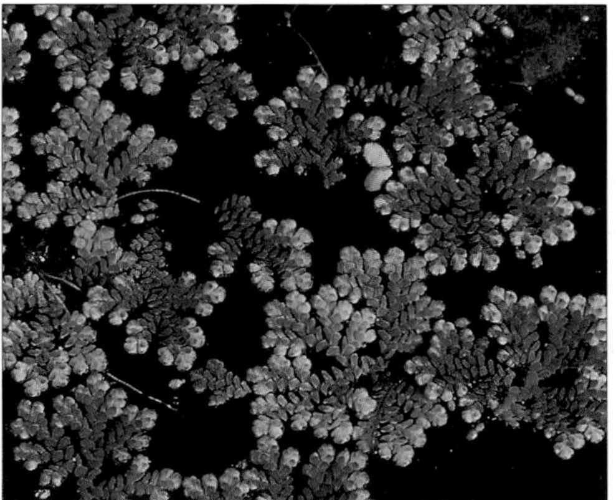

Fast-growing Floating Plants
Small free-floating plants such as Azolla filiculoides *spread rapidly, and are extremely useful for providing initial cover. By mid-summer, they will probably need thinning so that surface cover is not too dense.*

Consolidating Wet Ground
If your pond has boggy surrounds, plants with creeping, mat-forming root systems, such as Houttuynia cordata (above), Carex, *and* Persicaria *will soon grow to hold soil together and reduce surface evaporation.*

moving water, for example, so plants must be chosen with care for streams and around waterfalls. Ponds with informal soil surrounds require some plants that will root strongly and consolidate the edges. For small ponds, marsh marigolds (*Caltha palustris*) are ideal; for larger ponds, *Iris pseudacorus* or *Cyperus longus* could be used. If aiming to attract wildlife, this will also affect plant choice *(see pp. 54–55)*.

Ornamental Planting

Although you will be choosing plants for their visual contribution, you must bear in mind their suitability. The plants you choose and the way you arrange them may be restricted by the style of water feature and by climate and site.

Try to keep planting as simple as possible so that the water remains the focus of attention – planting should enhance rather than dominate the surroundings. Avoid using very vigorous plants in close proximity to less robust species, and be especially careful in small areas to choose plants that can be kept within their allotted space. Large species can be used as specimen plants, but smaller plants often look better grouped in twos and threes.

Colour Schemes

Some gardeners enjoy bright colours, others prefer subdued shades – it is entirely a matter of taste. Colour schemes can continue a theme throughout the season *(below)*, or become progressively richer: yellow *Ranunculus* and white callas and bogbean (*Menyanthes trifoliata*) will give a fresh look in spring, brightening dull brown surrounds, while in summer, vivid blue *Pontederia cordata* and rich, red *Lobelia cardinalis* stand out against a lush, leafy background. Plants with attractive foliage are particularly well complemented by water. Grasses, sedges, and ferns can be used to create both formal and informal looks.

Planting for Style

Formal Pool
To enhance the clear, symmetrical shapes of a formal water feature, a restrained planting scheme is especially important.

Informal Pond
This water garden makes generous use of plants; bear in mind, however, that plants grow rapidly and may congest the feature.

Planting for Colour

Bold Colours
Dark water and the lush greens of vigorously growing moisture-lovers are perfect backgrounds against which to use rich, bold colour.

Pastel Scheme
This low-key planting plan utilizes limited space by using white flowers, silvery foliage, and pale pebbles to light up a dull corner.

Flower Colour Through the Season

	Early spring	Late spring to early summer	Mid-summer to early autumn
White to cream	*Caltha palustris* var. *alba* *Leucojum aestivum* *Petasites japonicus* *Primula denticulata* var. *alba*	*Aponogeton distachyos* *Calla palustris* *Menyanthes trifoliata* *Ranunculus aquatilis*	*Aponogeton distachyos* *Filipendula ulmaria* 'Aurea' *Miscanthus sinensis* 'Zebrinus' *Sagittaria sagittifolia*
Yellow to orange	*Caltha palustris* 'Flore Pleno' *Lysichiton americanum* ♀ *Primula veris* ♀ *Ranunculus ficaria*	*Iris pseudacorus* *Narthecium ossifragum* *Nymphaea* 'Odorata Sulphurea Grandiflora'	*Inula hookeri* *Ligularia* 'Gregynog Gold' ♀ *Lysimachia nummularia* 'Aurea' ♀ *Myriophyllum verticillatum*
Pink to red	*Anagallis tenella* 'Studland' ♀ *Darmera peltata* ♀ *Nymphaea* 'Laydekeri Fulgens' *Primula rosea* ♀	*Alisma plantago-aquatica* *Nelumbo nucifera* 'Momo Botan' *Nymphaea* 'James Brydon' ♀ *Nymphaea* 'Marliacea Carnea'	*Astilbe* 'Venus' *Butomus umbellatus* ♀ *Filipendula purpurea* ♀ *Lythrum salicaria*
Purple to blue	*Myosotis scorpioides* *Primula denticulata* ♀ *Trillium erectum* ♀	*Iris versicolor* *Hosta fortunei* *Nymphaea* 'Blue Beauty' *Nymphaea capensis*	*Lobelia* x *gerardii* 'Vedrariensis' *Phragmites australis* 'Variegatus' *Pontederia cordata* ♀ *Veronica beccabunga*

Year-round Interest

Foliage plants can provide a changing, colourful display year-round. Most aquatic plants are herbaceous, but evergreen marginal plants include *Thalia, Acorus gramineus, Equisetum*, and *Carex*. Among the irises and grasses in particular there are many attractive variegated forms, and for autumn colour, *Darmera peltata* and *Lobelia cardinalis* provide a boost once the main flowering season is over. Texture can be varied too, from feathery astilbes and sword-like irises and reeds to magnificently broad-leaved gunneras and rheums. The seedheads of many plants are also decorative.

BUYING PLANTS

MOST AQUATIC NURSERIES have a good selection of water plants, although at certain times of the year the choice may be more limited. Any general garden centre should have a range of moisture-lovers among its stock. Examine plants carefully before making a choice; good suppliers will have plants on display that are clean, plump, and dense. Aquatic plants will either be bare-rooted or container-grown; they will be packed in plastic bags to make transportation easier. It is advisable to place the plants in another bag to avoid the possibility of leakage. Do not delay your journey home, and make sure that the plants remain moist.

CHOOSING YOUNG PLANTS

Mid-spring is the best time of year for purchasing plants, when the increasing day-length and warmer water will make it easier for them to re-establish in their new environment; there should also be little likelihood of frost. It is possible to plant through until late summer, but plants bought later in the year that have made more growth should be cut back before planting; they will not be at their best until the next season.

SELECTING DEEP-WATER PLANTS

Most deep-water plants survive winter by storing food reserves in large rhizomes or tubers; the young shoots grow to the surface in spring, and only when the leaves have unfurled can they manufacture food from sunlight again. For this reason it is essential to choose plants with a sound, fat tuber or rhizome that will nourish this early stage of growth.

Young deep-water plants are often sold bare-rooted, having been freshly divided from a parent plant. Buying containerized plants avoids root disturbance, although water plants generally suffer less transplant setback than other garden plants.

PLANTS ON DISPLAY *Aquatic nurseries should have a range of water plants on display, which will be grouped according to their requirements. This makes it possible to examine the plants thoroughly before making a purchase. It is best to visit aquatic nurseries during spring to mid-summer, when there will be a far greater variety of water plants to choose from.*

SELECTING HEALTHY PLANTS

FREE-FLOATING PLANTS

Stratiotes aloides *(water soldier) is a semi-evergreen perennial that resembles a pineapple top, with short, stubby roots. The rosette of dark olive-green leaves should be well formed and dense. A well-grown plant will produce creamy white flowers in mid-summer.*

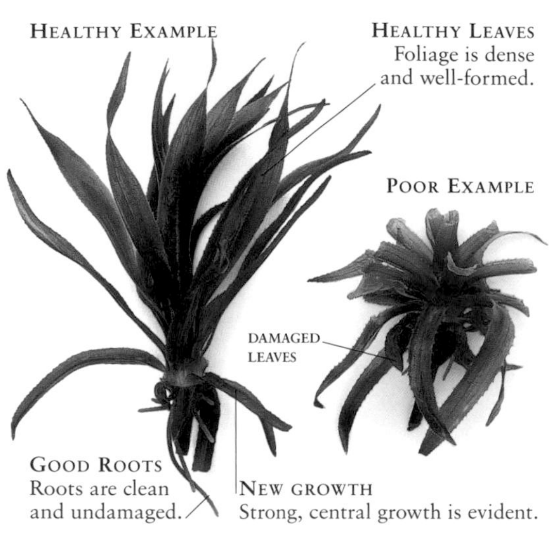

DEEP-WATER PLANTS

Healthy young water lilies will soon put on a fine display. Many water lilies increase by producing small plants that bud off from the main tuber (see above)*; these can immediately be used to increase stock* (see pp. 162–163).

CONTAINERIZED MARGINAL

Caltha palustris *(marsh marigold) is particularly useful for wildlife ponds, as it attracts insects early in the year. A healthy plant will be compact, with shiny, dark green foliage. The single, golden yellow flowers appear in spring.*

One reason for buying containerized plants is to obtain large specimens to create an "instant" effect, but these plants are expensive, heavy, and difficult to transport without damage. Given the right conditions, healthy young plants will soon make plenty of growth. Look for plants with several young folded leaves thrusting from the base – older leaves will probably die shortly after planting.

Selecting Oxygenators

Most aquatic nurseries or retailers will stock up to six different species of oxygenator; from autumn to early spring the choice may be limited to one or two that remain evergreen in the winter, such as *Lagarosiphon major*. Unless you have very strong preferences, buy as many different types as possible: all water conditions are different, and suit different plants. Excess plants can easily be thinned. Oxygenating plants are sold as cuttings, in bunches of six to nine stems held together with a small lead clasp near the base. The stems should be 15–30cm (6–12in) in length, have closely spaced leaves, and look plump and vigorous. Examine bunches carefully: if dirty, weak, or containing blanketweed (tiny, bright green strands that clump together like wet cottonwool) or jelly-like snail eggs, do not purchase them.

Rinsing New Plants
Rinse plants in water to wash out and inspect any insects, so that you do not introduce harmful ones into the pond.

Selecting Floating Plants

Floating plants are generally sold from tanks: the tiny plants such as duckweed *(Lemna)* and fairy moss *(Azolla)* are scooped out and packed in watertight plastic bags, with a small amount of water to keep them moist. Larger floaters like water hyacinth *(Eichhornia)* and water soldier *(Stratiotes aloides)* are sold individually and packed in plastic bags. Shops and outlets that do not have the facilities to keep plants in water tanks may stock vacuum-packed plants in airtight packs: these plants have a limited shelf life, so inspect them carefully before purchase.

Keeping Plants Moist
If you cannot plant immediately, keep oxgenating and free-floating plants in a bucket of water (change this daily if the delay is prolonged) and stand young containerized plants in water. Bare-rooted plants may be wrapped in wet newspaper, but should be planted on the same day.

Selecting Marginals and Moisture-lovers

Displays of bog and moisture-loving plants in aquatic or garden centres often look tired towards the end of the summer; late spring is a better time to buy. Use the same criteria to select specimens as you would any garden plant, choosing healthy, compact young specimens with plenty of fresh new growth thrusting up from the base; these will quickly become established in their new quarters. Marginal plants especially may grow away at a phenomenal rate; match the vigour of plants to your site, and do not buy too many plants at first.

Pre-planting Care

If planting is delayed, plants must be kept continually moist. Keep marginal and moisture-loving plants in a tray filled with 5cm (2in) of water; oxygenators and deep-water plants should be submerged in, ideally, pond- or rainwater. Plants can survive in this state for two to three weeks, after which time their condition will begin to deteriorate. Before planting, trim plants with a sharp knife to remove any damaged roots, stems, or foliage: water lilies in particular benefit from a little preparation *(see below)* before planting.

Preparing a Water Lily for Planting

1 Using secateurs or a sharp knife, cut back to within about 5cm (2in) of the tuber any roots that are either damaged or excessively long.

Old Roots
Trim back long, coarse roots.

New Shoots
Young shoots with furled leaves grow from the tuber.

2 Cut off any leaves that have unfurled close to the base, being careful not to damage any new growth. Retain all of the young, tightly rolled leaves that are still growing; they will soon reach the water surface.

Young Growth
Retain tightly rolled leaves, which are still growing.

Older Growth
Remove any unfurled leaves.

PLANTING TECHNIQUES

WATER PLANTS MAY be planted in aquatic containers, in purpose-built deep-water beds, or directly into soil on the bottom of a pond or on marginal shelves; some, such as free-floating plants and some oxygenators, are simply placed on the surface of the water. Containers are particularly useful for restricting plants with vigorous growth. Remember, however, that many plants will rapidly outgrow their containers, especially some of the more vigorous marginals, and will need attention. The condition of the water will influence the health of aquatic plants; check the water quality *(see p. 151)* before introducing them.

PREPARING THE POND

Fill the pond at least three days before planting to allow the water temperature to reach that of the surrounding atmosphere. Aquatic plants absorb nourishment through their top growth as well as their roots, so the condition of the water is important *(see pp. 136–137)*. Do not hose water directly onto a soil-bottomed pond or a marginal soil bed – this may disrupt the soil. Cover the soil with a sheet of polythene, and rest the end of the hose upon it. The action of the water spreading out over the sheet will help keep the soil in place. As the pond fills, the polythene should float up and can be retrieved.

PLANTING UNDER WATER

When planting in submerged soil layers and beds, there is usually nothing for it but to work standing in the pond. In fact, when planting marginal beds, standing in the deep zone usually enables you to work at a more comfortable height. Provided that the soil is of a suitable consistency *(see p. 150)* you should be able to firm it down adequately.

PLANTING IN CONTAINERS

Most water gardeners find planting baskets and crates more manageable for deep-water plants than a layer of bottom soil, except in very large informal ponds. Marginals also grow well in containers, which can be positioned in groups to give a more natural, mingled effect. An added advantage is that the plants can be moved around until the desired effect is achieved. Deep-water plants are best spaced evenly around the base of the pond to prevent stems growing through each other and tangling.

Plants may already be in containers when bought, but these can be rather small, since display space is often limited. It is worth potting them up to allow their roots to develop well. Any aquatic plant sold in an ordinary pot must be transferred into one with openwork sides. Choose a basket appropriate to the size of the plant (as a guide, a vigorous water lily needs a crate

POND ACCESS
In order to introduce planting baskets into the pond, it may be necessary to wade in and place the basket by hand. Thigh or, better still, chest waders will allow you to move in the pond freely. Try to move as gently as possible – any vigorous movement may stir up mud and distress fish.

PLANTING OXYGENATORS

PLANTING METHODS
Oxygenators can be planted directly into the soil beds of large, natural ponds; they will be able to root freely and their spread will be unrestricted. In smaller ponds, it is better to containerize the plants (right) *so that their growth can be controlled.*

LEAD CLASP
The weight of the lead pulls the oxygenator down to the bottom of the pond, where it can root.

1 LINE A PLANTING container with hessian and fill with damp compost. Firm down lightly. Make evenly-spaced holes 5cm (2in) deep and insert bunches of cuttings (here *Lagarosiphon major*).

2 FIRM IN THE PLANT with your fingers and trim off any excess hessian. Top-dress the plants with a 1cm (½in) layer of pea shingle to keep the soil in place. Lower the basket gently into the pond.

that is 40cm/16in across and 20cm/8in deep). If you need to add ballast to a container in order to keep large marginals stable *(see below)*, then choose a larger container to accommodate the extra material. Line the baskets if necessary *(see p. 151)*, fill with well-dampened soil or aquatic compost *(see pp. 150–151)*, firm lightly and make planting holes. Container-grown plants should be planted at the same depth as when in their original containers; most bare-rooted plants are tuberous or rhizomatous, and these need to be positioned fairly near the soil surface *(see right)*. Firm them in well, and add a layer of shingle that is approximately 1cm (½in) thick to prevent soil from drifting away. This layer of shingle is particularly necessary in ponds containing koi carp and other bottom-feeders, which can uproot plants as they nose around for food.

Either position containers by hand or, if you have a helper, thread two lengths of string through opposite sides of the basket. Holding the ends, you and your partner can stand facing each other across the pond and lower the plant into position. Depending on the depth of your pond, young deep-water plants may need a temporary plinth of bricks *(see right)*, or an inverted basket, to allow the new shoots to reach the surface quickly.

Oxygenating and Free-floating Plants

In ponds with a layer of bottom soil, bunches of oxygenators can simply be dropped in the water. The lead clasp around the bunches will pull them down to the bottom, where they will root. Oxygenators may also be planted in containers. A 30cm (12in) crate will accommodate several bunches. If several species of oxygenators are planted, keep each one to a separate crate.

For free-floating plants, such as *Azolla filiculoides* and *Stratiotes aloides*, simply float the plants from your hand on the surface of the water.

Planting in Surrounding Soil and in Bog Gardens

Planting in permanently moist soil is no different to planting in any bed or border. Planting crates are not necessary; plant directly into the soil. Do not add fertilizers or handfuls of rotted or concentrated manures where they may leach into water, and be careful not to compact the wet ground when working. Remember that, in permanently moist soil, plants will grow very vigorously: give them plenty of room, especially giants such as *Gunnera manicata* and *Rheum*, which will develop extensive root systems.

Planting Bare-rooted Deep-water Plants

1 Line the basket if needed and fill three-quarters full with dampened soil. After trimming, if necessary *(see p. 155)*, position the tuber or rhizome so that it is within 4cm (1½in) of the rim.

2 Add more soil and use your fingers to firm the soil, being very careful not to damage new shoots. Top-dress with pea shingle to prevent soil floating off the container once under water.

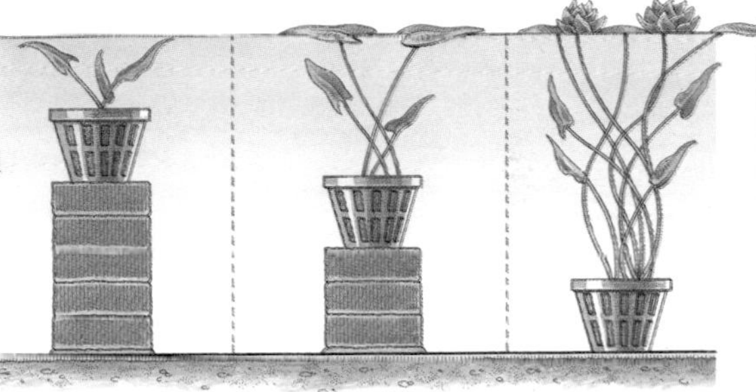

3 Place the container on a pier of bricks, so that it is initially supported close to the water surface. As new leaves appear, remove bricks gradually until the plant sits on the bottom of the pond.

Planting in Moist and Wet Soil

1 Dig a hole in the soil bed large enough to accommodate the root ball of the plant. Support the plant (here *Caltha palustris*) with one hand, and gently ease the root ball out of the container.

2 Place the plant in the hole at the same depth as it was in the container. Using your hands, thoroughly firm the soil all around the crown of the plant. Soak the entire area with water.

Stabilizing Plant Containers

Using a Brick
If a planting basket is to be used to house a tall, top-heavy marginal, place a brick or half-brick in the bottom of the container before introducing soil. This will anchor the basket so that it is unlikely to tip over.

Using Pebbles
Pebbles placed on top of the soil in the planting basket are even better than bricks for weighting down plants. This method does not use up soil space and provides a decorative finish.

ROUTINE PLANT CARE

IN ORDER TO ENSURE healthy and vigorous growth, plants must be well cared for. Routine maintenance includes many tasks common to all garden plants, although the techniques used may be modified. In this special environment, it is very important to remove any dying plant material, or it will decompose and cloud the water, affecting other life. Regular pond care *(see pp. 140–141)* will also help maintain clear, well-oxygenated water, essential to successful growth. If you have to enter the water to work, try to accomplish several tasks in one go: repeated excursions into the water, however careful your movements, will disrupt it and its inhabitants.

WATER PLANTS THROUGH THE YEAR

Spring is the busiest time of the year for the water gardener, with many key tasks to be performed. If attended to now, plants are more likely to be vigorous and trouble-free during summer, when they can be enjoyed at leisure. Remember that algae are among the first "plants" to grow, and pond water will temporarily be green and cloudy each spring until the pond's ecosystem adjusts itself to the start of a new growing season.

CUTTING BACK AND THINNING

Most plants used in and around water are herbaceous, and in cold climates, where old foliage has been left to shelter the crown of the plant over winter, spring is the time to cut all dead and dying leaves and stems back, together with remaining seedheads of grasses and similar plants. Be sure not to damage the growing points of new, emerging shoots.

Spring is also a good time to thin or divide many plants *(see pp. 160–161)* if they have begun to outgrow their allotted space. Oxygenating pondweed may be thinned at any time if it begins to choke the pond. Free-floating plants sink to the bottom of the pond during the winter, reappearing in spring. Divide clump-forming plants such as *Stratiotes aloides* when they return to the surface. Most floaters grow rapidly, and may need thinning again by summer. Water lilies and deep-water plants will need to be divided every three to four years – this will be evident the preceding summer when leaves become congested, with far fewer flowers appearing. Marginal plants will require more regular division, perhaps every other year, or they will outgrow containers and crowd the limited space on the edge of the pond. Similarly, moisture-loving plants will need to be divided quite frequently; if not, they will weaken and produce fewer flowers.

WORKING IN WET SOIL
Fork over footprints made in damp soil to prevent compaction, being careful to avoid plant roots. In very wet conditions, work as much as possible from a wooden board laid over the soil, in order to distribute body weight evenly.

CUTTING BACK GRASSES
Grasses and sedges will benefit from annual pruning in spring: cut the whole plant close to the base, and remove any debris to let light and air into the centre of the plant. Many species have sharp leaves, so wear thick gloves.

INTRODUCING PLANTS

Mid-spring, as growth begins and any danger of late frost is past, is an ideal time to introduce new plants to the pond *(see pp. 156–157)* and to the surrounding soil, so that they are able to benefit from the full growing season. Also, reintroduce any plants that have been protected from frost during winter *(see overleaf)*. When planting moisture-loving and marginal plants, it may be necessary to stand on the soil. Be sure to fork over any footprints afterwards; this will prevent the earth from compacting, thereby making it more accessible to growing roots.

FEEDING

Established water plants will benefit from the addition of slow-release fertilizers in spring; water lilies in particular need large amounts of nutrients in order to thrive. Most garden centres and all aquatic specialists will stock suitable slow-release fertilizers. These are generally sold in sachet form: a tape covering the perforated area is removed, and the sachet pushed well into the soil, to prevent its contents leaking into the water. The feed is released only at the rate that the plant can absorb it; little surplus enters the water to nourish the growth of algae.

Removing Unwanted Growth

Cutting off Decaying Leaves
Hold the plant firmly and use a sharp knife to remove any yellowing or dead leaves, until you reach healthy, green stems. If yellowing is excessive, lift the plant to see if it is diseased in any way (see pp. 164–165).

Duckweed and Surplus Floaters
Hold a plank vertically and draw it across the surface of the water to skim off duckweed, which is often naturally introduced into the pond by birds or on new plants. Dispose of the weed carefully, as it spreads easily.

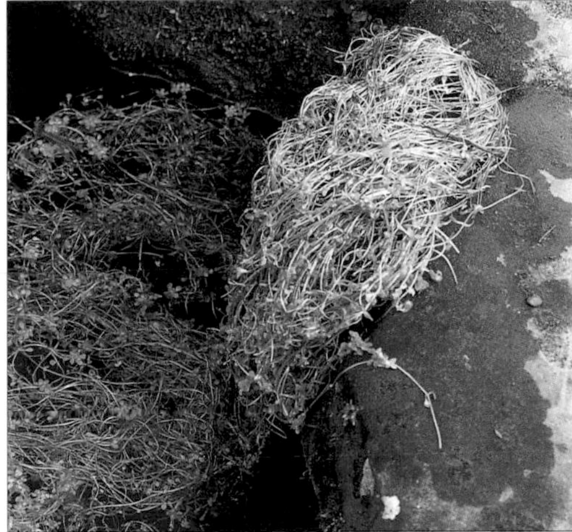

Protecting Pond Life
When thinning pond weed, drape it for a while on an edge or rock to allow small creatures to crawl or fall back into the water before disposal. In modest quantities, it can usefully be added to compost heaps.

Summer Tasks

Lushly-growing plants may renew their leaves frequently, and it is important to pick off, or trim with a sharp knife at the stem base, regularly those that are yellowing and dying. Deadhead all flowering water plants: in some, this encourages further flowers while in others it removes potential decaying material.

If you wish to collect seed for propagation *(see pp. 162–163)* remember that seeds of aquatic plants need to be sown when freshly gathered, so it is important to collect the seed when there is still sufficient warmth for germination to occur, preferably in mid- to late summer. In moist soil around the pond, do not deadhead plants with decorative seedheads, unless self-seeding plants are problematic. Weed regularly, watch water levels for any fall in long dry spells, and ensure that pond weed does not grow to smother the crowns of containerized marginals. Examine plants for signs of pests and diseases *(see pp. 164–165)*; they are susceptible to infections in summer, encouraged by the warm, humid conditions, and recognizing symptoms at an early stage is necessary for effective control.

Autumn Netting
In autumn, lay fine-mesh plastic netting over the pond, securing the edges with bricks or pegs. This will prevent leaves that are shed by the plants surrounding the pond entering the pond and decomposing. Every week or so, remove the netting and dispose of the leaves, then replace securely.

Preparing for Winter

As the growing season ends, collect any young plantlets, plant material, or winter buds *(see pp. 160–163)* intended for propagation purposes that need shelter during winter. Store in moist soil in frost-free conditions.

Half-hardy and tender aquatics will also need to be lifted from the pond in the autumn. Remove any dying foliage and insert the plants in containers filled with moist soil or sand, which will prevent them from rotting when daylight intensity is low. Place them under glass in a frost-free place until the following spring.

Once winter sets in, take any precautions necessary to protect the pond and its plants from severe cold weather *(see pp. 138–139)* and freezing over, such as erecting a temporary partial shelter. A thick mulch of clean straw around bog-garden and moisture-loving plants will help to protect their roots.

Tender Plants
Overwinter tender plants in a container filled with damp sand. Do not close the lid, but cover with a polythene bag with a few holes in it to allow air to enter.

DIVISION AND PROPAGATION

HOWEVER CAUTIOUS INITIAL stocking may be, it is likely that, with the vigorous growth stimulated by water, plants will outgrow their sites. In a container or small pool this can happen in a single season; in a large informal pond it can take years. The same methods used to control plant size by discarding the older, less productive growth in favour of young growth may also be used to gain a modest increase in stocks, and these are among the easiest methods of propagation. Other methods of propagating water garden plants *(see pp. 162–163)* include taking root or stem cuttings or, provided that the plant breeds true, growing from seed.

THINNING AND DIVIDING PLANTS

Many of the plants used in and around water features spread and multiply readily by vegetative means, producing new plantlets either from the rootstock or on runnering stems. Sometimes these detach naturally from the parent plant, often sinking to the bottom to remain dormant over winter, then growing the next spring (these may be known as "winter buds"). Sometimes they must be physically separated. Clump-forming plants that have a mass of roots may also be physically divided; provided that each has a portion of root and one or more shoots, small parts of the plant will grow independently of the parent. Whether these methods are used to control size, or to produce several new plants, depends entirely on how much space is available, but in all cases it is the older plant or portion of the plant that should be discarded, and the new growth retained.

Thinning and division should take place when plants are in active growth, ideally in spring so that any cut surfaces will heal quickly. Some moisture-lovers may also be divided in late summer or autumn *(see pp. 196–207)*. Dividing water plants in the dormant season is not recommended, as low water temperatures may cause the newly divided plants to rot.

THINNING OXYGENATORS AND SMALL FLOATERS

1 IN SPRING OR AUTUMN, thin out overgrown pond weed and small floaters by "combing" the water with a rake. For containerized plants, lift out the basket and trim some stems off with a sharp knife.

2 BE SURE TO leave enough of the plants to fulfil their functional roles. If possible, thin little and often. Drape surplus plants on the side temporarily *(see p. 159)* to allow any inhabitants to escape.

SEPARATING RUNNERS AND PLANTLETS

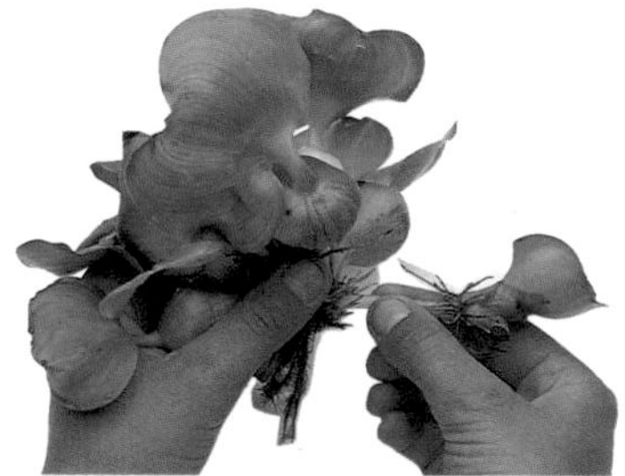

1 IN SPRING, remove young, vigorous plantlets from the parent, either snapping them off carefully from the perimeter of the parent, or severing the connecting stem on each side of the plantlet.

2 PLACE THE PLANTLET directly on the water surface, supporting it gently with your hand until it floats upright. Air sacs in the spongy leaf bases of *Eichhornia crassipes* keep it buoyant. Its roots will soon develop.

DIVIDING WATER LILIES

OVERGROWN PLANT
A water lily in need of thinning has crowded leaves that thrust out of, rather than float on, the water, and few flowers; its roots have exhausted the soil nutrients, so it produces more leaves and stems, which in aquatic plants can absorb food from the water.

CONGESTED CROWN
The growth of young stems and leaves to the surface is impeded by crowded, older foliage.

1 CAREFULLY LIFT THE plant and rinse off the soil. Remove all opened leaves, and cut the rhizome in two, retaining the part with the most vigorous young, emerging shoots. If desired, remove any suitable bud cuttings *(see p. 162)* for propagation.

2 TRIM LONG, COARSE roots, replant with the crown just below soil level, and reposition the water lily in the pond just as for a new young plant *(see pp. 156–157)*. Discard the old portion of the rhizome.

Dividing Rhizomatous Plants

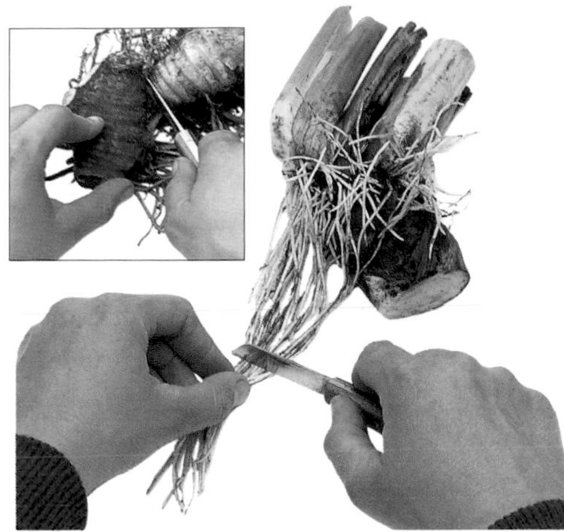

1 Lift the plant (here, *Iris pseudacorus*) and rinse soil off the roots. Large masses of fleshy rhizomes can be split apart with your hands; otherwise, use a knife to separate vigorous portions of the rhizome, each with a number of fibrous roots, strong young leaves, and shoots.

2 Use a sharp garden knife to trim the rhizome neatly, removing any isolated portions that do not show any new shoot growth *(inset)*. Trim all of the top growth back to 6–9cm (3–4in), and cut back long roots so that they can comfortably be accommodated in the crate.

3 Replant carefully, filling in fresh soil or compost around the rhizome, rather than pressing it into a hole, so that the roots are not compressed. Top-dress with shingle and reposition in the pond, on bricks if necessary to raise the trimmed top growth just above water.

Oxygenators and Free-floaters

Oxygenating pond weeds are extremely easy to thin. Surplus stems can either be pulled out by hand or raked out *(see facing page)*. These plants are extremely resilient, and will regrow no matter how roughly they are treated. For containerized oxygenators, lift the container out of the pond, and remove old growth with a sharp knife. The smaller free-floating plants can also be raked off, or hosed to the edge of the pond and scooped out. The larger, more succulent floaters such as *Pistia* and *Stratiotes* are worth handling with more care, separating and refloating only as many young plantlets as are required.

Tuberous and Rhizomatous Plants

Plants such as water lilies and most irises have tuberous or rhizomatous roots: that is, shoots grow up and fibrous roots grow down from a swollen, fleshy storage organ just below the soil surface. These organs grow and branch, developing new growing points at their tips from which fresh shoots emerge. As the new leaves grow to maturity, energy is stored in the new portion of the rhizome or tuber, until it is capable of surviving independently of the parent root system. The plant may be divided *(see above and facing page, below)*, and either the best new portion or, to increase stocks, two or three young plants replanted in either the water or pond surrounds straight away.

Fibrous-Rooted Plants

The majority of moisture-loving plants form thick clumps that expand in rich, moist soil to form a circular mass of fibrous roots. The older roots inside the clump become progressively less productive, and flowers appear only on the young growth around the edges. The whole clump may be lifted and divided into sections. Grasses and sedges often have quite shallow root masses that can be pulled apart by hand *(right, above)*; other herbaceous plants form dense, bulky rootballs *(right)* that must be separated with a garden fork or with a knife.

Dividing Clump-forming Plants

Dividing Grasses

Cut down taller grasses to 15–20cm (6–8in), then lift the clump with a mass of soil adhering to the rootball. Pull away sections with a root ball of about a handful in size from the edge of the clump, where growth is youngest and most vigorous. Discard the older, tired central portion, and replant the new portions.

New Growth
Take a handful of the root mass, not the top growth, and pull away firmly.

Dividing Dense Clumps of Tough Roots

Plants such as hostas develop into substantial clumps (left) *that may be too tough to divide by hand. Use a garden spade (or lever with two forks back to back), or cut through the mass with a sharp knife. With the rootball in pieces of a more manageable size, carefully separate small sections* (right) *with a good root system and several plump buds or shoots, and replant.*

Other Methods of Propagation

THE CONVENIENCE OF PROPAGATION by division *(see pp. 160–161)* is that the young plants obtained can immediately be planted out in situ. Propagation by other means, such as by taking root or stem cuttings, or from seed, tends to produce very young plants that, with a few exceptions, will not be viable if planted out or placed straight into the pond. They must be looked after in a separate environment, usually under glass, until they have grown sufficiently to survive. If you have the facilities to care for these young plants, however, the techniques involved are not difficult, and can produce a great many new plants, if desired.

Winter Buds

Some water plants, such as frogbit (Hydrocharis morsus-ranae), *produce swollen buds on their roots that naturally detach at the end of the growing season, over-wintering at the bottom of the pool and developing into plants in spring; some float to the surface and grow roots downwards, while some root into bottom mud and send shoots upwards.*

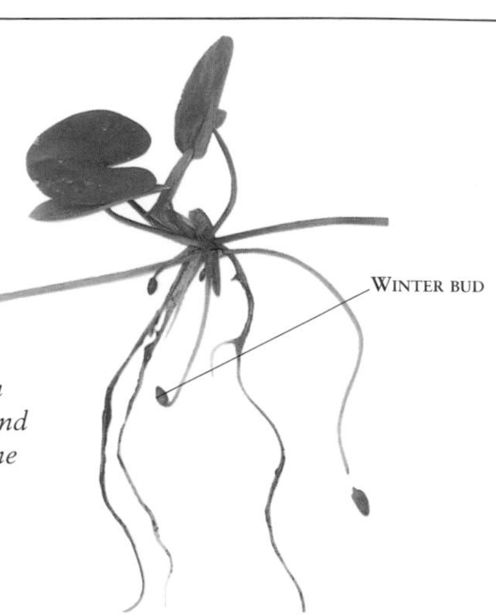

Root-bud Cuttings

When tuberous or rhizomatous plants are lifted, or bought bare-rooted, in spring, there may be tiny new growing points visible on the rootstock where shoots are only just emerging. While a section of the rootstock with only this growing point is unlikely to survive if planted out, it can be potted up and grown on. On rhizomes, cut off a 7–10cm (3–4in) portion of the rootstock behind the growing point. On tuberous water lilies, and at the base of plants such as *Butomus umbellatus*, the new growth may be emerging from a protruding nodule, or root bud; the entire bud should be pared out or snapped off.

Root buds and cuttings should be planted, either individually in small pots or in seed trays, in sifted soil or aquatic compost, with the growing tip just visible. The pots are then placed in a greenhouse in a shallow tray, with enough water in it to cover the soil. As the shoots grow, they will need to be potted on, and the water level raised accordingly. The young plants should be kept in cool but frost-free conditions over winter, and may be introduced to the pond as growth begins the following spring.

On some plants, such as *Hydrocharis morsus-ranae* and *Hottonia palustris*, nodule-like root buds *(see above right)* detach naturally and sink to the bottom of the pond where they remain dormant over winter (they are known as "winter buds", "water buds", or sometimes "turions"). Although they will naturally start into growth in spring, they may also be collected, potted up and grown on just as for root buds and cuttings.

Propagation by Root-bud Cuttings

1 CUT OUT THE swollen bud with its growing point from the rootstock. It may be necessary to cut through neighbouring leaf stalks to obtain all of the bud. Use a sharp knife; fungal infections are less likely to enter clean cuts. Rinse the bud thoroughly.

2 FILL A 10CM (4IN) basket with aquatic compost or sifted top-soil. Firm the bud into a hollow so that it sits securely on, rather than in, the compost. Top-dress with pea shingle to hold the bud in place.

3 IMMERSE THE POT in water that just covers the shingle. Keep the plant under glass and repot as it grows. Gradually immerse in deeper water, keeping the shoot tips above water. Plant out the next spring.

Taking Soft Stem Cuttings

1 WITH A SHARP KNIFE, detach a non-flowering shoot about 10cm (6in) long from the parent plant (here *Veronica beccabunga*). Carefully remove the lower leaves and any low sideshoots.

SHARP CUT
A clean cut decreases the likelihood of fungal growth.

2 WITH THE LOWER portion of the stem clear of leaves and sideshoots, cut the stem squarely across with a sharp knife to just below a node, or swollen area, where a leaf was removed.

ROOTING POWDER
Hormonal agent encourages roots to grow.

3 DIP THE PREPARED cutting into hormone rooting powder, which will encourage roots to grow from the nodal area. The cut surface will be sufficiently moist to allow enough powder to stick.

4 TAKE A FINE-MESH container, approximately 10cm (4in) square, and fill it with aquatic compost. Insert the cutting into the container, firm it in, and keep under glass until rooted.

Stem Cuttings

If oxygenating plants are looking ragged after winter or on emptying and cleaning a pond, or if more plants are required, new plants can easily be obtained from cuttings. These do not need to be rooted before being introduced into the water. Simply cut or pinch off healthy young shoots, 10–15cm (4–6in) long, and tie them in bunches of six to eight with florist's or garden wire. As with purchased oxygenators *(see p. 155)*, either weight the bunches and throw them into the water, or plant several bunches in a crate and immerse it.

Many marginal and moisture-loving plants may also be propagated from individual soft stem cuttings *(see facing page, below)*. These cuttings should be rooted under glass, with the soil kept either moist or wet, depending on the plant's needs. Cuttings from creeping bog plants such as *Veronica beccabunga*, *Ludwigia palustris*, and *Mentha aquatica* take particularly easily, and should have rooted after two to three weeks.

Propagation by Seed

Most moisture-lovers and some deep-water plants, including *Aponogeton distachyos*, *Orontium aquaticum*, and some lotus and tropical water lilies, may be grown from seed *(see right)*. Plants will take some time to develop and flower, so as a method of propagation it is recommended only for the patient gardener, or where lots of plants are required. Seed of most aquatic plants must be collected when ripe, in summer or autumn, and if not sown immediately, should be stored in phials of water. The seedlings must be grown in moist or permanently wet soil depending on the plant's natural growing environment.

Seeds of cultivars may not grow true to type; variation in offspring is likely unless precautions have been taken (difficult in open environments) to prevent cross-pollination. However, many species, particularly of native plants, grow well from seed. Marginals such as the water plantain *(Alisma plantago-aquatica)* are prolific seed producers, whose seed often floats for some distance to achieve effective spread.

Propagation by Sowing Seed

1 **Fill a standard** seed tray with aquatic compost or sifted garden loam, and water and compress it. Use a piece of folded paper to distribute the seeds evenly on the surface of the compost.

2 **Sieve a layer** of fine sand or compost over the seed. This will help to retain moisture around the seed coat. For aquatic plants, stand the seed tray in a deep tray of water, keeping it topped up to just below soil level. Keep seed of moisture-lovers well watered.

3 **Place the tray** in full light in a greenhouse until the seeds have germinated. When seedlings have two or three leaves, prick them out into individual modules. Pot on again when a good root system has developed. Keep young aquatic plants immersed in water as they grow. Overwinter in frost-free conditions and plant out the following spring.

Plant Care Through the Year

Spring	Summer	Autumn	Winter
• Trim off all dead and frost-damaged foliage from perennial plants. • If uprooting winter casualties, check first that there is no new growth at the base of the plant. If not, remove, and work compost into the soil before replanting. • Once the danger of frost has passed, introduce new plants, and reintroduce plants that were removed for protection over winter. • Divide crowded or overgrown plants as necessary *(see pp. 160–161)*. • Feed aquatic plants, especially water lilies, with slow-release fertilizer. Ordinary garden feeds may be applied only where they will not leach out into water. • Once all planting, replanting, and feeding has been done, mulch boggy areas of soil to conserve soil moisture. • Remember that a temporary "greening" of the water is natural in spring; do not take action unless it persists.	• Deadhead flowering plants where decorative seedheads are not desired. • Where plants are in containers, move them around if large plants grow to dominate smaller specimens. • Remove any dying or disease-affected foliage *(see p. 159)*. Congested foliage may be lightly thinned. • Make a note of plants that are becoming overgrown and congested, so that they may be thinned in autumn or the following spring. • Note gaps in the planting scheme where new plants could be accommodated when dividing crowded plants. • Check plants for symptoms of pests and diseases, and treat as necessary *(see pp. 164–165)*. • If algal growth is a problem, consider whether there are enough oxygenating and floating-leaved plants in the pond; it is not too late to introduce more.	• Collect and either plant or store any material for propagation, such as ripe seed or winter buds. • Check plants for symptoms of pests and diseases, and treat as necessary *(see pp.164–165)*. • If you have a greenhouse, take cuttings of tender and borderline hardy perennials, in case the parent plants do not survive the winter. • Remove frost-tender plants for overwintering *(see p. 159)*. Wash, dry, and store any containers from which plants have been removed. • In exposed areas, cut back tall grasses, reeds, and other plants, reducing their height by about half, to prevent wind rock and damage. • Protect moisture-loving plants against coming frosts with a mulch of straw.	• As severe weather sets in, take measures *(see p. 139)* to protect plants. • In prolonged freezing weather, containerized marginal plants and those in raised pools may be brought inside. Place them in a tray of water and leave them in a cool, light place. • Leave dying and frost-damaged foliage on perennial plants until spring to protect new growth below. • To ensure that the water environment remains healthy for dormant plants, make holes in ice sheets, and brush off snow to let light in. • Browse through specialist plant catalogues and order attractive new additions to your planting scheme.

Plant Pests and Diseases

Water plants are vulnerable to a number of pests and diseases that invade leaves, stems, and roots, especially during summer. Dividing and thinning plants *(see pp. 160–161)* will reduce the problem considerably; for example, most of the pests of water-lily foliage attack when the leaves are held well above water, often an indication of an overgrown plant. Be sure, also, to remove ageing or dying floating leaves. Creating an environment that will accommodate fish and frogs is worth considering, as these creatures are very efficient pest predators.

Plant Diseases

Brown Spot

Plants affected Water lilies and lotuses *(Nelumbo)*.
Cause A fungal infection that gains entry through insect bites or wounds on the leaf. As with many fungal leaf spots, older leaves are more susceptible, especially if infected leaves are promptly removed.
Symptoms Dark patches appear on the leaves; the patches become far more pronounced in cool, wet summers. In serious cases, the leaves can become so badly infected that they eventually disintegrate.
Treatment Remove and burn infected leaves immediately, cutting through the leaf stalk at the base. Although fungicides will control the disease, it is seldom serious enough to require chemical control measures. Make sure that the plant is kept in full vigour by thinning when necessary *(see pp. 160–161)*. It is also important to remove regularly any dying or yellowing leaves *(see pp. 158–159)*.

Primula Leaf Spot

Plants affected Primulas growing in moist ground.
Cause A fungal disease that attacks ageing leaves which have been wet for several hours, allowing spores to germinate and penetrate the leaf.
Symptoms Small, circular spots, usually brown, appear on the leaves of older plants, or on plants that are starved of nutrients, and lacking in vigour due to root weakness. These spots may coalesce.
Treatment Control involves good garden hygiene and adequate feeding. Where fertilizers may leach into pondwater, use a slow-release fertilizer. It is especially important to remove old leaf debris. Having removed and burned affected leaves, a wide-spectrum fungicide such as dithiocarbamate, mancozeb, or thiram should be sprayed over the entire plant, including the undersides of leaves; the application should be repeated after 14 days. Avoid frequent and heavy overhead watering.

Iris Leaf Spot

Plants affected Bulbous and rhizomatous irises.
Cause The fungus *Mycosphaerella macrospora* is attracted by mechanical injury to the leaves of the plant, and by wet weather. It produces spores that are spread on air currents, and by rain and water splashes. This disease usually develops after the leaf has been wet for several hours.
Symptoms Brown oval spots scattered at random; the spots become elongated as they stretch in the direction of the leaf veins. The centre of the spot is often lighter in colour, and may show the spores of the fungus. The spots sometimes coalesce as the disease gains a strong hold.
Treatment If it occurs early in the season, spray the affected plants with a wide-spectrum fungicide such as mancozeb. Make sure there is no risk of spray drift into the water. If infection occurs after flowering, remove affected leaves.

Honey Fungus

Plants affected A large range of plants, especially trees and shrubs.
Cause A damaging fungus produces discoloration of the foliage and progressive dieback of shoots. It then penetrates root tissue, affecting the plant's ability to transport water to its leaves. The fungus spreads through the soil by means of dark brown, root-like structures.
Symptoms White streaks of fungal growth develop within the dead tissue of the roots and crown. Plants may die rapidly, or may take several years to die.
Treatment Dead and dying plants should be removed immediately and, if possible, the soil should be changed in the vicinity of the infection. Chemical control is not practical on herbaceous material near water, which it may contaminate. Do not replant any herbaceous or woody specimens for a year; this will allow any remaining portions of fungus surviving on root fragments to die.

Powdery Mildew

Plants affected Some soft-stemmed marginals and moisture-loving plants, particularly *Caltha palustris*.
Cause A fungal infection that is encouraged by overcrowding, and by humid or damp air around the top growth and dryness around the roots.
Symptoms A white, powdery fungal growth develops on the leaf surface, and can spread to the underside of the leaf. The mildew may kill off small areas of leaf tissue that then drop away.
Treatment Remove the infected leaves promptly, and spray the plant with a suitable fungicide. New growth will regenerate from the crown.

Lotus Blight

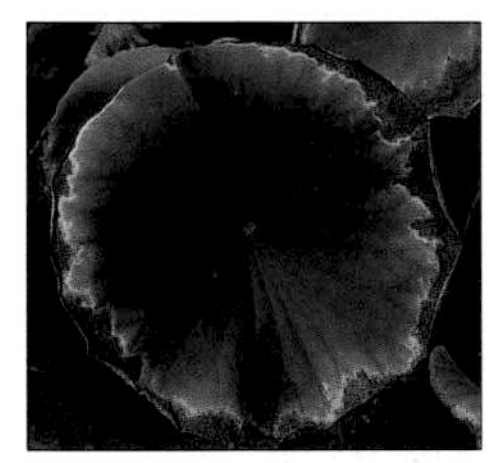

Plants affected Lotus *(Nelumbo)* species and cultivars.
Causes There are two disorders referred to as blight, both of which attack leaves: one a fungal blight, and the other a bacterial blight.
Symptoms Brown patches appear near the edges of the leaf, which later disintegrates.
Treatment Treatment for fungal blight involves spreading the entire surface of the growing bed with a fungicide in powder form. The bacterial blight is more resistant, and therefore less easy, to control with chemicals; treatment for this strain should include removing all infected tissue immediately.

Other Diseases

Water-lily leaf spot Dark patches form on water-lily leaves, which eventually rot. Diseased leaves should be removed and burned. Spray with benomyl after new leaves appear in spring; repeat every 10 to 14 days until flowering begins.

Rhizome rot The leaves of rhizomatous irises die back. Cut out any rotting parts of the rhizome and dust cut surfaces with a fungicidal powder.

Plant Pests

Snails

Plants affected Marginals and moisture-lovers (garden snail); most species of submerged plants (water snail).
Cause Garden snails and water snails eat small pieces of tissue from the leaves and stems of plants.
Symptoms Irregular, unsightly holes appear on leaves and stems. Snails are mostly active after dark or during wet weather.
Treatment Stocking fish can be useful, as they may eat the jelly-like strands of water snails' eggs, laid on the underside of floating leaves. Adult snails can be lured on to lettuce leaves left to float on the water in the evenings; they can then be netted off the following morning. Non-chemical controls for garden snails include laying traps overnight *(see* Slugs, *right)*.

Caddis Fly

Plants affected Young water lilies.
Cause Adult caddis flies that lay their eggs on or near water. The eggs swell up rapidly on contact with water, and hatch in about 10 days. The larvae spin protective cases that they cover with pieces of leaves, small stones, or pebbles, to form shelters. They float or swim around in their structures, feeding hungrily on any vegetation present, and are quite capable of destroying young water lilies whose foliage is underwater. They later pupate at the water's edge.
Symptoms Damaged water-lily leaves.
Treatment Remove by hand any of the well-disguised larval cases. In severe cases, remove all wildlife from the pond and treat the water with proprietary insecticide.

China Mark Moth

Plants affected Mainly water lilies, but occasionally other water plants.
Cause This common pest lays its eggs on floating foliage in late summer; the eggs hatch into leaf-eating caterpillars. These caterpillars eat the undersides of leaves, and form shelters by weaving silky cocoons with the pieces of foliage.
Symptoms Extensive damage, manifested by leaves with oval shapes cut from the leaf margins. It is common to see pieces of decomposing foliage floating nearby.
Treatment Remove the caterpillars' cases from the underside of the leaves. Any severely damaged leaves should be removed by hand and burnt, as any dormant cocoons inside the leaves may hatch if thrown onto the compost heap.

Slugs

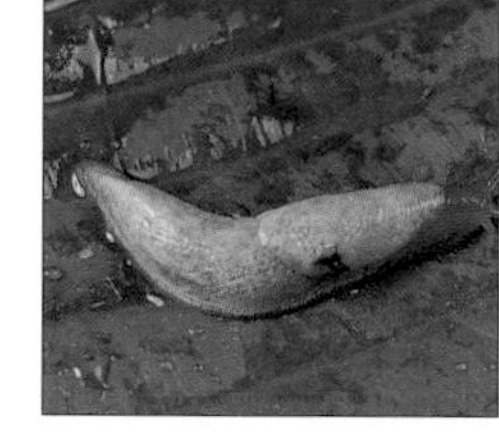

Plants affected Any number of soft-leaved plants growing in moist ground, particularly hostas.
Cause Several species of slug that feed on plant tissue.
Symptoms Irregular holes appear in the foliage, and in severe cases whole stems can be stripped.
Treatment As slugs can never be completely eliminated from gardens, control measures should be concentrated on protecting vulnerable plants. Avoid heavy organic mulches. Cultivating soil regularly will destroy eggs. Encourage predators such as frogs and thrushes. Non-chemical controls include laying overnight traps such as hollowed-out potatoes or grapefruit skins. Half-filled jars of beer sunk in the ground will attract slugs, which fall in and drown.

Iris Sawfly

Plants affected Water-loving irises, particularly *Iris pseudacorus*.
Cause Bluish-grey larvae, up to 2cm (¾in) long, eat the edges of the leaves in summer.
Symptoms Large chunks of foliage are eaten from the sides of the leaves, with noticeable saw-edged margins to the cut surfaces. In severe attacks, the leaves can be reduced to a skeletal central vein.
Treatment The most effective measure of control is the diligent hand removal of caterpillars as soon as the first signs of attack are seen. The caterpillars are quite conspicuous – slide the leaves through finger and thumb to collect and dispose of them. Remove any severely damaged leaves by cutting through the leafstalk at the base, and destroy.

Figwort Weevil

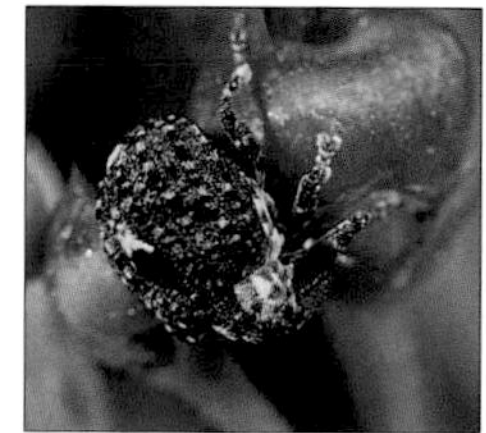

Plants affected Figwort *(Scrophularia auriculata)*, *Phygelius*, *Verbascum*.
Cause Small beetles infest the shoot tips of plants. The beetles have a snout-like projection that makes incisions in plant tissue, into which the females sometimes lay their eggs. The larvae that develop are slug-like in appearance; they attack leaves and occasionally flowers. They then envelop themselves in a brown cocoon attached to the top of the plant.
Symptoms Holes and brown patches appear on the affected plants' leaves.
Treatment If possible, remove the weevils by hand. In severe cases, it will be necessary to remove all wildlife from the pond and treat the water with proprietary insecticide.

Water-lily Beetle

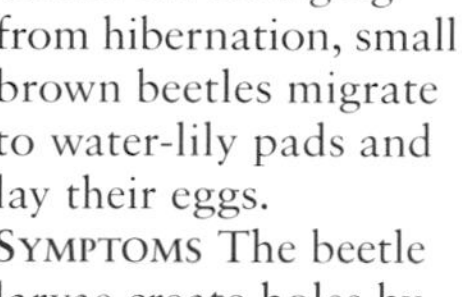

Plants affected Water lilies.
Cause On emerging from hibernation, small brown beetles migrate to water-lily pads and lay their eggs.
Symptoms The beetle larvae create holes by stripping the surface layer of tissue from the leaves; the leaves will eventually shrivel and rot. Adult beetles also feed on flowers.
Treatment Since the beetles hibernate in poolside vegetation, cutting down herbaceous plant material in autumn *(see pp. 158–159)* will remove the beetles' winter protection. Water-lily leaves should be sprayed frequently throughout the summer with a strong water jet in order to dislodge the larvae, which will be devoured by any fish present. Adult beetles and larvae may be removed by hand.

Leafhoppers

Plants affected Soft- or fleshy-leaved marginals, whose leaf tissue is vulnerable to attack.
Cause Small, green leafhoppers, which can transmit viral diseases. With their creamy yellow nymphs they suck the sap from the undersides of plant leaves.
Symptoms Small, pale green or yellow spots appear on the upper leaf surfaces. Severe infestation causes the leaves to turn brown.
Treatment Hose the leaves frequently with a jet spray to dislodge the leafhoppers. If there are fish present, the pests will be eaten. To minimize the risk of attack, make sure that plants do not become congested, allowing insects to move easily from leaf to leaf; divide the rootstock of water lilies *(see p. 160)* every two to three years.

Other Pests

Iris flea beetle Bluish-black beetles attack waterside irises in mid-summer. Small longitudinal leaf areas become devoid of tissue. Control by frequent spraying with a strong jet of water.
Vine weevil These dull black beetles attack several moisture-loving perennials, especially hostas, primulas, and astilbes. Irregular notches are eaten out of the margins of the leaf. Most damage is done by the larvae, which eat the roots until the plant wilts. Remove the weevils by hand.
Red spider mite These tiny mites gather on the undersides of water-lily leaves and other aquatic foliage held above water. Remove by hand or drown by weighting down the leaves for two days with nets.

FISH FOR WATER FEATURES

THE ORNAMENTAL ATTRIBUTES of fish have been recognized and appreciated for centuries. The first people to keep and breed fish for their decorative qualities were the ancient Egyptians. There is also strong evidence to suggest that the most popular of ornamental fish, the goldfish – which is closely allied to the carp – was selectively bred in China as far back as AD 970.

CREATING A BALANCED ENVIRONMENT FOR FISH

With the availability of exotic fish from habitats all around the world, it has become even more important to create an environment suitable for mixed populations of fish *(see pp. 168–169)*. Whether a garden water feature is large or small, formal or informal, the basic requirements for keeping fish remain the same – clear, well-oxygenated water, varied depths, adequate shelter and shade, and food.

WILDLIFE POND
Much of the charm of a wildlife pond lies in the sheer variety of wildlife it attracts. Unfortunately, this variety means that the inhabitants of such a pond, including its fish, are more susceptible to a range of predators. Because they are not highly-coloured ornamental fish – and hence cheaper to replace – native varieties such as roach (left)*, dace, and rudd, are ideally suited to wildlife ponds.*

GOLDFISH FEEDING
Although a well-planted pond should ensure that these goldfish obtain most of the food they need, some supplementary feeding will be necessary. Fish that become used to regular feeding at the same place each day will soon learn to assemble at the surface of the water at the right time and in the right spot.

FISH IN A FORMAL POOL
Much of the pleasure of fish-keeping derives from viewing the fish at close quarters. This raised formal pool, with its submerged and floating-leaved plants, provides an ideal environment for fish, as well as an ideal platform from which to view them.

INFORMAL POND
Although clear water allows an unimpeded view of fish, crystal clear water is not necessarily the kind of environment fish prefer. Many species feel insecure in water that leaves them clearly visible to aerial predators such as herons and kingfishers. Carp, for instance, will disturb mud at the bottom of the pond in order to create a more opaque habitat.

Although fish need room in which to swim about freely, even a barrel will accommodate one or two small goldfish. Deep-water ponds have distinct advantages over shallow ponds: as well as being suitable for fish that feed at different levels *(see pp. 168–169)*, the water remains at a more constant temperature, and retains more dissolved oxygen during hot weather. If a pond is too shallow, and there are no crannies in which to hide, fish will become stressed and dart about, stirring up mud at the bottom of the pond and disturbing plants.

Provided that they are fed, a suitably constructed pond without plants, but with a sophisticated filtration system *(see right, below)*, will give fish all they need. However, most gardeners prefer a more natural, "planted" environment in which the plants themselves fulfil the fish's requirements for clear water, food, shelter, and shade *(see right, above)*. Even algae, which can become a problem if allowed to spread unchecked, are useful components in the ecology of a fish pond; not only are algae the first link in the food chain, they also provide a breeding ground for creatures on which fish can feed.

FISH BEHAVIOUR

Like all vertebrates, the behaviour of fish comprises two components: instinct and learning, the latter demonstrated by a fish's ability to appear at the same time and in the same place for feeding – one of the pleasures of fish-keeping. Although many species prefer to remain solitary – except in the spawning season – other species such as roach, dace, and minnows form shoals and must spend their lives in the company of their own species. Solitary species tend to be predatory, and are often large. In contrast, shoaling species tend to be smaller and, most commonly, omnivorous, gathering together for mutual protection and to share food.

KEEPING THE WATER CLEAN

USING PLANTS AS NATURAL FILTERS
Plants can be used to create a healthy environment for fish. Aside from their "filtering" qualities, oxygenating plants (see pp. 148–149, 178–179) *and floating-leaved plants provide vital shade for fish.*

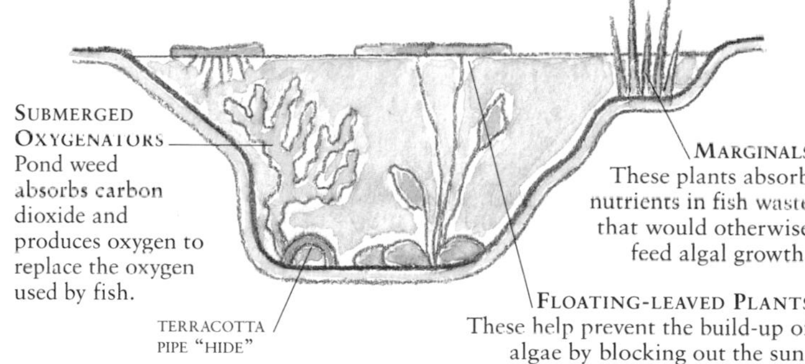

ARTIFICIAL FILTRATION SYSTEM
If a crystal clear, plant-free pool is desired, a biological filtration system (see pp. 70–73) *should be supplemented by a UV clarifier to help keep the water clear of algae, and a magnetic descaler, which is designed to control limescale.*

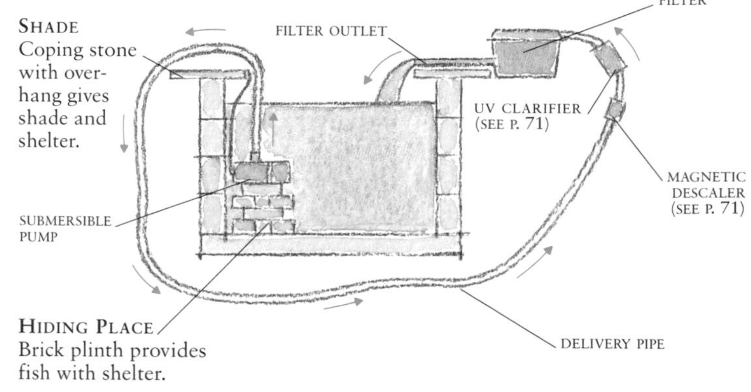

Fish Species and their Requirements

Different species of fish have different environmental preferences. Wildlife ponds, for example, are more suitable for hardy, native fish, while exotic fish will look their best in the sheltered environs of informal or formal ornamental ponds. Since fish feed at different water levels, establish the preferences of your chosen fish before buying and introducing them to the pond. Koi, which require a water depth of at least 1m (3ft), would be unsuited to a shallow pond, while orfe, which swim in the upper layers of the water, require a pond with a large surface area. A pond with adequate depth and surface area can accommodate several species.

Varieties of Goldfish

The many types of goldfish and shubunkin all belong to the same species, *Carassius auratus*. They like rich, weedy ponds that have plenty of cover and a muddy bottom. They breed easily, normally maturing in their third or fourth year, and often live for more than 10 years. The single-tailed varieties are hardy; unlike the twin-tailed varieties, they can tolerate the icy waters of cold winters.

SINGLE CAUDAL FIN (TAIL)

Common Goldfish
Usually orange-red in colour, this fish feeds at all levels. It is generally no longer than 15cm (6in), and is easily bred. Being hardy, it is ideal for most garden ponds, and will tolerate water as warm as 35°C (95°F), but not for extended periods.

Exotic Goldfish

For the more adventurous fish-keeper, there are many exotic forms of goldfish to choose from. Originally bred in China and Japan, they are available in many different shapes, sizes, and colours. The more popular varieties include the Celestial, with its peculiar upturned eyes, the Bubble-eye, with enlarged fluid-filled sacs beneath its eyes, the Oranda, with a "hood" that covers its entire head, and the short, plump Pearlscale. All these twin-tails prefer very clean water. They should be brought indoors during the winter.

HIGH DORSAL FIN

DOUBLE CAUDAL FIN

Fantail Goldfish
The metallic-orange Fantail has an egg-shaped body and seldom exceeds 9cm (3½in) in length. It is less hardy than the Common Goldfish, although it is just as easily bred. If the water temperature drops below 15°C (59°F), the Fantail should be moved indoors. It feeds at all levels.

Mottled Colours
The coloration of shubunkins depends on both their strain and on the formation of their scales.

Sarasa Comet (Red Cap)
A comet's colours depend on its strain. Sarasas have a white or silver base colour, feed at all levels, and breed easily. Although hardy, they thrive best in temperatures of 8–20°C (46–68°F).

Bristol Shubunkin
Shubunkins can grow to lengths of 38cm (15in). The popular varieties, like this one, feature black, red, purple, blue, and brown scales beneath pearly scales. Most shubunkin types are hardy, and feed at all levels. They breed easily, and tolerate temperatures as low as –15°C (5°F).

Forked Tail
All comets have one deeply forked caudal fin, which may be almost as long again as their bodies.

Gold Comet
Growing to lengths of up to 38cm (15in), the Gold Comet needs a lot of space in which to swim. It is very hardy, and can tolerate temperatures as low as 0°C (32°F) and as high as 40°C (104°F). Comets breed easily and, like most goldfish, feed at all levels.

Moor
The egg shaped Moor should ideally have a velvety, jet-black body with no silver showing through. Some Moors have normal eyes, and some have "telescopic" eyes, which protrude on conical supports. They grow to approximately 11cm (4½in), feed at all levels, and are easily bred. They should be kept indoors in winter.

THE CARP FAMILY

The size and shape of carp vary greatly, as do their habits, habitats, and choice of food. Most carp will eat small invertebrates rather than other fish, while others are omnivorous, eating both plants and invertebrates. Yet others, including the Grass Carp, are completely herbivorous.

SPECIALITY KOI

The more exotic, highly bred koi carp are classified by scale types, patterns, and colours – single-colour, two-colour, and multi-colour. Because koi are viewed from above by show judges, their colours and patterns have been specifically developed for this purpose. To house and display koi well, pools must be deep, with crystal-clear water.

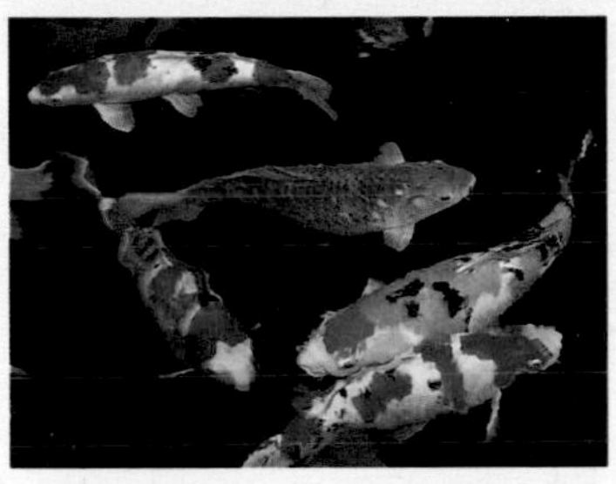

ORNAMENTAL KOI

CRUCIAN CARP *(Carassius carassius)*
This boisterous fish is not suited to small ponds. It is a bottom-level feeder that can grow up to 60cm (24in) long. It thrives in weedy habitats, is easily bred, and will tolerate temperatures of 0–20°C (32–68°F).

PLANT EATER The wide-mouthed Grass Carp feeds on vegetative matter.

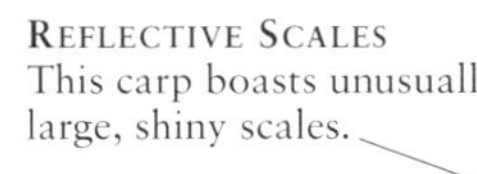

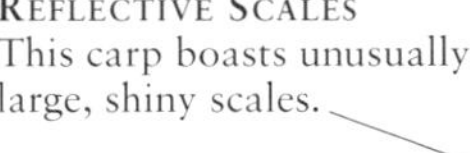

REFLECTIVE SCALES This carp boasts unusually large, shiny scales.

GRASS CARP *(Ctenopharyagodon idella)*
The silver-grey Grass Carp has a wide mouth adapted for feeding on plants. It has a huge appetite, and grows very quickly, up to a length of 60cm (24in). A middle- to bottom-level feeder, it is easily bred, and will thrive in large ponds in temperatures of 0–20°C (32–68°F).

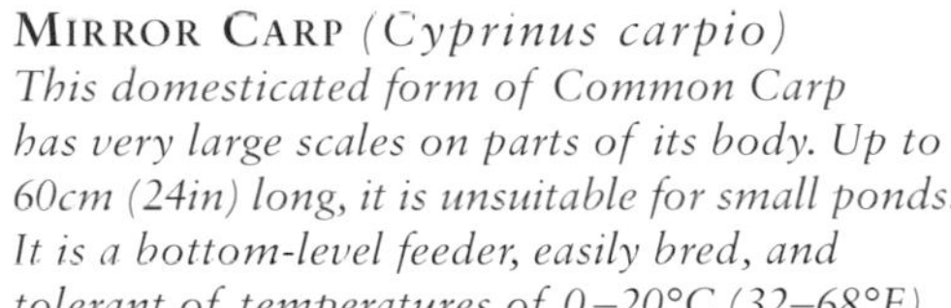

MIRROR CARP *(Cyprinus carpio)*
This domesticated form of Common Carp has very large scales on parts of its body. Up to 60cm (24in) long, it is unsuitable for small ponds. It is a bottom-level feeder, easily bred, and tolerant of temperatures of 0–20°C (32–68°F).

KOI *(Cyprinus carpio)*
Not all koi are expensive, only those intensively bred for special colours and patterning (see box, left). Because they grow to 60cm (24in) in length, koi are unsuitable for very small ponds. Hearty eaters, especially of plants, they need an efficient filtration system to deal with their waste. Koi feed at all levels, are easily bred, and prefer temperatures of 0–20°C (32–68°F).

OTHER FISH

Decorative alternatives to goldfish and koi include lively orfe and rudd, while more subtly coloured fish for large, natural ponds include roach and the steely-grey dace, which darts about just beneath the water's surface. Smaller wildlife ponds can accommodate bitterling and sticklebacks, popular with children; minnows, best introduced in groups of 8–10, will thrive in a stream.

ROACH *(Rutilus rutilus)*
Roach, which grow to a length of 25cm (10in), are unsuitable for small ponds. They tolerate both clear and muddy water, but prefer well-oxygenated water. They are middle-level feeders, and spawn when the water temperature rises above 54°F (12°C).

RUDD *(Scardinus eryphtyhrophthalmus)*
This lively, gold or silver fish reaches 25cm (10in) in length. It will breed freely in a spacious pond that has plenty of underwater foliage. It is a surface-feeder and tolerates a wide range of temperatures, up to a maximum of about 38°C (102°F).

GOLDEN ORFE *(Leuciscus idus)*
Unsuitable for small ponds, these hardy fish grow to 45cm (18in) or larger. Active surface-feeders, orfe spawn when the water temperature rises above 10°C (50°F).

BITTERLING *(Rhodes ceriseus)*
This bottom feeder grows to 5–9cm (2–3½in) in length, and prefers temperatures of 10–20 °C (50–68°F). Breeding is complex, as the female needs a freshwater mussel in which to lay her eggs.

SCAVENGING FISH

Because scavenging fish are omnivorous, they are very useful in keeping the pond clean. The most common scavenger is the greyish, olive-green tench, which can grow to a length of 30cm (12in). Another is the catfish, which will grow up to 30cm (12in) long; before introducing this fish, however, consideration should be given to the fact that it is aggressive and will eat small fry, snails, and exotic fish.

BUYING AND INTRODUCING FISH

THE IDEAL TIME to buy fish is late spring or early summer, when the water temperature reaches about 10°C (50°F). Just as important as the selection of healthy fish is the way in which the fish are transported and introduced into the pond, and the readiness of the pond itself. Always test the acidity or alkalinity of pond water with a pH test kit *(see p. 151)*, and use a pH adjuster, available in powder form, to remedy any imbalance. As a precaution against disease, fish can be disinfected with a proprietary fungal cure before introducing them.

SELECTING FISH

The first step in buying healthy fish is to choose a reputable supplier, who will allow you to pick out and inspect individual fish, and who will have an oxygen cylinder on site to inflate a carrying bag with enough oxygen *(see facing page)* for a long journey home. Avoid buying fish from tanks that are connected to each other; this exchange of water increases the risk of water-borne diseases. Also avoid buying fish from a crowded selling tank, as this environment provides ideal conditions for the incubation of many pests and diseases *(see pp. 174–175)*. If possible, buy fish that are no more than 7–12cm (3–5in) long. Bigger fish not only cost more, some may find it harder to acclimatize to a new environment. Inexperienced fish-keepers should not invest in exotic and expensive varieties of fish at the outset, as these fish often have specialist requirements. If a fish becomes ill, a good supplier or an aquatic centre will be able to offer advice; failing this, they will be able to recommend a veterinary practice specializing in fish.

BRIGHT EYES
Always choose a fish with bright eyes. Cloudy eyes are indicative of ill-health.

DORSAL FIN
A healthy fish should carry a sturdy dorsal fin that is fully erect.

CAUDAL FIN
Make sure that the delicate tail fin is intact.

VENTRAL FINS
When swimming, a fish's fins should be held away from the body.

FLAT SCALES
The scales of a healthy fish lie flat against its body.

CHOOSING A HEALTHY FISH
Always select a fish with bright eyes and a sturdy body. The fish should be lively, its large dorsal fin erect, and its two ventral fins well expanded. A healthy fish will swim effortlessly, with its fins erect; it will also be able to remain perfectly still in the water. If a fish regularly sinks, or bobs to the surface of the water, it may have a swim-bladder disorder. Highly coloured fish may not be ideal purchases, as the strong coloration could mean that they have been freshly imported, or reared in outdoor ponds, which would make them susceptible to diseases. More subdued colours are an indication that the fish has been in quarantine for some time – probably under cover – and will therefore be less prone to disease.

FIN ROT

FUNGUS (COTTONWOOL DISEASE)

WHITE SPOT

DULL EYES

MOUTH FUNGUS

INTERNAL AILMENT
Fish with an internal ailment may trail colourless excreta.

DROPSY
Bristling scales are one indication that a fish has dropsy.

SIGNS OF AN UNHEALTHY FISH
Check that small fish in particular do not have damaged or missing scales, as the exposed tissue beneath the scales will be vulnerable to secondary fungal infection. Because larger fish are more aggressive, it is more common for them to have some missing scales. If the spine of a fish appears to be bent, it could be the result of damage to its nervous system. A bloated body, bulging eyes, and bristling scales are indicative of dropsy (see pp. 174–175).

Transporting and Introducing Fish

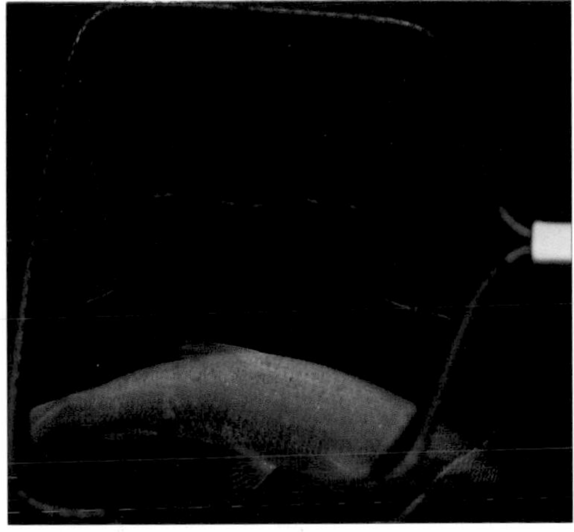

1 **Trawl a wide,** soft mesh net underneath the selected fish. To prevent the fish from panicking and damaging itself, be as gentle as possible. Do not take the fish out of the water.

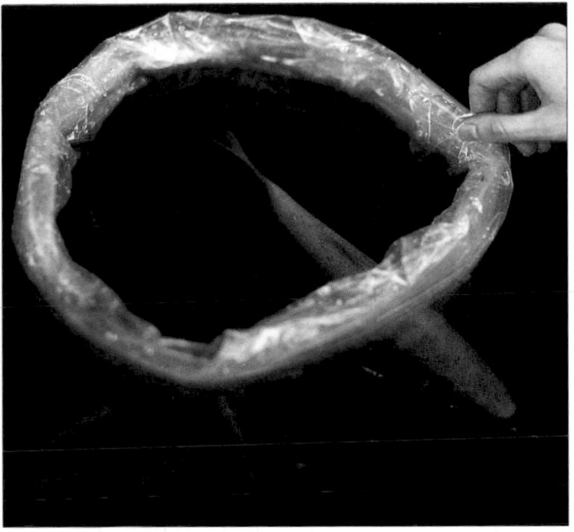

2 **To make the** polythene bag more manageable, roll down the top as shown. Fill the bag with 5–8cm (2–3in) of water from the holding tank. Tip the fish gently from the net into the bag.

3 **If the journey home** will take more than four hours, inflate the bag with oxygen from the supplier's cylinder, then seal. Do not leave fish in a sealed bag for more than 36 hours.

4 **To support the bag** and maintain the level of the water inside it, place in a cardboard or styrofoam box for the journey home. Cover the box: light can cause the fish unnecessary stress.

5 **Float the unopened** bag on the pond until the water temperature in the bag matches that of the pond. To further acclimatize the fish, add a little pond water to the bag a few times, and reseal.

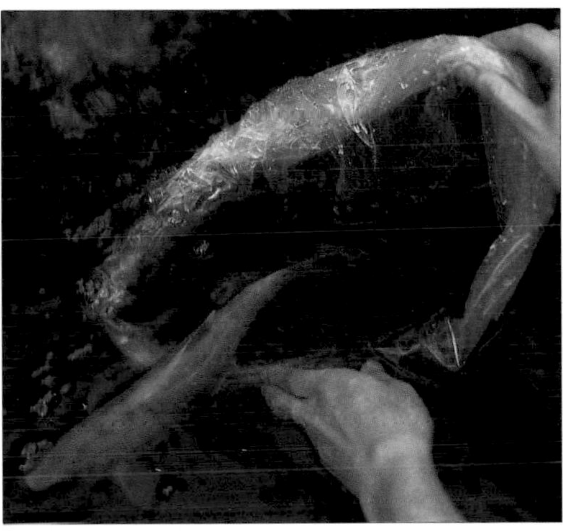

6 **Use a pH kit** to test that the chemical composition in the bag and the pond are the same, then release the fish. Once it swims around happily, give it small quantities of food.

Guide to Stocking Levels

To achieve a healthy balance of submerged pond life, stock with a number of small fish rather than a few large ones that will swiftly devour other members of the food chain.

The number of fish your pond will support depends on its surface area (because it is this factor that chiefly determines how much oxygen will be available to them) and the length of the fish when mature (because their size determines their oxygen needs). An area of 30cm x 30cm (1ft x 1ft) will support a fish 5cm (2in) long, from nose to tail. While an area three times as big will accommodate three such small fish, it could instead be allocated to one 15cm (6in) fish. You can therefore divide your pond into equal portions to support a number of same-sized fish, or, for a mixed population of differently-sized fish, allocate an appropriate area to each *(see right)* as space allows.

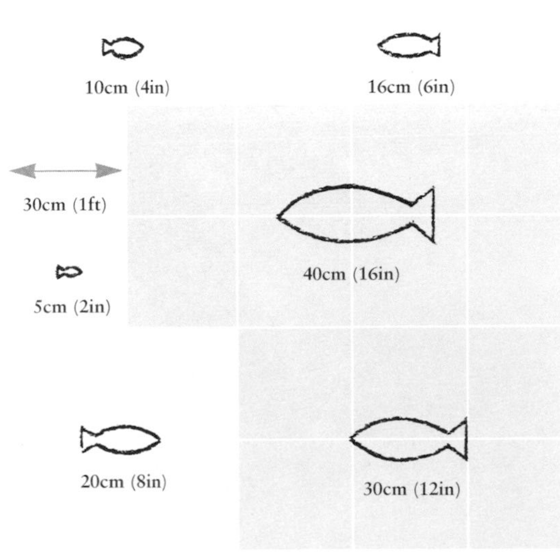

How Many Fish?
Exclude areas of marginal planting when calculating the surface area of clear water (this can include areas covered by floating foliage). Never overstock a pond. All fish, large or small, need enough space in which to swim freely.

ROUTINE FISH CARE

THE NATURAL ECOLOGY of a pond takes months, if not years, to establish itself *(see pp. 136–137)*. However, while it is advisable to wait several weeks before putting fish into a newly constructed pond, the addition of a proprietary dechlorinator and water conditioner, stocked by fish suppliers, can reduce this time to two weeks or so.

A WELL-PLANTED POND
Fish are happiest in a pond that provides shade and shelter, and has a variety of submerged, floating, and deep-water plants. The pond should not be overstocked, and should be well-maintained, so that the fish are less susceptible to water-borne diseases (see pp. 174–175). *Clean water is not only beneficial to their health; it also allows them to be seen.*

AN IDEAL HABITAT

A well-planted pond makes an ideal habitat for fish. Submerged plants provide a spawning ground, cover, and food, as well as oxygen during the daylight hours, while floating-leaved plants create shade. Additional cover can be provided by placing corrugated tiles or terracotta piping on the bottom of the pond. The pond should not have any rough edges that fish could rub themselves raw against; this could lead to infection. If planning to keep boisterous fish such as koi, which tend to stir up mud at the bottom of the pond, it is essential to install a mechanical filter *(see pp. 70–73)*. In hot weather, a hose with a spray attachment or sprinkler can be used in an emergency, if fish are distressed and gasping for air. The pH levels of pond water should be maintained between 6.5 and 7.5 *(see p. 151)*. To lower the risk of diseases being transmitted, avoid over-stocking.

FEEDING FISH

During winter, fish are semi-dormant and will not require feeding, as they will live off reserves of fat and occasional stray food items. As spring advances and fish become more active, they will need an increasingly rich diet. If the pond is not yet well enough established to satisfy their food requirements, most good-quality, pre-packed fish food will adequately supplement any diet deficiencies. Feed fish once a day as the temperature rises and the fish begin actively to search for food. This frequency can be raised gradually to several feeds per day as the season progresses. Specialist foods such as shredded shrimps, which are rich in protein, will provide a dietary boost during the breeding period. Never overfeed fish, as uneaten food will decompose and pollute the water.

EATING HABITS
A useful rule is to provide fish with no more food than they can eat within 3–5 minutes. All fish, even bottom-feeders, can be tempted to the surface with floating pellets of food. Even if fish are fed regularly with manufactured food, they will automatically supplement this diet with live foods such as gnat and mosquito larvae.

PREPARED FISH FOODS

FROZEN FOOD

Frozen or freeze-dried natural aquatic foods such as shredded shrimp, dried flies, and ants' eggs are rich in protein and contain all the nutrients that fish need.

DRIED FISH FOOD
Floating pellets and flakes are prepared to provide a balanced and nutritious diet for fish. Crumb food, although less nutritious, does give fish essential roughage.

PELLETS

CRUMB FOOD

FLAKED FOOD

Inspecting Fish

To remove a fish from the pond, always have a large bowl or bucket ready. Rather than chase fish round the pond, causing them stress in the process, it is advisable to attract them to a secluded area with a sprinkling of food. If the fish is a small specimen – say, 10cm (4in) long – gently trap it in a soft net, then lift the net out of the water and release the fish into a bowl filled with pond water. Alternatively – and preferably – scoop the fish out of the net with a small bowl, without removing the net from the water, and release it into the larger holding bowl.

Under no circumstances should large fish (carp, for example) be lifted out of the water in a net. First net the fish gently, then lower the holding bowl into the pond and guide the fish into it.

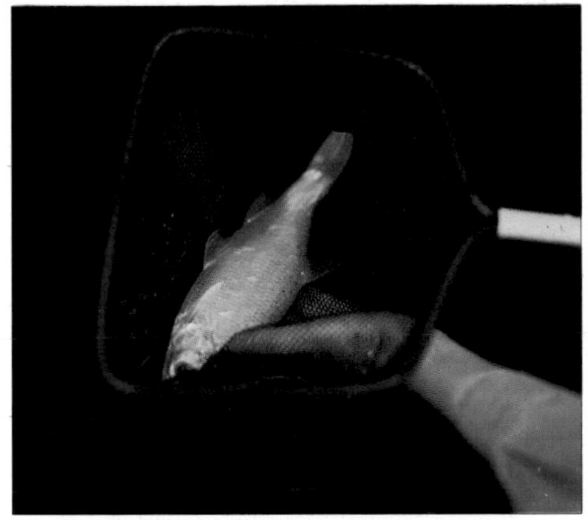

Signs of Ill Health
When inspecting a fish for signs of ill health, it will be necessary to look at it closely, and in reasonably clear water. Small fish may be lifted out of the pond in a soft net, and placed in a holding bowl filled with pond water. Net large fish, but rather than lifting them out of the water, guide them into a holding bowl.

Breeding Fish

Whether or not fish breed depends on the population of the pond: if overstocked, the female will re-absorb her own eggs; if fry develop, most will not survive. The breeding season occurs between spring and mid-summer, but unless they have reached a certain size, fish will not breed. Goldfish, shubunkin, and carp, for instance, must be at least 8cm (3in) long. Most pond fish lay and fertilize their eggs externally. Three or four days after the male has fertilized the female's eggs by spreading his milt over them, the fry begin to develop. During summer, professional fish breeders use a method known as hand-stripping to selectively breed fish. This should not be attempted by novice fish-keepers, as it involves the delicate task of removing the female fish's ova and the male's milt.

Roach Fry
This roach fry started out as a minute and transparent organism, and only began to look like a fish after two or three weeks. Depending on her size, a female roach may lay between 5,000 and 200,000 eggs, which hatch in 5–10 days, depending on the temperature of the water. Males usually mature in their second or third year, females in their third or fourth year.

Lighting and Fish

Only use lighting in a fish pond if the pond is large enough to allow fish – if disturbed by the light – to take refuge in other, unlit nooks and crannies in the pond. Never light up the entire area of a fish pond, or leave the lights on all night.

Seasonal Checklist for Fish Care

Spring	Summer	Autumn	Winter
• Use a testing kit *(see p. 151)* to evaluate the water's pH levels. • Introduce new fish *(see pp. 170–171)*. • When the water temperature rises above 5–6°C (41–43°F), start feeding fish with high-protein food, and supplement with dried or frozen food or daphnia *(see p. 172)*. • Reintroduce fish overwintered indoors *(see p. 139)*. • Inspect fish for parasites or disorders they may have picked up during the winter *(see pp. 174–175)*. • Remove algae *(see pp. 140–141)*. • Keep an eye out for herons, which become active in the spring when food is not yet plentiful *(see p. 174)*. • Take precautions against predators by erecting a netting fence, approximately 45–60cm (18–24in) high, around the perimeter of the pond *(see p. 174)*.	• Introduce new fish *(see pp. 170–171)*. • Top up water lost through evaporation *(see pp. 138–141)*. • Check water-lily leaves for pests, then hose them into the water to supplement the fish's diet. • Regulate feeding, as more natural foods are available to the fish. • Check fish regularly for pests and diseases, especially in very hot weather *(see pp. 170–171, 174–175)*. • If necessary, remove fry to a separate pond or to a bucket of water taken from the pond until they grow larger. • In hot spells, if fish are surfacing and gasping, use a hose with a spray attachment or a sprinkler to rapidly increase oxygen content of the water.	• Feed fish when the weather is warm and bright *(see p. 172)*. • To build up fish for the winter months, supplement their diet with high-protein foods *(see p. 172)*. • Remove tender species of fish and keep under cover for the winter • Net the pond to protect it from falling leaves and debris. Keep an eye out for herons as they prey more heavily on fish to build up their own reserves for the winter months *(see p. 174)*.	• Cease feeding fish as they become semi-dormant. • Place terracotta pipes at the bottom of the pond to provide fish with shelter from predators. • If freezing temperatures are forecast, install a pool heater *(see p. 139)*, or place one or more floats in the water, or cover a section of the pond *(see pp. 138–139)*. • If a pond ices over, make an air hole by placing a pan of boiling water on the ice. Never break ice with a hammer; the shock vibrations are harmful to fish.

FISH PESTS AND DISEASES

ALTHOUGH FISH ARE vulnerable to a range of pests and diseases, a healthy pond environment can minimize these hazards. Ensure that the pond has different depths and varied planting, and avoid overstocking with fish *(see pp. 170–171)*. Cleaning the pond regularly *(see pp. 140–141)* and maintaining a balanced ecosystem *(see pp. 136–137)* are equally important. Most fish diseases are curable, and treatments for many are available from pet shops or garden centres. If a fish displays symptoms or behaves abnormally, move it into a separate container *(see p. 171)*, away from other fish, while you seek advice and treatment.

FISH PESTS

DRAGONFLY AND DAMSELFLY LARVAE

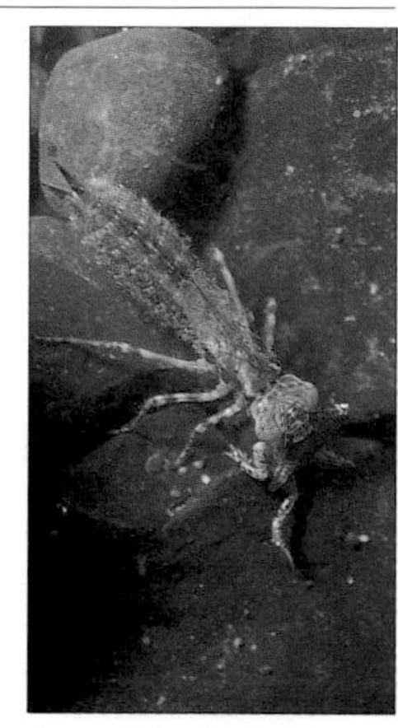

Dragonflies can spend up to five years as nymphs (larvae) under water, but only have one or two months of adult life. The colour of these scorpion-like nymphs *(right)* varies from green to brown and grey. They spend most of their time at the bottom of the pond, where they prey on small fish. They catch the fish by shooting out their "mask", which is an extension of the lower jaw that resembles the claws of a lobster. These claws grip the prey and draw it back into the mouth, where it is injected with digestive fluids. Dragonfly larvae are difficult to control; the only sure method is to remove the larvae by hand. Damselfly larvae present a lesser, though still considerable problem; they, too, should be removed by hand.

HERON

The most common species in temperate climates is the grey heron, which stands about 1m (3ft) tall. Because it is unable to swim, the heron obtains its food by wading in shallow water or standing in the water on one leg, its head hunched into the tops of its wings. Without warning, the bird will stretch out its long neck and stab a passing fish with its dagger-like beak. Having identified a fish pond as an excellent source of food, the heron will hunt relentlessly. Control is not easy, and if visits persist, it may become necessary to erect a netting fence, 45–60cm (18–24in) high, around the edges of the pond. The fence should be strong enough to keep these large birds out; a netting roof spread across it will also stop small diving birds getting through. Koi keepers often build ornamental pergola-like structures over their ponds; this structure can then easily be covered with netting when necessary.

FISH LICE

Fish lice can affect most pond fish, irrespective of size. Lice attach themselves to the body of the fish, and cause damage to the tissues. Sometimes this results in death. It is possible to remove the clearly visible parasites by lifting them off gently with a pair of forceps. Another method of removing them is to hold the fish in a soft net and dab a little paraffin on the lice with a small paint brush. Dip the fish in a solution of proprietary antiseptic to reduce the risk of secondary infection.

WATER BOATMAN

The most common species of water boatman is oval, with a brown back, and a black underbelly with a conspicuous brown triangular mark in the centre. The water boatman is often called a back-swimmer because of its habit of swimming upside down. Although it is only 1.5cm (½in) long, it can kill a small fish by injecting poison through its piercing mouthparts. Control is very difficult, as the adults fly from pond to pond on summer evenings. Netting them off as seen is the only effective control.

WHIRLIGIG BEETLE

Only 3–6mm (⅛–¼in) long, these black, oval beetles congregate in groups and gyrate on the surface of the water. Although they are air-breathing insects, they spend nearly half their lives in water and can, when necessary, create an air bubble to keep themselves supplied with oxygen as they dive to the bottom of the pond in search of food. They feed on other aquatic insects, but will also attack fish fry. The only method of control is to net off the adults from the water surface.

GREAT DIVING BEETLE

This insect, which is capable of storing oxygen in its wing cases, spends most of its three-year lifespan in water. It flies at night, and swims on the surface of the water before diving for prey. It has a dark brown body with a distinctive yellow or gold edge, and reaches a length of 5cm (2in). In addition to preying on newts and tadpoles, this beetle can kill small fish with its ferocious bite. There are no effective methods of control; if a beetle is seen, remove it with a net.

WATER SCORPION

Although these creatures resemble land scorpions, the tail of a water scorpion is a harmless breathing tube. About 2.5cm (1in) long, the water scorpion lives in shallow water, and watches for prey from the leaves of plants. When a small fish passes by, the insect grabs and holds the victim with its pincer-like front legs, while its sharp mouthparts pierce and kill it. Rigid pond hygiene is one method of control; the other is to remove the insect by hand when its tail is seen on the surface.

OTHER PESTS

Amphibians are not normally considered pests, although amorous male bullfrogs may, on rare occasions, grab a passing fish. A strong netting fence approximately 45–60cm (18–24in) high can be an effective barrier against predators – such as storks and herons – that prefer to approach the pond on foot; small, airborne predators such as kingfishers will, however, always get through. A perimeter fence will also help to keep out fish-loving cats and, in certain areas, "escaped" pests such as mink and turtles.

FISH DISEASES

DROPSY

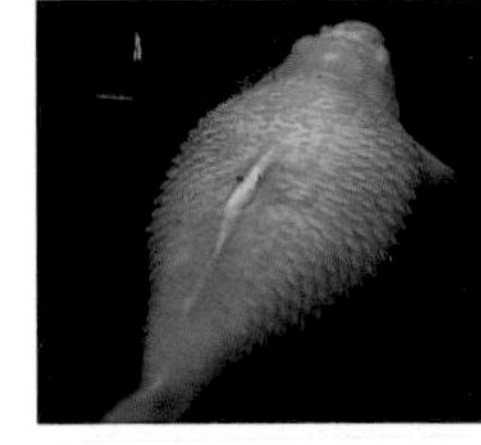

FISH AFFECTED Dropsy is an uncommon disease, but it is, unfortunately, one that can affect most pond fish.
SYMPTOMS The body of an affected fish becomes severely bloated, and the eyes protrude. The most distinctive symptom to look for is bristling scales which, once the disease has taken hold, resemble an open pine cone.
TREATMENT Treatment is difficult to prescribe, owing to the many possible causative agents. One of the most common causes of dropsy is bacterial septicaemia. Broad-spectrum type antibiotics – prescribed by a vet specializing in fish – administered to the affected fish and its contacts may be beneficial in some cases. Improved water quality, reduction of stress, and good-quality food also sometimes help.

FIN OR BODY ROT

FISH AFFECTED This is a fairly common disease that mainly affects long-finned goldfish and shubunkins.
SYMPTOMS A whitish line develops along the outer fin and tail. The area also becomes ragged and bloodshot. This is due to the disintegration of the soft tissue between the bony rays of the tail. The condition may be complicated further by a fungal attack.
TREATMENT The disease is progressive and will cause death if the condition reaches other parts of the fish's body. However, treatment is effective if administered at the early stages of the disease. Capture the fish in a soft net, then remove the damaged tissue carefully with a pair of sharp scissors. Afterwards, use a fungal cure based on malachite green or methylene blue.

ULCER DISEASE

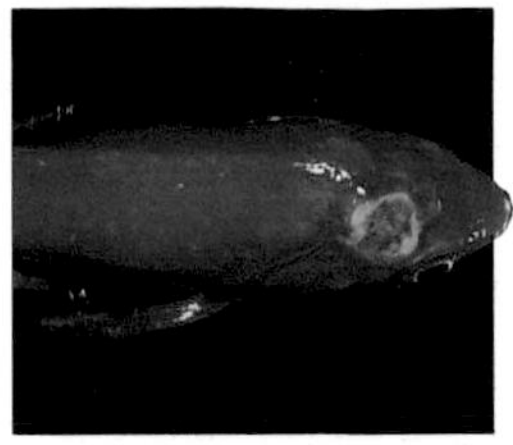

FISH AFFECTED All types of fish are susceptible to this bacterial disease.
SYMPTOMS Pathogenic bacteria are very common in pond water, and will cause disease if the fish are at all vulnerable. The bacteria associated with ulcer disease can produce a wide range of symptoms that are easily detected, from shredded dorsal, tail, and ventral fins, to ulcers on the body, haemorrhagic (bloody) spots, and a "pop-eye" appearance.
TREATMENT Like many of the diseases that affect pond fish, this one can be cured if it is caught early enough and treated – under the guidance of a vet specializing in fish – with antibiotics such as tetracyline or chloramphenicol. Fish foods that contain antibiotics are also available from vets and good fish stockists.

WHITE SPOT

FISH AFFECTED A widespread disease affecting most pond fish, especially newly purchased fish.
SYMPTOMS A number of white spots resembling grains of salt will be found on the body, fins, and tail of the fish. The spots are caused by tiny parasites burrowing into the skin of the fish. However, do not confuse this with the white pimples that appear on the gill plates of male fish during the mating season. Because of the itchiness caused by white spot, fish will rub themselves against objects.
TREATMENT Treatment is only effective in the very early stages of the disease. Place the fish in a holding tank and, by adding warm water, gradually raise the temperature to 16–18°C (60–65°F) to encourage the parasites to swarm. Then add a proprietary cure to the water. Change the water every three days and continue treatment until the fish is healthy. Effective and easy-to-use "whole-pond" treatments against white spot are now available; these present more practical alternatives than the treatment of individual fish, especially if more than one specimen in the pond is affected.

SKIN AND GILL FLUKES

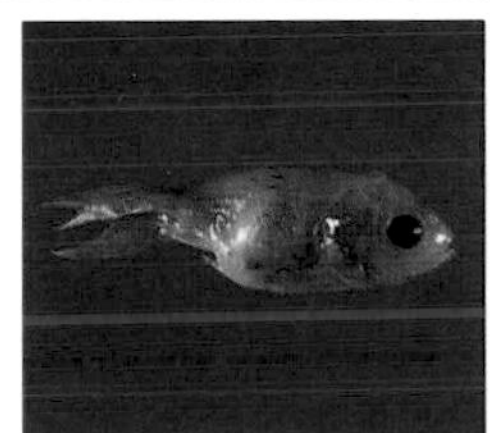

FISH AFFECTED All types of fish.
SYMPTOMS Invisible to the naked eye, flukes are microscopic flatworms that use hooks to attach themselves to the fish. The skin fluke causes irritated patches on the skin and fins, while the gill fluke causes inflamed gill tissues and loss of colour. Both lead to excessive production of mucus, and scratching against objects. The breathing rate of the fish will increase, its fins will twitch, and it will swim about in an agitated state, often rushing to the surface of the water as if short of air.
TREATMENT Commercial medications are available, including a parasite cure based on dimethyltrichlorohydroxyethyl phosphonate. Salt baths containing 10–15g (¼–½oz) salt (pure sodium chloride or rock salt, *not* household salt) to 1 litre (35fl oz) of water are also effective, as is immersion in a very dilute formalin solution: 20ml (7fl oz) formalin in 100 litres (11 gallons) of water. Formalin is stressful to fish; they should only remain in the solution for 30–40 minutes. Immersing fish in a dilute methylene blue solution over an extended period may also produce results.

FISH TUBERCULOSIS

FISH AFFECTED All types of fish.
SYMPTOMS This common fish disease is caused by bacteria. Symptoms can range from the development of ulcerated swellings and "rotting" fins, to the loss of coloration. Gradual consumption, causing the fish to lose weight and condition progressively, is also symptomatic of the disease.
TREATMENT The tuberculosis bacteria will spread very quickly through the pond; it is essential, therefore, to remove affected fish from the pond as soon as the symptoms become evident. In cases of suspected tuberculosis, always consult a vet specializing in fish. Some proprietary antibiotics may produce a cure during the early stages of the disease. However, in the long term, fish almost invariably die.
WARNING When treating fish affected by this disease, always wear protective gloves, especially if there are cuts or grazes on your skin. Fish tuberculosis can, albeit rarely, affect humans, resulting in localised nodular growths which, while not normally presenting a major health problem, can nevertheless prove stubborn to treat.

OTHER FISH DISEASES

Mouth fungus affects all types of fish. The area round the mouth develops white or cream-coloured growths which, in severe cases, can extend to the jaw bones, killing off tissue as the disease progresses. Treat with a proprietary medication based on malachite green, phenoxethol, and acriflavine. Antibiotics can also be effective; always consult a vet specializing in fish before using them.

Fungus or *cottonwool disease* affects all types of fish, but usually only fish already weakened by stress, injury, or infection. Cottonwool-like growths appear on the fins, gills, eyes, and mouth of the fish, usually at a point where damage to the tissues has already occurred. Proprietary treatments are available, but these are only effective for large fish. Follow the instructions carefully.

FURTHER INFORMATION

- Fish Species and their Requirements – pp. 168–169
- Buying and Introducing Fish – pp. 170–171
- Routine Fish Care – pp. 172–173

The Plant Catalogue

Submerged Plants • Floating-leaved Plants
Water Lilies • Lotuses • Marginal Plants
Moisture-loving Plants

Throughout the catalogue, symbols are used for a quick reference to plants' growing requirements; a key can be found on page 4. Plants that hold the Royal Horticultural Society's Award of Garden Merit are also indicated. Detailed descriptions of a number of other plants can be found in *Water Garden Designs* (pp. 16–44).

Blending into the Garden *(left)*
Carefully chosen and positioned plants will soon make a water feature look established. A wide range of moisture-loving plants can be used to soften and disguise pond edges.

Submerged Plants

Unless an advanced filtration system is to be installed in a pond, plants whose leaves are at least partially submerged in the water are essential to maintain clear, well-oxygenated water (*see pp. 152–153*). These plants are often listed as "oxygenators" in plant catalogues, and are also known generally as "pond weed". Most such plants root at the bottom of the pond, in a soil layer or baskets, and are entirely submerged. Their stems are not robust enough to be self-supporting out of the water, although they occasionally thrust flower spikes above the surface. Others, such as *Myriophyllum*, are able to grow above and below the water. An oxygenating role can also be performed by certain free-floating plants that float not on, but just below the surface, with only part of their leaves above water. Their floating leaves additionally provide valuable shade, and their suspended roots absorb nutrients from any fish waste, preventing a build-up of toxic material. All plants in this category can be fast-growing, and must be regularly thinned so that they do not dominate the pond; during the night, they deplete the water of oxygen, and produce carbon dioxide. A fountain playing at night can effectively combat this effect.

***

Ceratophyllum demersum (hornwort)
Deciduous, submerged perennial, with slender stems and whorls of forked leaves. It tolerates shade and thus will grow in deeper water than many oxygenators. Young plantlets break away from the main plant, and may sink as winter buds. Also propagate from cuttings in summer. S indefinite, water depth to 60cm (24in).

***

Fontinalis antipyretica
Evergreen, perennial moss with branched stems bearing olive-green, scale-like leaves. Best grown in cold streams (it is much less vigorous in still water); plant by weighting the plants between boulders, on which roots will cling and spread. Propagate by division in spring. H 8cm (3in), S indefinite, water depth to 44cm (18in).

***

Hottonia palustris (water violet)
Deciduous perennial forming spreading masses of light green, deeply divided foliage, held both below and above the water surface. Pale lilac flower spikes emerge above the water in spring. Thin periodically; to propagate, take stem cuttings in spring or summer. H 30–90cm (1–3ft), S indefinite, water depth to 45cm (18in).

***

Lagarosiphon major, syn. *Elodea crispa*
Semi-evergreen perennial forming dense, submerged masses of branching, fragile stems covered in reflexed, linear leaves. Tiny, translucent flower spathes develop in summer. Thin in summer and cut back in autumn. Propagate from stem cuttings in spring or summer. S indefinite, water depth to 1m (3ft).

Myriophyllum verticillatum (milfoil)
Perennial with spreading stems and tightly packed, delicate, bright green leaves, ideal for shallow water, where stems extend above the surface with the spikes of inconspicuous, yellowish flowers. Propagate from stem cuttings in spring or summer. S indefinite, water depth to 44cm (18in).

Potamogeton crispus (curled pondweed)
Perennial with seaweed-like submerged leaves, bearing crimson and creamy-white flowers just above the water in summer. Spreads rapidly in mud-bottomed pools and tolerates cloudy or shady water better than any other oxygenator. Propagate from stem cuttings in spring or summer. S indefinite, water depth to 1m (3ft).

Ranunculus aquatilis (water crowfoot)
Annual or perennial, holding its flowers and some of its leaves just above water. Best in large, wildlife ponds or streams at a depth of 15–60cm (6–24in), where it can spread and root in mud bottoms. Propagate from fresh seed or by division in spring or summer. S indefinite, water depth to 1m (3ft).

Stratiotes aloides (water soldier, water aloe)
Semi-evergreen, free floating perennial forming "pineapple-top" rosettes of spiky leaves, held partly below and partly above the water. Thin regularly. New plants form as small water buds on spreading stems: they may be separated in summer. H 40cm (16in), S indefinite, water depth to 1m (3ft).

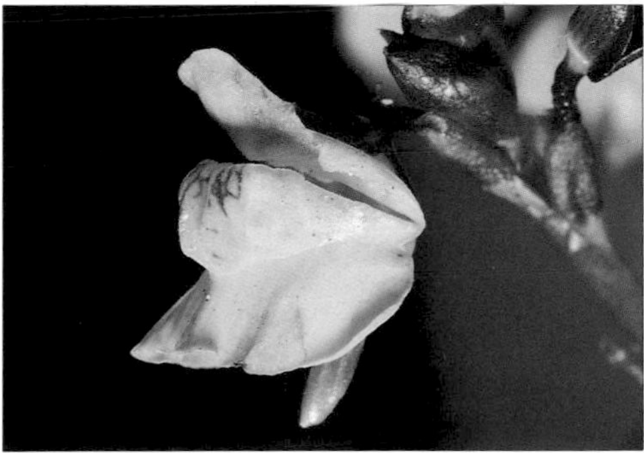

Utricularia vulgaris (greater bladderwort)
Deciduous, frost-hardy, free-floating perennial with feathery, bronze-green, bladder-like leaves that trap insects. Pouched, bright yellow flowers, with red-brown streaks, are held 25cm (10in) above the water in summer. Propagate by separating young plantlets in spring or summer. S 60–90cm (2–3ft), water depth to 1m (3ft).

FLOWING FOLIAGE
Leaves twist and spiral in water currents.

Vallisneria spiralis (eelgrass, tape grass)
Half-hardy to frost-tender perennial, evergreen in the tropics, grown for its spiralling, strap-shaped leaves, which can be 80cm (32in) long. Greenish flowers, held on spiralling stalks, are produced year-round. Propagate by division in spring or summer. S indefinite, water depth at least 30cm (12in).

ALSO RECOMMENDED

Callitriche hermaphroditica, syn. *C. autumnalis*
Ceratopteris pteridioides (frost-tender)
Egeria densa, syn. *Anacharis densa*, *Elodea densa* (frost-tender)
Hygrophila polysperma rubra (frost-tender)
Myriophyllum aquaticum (*see p. 27*)

Where specific page references are not given for descriptive plant entries found in other sections, brief details are given in the Plant Index (*see pp. 210–212*).

Floating-leaved Plants

PLANTS WITH FOLIAGE FLOATING on the water surface are essential to maintain clear water. By blocking a proportion of sunlight, they check the growth of algae, which thrive only in well-lit water. They also provide shade and shelter for pond life. Among those that are anchored by their roots in bottom soil or planting crates, the true water lilies (*Nymphaea*) are the most popular *(see pp. 182–187)*. In conditions where they are unsuitable, however, there are other more adaptable plants such as pond and fringe lilies *(Nuphar* and *Nymphoides)*, or plants such as water hawthorn, with its long season of headily scented flowers. Other plants in this category, such as *Trapa natans*, float completely, their suspended roots absorbing dissolved nutrients and any fish waste. Floaters tend to multiply rapidly and should be used and controlled with care. Some, such as *Eichhornia*, the water hyacinth *(see p. 26)* and water lettuce *(Pistia stratiotes)*, while not invasive in temperate climates, are so vigorous in tropical waters that their introduction may be prohibited in certain areas; for example, in parts of the southern United States. In temperate climates, the majority of floaters are deciduous, sinking to the bottom in winter and floating back to the surface in spring.

Aponogeton distachyos
(Cape pondweed, water hawthorn)
Deep-water perennial that may be almost evergreen in mild winters, producing heavily scented white flowers in forked clusters, either in two flushes or throughout the summer. Propagate from fresh seed or by division in spring. S 1.2m (4ft), water depth to 60cm (2ft).

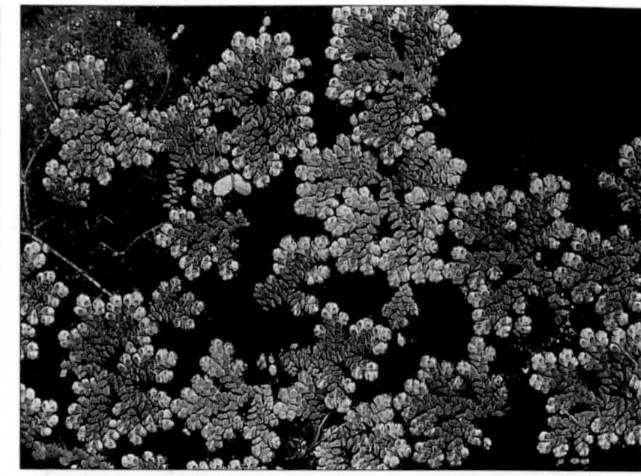

Azolla filiculoides, syn. *A. caroliniana*
(fairy moss, water fern)
Tiny, free-floating, perennial fern that multiplies to form clusters of soft, pale green leaves, each with a single fine root, that turn purplish-red in autumn. Useful for rapid, temporary cover in a new pond while other plants grow. Can be invasive: in summer, thin regularly. S indefinite.

Hydrocharis morsus-ranae (frogbit)
Perennial free-floater with rosettes of kidney-shaped, shiny leaves and papery white flowers with a yellow centre. It prefers still, shallow water (it may root in mud), providing useful shelter for creatures, but is vulnerable to snail damage. New plantlets form on runners.
S indefinite, water depth to 30cm (12in).

Marsilea quadrifolia (water clover)
Scrambling, perennial fern with long, creeping roots. The shamrock-like leaves, downy when young, float on the surface on stalks 8–15cm (3–6in) long, or may stand above the water in muddy shallows; it is a popular marginal in tropical pools. Propagate by division.
S indefinite, water depth to 60cm (24in).

Nuphar japonica (Japanese pond lily)
Deciduous perennial, with heart-shaped floating leaves and round, yellow flowers, held just above the surface in summer. Grows in still or slowly moving water, but requires more sun to flower freely than *Nuphar advena* and *N. lutea*. Propagate and thin by division in spring. S 1m (3ft), water depth to 30cm (12in).

Polygonum amphibium
(willow grass, amphibious bistort)
Amphibious perennial with long-stalked, floating leaves borne on stems that root at the nodes. In mid-summer, pink flowers are held above the water. Will also grow in boggy margins. Propagate by division. S indefinite, water depth to 45cm (18in).

Salvinia auriculata (butterfly fern)
Free-floating, perennial fern, evergreen in tropical areas (min. temp. 10°C/50°F), forming spreading colonies. The leaves, pale green or purplish-brown and covered in silky hairs, are tightly packed on branched stems. Remove faded foliage and thin by separating young plants in summer. H 2.5cm (1in), S indefinite.

Nymphoides peltata
(fringed water lily, water fringe)
Deciduous, rhizomatous perennial with small, floating, mid-green leaves, often splashed with brown and, throughout summer, small, fringed, yellow flowers held 5–8cm (2–3in) above the water. Propagate by division in spring. S 60cm (24in), water depth 15–45cm (6–18in).

Pistia stratiotes (water lettuce)
Deciduous, free-floating aquatic, evergreen in tropical waters (min. temp. 10°C/50°F). Slightly overlapping, velvety, pale green leaves, arranged like a culinary lettuce, are whitish-green on the underside. Thin and separate new plantlets in summer. H 22–30cm (9–12in), S indefinite, water depth to 1m (3ft).

Victoria amazonica
(Amazon water lily, royal water lily)
Tropical perennial (min. temp. 30°C/85°F) often grown as an annual, with rimmed leaves up to 2m (6ft) across. The night-blooming flowers, which last two days, open white then turn pink. Propagate from seed in winter or early spring. S 6m (20ft), water depth 60–90cm (2–3ft).

WATER LILIES

THE RANGE OF WATER LILIES *(Nymphaea)* available is increasing, with new cultivars continually being developed, many in North America. All have flowers that either float, or (particularly the tropical water lilies) stand just above the water surface. Many are delicately perfumed, and some change colour as they open and mature. There are species and cultivars to suit most climatic conditions, size of pond, and planting depth, although all share a need for a sunny, sheltered position and still or nearly still water. Hardy examples will survive outside, even if the surface of the pond is frozen. The old foliage sinks and dies in winter, new leaves appearing in the following spring. Tropical water lilies may bloom by day or by night. In cool climates, some may be grown as annuals, while others are small enough to flourish in containers in heated glasshouses or conservatories. If neglected, water lilies become coarse and congested, with few flowers. By regularly removing fading leaves and flowers, and lifting, dividing, and replanting *(see pp. 160–163)*, an elegant display will be preserved. Water lilies may be propagated *(see p. 160)* by division, separating root buds or plantlets in spring or early summer; species may also be grown from seed.

Nymphaea alba (common white water lily)
One of the few water lilies indigenous to Europe, *N. alba* is a prolific flowerer and is best in a large pond. Its round, dark green pads are 30cm (12in) in diameter. The semi-double flowers, 20cm (8in) across, are magnolia-white with yellow stamens. S 1.5–2m (5–6ft), water depth 30–90cm (1–3ft).

Nymphaea 'Aurora'
Of all the lilies whose flowers change colour, this has the widest range of shades. It is a small cultivar, with olive-green leaves mottled with red-purple. The semi-double flowers are cream in bud, opening to yellow, then turning orange to flecked blood-red, with orange stamens. S 75cm (30in), water depth 30–45cm (12–18in).

Nymphaea 'Blue Beauty'
A free-flowering cultivar with exceptional colouring. The wavy-edged leaves may be brown-flecked, with purplish undersides. The sweetly scented, semi-double flowers have rich blue petals and deep yellow stamens. Plant only once the weather becomes warmer in spring. S 1.2–2.2m (4–7ft), water depth 30–60cm (1–2ft).

Nymphaea capensis (Cape blue water lily)
This adaptable species will grow well in any size of pond. Its large, wavy-edged leaves can be 40cm (16in) in diameter. The semi-double, star-shaped flowers, up to 25cm (10in) across, are light blue with yellow stamens, and held well above the water. S 1.5–2.5m (5–8ft), water depth 30–60cm (1–2ft).

Nymphaea 'Caroliniana Nivea'
A hardy cultivar for larger ponds, performing best when planted in a large crate or basket that allows a substantial root system to develop. The leaves are almost round; the flowers semi-double, star- to cup-shaped, fragrant, ivory-white, with yellow stamens. S 1.2–1.5m (4–5ft), water depth 30–60cm (1–2ft).

Nymphaea 'Escarboucle'
Excellent for most ponds in cool climates, and stays open later in the afternoon than most red-flowered cultivars. Brown-tinged young leaves mature to deep green; the semi-double flowers are bright crimson with golden stamens, their outer petals tipped white. S 1.2–1.5m (4–5ft), water depth 30–60cm (1–2ft).

Nymphaea 'Firecrest'
Needs ample space and a planting basket at least 60cm (2ft) wide and 30cm (1ft) deep. Its deep purple young leaves mature to green. The semi-double, star-shaped pink flowers, held just above the water, have orange inner stamens and outer stamens tipped with deep pink. S 1.2m (4ft), water depth 30–45cm (12–18in).

Nymphaea 'Froebelii'
A good choice for shallow water, ideal for barrels or small ponds. Bronzed young leaves mature to small, round or heart-shaped, pale green pads. The deep red flowers, 10–13cm (4–5in) across, are first cup-shaped, then star-shaped, with orange-red stamens. S 1m (3ft), water depth 15–30cm (6–12in).

Nymphaea 'Gladstoneana'
A vigorous, free-flowering cultivar, which will grow large unless regularly thinned. The bronzed young leaves mature to almost round, dark green pads, with crimped edges. Flowers are semi-double, star-shaped, waxy-petalled, with bright yellow stamens. S 1.5–2.4m (5–8ft), water depth 45–60cm (18–24in).

Nymphaea 'Gonnère'
This magnificent white cultivar is ideal for any size of pond. Its slightly bronzed young leaves mature to round, pea-green pads, up to 22cm (9in) across. The fully double, globe-shaped, fragrant white flowers, 10–15cm (4–6in) across, stay open until late in the afternoon. S 1–1.2m (3–4ft), water depth 30–45cm (12–18in).

Nymphaea x *helvola*
A small, free-flowering water lily, ideal for small, shallow ponds or containers. The oval, heavily mottled, purplish leaves have purple undersides. The small, semi-double, clear buttercup-yellow flowers are cup-shaped at first, opening fully to a star shape. S 60cm (2ft), water depth 15–22cm (6–9in).

Nymphaea 'James Brydon'
A popular red-flowered cultivar for barrels or small to medium-sized ponds, and resistant to crown rot. Its purplish-brown young leaves mature to dark green pads. The double flowers, their petals suffused with brilliant rose-red, are 10–12cm (4–5in) across. S 1–1.2m (3–4ft), water depth 30–45cm (12–18in).

Nymphaea 'Lucida'
This free-flowering cultivar is suitable for any size of pond. Its large leaves are heavily marked with dark purple, and the star-shaped flowers, 12–15cm (5–6in) in diameter, have red inner petals and outer petals of pale pink with deeper pink veins. S 1.2–1.5m (4–5ft), water depth 30–45cm (12–18in).

Nymphaea 'Laydekeri Fulgens'
One of the first cultivars to bloom in spring, flowering freely through the summer, and suitable for any size of pond. The young leaves are blotched with purple, maturing to plain green. Semi-double, burgundy-red flowers have orange-red stamens. S 1.2–1.5m (4–5ft), water depth 30–45cm (12–18in).

Nymphaea 'Marliacea Albida'
Popular cultivar that reliably produces a high proportion of blooms for its limited spread of leaves. Slightly bronzed young foliage matures to deep green pads, tinged red-purple beneath. The cup-shaped, semi-double flowers are white with yellow stamens. S 1–1.2m (3–4ft), water depth 30–45cm (12–18in).

Nymphaea 'Marliacea Carnea'
A vigorous, pink-flowered cultivar, only suitable for medium-sized to large ponds. The purplish young leaves mature to large, deep green pads. The light pink, semi-double flowers, with yellow stamens, can be up to 20cm (8in) in diameter. S 1.2–1.5m (4–5ft), water depth 30–45cm (12–18in).

Nymphaea 'Marliacea Chromatella'
One of the most reliable yellow water lilies for any size of pond. Its coppery young leaves, with purple streaks, mature to an attractive purple-mottled mid-green. Semi-double, primrose-yellow flowers, 15cm (6in) in diameter, are borne in abundance. S 1.2–1.5m (4–5ft), water depth 30–45cm (12–18in).

Nymphaea 'Odorata Sulphurea Grandiflora'
Cultivar whose yellow flowers tend to open only from late morning to early afternoon, but are reliably produced throughout summer. Its dark green leaves are speckled with maroon; the semi-double flowers are sweetly scented, with yellow stamens. S 1–1.2m (3–4ft), water depth 30–45cm (12–18in).

Nymphaea 'Pearl of the Pool'
This cultivar flowers best when given a large planting basket or crate. Its bronzed young leaves mature to plain green pads, their lobes sometimes overlapping. The star-shaped, fragrant, pink flowers are 12–15cm (5–6in) in diameter, with orange stamens. S 1.2–1.5m (4–5ft), water depth 30–45cm (12–18in).

Nymphaea 'Pink Sensation'
One of the finest pink cultivars, with flowers that stay open late into the afternoon. Leaves are purplish when young, later turning deep green. The pink flowers open to a star shape, 12–15cm (5–6in) across, with yellow inner and pink outer stamens. S 1.2m (4ft), water depth 30–45cm (12–18in).

☼ ▦ ❄❄❄

Nymphaea 'Ray Davies'
A recently introduced cultivar suitable for small or medium-sized ponds, noted for its evenly coloured and shaped flowers. Its leaves are a glossy plain deep green, and the fully double flowers are pale pink, with a showy ring of golden stamens in the centre. S 1m (3ft), water depth 30–45cm (12–18in).

☼ ▦ ❄❄❄

Nymphaea 'Rose Arey'
Best given a large planting container that will allow a substantial root system to develop. Its purple young leaves mature to green; the aniseed-scented, semi-double flowers open deep pink, paling with age, with golden stamens, orange-pink towards the edges. S 1.2–1.5m (4–5ft), water depth 35–60cm (14–24in).

☼ ▦ ❄❄

Nymphaea 'Sunrise'
Although frost-hardy, this cultivar needs a warm temperate climate to flower well. Purple-mottled when young, the leaves mature to plain green, round to oval pads, up to 20cm (8in) across. The flowers are semi-double, with long yellow petals and yellow stamens. S 1.2–1.5m (4–5ft), water depth 35–45cm (14–18in).

☼ ▦ ❄❄❄

Nymphaea 'René Gérard'
A large-leaved cultivar that looks best in medium-sized to large pools. Its bronzed young leaves mature to round, plain green pads, up to 30cm (12in) in diameter. The flowers are rose-red, their outer petals heavily flecked with pale pink; the stamens are yellow. S 1.5m (5ft), water depth 30–45cm (12–18in).

☼ ▦ ❄❄❄

Nymphaea 'Robinsoniana'
A free-flowering cultivar with attractively contrasting flowers and foliage. Its light purple leaves have deep purple blotches and deep red undersides. Star-shaped flowers with cupped centres, 11–13cm (4½–5in) across, have orange-red petals and orange stamens. S 1.2–1.5m (4–5ft), water depth 30–45cm (12–18in).

☼ ▦ ◈

Nymphaea 'Saint Louis Gold'
Tropical cultivar with smaller but more richly-coloured flowers than the similar 'Saint Louis'. The purple-blotched young leaves become large, plain green pads. Semi-double, fragrant flowers, held above the water, are first a mustard-gold colour, fading to lemon. S 2.4–3m (8–10ft), water depth 37–60cm (15–24in).

Nymphaea 'Vésuve'
Cultivar with a long flowering season; in addition, its blooms are open for much of the day. The dark green leaves are almost circular, up to 25cm (10in) across. The flowers, an even, glowing cerise with orange stamens, are star-shaped, with inward-curving petals. S 1.2m (4ft), water depth 30–45cm (12–18in).

Nymphaea 'Virginalis'
One of the most reliably free-flowering white cultivars for a cool climate. The purple or bronzed young leaves mature to plain green pads, with overlapping lobes. The cup-shaped, day-blooming, fragrant white flowers have yellow stamens. S 1–1.2m (3–4ft), water depth 37–45cm (15–18in).

Nymphaea 'Virginia'
A free-flowering cultivar, with purplish deep green leaves and star-shaped, semi-double, very pale yellow (often near white) flowers, 10–15cm (4–6in) across, and distinctively star-shaped, with numerous, narrow chrysanthemum-like petals. S 1.5–1.8m (5–6ft), water depth 35–50cm (14–20in).

Nymphaea 'William Falconer'
A compact, vividly coloured cultivar that is suitable for a medium-sized pond. Its leaves are maroon when young, maturing to dark green with heavy purple veining. The medium-sized, rounded, deep cherry-red flowers open to reveal yellow stamens. S 1.2m (4ft), water depth 45–75cm (18–30in).

Nymphaea 'Wood's White Knight'
A vigorous, night-blooming cultivar for a large, tropical pond. The almost circular leaves, up to 37cm (15in) across, have unusual scalloped edges. The large, narrow-petalled flowers open wide around central yellow stamens, giving a daisy-like effect. S 2.4–3m (8–10ft), water depth 40–60cm (16–24in).

Also Recommended

N. 'Amabilis' Pink flowers. Hardy, S 1.5–2.3m (5–7ft), WD 30–45cm (12–18in).

N. 'American Star' Salmon flowers. Hardy, S 1.2–1.5m (4–5ft), WD 30–45cm (12–18in).

N. 'Attraction' (see p. 37)

N. caerulea Pale blue flowers. Half-hardy, S 2.4–3m (8–10ft), WD 45–90cm (18–36in).

N. 'Charlene Strawn' Lemon flowers. Hardy, S 1–1.5m (3–5ft), WD 30–45cm (12–18in).

N. 'Charles de Meurville' Pink flowers. Hardy, S 1.2–1.5m (4–5ft), WD 30–45cm (12–18in).

N. 'Ellisiana' Red flowers. Hardy, S 90cm (3ft), WD 22–40cm (9–16in).

N. 'Emily Grant Hutchings' Deep pink flowers. Frost-tender, night-blooming. S 2m (6ft), WD 30–60cm (2–3ft).

N. 'General Pershing' Lilac flowers. Tropical, S 1.5–2m (5–6ft), WD 30–45cm (12–18in).

N. gigantea Purple-blue flowers. Tropical, S 2–3m (6–9ft), WD 45–90cm (18–36in).

N. 'Indiana' Apricot to orange flowers. Hardy, S 75cm (30in), WD 15–30cm (6–12in).

N. 'Louise' Red flowers. Hardy, S 1.2–1.5m (4–5ft), WD 30–45cm (12–18in).

N. mexicana (see p. 26)

N. 'Splendida' Pink flowers. Hardy, S 1.2–1.5m (4–5ft), WD 37–60cm (15–24in).

N. tetragona alba White flowers. Frost-hardy, S 60–90cm (2–3ft), WD 15–22cm (6–9in).

LOTUSES

WITH THEIR STRIKING LEAVES and exquisite mid-summer flowers, lotuses *(Nelumbo)* are exceptionally beautiful plants. They require an open, sunny position, and many need at least semi-tropical conditions. Very hot summers enable some lotuses to survive cold winters, but in temperate climates they can be grown in containers, either sited permanently in a heated conservatory or brought under cover for the winter. The rhizomatous roots may also be stored over winter *(see p. 158)*. Lotuses can be planted in water 15–60cm (6–24in) deep, and are thus suitable both for the margins and deeper, central areas of the average pond. However, the roots spread rapidly, and are best confined in planting baskets or crates. At first, the young leaves lie on the water surface; however, the stout leaf stalks soon thrust the foliage into the air. The leaves are large, bluish-green, and plate-like, with a waxy coating. The flowers, usually held just above the leaves, last for about three days, opening in the morning and closing by mid-afternoon. The petals fall to expose a delightful seedhead resembling a pepperpot or watering-can rose. Lotus species are grown from seed in spring; selections and cultivars must be propagated by division in spring.

Nelumbo nucifera 'Alba Grandiflora'
Vigorous, deciduous perennial with wavy-edged leaves. Its large, white flowers have broad, oval petals and tufts of golden stamens. Sometimes referred to as the "magnolia lotus", 'Alba Grandiflora' is widely held to be the finest white-flowered cultivar. H 1.2–2m (4–6ft), S indefinite.

Nelumbo lutea (American lotus, water chinquapin)
Vigorous, deciduous perennial with rounded leaves and yellow flowers, their petals fading gently towards the tips. The seedheads, 10cm (4in) in diameter, are a traditional food of native Americans. Grows well in shallow water. H 0.7–1.5m (2½–5ft), S indefinite.

Nelumbo nucifera (sacred lotus, Asian lotus)
Very vigorous, deciduous perennial, holding its leaves, which can be 90cm (3ft) across, very high above the water. The flowers have a pleasant fragrance, and are large, opening rose-pink then fading to a pale flesh tone. The seed capsule turns from yellow to brown.
H 1.5–2.2m (5–7ft), S indefinite.

Nelumbo nucifera 'Momo Botan'
Deciduous perennial, smaller than most lotuses, needing water no deeper than 30cm (12in). The peony-like double flowers are rose pink, with yellow at the petal bases. It has a longer flowering season than most lotuses, and the flowers also stay open for longer, sometimes all night. H 0.6–1.2m (2–4ft), S 1m (3ft).

Nelumbo nucifera 'Mrs Perry D Slocum'
Deciduous perennial with glaucous leaves. It is exceptionally free-flowering, the blooms in many ways resembling those of the rose 'Peace'. The petals are pink-flushed yellow on the first day, pink and yellow on the second day, and cream-flushed pink on the third day. H 1.2–1.5m (4–5ft), S indefinite.

Nelumbo nucifera 'Pekinensis Rubra' (red lotus)
Deciduous perennial with leaves 50–60cm (20–24in) across. The slightly fragrant flowers, 20–30cm (8–12in) in diameter, are deep rose-red, later turning pink. The seed capsules, which are large and yellow, later develop a green rim. H 1.2–2m (4–6ft), S indefinite.

Nelumbo nucifera 'Rosea Plena'
Vigorous, free-flowering, deciduous perennial with leaves 45–50cm (18–20in) in diameter. The double, rose-pink flowers turn yellow towards the petal bases. While the flowers are large, up to 33cm (13in) across, the seed capsule is unusually small, only 2.5cm (1in) in diameter. H 1.2–1.5m (4–5ft), S indefinite.

Nelumbo 'Perry's Giant Sunburst'
Deciduous perennial with blue-green leaves, 43–53cm (17–21in) across. The pleasantly fragrant, large flowers, 25–35cm (10–14in) in diameter, are a rich creamy colour, with buttery yellow stamens. They are held well above the leaves on robust, erect stalks. H 1.4–1.7m (4½–5½ft), S indefinite.

Nelumbo 'Perry's Super Star'
Deciduous perennial with blue-green leaves. The sweetly scented flowers change from rich pink to yellow, culminating in a creamish colour, with pink tips.They are unusual in having six to eight green-tipped petals near the centre of the flower. H 1–1.2m (3–4ft), S indefinite.

Nelumbo 'Shiroman', syn. var. *alba plena*
Vigorous deciduous perennial, with leaves 60cm (24in) in diameter. The slightly fragrant, large, double flowers, 25cm (10in) across, are creamy white in colour with golden stamens in the centre. This rapidly spreading lotus should only be sited in a medium to large pond. H 0.9–1.5m (3–5ft), S indefinite.

Also Recommended

N. 'Alba Striata' White-flowered, with jagged red petal margins.
N. 'Angel Wings' White-flowered.
N. 'Baby Doll' White-flowered.
N. 'Ben Gibson' Pink-flowered.
N. 'Charles Thomas' Pink-flowered.
N. 'Debbie Gibson' Cream-flowered.
N. 'Empress' White-flowered.
N. 'Kermesina' Rose pink to bright red flowered.
N. *lutea* 'Flavescens' Yellow-flowered.
N. 'Maggie Belle Slocum' Pink-flowered.
N. *nucifera* 'Chawan Basu' Cream-flowered.
N. 'Sharon' Pink-flowered.
N. 'Shirokunshi' (tulip lotus) White-flowered.
N. 'Suzanne' Pink-flowered.
N. 'The Queen' Ivory-flowered.

Marginal Plants

Marginals inhabit shallow water, usually around the edges of a pond. While most of their top growth is visible above the water surface, their bases and roots are under water, although many also grow well in marshy, saturated soil. Their vertical presence contrasts well with the flat water surface and the floating leaves of plants such as water lilies. Marginals planted around wildlife ponds can provide cover for birds, aquatic insects, and other small creatures. But while generally used in informal ponds, marginals placed in baskets on shelves break the rigidity of formal edges. It is important to position marginals in the depth of water that best suits each individual plant. Some prefer a water depth of only 2.5–5cm (1–2in), while others tolerate a depth of up to 30cm (12in). Lotuses *(see pp. 188–189)* may also be used as marginals, given tropical conditions and a minimum depth of 16cm (6in). Many marginal plants grow very quickly, and where space is limited they should be contained in isolated planting beds or planting crates. Some of the more robust rhizomatous species, such as reedmaces *(Typha)*, develop sharply pointed roots that can pierce flexible liners. Using planting crates will protect the liner.

Calla palustris (bog arum)
Deciduous or semi-evergreen perennial with long, creeping rhizomatous roots. White, arum-like flower spathes, echoing the leaves in shape, appear in spring, followed by clusters of red or orange berries. Propagate from seed in late summer or by division in spring. H 25cm (10in), S 30cm (12in), water depth to 5cm (2in).

Acorus calamus 'Variegatus' (myrtle flag, sweet flag)
Deciduous, rhizomatous perennial with iris-like leaves, mid-green with cream stripes, with some wrinkling along the edges. Small, conical flowers emerge just below the leaf tips. Propagate by division in spring. H 75cm (30in), S 60cm (24in), water depth to 22cm (9in).

Alisma plantago-aquatica (water plantain)
Rhizomatous perennial with rosettes of oval leaves held on long stalks above the water. Dainty, pinkish white flowers open in summer. Self-seeds readily in wet soil; the seeds are also a food source for wildlife. Propagate from seed in late summer or by division in spring. H 75cm (30in), S 45cm (18in), water depth to 25cm (10in).

Butomus umbellatus (flowering rush)
Perennial with bronze shoots that develop into thin, olive-green leaves. Rose-pink flowers are borne above the leaves on tall, cylindrical stems in summer. Best grown in open ground; if containerized it needs regular dividing and repotting. Propagate by division. H 60cm–1.2m (2–4ft), water depth 5–40cm (2–16in).

Cyperus papyrus (paper reed, papyrus)
Evergreen, perennial, frost-tender sedge with stout, leafless stems, triangular in cross-section. Mop-head tufts of fine, pendulous leaves and flower sprays with as many as 100 rays develop in summer. Best sheltered from wind. Propagate from seed or by division in autumn. H 3–5m (10–15ft), S 1m (3ft), water depth to 25cm (10in).

Eriophorum angustifolium (common cotton grass)
Evergreen marsh or marginal plant, forming dense tufts of grass-like leaves. Flowers form as white, downy "cotton balls". Best in acid conditions, such as peaty soil. Propagate from seed or by division in autumn. H 30–45cm (12–18in), S indefinite, water depth to 5cm (2in).

Glyceria maxima var. *variegata* (variegated water grass, sweet grass, manna grass)
Deciduous, perennial aquatic grass with leaves striped with creamy-white, often flushed pink at the base. Flowers are open heads of greenish spikelets in summer. Propagate from seed or by division in autumn. H 80cm (32in), S indefinite, water depth to 15cm (6in).

Houttuynia cordata 'Chameleon', syn. *H. cordata* 'Variegata'
Spreading, rooting, often invasive perennial. Red stems bear aromatic leaves splashed with yellow and red. Insignificant flowers with white bracts are produced in spring. Propagate by lifting runners in spring. H 15–60cm (6–24in), S indefinite, water depth no more than 5cm (2in).

Iris laevigata 'Alba'
Deciduous perennial forming clumps of sword-shaped leaves with no midrib. Sparsely branched stems bear white, broad-petalled, beardless flowers. Can also be grown in moist soil, but must not dry out. Divide rhizomes in late summer to propagate. H 60cm–1m (2–3ft), S indefinite, water depth to 7–10cm (3–4in).

Iris laevigata 'Mottled Beauty'
Deciduous perennial forming clumps of sword-shaped, soft green leaves without a midrib. The white flowers are broad-petalled and beardless; the fall petals are spotted pale blue. Also grows well in moist soil. Divide rhizomes in late summer to propagate. H 60cm–1m (2–3ft), S indefinite, water depth 7–10cm (3–4in).

Iris versicolor (blue flag, wild iris)
Deciduous, clump-forming perennial with narrow, grey-green leaves. Each branched stem bears three to five violet-blue flowers. Fall petals are white veined with purple, yellow-blotched at the base. Also grows in wet soil. Divide rhizomes in late summer to propagate. H 60cm (2ft), water depth to 5–7cm (2–3in).

Ludwigia palustris (water purslane)
Deciduous, half-hardy perennial that forms mats of branched, creeping stems in shallow water or mud. The leaves may become suffused with purple, particularly in full sun. Tiny, bell-shaped flowers appear in summer. Propagate from seed in spring. H 50cm (20in), S indefinite, water depth to 30cm (12in).

Lysichiton camtschatcensis
Vigorous, deciduous perennial with a stout rhizome. White, arum-like spathes surrounding erect spikes of small flowers appear in early spring, before the bright green, paddle-like, leathery leaves. Propagate from fresh seed in late summer. H 75cm (30in), S 60–90cm (24–36in), water depth 2.5cm (1in).

Narthecium ossifragum (bog asphodel)
Deciduous perennial with slender, rigid fans of reddish green leaves and, in summer, erect spikes of star-shaped, yellow flowers that mature to orange. Needs acid conditions; grow in peaty soil or pure sphagnum moss. Propagate by division or from seed. H 20–30cm (8–12in), S 20–30cm (8–12in), water depth 2.5cm (1in).

Lysichiton americanus (yellow skunk cabbage)
Vigorous, deciduous perennial that grows well in deep, moist soil and in still or moving water. Yellow spathes appear in early spring, followed by big, strongly veined leaves. Propagate from fresh seed in late summer. H 1.2m (4ft), S 75cm (2½ft), water depth 2.5cm (1in).

Menyanthes trifoliata (bog bean, buckbean, marsh trefoil)
Deciduous perennial with three-lobed, olive green leaves held on tall, sheathed stalks. Dainty, white to purplish flowers open from pink buds in late spring. Divide congested plants or propagate from stem cuttings in spring. H 23cm (9in), S indefinite, water depth 5cm (2in).

Orontium aquaticum (golden club)
Deciduous, rhizomatous perennial tolerating fairly deep water, on which the leaves, bluish-green with a silvery sheen on the underside, will float. The poker-like flowerheads stand well above the water. Propagate from fresh seed or by division in spring. H 30–45cm (12–18in), S 60cm (24in), water depth to 30cm (12in).

Phragmites australis 'Variegatus'
Variegated reed grass with leaves striped with bright yellow, fading to white and, in summer, heads of soft purple flowers. Also grows well in moist soil, but will be invasive. It is only suitable for large, natural poolsides. Propagate by division in spring. H 1.2–1.8m (4–6ft), S indefinite, water depth 7cm (3in).

Ranunculus lingua 'Grandiflorus' (greater spearwort)
Deciduous perennial bearing yellow flowers in late spring. Leaves are heart-shaped and long-stalked on non-flowering shoots; pointed and short-stalked on flowering shoots. Propagate from fresh seed or by division in spring. H 1.5m (2–5ft), S 2m (6ft), water depth 7–15cm (3–6in).

Peltandra undulata, syn. *P. virginica* (green arrow arum)
Deciduous perennial with arrow-shaped, bright green leaves. Narrow, yellow or white flower spathes, green-tinged when young, appear in summer, followed by green berries. Propagate from seed or by division in spring. H 90cm (3ft), S 60cm (2ft), water depth 5–7cm (2–3in).

Pontederia cordata (pickerel weed)
Robust, deciduous perennial that forms dense clumps of stems bearing smooth, narrowly heart-shaped leaves. In late summer, compact spikes of soft blue flowers develop from within a leaf at the stem tip. Propagate from fresh seed or by division in spring. H 75cm (30in), S 45cm (18in), water depth 13cm (5in).

Sagittaria latifolia (American arrowhead, duck potato, wapato)

Deciduous, runnering perennial with soft green leaf-blades and whorls of white flowers in summer. Develops tubers at the ends of subterranean stems that may be separated from the parent for propagation purposes. H 1.5m (5ft), S 60cm (2ft), water depth 15cm (6in).

Schoenoplectus lacustris subsp. *tabernaemontani* 'Zebrinus'

Perennial, spreading rush with a tough, creeping rhizome. Dark green stems have horizontal cream banding. Flowers are white and brown, in spike-like heads, in summer. Propagate by division in spring. H 1.5m (5ft), S indefinite, water depth 7–15cm (3–6in).

Scrophularia auriculata 'Variegata' (water figwort)

Evergreen perennial with striking, cream-edged foliage. The greenish-purple flowers are popular with bees but may be removed to prevent rampant self-seeding. Propagate by division or from softwood cuttings in summer. H 90cm (3ft), S 60cm (2ft), water depth 7cm (3in).

Saururus cernuus (lizard's tail, swamp lily, water dragon)

Deciduous perennial with erect stems carrying heart-shaped, bright green leaves. Spikes of waxy, fragrant flowers appear in summer. Looks best completely surrounded by water. Propagate by division in spring. H 23cm (9in), S 30cm (12in), water depth 10–15cm (4–6in).

Thalia dealbata

Evergreen, half-hardy perennial with bold, long-stalked, blue-green leaves with a white, mealy coating. Spikes of tubular, violet flowers are carried high above the leaves in summer, followed by decorative seed heads. Propagate from seed or by division in spring. H 1.5m (5ft), S 60cm (2ft), water depth to 15cm (6in).

Typha latifolia 'Variegata'
Deciduous perennial forming large clumps of wide, cream-striped leaves. Cylindrical "bulrush" heads amongst the foliage comprise light brown male flowers held above the dark brown female flowers. Propagate from seed or by division in spring. H 1–1.2m (3–4ft), S indefinite, water depth 25cm (10in).

Zantedeschia aethiopica 'Crowborough'
Half-hardy tuberous plant (hardier under 30cm/12in of water), ideal in a formal setting, with dark, glossy leaves and, in summer, a succession of large, fragrant, white flower spathes, with a central yellow spike. Propagate by offsets in winter. H 45cm–1m (1½–3ft), S 35–45cm (14–18in), water depth to 30cm (12in).

Veronica beccabunga (brooklime)
Semi-evergreen perennial with white-centred blue flowers and fleshy, creeping, rooting stems; an excellent scrambling plant for the water's edge. Replace old, straggly specimens; propagate by cuttings in summer, or from seed or by division in autumn. H 10cm (4in), S indefinite, water depth 7cm (3in).

Zantedeschia aethiopica 'Green Goddess'
Half-hardy tuberous plant with, throughout the summer, white-splashed green, arum-like flower spathes, each with a central yellow spike. It is ideal for a sunny corner of a formal pool. Propagate by separating offsets in winter. H 45cm–1m (1½–3ft), S 45–60cm (18–24in), water depth 15–22cm (6–9in).

Also Recommended

Acorus gramineus 'Pusillus'
Caltha palustris *(see p. 37)*
Colocasia esculenta 'Fontanesii' (frost-tender)
Equisetum japonicum
Houttuynia cordata 'Flore Pleno' *(see p. 21)*
Iris pseudacorus 'Variegata' *(see p. 43)*
Isolepis cernua
Juncus effusus 'Spiralis' *(see p. 27)*
Juncus ensifolius
Mentha aquatica *(see p. 43)*
Myosotis scorpioides *(see p. 32)*
Sagittaria sagittifolia *(see p. 47)*
Typha minima *(see p. 32)*

Where specific page references are not given for plant entries found in other sections, brief details are given in the Plant Index *(see pp. 210–213)*.

Moisture-loving Plants

There is a wide range of plants that not only tolerate but positively thrive in moist soil. They include not only those plants seen growing naturally by streams and poolsides, but also many that, although traditionally raised in more normal soil conditions, will excel in this fringe environment, growing with a vigour and lushness they seldom exhibit in drier soil in high summer. Moisture-loving plants are often referred to, and may be offered for sale, as "bog plants", but this is a misleading description. While boggy soil saturated with water is ideal for many shallow-water aquatic plants (*see* Marginal Plants, *pp. 190–195*), nearly all moisture-lovers need good drainage and will not tolerate waterlogging. They can be used in surrounding beds to bridge the gap between aquatic plants contained in formal, enclosed pools and the rest of the garden, provided that they are given moisture-retentive soil and are well-watered in dry spells. Alternatively, they can be used to edge informal clay-bottomed or lined ponds, planted above the waterline yet where the soil is still naturally damp. Many moisture lovers are spreading, and will mingle informally.

Ajuga reptans 'Multicolor', syn. 'Rainbow', 'Tricolor'
Hardy, evergreen perennial whose stems spread and root to form a creeping mat. The blue spring flowers with purple bracts are carried on spikes 10–13cm (4–5in) high above bronze-pink leaves splashed with gold. Propagate by division in spring. H 10–13cm (4–5in), S 45cm (18in).

Anagallis tenella 'Studland' (bog pimpernel)
Hardy, creeping perennial that roots freely as its stems spread. Mats of small, rounded leaves are brightened by a profusion of star-shaped, sweetly scented, deep pink flowers in spring. Plants are short-lived; propagate from soft tip cuttings in spring or early summer.
H 5–10cm (2–4in), S 15–30cm (6–12in).

Vivid Leaves
Bright, striking foliage borne on upright stems.

Edible Stem
Stems may be candied for culinary use.

Angelica archangelica (angelica)
Short-lived perennial, often grown as a biennial, that grows rapidly, becoming a very large plant. Self-seeding freely, its lifespan may be prolonged by deadheading. The bright green, deeply divided leaves are aromatic; yellow-green flowerheads appear in late summer. Propagate from seed. H 2m (6ft), S 1m (3ft).

Arisaema candidissimum
Frost-hardy, tuberous perennial that appears in early summer; erect stems support hooded spathes that are pink-and-white striped within, followed by large, three-lobed leaves that fade in autumn to a straw colour, surrounding spikes of red fruits. Propagate from seed or offsets. H 15cm (6in), S 30–45cm (12–18in).

Aruncus dioicus (goat's beard)
Hardy, herbaceous perennial, forming dense hummocks of broad, fern-like leaves, bronze-green in spring, turning light green by summer. Large, creamy plumes of flowers gradually turn brown on the more feathery male plants, while seed pods form on females. Propagate from seed or by division. H 1.5–1.8m (5–6ft), S 1m (3ft).

❄❄❄

Astilbe 'Venus'
Summer-flowering, hardy perennial with plumes of shell-pink flowers. The dark green foliage has a coppery tint when young. The dried, brown flowerheads are attractive in winter, so should not be removed until the following spring. Propagate by division in spring or autumn. H 1m (3ft), S 1m (3ft).

❄❄❄

Chelone obliqua (turtle head, shellflower)
Hardy, herbaceous perennial. Its upright stems support serrated, dark green leaves. In late summer and autumn it produces terminal heads of rich reddish-purple, penstemon-like flowers. Propagate from seed or by division in spring or autumn, or from soft tip cuttings in summer. H 1m (3ft), S 50cm (20in).

❄❄❄

Carex elata 'Aurea', syn. *Carex stricta* 'Bowles' Golden' (Bowles' golden sedge)
Hardy, evergreen perennial, with golden-yellow tufts of grassy foliage. Inconspicuous brown flowers, forming blackish spikelets, are held among the leaves in summer. Will also grow well in shallow water. Propagate by division in spring. H 15in–3ft (38cm–1m), S 1m (3ft).

❄❄❄

Carex pendula (pendulous sedge)
Hardy perennial with grass-like leaves. Tall, triangular stems support graceful, pendulous spikes of brown flowers, very striking when reflected in a still pool. Will also grow well in very shallow water, and is ideal for the margins of a wildlife pool. Propagate by division in spring. H 60–90cm (2–3ft), S 45cm (18in).

❄❄❄

Cimicifuga simplex (bugbane)
Herbaceous perennial that will grow well in light shade. This species is one of the last to flower, sometimes well into late autumn. The flowers are slightly fragrant, held in delicate spikes on dark, wiry stems; plants benefit from staking in open sites. Propagate from seed or by division in spring. H 1.2m (4ft), S 45cm (18in).

Cornus stolonifera 'Flaviramea'

Cornus stolonifera 'Flaviramea'

Vigorous, deciduous, spreading shrub suited to moist or well-drained soils, chiefly grown for its bright, greenish-yellow young stems, which can be renewed by hard pruning in early spring. Propagate from softwood cuttings in summer, or from hardwood cuttings in autumn or winter. H 1.2–2m (4–6ft), S 4m (12ft).

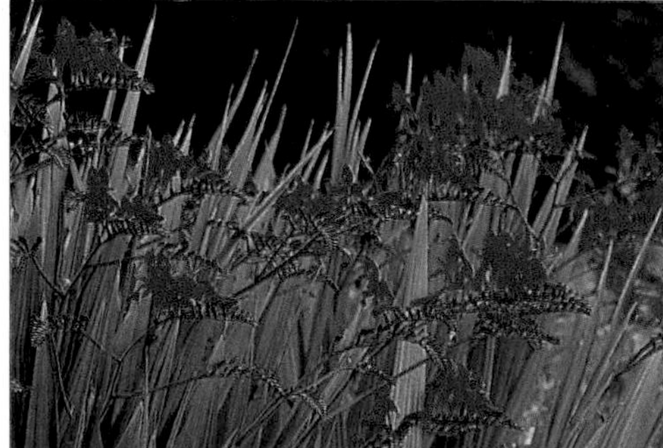

Crocosmia 'Lucifer'

Vigorous, clump-forming, cormous plant that grows in moist or dry soils. Erect, sword-like, bright green leaves surround purple, wiry stems that support flame-red, trumpet-shaped flowers in dense, branching spikes in mid-summer. Propagate by division in spring. H 1.2m (4ft), S 25–30cm (10–12in).

Filipendula purpurea

Herbaceous perennial, forming informal clumps of deeply divided leaves and dense clusters of tiny, fragrant, rose-pink flowers in summer, followed by bronze-red seedheads. It is susceptible to mildew if soil becomes dry. Propagate in autumn from seed or by division. H 1.2m (4ft), S 60–90cm (2–3ft).

Filipendula ulmaria 'Aurea'

Herbaceous perennial, with beautifully divided leaves, golden-green in spring, turning to pale green. Branching heads of creamy flowers are carried above the foliage in mid-summer. Deadhead promptly to encourage new growth. Propagate in autumn from seed or by division. H 60cm (2ft), S 45cm (18in).

Filipendula vulgaris (dropwort)

Interesting perennial for the fringes of moist soil, with mat-forming, carrot-like foliage that may be used in salads. Flowers are borne in branching, creamy heads, tinged pink on the undersides. 'Multiplex' is a double-flowered cultivar. Propagate in autumn from seed or by division. H 60–75cm (2–2½ft), S 60cm (2ft).

Gunnera manicata
Large perennial with enormous, jagged leaves, up to 1.5m (5ft) across, borne on thick stems. Conical clusters of green flowers appear in spring, followed by rust-brown seeds. Protect from wind and, in cool climates, mulch for protection in winter. Propagate from seed or by division in spring. H and S 2.1–3m (7–10ft).

Hemerocallis fulva 'Flore Pleno'
Vigorous, herbaceous perennial forming mounds of light green, strap-like leaves. In mid- to late summer it produces spikes of rich orange-buff, trumpet-shaped, double flowers, longer-lasting than the blooms of many other daylilies. Propagate by division in autumn or spring. H 1–1.2m (3–4ft), S 75cm (2½ft).

Hosta fortunei var. *albopicta*
Vigorous, clump-forming perennial with spectacular leaves nearly 30cm (12in) long. These are pale green, with dark veins and creamy yellow centres fading to dull green. Pale violet flowers are borne on graceful stalks in early summer. Propagate by division in spring. H 75cm (2½ft), S 1m (3ft).

Hosta fortunei var. *aureomarginata*
Herbaceous, clump-forming perennial with mid-green leaves that are smaller than those of many hostas, and have irregular cream margins. Pale violet, trumpet-shaped flowers are held well above the foliage on graceful stalks in mid-summer. Propagate by division in spring. H 75cm (2½ft), S 1m (3ft).

Hosta 'Frances Williams'
Vigorous, herbaceous, clump-forming perennial. The large, heart-shaped, deeply ribbed and puckered leaves are glaucous blue, with a wide, creamy margin. In early summer, the pale lavender-blue of the flowers makes a cool contrast to the foliage. Propagate by division in spring. H 1m (3ft), S 1.5m (5ft).

☼ 💧 💧 ❄❄❄

Inula hookeri

Herbaceous perennial that forms spreading clumps of branched stems. It has oval, light green to yellow leaves and a mass of woolly buds that, in mid- to late summer, open into slightly scented, greenish-yellow, finely petalled, daisy-like flowers. It can be invasive. Propagate from seed or by division. H 75cm (2½ft), S 1m (3ft).

☼ 💧 💧 ❄❄❄

Iris ensata (syn. *I. kaempferi*) 'Blue Peter'

Rhizomatous, herbaceous perennial with dense tufts of bold, sword-shaped leaves and blue flowers, 8–15cm (3–6in) across. Dislikes lime. Can be used as a shallow marginal, provided that it is removed from saturated soil in winter. Propagate by division in late summer. H 60–90cm (2–3ft), S indefinite.

☼ 💧 💧 ❄❄❄

Iris sibirica (Siberian flag)

Rhizomatous, herbaceous perennial with upright sheaves of grass-like leaves. Each stem bears two or three dark-veined blue or blue-purple flowers, 5–10cm (2–4in) across. An adaptable plant that will also flourish in dry soil. Propagate from seed or by division in late summer. H 45cm (18in), S 90cm (3ft).

☼ 💧 💧 ❄❄❄ 🏆

Kirengeshoma palmata

Erect, herbaceous perennial, forming clumps of large, rounded leaves, hairy on both sides with irregularly cut edges. The funnel-shaped flowers, pale yellow and waxen, hang in loose sprays on purplish stems in late summer. Dislikes lime. Propagate from seed or by division in autumn or spring. H 1m (3ft), S 60cm (2ft).

☼ 💧 ❄❄❄

Leucojum aestivum (summer snowflake)

Bulb with glossy, strap-shaped, daffodil-like leaves of rich green. In springtime, sturdy, green stems produce loose clusters of bell-shaped flowers resembling large snowdrops, with white petals tipped with green. Propagate from seed in autumn, or by division in autumn or spring. H 15–60cm (6–24in), S 15–30cm (6–12in).

☼ 💧 ❄❄❄ 🏆

Ligularia 'Gregynog Gold'

Clump-forming, herbaceous perennial with large, richly veined, deep green leaves. In mid- to late summer, daisy-like, orange-yellow flowers are borne in large, pyramidal spikes. Tends to wilt quickly on bright, windy days or during dry spells. Propagate from seed or by division in spring. H 2m (6ft), S 60cm (2ft).

Ligularia przewalskii

Elegant, clump-forming, herbaceous perennial with dark green, deeply lobed basal leaves. The stems are dark purple and carry narrow spikes of small, ragged, daisy-like yellow flowers in mid- to late summer. Plants tend to wilt in bright sunshine. Propagate from seed or by division in spring. H 2m (6ft), S 1m (3ft).

Lobelia 'Bees' Flame'

Clump-forming, half-hardy perennial with oval or lanceolate, bronze-red leaves and tall, strong spikes of large, velvety, luminous scarlet flowers in late summer. Do not leave in wet soil over winter, and in cool temperate climates provide a protective winter mulch. Propagate by division in spring. H 1m (3ft), S 30cm (12in).

Lobelia 'Cherry Ripe'

Herbaceous, clump-forming perennial with spikes of scarlet flowers from mid- to late summer. The fresh green leaves are often tinged with bronze. Like 'Bees' Flame', this half-hardy cultivar should be given a protective winter mulch in cool temperate climates. Propagate by division in spring. H 1m (3ft), S 25cm (10in).

Lobelia 'Will Scarlet'

Half-hardy, clump-forming perennial with dark green leaves tinged with red. It produces tall spikes of bright scarlet, two-lipped flowers in late summer. In temperate climates, protect in winter with a mulch, or lift from wet soil and overwinter in pots under glass. Propagate by division in spring. H 1m (3ft), S 30cm (12in).

Lobelia x *gerardii* 'Vedrariensis'

Clump-forming, vigorous, hardy, herbaceous perennial. Produces long-lasting, dense spikes of two-lipped flowers on stout stems in late summer and early autumn, in varying tones of rich violet-purple. The basal rosettes of oval leaves are dark green tinged with red. Propagate by division in spring. H 1m (3ft), S 30cm (12in).

☼ ♦ ◊ ❄❄❄ 🏆

Lysimachia nummularia 'Aurea' (creeping Jenny, moneywort)

Prostrate, carpeting, herbaceous perennial with bright yellow flowers in summer. The rooting stems produce soft yellow leaves that darken in late summer or in shade. Can be invasive. Propagate by division in spring or from seed in autumn. H 2.5–5cm (1–2in), S indefinite.

☼ ♦ ◊ ❄❄❄ 🏆

Mimulus cardinalis

Erect, branching perennial producing, from mid-summer onwards, sprays of snapdragon-like flowers. It can become untidy in late summer and should be cut back to prompt new growth. Propagate from seed or by division in spring, or grow as an annual where winters are severe. H 60–90cm (2–3ft), S 90cm (3ft).

☼ ♦ ◊ ❄❄❄

Mimulus luteus (yellow musk)

Spreading perennial with prolific, snapdragon-like yellow flowers, sometimes with browny-red spots, produced in succession from mid-summer onwards above lush, hairy, mid-green foliage. A rampant self-seeder, ideally suited for a large, informal wildlife pond. May also be propagated by division. H and S 45cm (18in).

☼ ♦ ◊ ❄❄❄ 🏆

Macleaya microcarpa 'Kelway's Coral Plume'

Imposing herbaceous perennial with spikes of cream or white flowers. Leaves are grey or olive-green above, and downy white below, on glaucous stems. Chop through roots to control spread. Divide in spring or take root cuttings in winter. H 2–2.5m (6–8ft), S 1–1.2m (3–4ft).

☼ ♦ ◊ ❄❄❄

Miscanthus sinensis 'Zebrinus'

Clump-forming, perennial grass that makes a distinctive specimen plant. Tough stems and leaves develop transverse yellow bands from mid-summer onwards. The flowers are silky-white on pinkish-brown spikelets, held in fan-shaped heads in autumn. Propagate by division in spring. H 1.2m (4ft), S 45cm (18in).

Osmunda regalis (royal fern)
Elegant, deciduous fern. Mature plants bear sterile fronds to 1.5m (5ft), in a pale, copper-tinted green that deepens to rich russet. Pale brown, fertile flower spikes appear at the tips of taller fronds. Protect the base with a mulch in winter. May be propagated by division in winter. H 2m (6ft), S 1m (3ft).

Persicaria bistorta 'Superba'
Vigorous, clump-forming, herbaceous perennial with dense, dock-like basal foliage. Erect, broad, bottlebrush-like spikes of soft pink flowers are produced over a long period. Plants can become invasive. Propagate from seed or by division in spring or autumn. H 60–75cm (2–2½ft), S 60cm (2ft).

Parnassia palustris (grass of Parnassus)
Small perennial, often evergreen, with low tufts of heart-shaped, pale or mid-green leaves. Buttercup-like white flowers, with dark green or purplish green veins, are borne on erect stems in late spring and early summer. Not easy to establish in cultivated conditions. Sow seed in autumn. H 20cm (8in), S 6cm (2½in).

Persicaria campanulata
Stout, spreading, mat-forming, herbaceous perennial with attractively crinkled, dark green leaves that are silver or buff on the underside. From mid-summer onwards it produces a long-lasting display of small, pale pink or white, bell-shaped flowers. Propagate from seed or by division in spring or autumn. H and S 1m (3ft).

Petasites japonicus (butterbur)
Spreading perennial with stout rhizomatous roots. Dense cones of small, greenish-white, daisy-like flowers are followed by impressive leaves, up to 1m (3ft) across. A dramatic specimen for informal ponds, but can be difficult to control. Propagate by division in spring or autumn. H 1m (3ft), S 1.5m (5ft).

Phalaris arundinacea var. *picta*
(gardener's garters)

Rhizomatous grass with broad, brightly white-striped leaves that turn to a biscuit colour in winter. Bears narrow clusters of flower spikelets in summer. Contrasts well with green or purple foliage, but can be invasive. Propagate by division in spring. H 1m (3ft), S indefinite.

Primula beesiana

Compact, perennial "candelabra primula" with rosettes of oval, slightly toothed leaves, waxy white-powdered below. Mid-summer-flowering, in rose-purple with a yellow eye. Mixes well with many other candelabras, particularly *P. pulverulenta*. Propagate from seed when fresh or in spring. H 60–90cm (2–3ft), S 90cm (1ft).

Phlox paniculata 'Norah Leigh'

Upright, herbaceous perennial with attractive foliage; leaves are cream with a thin, central zone of green. Pyramidal heads of fragrant, pale pink flowers appear in summer. Propagate from seed in autumn or spring, by division in spring, or from root cuttings in winter. Dislikes chalky or clay soils. H and S 60cm (2ft).

Physostegia virginiana subsp. *speciosa* 'Variegata'

Erect perennial with toothed, cream-edged leaves and, in late summer, spikes of hooded, purple-pink blooms. These have hinged stalks, allowing the flowers to be moved into different positions, where they will remain. Propagate by division in spring. H 1m (3ft), S 60cm (2ft).

Primula bulleyana

Compact, upright, herbaceous perennial with rosettes of oval or lance-shaped, dark green, toothed leaves. The candelabra flowers, deep orange or sometimes mauve, appear in early summer and maintain a vivid display for many weeks. Seeds readily, making good ground cover on moist soil. H 60cm (2ft), S 30cm (1ft).

Primula florindae (giant cowslip)
Bold, upright, clump-forming, herbaceous perennial, one of the most vigorous of the waterside primulas. Established plants produce several stems with long, drooping heads of fragrant, white-powdered, sulphur yellow bells. Propagate from seed when fresh or in spring. H 60–90cm (2–3ft), S 30–60cm (1–2ft).

Primula prolifera
Vigorous, herbaceous perennial. Basal rosettes of rich green leaves surround tall, green flower stems with orange buds. The golden-yellow, white-powdered flowers open in early summer. A good choice for mass planting by streams. Propagate from seed when fresh or in spring. H 90cm (3ft), S 60cm (2ft).

Primula japonica 'Miller's Crimson'
Vigorous, upright, clump-forming, herbaceous perennial with pale green leaves that are oval to lance-shaped, toothed, and coarse. In early summer, sturdy spikes of intense crimson flowers are produced. Unusually for a selected cultivar, it breeds true from seed. May also be divided. H 30–60cm (1–2ft), S 30–45cm (1–1½ft).

Primula pulverulenta
One of the most elegant candelabra primulas, although slightly smaller than many. This clump-forming species has red tubular flowers with purple-red eyes, on floury stems. The mid-green leaves are broadly lance-shaped and toothed. Propagate from seed when fresh or in spring. H 60cm (2ft), S 30–45cm (1–1½ft).

Primula rosea
Clump-forming perennial that, in early spring, bears small, flat heads of rose-pink flowers, often flushed bronze when young. Less vigorous than most primulas and waterside plants; care is required to prevent it from being smothered. Propagate from seed when fresh or in spring. H 10–15cm (4–6in), S 15–20cm (6–8in).

◧ 💧 💧 ❄❄❄

Pulmonaria angustifolia subsp. *azurea*
Herbaceous perennial that makes slow-growing ground cover in a wide range of conditions. Narrow, lance-shaped, rough leaves open as rich blue flowers, sometimes pink-tinged, appear. These are a good nectar source around a wildlife pond. Propagate by division in spring or autumn. H 23cm (9in), S 20–30cm (8–12in).

◧ 💧 ❄❄❄

Rheum palmatum 'Atrosanguineum'
Stout, clump-forming cultivar grown for its large, deeply cut leaves. Rich red-purple when young, they retain this colour on the undersides in maturity. Dense spikes of small, rust-red flowers appear in early summer. Grows best in deep, moist soil. Propagate from seed in autumn or by division in spring. H and S 2m (6ft).

◧ 💧 💧 ❄❄❄ 🏆

Rodgersia podophylla
Clump-forming perennial with large, attractive leaves, bronze-veined when young, turning green, then copper. The flowers are cream, occasionally pink. A good substitute for gunnera in a small garden. Must have shelter from wind. Propagate by division in spring or from seed in autumn. H 1.2m (4ft), S 1m (3ft).

◧ 💧 💧 ❄❄❄

Rodgersia sambucifolia
Rhizomatous perennial, forming clumps of emerald green, sometimes bronze-tinged leaves. Astilbe-like heads of pink or white flowers appear in summer. Well-suited to the woodland water garden or at the side of a woodland stream. Propagate by division in spring or from seed in autumn. H 1–1.2m (3–4ft), S 1m (3ft).

☐ 💧 ❄❄❄

Senecio smithii
Bushy, herbaceous perennial whose woolly stems are clothed with long, serrated, leathery, dark green leaves. Terminal clusters of white, daisy-like flowers with yellow centres are held above the foliage in early summer, followed by attractive, fluffy white seed heads. Propagate by division in spring. H 1–1.2m (3–4ft), S 1m (3ft).

Trillium erectum (stinking Benjamin, birthroot, squawroot)
Clump-forming perennial with mid-green leaves borne in whorls of three. Maroon-purple spring flowers are unpleasant-smelling but attractive, with an indigo centre and pale anthers. Propagate by division in late summer or from seed in spring. H 30–45cm (12–18in), S 30cm (12in).

Trollius europaeus (globe flower)
Compact, herbaceous perennial resembling a large, double buttercup, with thick, fibrous roots and rounded, deeply divided, mid-green leaves. Solitary, globose, many-petalled, lemon to mid-yellow flowers appear in spring. Propagate by division or from seed in early autumn. H 60cm (24in), S 45cm (18in).

Trollius pumilus
Small, tuft-forming perennial with fibrous roots and basal green leaves that are crinkled and finely divided. Solitary cup-shaped flowers, yellow on the interior, dark wine-red or crimson outside, appear through late spring and early summer. Propagate by division or from seed in early autumn. H and S 15cm (6in).

Veratrum album (false helleborine)
Clump-forming, potentially harmful perennial with oval, deeply pleated, dark green leaves. These form arching mounds of foliage below dense terminal heads of palest green summer flowers. Ideal in a woodland setting, but prone to slug damage. Propagate by division or from seed in autumn. H 2m (6ft), S 60cm (2ft).

Also Recommended

Alnus incana
Arundo donax
Astilbe 'Fanal'
Brunnera macrophylla
Carex hachijoensis 'Evergold'
Darmera peltata (*see p. 47*)
Deschampsia cespitosa
Dryopteris filix-mas (*see p. 39*)
Eupatorium purpureum
Gentiana asclepiadea
Geum 'Borisii'
Gunnera tinctoria (frost-hardy)
Heuchera sanguinea
Hosta undulata var. *aureomarginata* (*see p. 30*)
Juncus ensifolius
Liatris spicata
Ligularia dentata 'Desdemona'
Ligularia 'The Rocket' (*see p. 37*)
Lobelia cardinalis (*see p. 21*)
Lobelia 'Cinnabar Rose'
Lysimachia nummularia
Lythrum salicaria
Matteuccia struthiopteris (*see p. 36*)
Metasequoia glyptostroboides
Miscanthus sinensis 'Gracillimus'
Persicaria amplexicaulis
Phalaris arundinacea var. *picta* 'Feesey'
Primula denticulata
Rheum palmatum
Onoclea sensibilis
Salix hastata 'Wehrhahnii' (*see p. 20*)

Where specific page references are not given to plant entries found in other sections, brief details are given in the Plant Index (*pp. 210–213*).

Glossary

ACIDIC (of soil, water) With a *pH* value of less than 7.
AGGREGATE Similar to *ballast*, a loose mixture of crushed stone and sand used to reinforce *cement*.
ALGAE Microscopic, non-flowering plants, mostly aquatic.
ALGICIDE A proprietary substance for controlling algae.
ALKALINE (of soil, water) With a *pH* value above 7.
ALPINE A term loosely applied to rock-garden plants.
AMPHIBIOUS Able to live both on land and in water.
ANAEROBIC An environment low in, or free of, oxygen, conducive to certain bacterial activity.
ANNUAL Plant that flowers, sets seed, and dies within one growing season.
ANTHER The part of a stamen that produces pollen (the male cells).
AQUATIC COMPOST A proprietary planting mixture composed mainly of loam, sometimes with a small proportion of silt and sand.
AQUATIC PLANT Any plant that can grow with its roots surrounded by water, either free-floating or in saturated soil.
ARMOURED CABLING Cabling with reinforced protective covering for safety.
AXIL The upper angle formed where a leaf joins a stem, or where a stem joins a branch.

BACKFILL To fill in a hole around the object occupying it, for example a rigid pool unit or a plant's root ball.
BALLAST A sand and gravel mix used in making *concrete*.
BARBELS The spines or bristles hanging down from the jaws of certain fish.
BARE-ROOTED Plants sold with their roots bare of soil.
BASAL Growing at the base of a stem or from the *crown* of a plant.
BATTEN A narrow strip of wood.
BEARER A supporting beam or plank on which *joists* rest.
BEDDING MORTAR A mixture of sand and *cement* used for laying paving stones.
BENTOMAT A waterproof lining material containing *bentonite*.
BENTONITE A powder derived from fossilized volcanic ash which, when mixed with water and added to clay, swells into a water-resistant gel.
BIENNIAL A plant that flowers and dies in its second growing season.
BLEED (of plants) To lose sap from a cut or wound.
BLUE MOTTLING An indication on the surface that the soil below is waterlogged.
BOG GARDEN An area where the soil is permanently damp.
BOG PLANT Plants that will grow and thrive with their roots in wet soil; many will also grow in shallow water, and are more properly called *marginal plants*.
BOLSTER CHISEL A steel chisel with a wide blade used with a *club hammer* for cutting bricks, pavers, or blocks.
BRACT A modified leaf at the base of a flower. Bracts may resemble normal leaves, or be small and scale-like, or large and brightly coloured.
BREEZE BLOCK An undecorative, moulded concrete block.
BRICKLAYER'S TROWEL A pointed, flat-bladed trowel used to lift, shape, and apply mortar to brickwork.
BUD A condensed shoot containing an embryonic leaf, leaf cluster, or flower.
BUILDER'S SQUARE Timber triangle used to check the accuracy of right-angles.
BULB A modified, usually underground, stem acting as a storage organ, generally comprising layers of tightly packed fleshy scale leaves on a basal plate from which roots grow downwards. An outer papery layer called the *tunic* may be present.
BULBIL A small, bulb-like organ usually borne in a leaf axil, or occasionally on a stem or in a flowerhead. Can be separated and used for *propagation*.
BULBLET A small bulb that develops from the basal plate of a mature bulb, usually outside the *tunic*. Can be separated and used for *propagation*.
BUTYL Strong, durable, waterproof material made of rubber.

CALYX The collective term for the sepals; the outer whorl of usually green segments which enclose a flower in bud.
CEMENT A fine, grey powder comprising calcined limestone and clay, which is mixed with sand and water to make *mortar*, or, with the addition of *ballast*, *concrete*.
CHAMFER To bevel symmetrically a right-angled edge or corner.
CIRCUIT BREAKER See *Residual current device*.
CLUB HAMMER A heavy, mallet-shaped hammer used with a *bolster chisel* to cut walling stones.
COCOON A protective envelope secreted by an insect *larva* in which a *pupa* develops.
CONCRETE A mixture of sand, *cement*, water, and small stones, which sets to form an extremely strong, durable building material; often used to make foundations.
CONDUIT A tube or duct conducting water or enclosing cables.
CONIFER Cone-bearing tree, usually evergreen, but occasionally deciduous.
COPING The top course of stones or bricks in a wall; often, flat or sloping stones that differ from those used in the wall, for decorative effect or to allow rainwater to run off.
CORM A bulb-like, underground organ, consisting of a swollen stem or stem base, often surrounded by a papery *tunic*.
COUNTERSUNK SCREW A screw with a head that, when fully screwed down, lies flush with the surface.
CROWN The basal part of a *herbaceous* plant where roots and stems join at soil level and from where new shoots are produced.
CULTIVAR A distinct plant variation which has originated in cultivation, not in the wild. An abbreviation of "cultivated variety", often itself abbreviated to "cv".
CULVERT An aperture in e.g. brickwork that allows water to flow out from a concealed header pool or tank.
CUTTING A portion of a plant (a leaf, stem, root, or bud) that is cut off to be used for propagation. A hardwood cutting is taken from mature wood of both deciduous and evergreen plants at the end of the growing season; a semi-ripe cutting is taken from half-ripened wood during the growing season, while a softwood, soft stem, or soft tip cutting is taken from young, green growth during the growing season.
CV Abbreviation of *cultivar*.

DATUM PEG A wooden peg driven into the ground; the top of, or a mark on, the peg is used as a reference point to establish a horizontal level.
DEADHEADING The removal of spent flowers or flowerheads.
DECIDUOUS Of plants that shed their leaves at the end of the growing season and renew them at the beginning of the next.
DELIVERY PIPE The pipe that runs from a pump to the water outlet in a recirculating feature.
DIBBER A tool used for making holes in soil or compost into which seedlings or cuttings are inserted.
DIEBACK The progressive death of shoots from the tip downwards as a result of damage or disease.
DIVISION A method of thinning or increasing plants by dividing them into pieces, each with a portion of the root system and one or more shoots (or dormant buds).
DORMANCY The state of temporary cessation of growth in plants, and slowing down of other activities, usually during winter.
DOUBLE FLOWER A flower with more than the normal number of petals in several rows, with few or no stamens visible or present.

ELBOW JOINT A length of connecting pipe bent to form a right-angle.
ENGINEERING BRICK A dense, hard, water-resistant brick, dark in colour and hence inconspicuous under water.
EVERGREEN Plants that retain their foliage for more than one growing season.

FALLS (of irises) The horizontal or, more often, pendent petals at the base of the flower.
FAMILY In plant classification, a grouping together of related plant genera.
FLEXIBLE LINER A waterproof *butyl*, *PVC*, or plastic material.
FLOW ADJUSTER An adjustable valve used to control water flow.
FOOTING A narrow trench *foundation*, usually for a wall.
FOUNDATION A solid base, often of *concrete*, on which a structure stands.
FROG The hollow in a brick.
FROND The leaf-like organ of a fern. Some ferns produce both barren and fertile fronds, the latter bearing spores.
FROST HARDY A plant usually able to withstand light frosts, provided that they are not prolonged.
FROST TENDER A plant vulnerable to frost damage.
FRY Young fish.
FULLY HARDY A plant able to withstand year-round climatic conditions, including frost, without protection.
FUNGICIDE A proprietary substance for controlling diseases caused by fungi.

GALVANIZED Of metal objects such as nails, with a protective coating of zinc to protect them from rusting.
GENUS A category in plant classification between *family* and *species*, denoting a group of related species linked by a range of common characteristics. For example, all species of forget-me-not belong to the genus *Myosotis*.
GERMINATION The starting of a seed into growth.
GILL The breathing organ of a fish.
GLABROUS Completely smooth.
GLAUCOUS With a blue-green, blue-grey, grey, or white bloom.
GLOBOSE Shaped like a globe.

HABIT Characteristic, natural form of growth of a plant – upright, prostrate, weeping, etc.
HALF-HARDY A plant not able to tolerate frost, but generally able to withstand lower temperatures than frost-tender plants.
HARDCORE Broken bricks, concrete, or stones used to create a firm base for foundations or paving.
HARDPAN A virtually impermeable layer of compacted soil.
HARDWOOD CUTTING See *Cutting*.
HARDWOOD TIMBER Timber cut from deciduous trees.
HARDY See *Fully hardy*.
HEAD The height of a water outlet above the level of the *reservoir pool*.
HEADER POOL The uppermost pool in a recirculating water feature.
HERBACEOUS A non-woody plant whose upper parts die down to a rootstock at the end of the growing season.
HOSE CONNECTOR A moulded plastic joint used to join two pipes together.
HUMUS Decomposed *organic* matter that enriches soil.
HYBRID The offspring of genetically different parents, which are usually of distinct species.
HYPERTUFA A *concrete* mix incorporating some *organic* matter, encouraging mosses and algae to grow on its surface for an "antique" effect.

INFLORESCENCE A group of flowers borne on a single stem.
INVASIVE Tending to spread.

JOIST A wooden supporting beam that runs beneath and usually perpendicular to planks, used e.g. for flooring, decking, or bridges.

LARVA The active immature stage of some insects.
LEACHING The loss of nutrients from the *topsoil*, carried downwards by water.
LEAF AXIL See *Axil*.
LOAM A term used for soil of medium texture, often easily worked, that contains more or less equal parts of sand, silt, and clay, and is usually rich in *humus*.
LOBE Of a leaf shape, where the margin is indented at one or more points.
LOG ROLL Edging material made from wooden stakes.
LUMP HAMMER See *Club hammer*.

MARGINAL PLANTS Plants that grow partially submerged in shallow water or in boggy soil at the water's edge.
MARGINAL SHELF A shallow planting area created for marginal plants.
MEALY A sprinkling or covering of powder resembling meal.
MIDRIB The primary, usually central vein of a leaf or leaflet.
MOISTURE-LOVERS Plants that thrive in moist soil. Unlike bog plants, moisture-lovers need some soil drainage and do not tolerate waterlogged conditions.
MORTAR A mixture of *cement*, sand, and water used to bond bricks and stones, and for *pointing* and *rendering*.
MULCH Various materials, for example bark chippings, applied in a layer to the soil surface in order to suppress weeds, conserve moisture, and maintain a cool, even root temperature.

NACREOUS A mother-of-pearl sheen.
NATIVE Plants originating in the country where they are grown.
NECTAR Sugary liquid secreted by flowers, which is often attractive to pollinating insects.
NEUTRAL (of soil) With a *pH* value of 7, i.e., neither acid nor alkaline.
NODE The point on a stem where leaves, shoots, or flowers arise.
NON-RETURN VALVE A valve that allows water to flow in one direction only.

OFFSET A young plant that arises by natural, vegetative reproduction, usually at the base of the parent plant.
ORGANIC 1) Chemically, referring to compounds containing carbon derived from decomposed plant or animal organisms. 2) Loosely, applied to *mulches*, composts, or similar materials derived from plant materials that have the effect of improving soil texture and quality.
ORNAMENTAL A plant grown for its decorative qualities.
OVERWINTER (of plants) Usually, to survive the winter by being given some protection against frost: for example a *mulch*, or cover under glass.
OXYGENATOR Submerged aquatic plant which performs a key functional role in ponds; the leaves and stems release oxygen into the water as a by-product of *photosynthesis*.

PANICLE A branched *inflorescence* often consisting of several racemose branches (see *Raceme*).
PEA SHINGLE Fine gravel, often used as a top-dressing for soil.
PERENNIAL A plant that lives for more than three seasons, commonly applied to herbaceous plants.
pH A measure of *acidity* or *alkalinity*.
PHOTOSYNTHESIS The production of organic compounds required for growth in plants by a complex process involving chlorophyll (the principal green plant pigment), light energy, carbon dioxide, and water.
PINNATE Leaves with leaflets arranged on either side of a central stem, usually in opposite pairs.
PLANTLET Usually used to describe a small plant produced naturally by the parent plant that can be detached and grown on separately as a method of propagation.
PLUMB-LINE A length of string with a metal weight attached, used to determine vertical alignment.
POINTING Filling the joins in brickwork and stonework with mortar.
POLLINATION The transfer of pollen from *anthers* to *stigmas*.
POLYETHYLENE A material closely related to polythene, but with a stronger and more durable consistency.
POT BOUND A plant whose growth is restricted by the size of its container; its roots become congested and tangled.
POTTING ON Transferring a young plant to a larger container once it has outgrown its module or original pot.
PREFORMED UNIT Ready-made, rigid mouldings for pools and streams.
PRICKING OUT The transplanting of seedlings from their germinating bed, tray, or pot to positions where they have more room to grow.
PROPAGATION The increase of plants by seed (usually sexual) or by vegetative (asexual) means.
PUDDLING Coating with a mixture of wet clay that is impervious to water.
PUPA The inactive, immature stage of an insect, during which it metamorphoses into the adult stage, often in a *cocoon*.
PVC A strong, durable waterproof material made of vinyl chloride.

RACEME An unbranched flower cluster with, usually, many stalked flowers borne on a long stem.
RECONSTITUTED STONE Natural stone *aggregate* cast in preformed shapes such as slabs or blocks.
REINFORCING FIBRES Synthetic fibres – based on polypropylene – which are mixed with cement-based materials to provide extra strength and elasticity.
RENDER To cover a surface with *mortar* or *cement* in order to produce a smooth finish.
RESERVOIR POOL A pool at the lowest point of a water feature.
RESIDUAL CURRENT DEVICE (RCD) Often called a circuit breaker, used as a safety measure; an automatic switch halts electricity flow in the event of a short-circuit, or if the current exceeds a pre-set safe value.
RHIZOME A specialized, usually horizontally creeping, swollen or slender, underground stem that acts as a storage organ and produces aerial shoots at its apex and along its length.
ROOT BALL The roots and accompanying soil visible when a plant is removed from a container or lifted from open ground.
ROSETTE A circular cluster of leaves growing from the base of a shoot.
RUNNER A horizontally spreading stem that runs above ground and roots at the *nodes* to form new plants.
RUST A fungal disease affecting plants.

SEALANT, SEALING COMPOUND A proprietary compound used to waterproof cement, timber, etc.
SEDGE A grass-like plant with triangular stems, usually growing in wet areas.
SELF-SEEDING Shedding fertile seeds that grow into young plants around the parent plant.
SEMI-DOUBLE FLOWER With two or three times the normal number of petals, usually in two or three rows.
SEMI-EVERGREEN Plants that retain some leaves or lose older leaves only in winter.
SEMI-RIPE CUTTING See *Cutting*.
SETT A granite paving block, often cuboid in shape.
SHARP SAND A sand composed of hard, angular particles, used in specific mixes with cement and water for rendering walls and similar surfaces.
SHINGLE Small, rounded stones.
SHUTTERING A timber frame forming a mould into which concrete is poured to create side-walls.
SOFT SAND Fine sand.
SOFT-TIP CUTTING See *Cutting*.
SOFTWOOD CUTTING See *Cutting*.
SOFTWOOD TIMBER Timber cut from coniferous trees.
SPATHE A large *bract* that encloses an *inflorescence*.
SPAWN The mass of eggs deposited by fish or amphibians.
SPECIES A category in plant classification denoting closely related plants within a single *genus*.
SPHAGNUM Mosses common to bogs; their moisture-retentive character makes them ideal components of some growing media.
SPILL STONE A flat stone set at the point at which water falls from one level to another.
SPIRIT LEVEL A tool for checking horizontal levels.
STAMEN The male organ of a flower.
STERILE Infertile, not bearing spores, pollen, or female reproductive organs (the pistil). Also, not producing flowers or viable seeds.
STIGMA The part of the female portion of the flower that receives pollen.
STRAIGHT-EDGE A straight length of timber on which to rest a spirit level.
SUBMERGED PLANTS Plants that for the most part have totally submerged foliage and, in many cases, emergent flowers.
SUBMERSIBLE PUMP A water-recirculating pump that is housed, and runs, under water.
SUBSOIL The layer of soil beneath the *topsoil*, usually less fertile and of poorer structure.
SUMP A pool or container into which water drains.
SURFACE PUMP A water-recirculating pump housed and running on dry land.

TAMP To compress firmly.
TERMINAL At the tip of a shoot, stem, or branch.
THINNING The removal of a proportion of a plant to improve the vigour and quality of the remainder.
TOOTHED Small or narrow indentations around the margin of a leaf or flower.
TOPSOIL The top layer of soil, which contains plant nutrients.
TRANSFORMER An apparatus for reducing or increasing the voltage of electrical currents.
TRANSPIRATION Loss of water by evaporation from the leaves and stems of plants.
TRIFOLIATE With leaflets in threes.
TRUE Of plant breeding, plants that when self-pollinated reliably produce offspring very similar to their parents.
TUBER A thickened, usually underground, storage organ derived from a stem or a root.
TUNIC The often papery outer layer of a *bulb* or *corm*.
TURION See *Winter bud*.

ULTRAVIOLET LIGHT (UV) Radiation with a wave-length less than that of visible light; a component of sunlight.
UNDERLAY Cushioning material laid under flexible liner as a form of protection.
UV FILTER AND MAGNET A combination filter system that prevents the build-up of minerals on which algae thrive.

VARIEGATED Marked with various colours in an irregular pattern, particularly of leaves with yellow or white markings.
VARIETY Botanically, a naturally occurring variant of a wild *species*.

WALL TIE A metal strip or wire figure-eight mortared into brickwork to cross the gap between double walls, giving them more stability.
WATER TABLE The level in soil below which water will not drain away; hence, the water level of natural ponds in the locality.
WICK EFFECT Tendency of water to move from a pond to surrounding soil, drawn by plants' root systems.
WINTER BUD A fleshy bud that detaches from the parent aquatic plant, overwintering at the bottom of a pond and growing into a new plant the following spring. Also called a *turion*.
WHORL A cluster of three or more flowers, buds, leaves, or shoots that are arranged around a stem at about the same level.

X Sign denoting a hybrid, produced from crossing two genetically distinct plants.

PLANT INDEX

A

Abies (firs) Tall, fully hardy conifers with whorled branches and soft needles. *A. koreana*, the Korean fir (H to 10m/30ft), bears upright, violet-blue cones from early maturity.
Acer (maples) Fully to frost-hardy, deciduous or evergreen shrubs and trees for well-drained soil, grown for their foliage or decorative bark; many, particularly the Japanese maple *(A. palmatum)*, display brilliant autumn colour.
Acorus Fully to frost-hardy aquatic perennials, grown for their often aromatic grass-like foliage. Need an open, sunny position. *A. calamus* prefers shallows; *A. gramineus* can grow largely submerged.
calamus 'Variegatus' 190
Ajuga Hardy annuals and perennials for moist soil and sun or shade. The small, semi-evergreen *A. reptans* makes excellent ground cover.
reptans 'Multicolor' 196
Alchemilla Hardy perennials bearing sprays of tiny, greenish-yellow flowers in summer. *A. mollis* (H & S 50cm/20in) tolerates shade and moist, but not wet, soil.
Alder see *Alnus*
Alisma Fully to frost-hardy, deciduous, perennial marginals grown for their foliage and flowers. Require a sunny position.
plantago-aquatica 190
Allium Fully to frost-hardy perennials needing sun and well-drained soil. Most have small flowers packed together in dense, spherical or shuttlecock-shaped heads on stout stalks.
Alnus (alders) Fully hardy, deciduous trees and shrubs that thrive in any soil and in wet conditions.
Amazon water lily see *Victoria amazonica*
American arrowhead see *Sagittaria latifolia*
American lotus see *Nelumbo lutea*
Amphibian bistort see *Polygonum amphibium*
Anagallis Fully to frost-hardy annuals and creeping perennials, grown for their flowers. Need moist soil and an open, sunny position. All enjoy moist soil, particularly the hardy *A. tenella* (H 5–10cm/2–4in, S 15–30cm/6–12in), or bog pimpernel.
tenella 'Studland' 196
Angelica Hardy, summer-flowering, often short-lived perennials, some with culinary/medicinal uses.
archangelica 196
Anthemis Fully to frost-hardy, carpeting and clump-forming perennials, some evergreen, grown for their daisy-like flower heads and fern-like foliage. Need sun and well-drained soil.
Aponogeton Frost-hardy to tender, perennial deep-water plants, grown for their floating foliage and scented flowers. Need an open, sunny position.
distachyos 180
Arisaema Fully to half-hardy, tuberous perennials, grown for their large, hooded spathes. Need sun or partial shade and moist, humus-rich soil.
candidissimum 196
Artemisia Evergreen, semi-evergreen, or deciduous shrubs, sub-shrubs, and perennials, grown for their silvery, aromatic foliage. Fully to half-hardy; enjoy well-drained soil and a sunny position.
Aruncus Hardy perennials forming hummocks of broad, fern-like leaves and plumes of white flowers in summer.
dioicus 196
Arundo Large, half-hardy perennial grasses for full sun and moist or well-drained soil. *A. donax*, the giant reed, can reach 6m (20ft) in height.
Asian lotus see *Nelumbo nucifera*
Asplenium Fully hardy to frost-tender, semi-evergreen or evergreen moisture-loving ferns. Most prefer partial shade but *A. trichomanes* (H 15cm/6in, S 15–30cm/6–12in) tolerates full sun.
Astilbe Hardy, summer-flowering perennials preferring moist soil and, usually, partial shade. Flowerheads remain handsome even when brown in winter.
'Venus' 197
Aucuba Fully to frost-hardy, bushy, evergreen shrubs for sun or shade and any but waterlogged soil, grown for their glossy foliage and fruits (formed only where plants of both sexes grow).
Azalea see *Rhododendron*
Azolla Frost- to half-hardy, deciduous free-floating ferns. Can be invasive.
filiculoides 180

B

Banana water lily see *Nymphaea mexicana*
Betula (birches) Fully hardy, deciduous trees, most upright and slender; *B. pendula* is the weeping birch. Prefer a sunny position and any moist but well-drained soil.
Birthroot see *Trillium erectum*
Blue flag see *Iris versicolor*
Bog arum see *Calla palustris*
Bog asphodel see *Narthecium ossifragum*
Bog bean see *Menyanthes trifoliata*
Bowles' golden sedge see *Carex elata* 'Aurea'
Brooklime see *Veronica beccabunga*
Brunnera Hardy, spring-flowering perennials, suited to light shade and moist soil.
macrophylla 39
Buckbean see *Menyanthes trifoliata*
Bugbane see *Cimicifuga simplex*
Butomus One species of hardy, rush-like marginal.
umbellatus 190
Butterbur see *Petasites japonicus*
Butterfly fern see *Salvinia auriculata*

C

Calla One species of hardy, perennial marginal plant.
palustris 190
Callitriche Hardy, perennial, submerged oxygenating plants needing full sun. *C. hermaphroditica* thrives in up to 50cm (20in) of still or moving water.
Caltha Hardy, deciduous perennials including some bog plants, grown for their yellow flowers. *C. palustris* is the marsh marigold; var. *palustris* (H 60cm/24in, S 45cm (18in) is more creeping in habit; 'Flore Pleno' has double flowers.
palustris 37
Camellia Fully to frost-hardy evergreen shrubs and trees grown for their glossy leaves and attractive flowers, borne from late winter to spring. Must have well-drained soil.
Canna Frost-tender, rhizomatous perennials, grown for their striking flower spikes. Require a warm, sunny position and humus-rich, moist soil. Some species, such as *C. flaccida* and *C. glauca*, can be grown as marginal plants, but must be lifted over winter.
glauca 25
Cape blue water lily see *Nymphaea capensis*
Cape pondweed see *Aponogeton distachyos*
Cardinal flower see *Lobelia cardinalis*
Carex Fully hardy to frost-tender evergreen, rhizomatous perennials that form dense, grass-like tufts. Several have variegated or golden foliage.
elata 'Aurea' 197
pendula 197
Cedrus (cedars) Hardy, evergreen conifers or shrubs for warm, well-drained sites in full sun. *C. deodara* (H to 25m/80ft) has grey-green leaves and glaucous cones; branch tips have an elegant, arching habit.
Centaurea Hardy annuals and perennials for any well-drained soil, grown for their flowers, with slender ray petals around a thistle-like centre.
Ceratophyllum Fully to half-hardy, submerged perennials. Prefer sun, but tolerate shade better than most oxgenators.
demersum 178
Ceratopteris Frost-tender, free-floating, spreading aquatic ferns needing full sun.
Chelidonium (celandine) One species, *C. majus* (H 60–90cm/24–30in, S 30cm/ 12in), of hardy, yellow-flowered perennial that rapidly forms ground cover, thriving in moist but not wet soil. The cultivar 'Flore Pleno' has double flowers.
Chelone Hardy, summer- and autumn-flowering, moisture-loving perennials.
obliqua 197
Cimicifuga Hardy, moisture-loving perennials grown for their flowers, despite their unusual, slightly unpleasant smell.
simplex 197
Colchicum Spring- and autumn-flowering cormous perennials, whose short-stalked, goblet-shaped flowers usually appear before their leaves. Fully to frost-hardy; need full sun and well-drained soil.
Colocasia Frost-tender, deciduous or evergreen perennials, grown for their foliage. *C. esculenta* 'Fontanesii' (H 1.1m/3½ft, S 60cm/2ft) will grow in shallow water or wet soil, in sun or light shade.
Common cotton grass see *Eriophorum angustifolium*
Common white water lily see *Nymphaea alba*
Corkscrew rush see *Juncus effusus* 'Spiralis'
Cornus Fully to half-hardy deciduous shrubs and deciduous or evergreen trees, needing moist but well-drained soil. Trees, such as *C. controversa* (H & S 15m/50ft), are grown for their habit, foliage, and pink, cream, or white bracts; the shrubs are often regularly cut back to renew their colourful young stems.
stolonifera 'Flaviramea' 198
Crocosmia Frost-hardy cormous plants, grown for their brightly coloured flowers, produced mainly in summer. Thrive in moist but well-drained soil and an open, sunny site.
'Lucifer' 198
Cryptomeria Hardy, coniferous trees and shrubs noted for their tolerance of heavy clay soils. There are several small cultivars of *C. japonica* with attractive foliage colours.
Curled pondweed see *Potamogeton crispus*
Cyperus Clump-forming sedges, grown for their slender leaves and flower spikelets. *C. papyrus* is frost-tender, but *C. longus* (H 1.5m/5ft, S indefinite) and the smaller *C. latifolius* are fully hardy. All prefer full sun and moist soil.
papyrus 190

D

Darmera A genus of only one species of hardy, moisture-loving perennial.
peltata 47
Daylily see *Hemerocallis*
Deschampsia Fully hardy, perennial grasses. *D. cespitosa* has dense, dark green leaves and pale brown flower spikelets in summer. Tolerates sun or shade.
Dianthus (pinks, carnations) Fully to half-hardy, evergreen or semi-evergreen, mainly summer-flowering perennials, annuals, and biennials, grown for their mass of flowers, often scented. All need sun and well-drained soil.
Diascia Frost-hardy, summer- and autumn-flowering annuals and perennials, grown for their flowers, in shades of pink. Need sun and moisture-retentive but well-drained soil.
Dierama Frost- to half-hardy, evergreen, summer-flowering, moisture-loving cormous plants with rows of pendent flowers on long, arching, wiry stems.
Dropwort see *Filipendula vulgaris*
Dryopteris Fully to half-hardy, deciduous or semi-evergreen ferns. Must have shade and moist soil.
filix-mas 39
Duck potato see *Sagittaria latifolia*

E

Eelgrass see *Vallisneria spiralis*
Egeria Frost-tender, semi-evergreen or evergreen, floating or submerged aquatics. *E. densa* forms thick masses of long, wiry stems with small, whorled leaves; white flowers are held above water in summer.
Eichhornia Frost-tender, evergreen or semi-evergreen aquatic plants, needing an open, sunny position in warm water.
crassipes 26
Elaeagnus Fully to frost-hardy, deciduous or evergreen shrubs and trees for well-drained soil. The usually fragrant flowers are followed, in many cases, by showy fruits. Evergreen species such as *E.* x *ebbingei* (H & S 5m/15ft) make good hedges in sun or shade.
Epimedium Hardy, spring-

flowering perennials, some evergreen. Make good ground cover in partial shade and moist, humus-rich but well-drained soil.
Equisetum (horsetail) Primitive, rush-like, non-flowering rhizomatous perennials with curious jointed stems. *E. japonicum* is one of several species that will grow in water. Best containerized as can be invasive.
Erica (heaths, heathers) Ericaceous, evergreen shrubs for well-drained soil, many low-growing with wiry stems. *E.* x *veitchii* is one of the larger tree heaths (H to 2m/6ft, S 1m/3ft), with dense clusters of white, bell-shaped flowers from mid-winter to spring; it is more lime-tolerant than many heathers.
Eriophorum Perennial, grass-like plants, often remaining green in winter, with the leaves dying at flowering time, when they bear spikelets of cotton-like tufts. Enjoy full sun and boggy, acidic conditions.
angustifolium 190
Erodium Fully to half-hardy mound-forming perennials, suitable for rock gardens. Require sun and well-drained soil.
Eupatorium Fully hardy to frost tender perennials, sub-shrubs, and shrubs. *E. purpureum* is an upright perennial (H to 2.2m/7ft, S to 1m/3ft) with pink flowerheads on purplish stems that thrives in moist soil and in sun or partial shade.

Fairy moss see *Azolla filiculoides*
False helleborine see *Veratrum album*
Fargesia Hardy to frost-hardy bamboos, remaining evergreen in most winters, forming large, dense clumps of arching stems. *F. murieliae* (H 4m/12ft, S indefinite) is fully hardy, thriving in moist but well-drained soil and in full sun or partial shade.
Fatsia One species, *F. japonica*, of frost-hardy, evergreen shrub, grown for its glossy foliage and flowers. Grow in sun or shade, in fertile, well-drained soil.
Filipendula Hardy, spring- and summer-flowering perennials, many species thriving in moist soil.
purpurea 198
ulmaria 'Aurea' 198
vulgaris 198
Flag see *Iris*
Flowering rush see *Butomus umbellatus*
Fontinalis Fully hardy, evergreen, submerged oxygenating plants.
antipyretica 178
Fringed water lily see *Nymphoides peltata*
Frogbit see *Hydrocharis morsus-ranae*

G

Gardener's garters see *Phalaris arundinacea*
Gentiana Hardy annuals, biennials, and perennials, many suitable for rock gardens. The perennial *G. asclepiadea* (H 90cm/3ft, S 60cm/2ft) will grow in sun or partial shade, in moist but well-drained soil.
Geranium (cranesbills) Fully to half-hardy perennials, some semi-evergreen, grown for their attractive flowers. Many make good ground cover in any but waterlogged soil.
Geum Fully hardy, summer-flowering perennials. Best in sun and moist but well-drained soil.
Giant cowslip see *Primula florindae*
Gleditsea Deciduous, usually spiny trees, grown for their foliage. Fully hardy, but young plants may suffer frost damage. *G. triacanthos* 'Sunburst' (H to 12m/40ft) has bright yellow leaves in spring.
Globe flower see *Trollius europaeus*
Glyceria Hardy, deciduous, sun-loving grasses with creeping roots, arching leaves and feathery flowerheads. *G. maxima* can form large stands in pool margins.
maxima var. *variegata* 191
Goat's beard see *Aruncus dioicus*
Golden club see *Orontium aquaticum*
Grass of Parnassus see *Parnassia palustris*
Greater bladderwort see *Utricularia vulgaris*
Greater spearwort see *Ranunculus lingua*
Green arrow arum see *Peltandra undulata*
Griselinia Frost- to half-hardy genus of evergreen shrubs and trees, with inconspicuous flowers, grown for their foliage. Require sun and fertile, well-drained soil. *G. littoralis* (H 6m/20ft, S 5m/15ft) thrives in exposed, coastal sites.
Gunnera Summer-flowering perennials, the larger, clump-forming species grown mainly for their huge leaves. The slightly tender *G. tinctoria* (H & S at least 1.5m/5ft) is more compact in habit than the hardier *G. manicata*.
manicata 207

H

Hedera (ivies) Mostly hardy, evergreen, self-clinging climbers, grown for their foliage. All prefer well-drained soil; variegated ivies need more light than those with plain green leaves, which tolerate deep shade. Small, yellowish-green flowers are produced on mature plants only, followed by black or yellow fruits.
Hemerocallis (daylily) Hardy perennials, some semi-evergreen, for full sun and moist soil. Flowers are borne in succession, each one lasting for only a day.
fulva 'Flore Pleno' 199
Hepatica Hardy perennials, some semi-evergreen, flowering in early spring before new leaves are properly formed. Must have partial shade and moist, humus-rich soil.
Heuchera Fully to frost-hardy, evergreen, summer-flowering perennials forming large clumps of leaves, often, as with *H. sanguinea* (H & S 60cm/2ft), tinted with bronze or purple. Make good ground cover.
Hornwort see *Ceratophyllum demersum*
Hosta Hardy, shade- and moisture-loving perennials, grown mainly for their decorative foliage. They form large clumps, making excellent ground cover.
'Frances Williams' 199
fortunei var. *albopicta* 199
fortunei var. *aureomarginata* 199
undulata var. *albomarginata* 30
venusta 20
Hottonia Fully hardy, submerged perennials for still or moving water, grown for their handsome foliage and flowers.
palustris 178
Houttuynia One species, *H. cordata*, of hardy perennial for moist or wet soil, or shallow water. With its spreading rhizomes, it makes good ground cover, although it can be invasive.
cordata 'Flore Pleno' 21
cordata 'Chameleon' 191
Hydrocharis One species of hardy, free-floating perennial.
morsus-ranae 180
Hygrophila Frost-tender, deciduous or evergreen, aquatic perennials; *H. polysperma* is a spreading, submerged oxygenator with pale green leaves.

I

Inula Hardy, summer-flowering, clump-forming, sometimes rhizomatous perennials.
hookeri 200
Iris Upright, rhizomatous or bulbous (occasionally fleshy rooted) perennials, some evergreen, grown for their strap-like leaves and distinctive, colourful flowers. Many prefer well-drained, sun-baked soil, but beardless species such as *I. pseudacorus*, *I. sibirica*, and the Japanese irises *I. laevigata* and *I. ensata*, will thrive equally well in shallow water or moist soil.
ensata 'Blue Peter' 200
laevigata 'Alba' 191
laevigata 'Mottled Beauty' 191
laevigata 'Snowdrift' 24
laevigata 'Variegata' 25
pseudacorus 43
sibirica 200
versicolor 191
Isolepis *I. cernua* is a grass-like hardy perennial that will grow in shallow water or wet soil, forming tuft-like clumps up to 30cm (12in) in height.
Ivy see *Hedera*

J

Japanese maple see *Acer*
Japanese pond lily see *Nuphar japonica*
Juncus Hardy, perennial grasses for full sun or partial shade. Both *J. effusus* and the smaller *J. ensifolius* (H 80cm/32in, S 45cm/18in) will thrive in shallow water or moist, heavy soil.
effusus 'Spiralis' 27
Juniperus Hardy, evergreen conifers, with a variety of forms and foliage colours. While *J.* x *media* grows to heights of up to 15m (50ft) it has many cultivars that make excellent small garden trees: 'Pfitzeriana' grows to 3m (10ft), while 'Plumosa' is no taller than 1m (3ft), though widely spreading.

K

Kingcup see *Caltha palustris*
Kirengeshoma Hardy, late summer- and autumn-flowering, moisture loving perennials.
palmata 200

L

Lagarosiphon Fully hardy, semi-evergreen submerged perennials, with attractive foliage; *L. major* is one of the most popular and widely available oxygenating plants.
major 178
Lavandula (lavenders) Fully to half hardy, evergreen shrubs for sun and well drained soil, grown for their scented flowers and aromatic, usually grey-green leaves.
Leucojum (snowflakes) Fully to frost-hardy bulbs, grown for their pendent, bell-shaped, white or pink flowers, borne in autumn or spring. Some species prefer sun and well-drained soil; others thrive in damp ground and partial shade.
aestivum 200
Liatris Hardy, summer-flowering perennials with thick rootstocks. Prefer full sun and moist but well-drained soil. *L. spicata* (H 60cm/24in, S 30cm/12in) bears erect spikes of densely packed, rose-purple flowers.
Ligularia Fully to half-hardy perennials grown for their foliage and large, daisy-like flower heads.
'Gregynog Gold' 200
przewalskii 201
'The Rocket' 37
Liquidambar Fully to frost-hardy deciduous trees, with inconspicuous flowers, grown for their maple-like foliage and autumn colour.
Lobelia Perennial species and hybrids such as *L. cardinalis* and *L.* x *gerardii*, and many perennial named cultivars, such as 'Queen Victoria' and 'Cinnabar Rose', thrive in moist but well-drained soil. Unlike the creeping and trailing annuals, perennials grow to around 1m (3ft) in height, with brilliantly coloured flower spikes.
'Bees' Flame' 201
cardinalis 21
'Cherry Ripe' 201
x *gerardii* 'Vedrariensis' 201
'Will Scarlet' 201
Lonicera (honeysuckles) Fully hardy to frost-tender, deciduous, semi-evergreen, or evergreen shrubs and, mainly, twining climbers, grown for their tubular, usually fragrant flowers.
Lotus see *Nelumbo*
Ludwigia Frost-tender, floating or creeping aquatic plants, forming partially submerged mats of foliage in shallow water.
palustris 192
Lychnis Hardy, summer-flowering perennials, annuals and biennials grown for their attractive flowers. The perennial *L. coronaria* (H 45–60cm/18–24in, S 45cm/18in) bears rose-pink flowers on branching stems above grey foliage.
Lysichiton Fully hardy, deciduous perennials for shallow water or boggy soil, grown for their handsome flower spathes and foliage. Tolerate light or partial shade (although they grow better in sun) and both still and moving water.
americanus 192
camtschatcensis 192
Lysimachia Fully to half-hardy, summer-flowering perennials, some creeping in habit, such as the green-leaved, yellow-flowered *L. nummularia*; its cultivar 'Aurea' has yellow foliage.
nummularia 'Aurea' 202
Lythrum Hardy, summer-flowering perennials that thrive by water and in bog gardens in sun or semi-shade. The pink-flowered *L. salicaria* (H 1m/3ft, S 45cm/18in), which readily self-seeds and can be invasive, is a popular nectar source for winged insects.

M

Macleaya Fully hardy, summer-flowering perennials for sun and moist but well-drained soil. *M. microcarpa*, the plume poppy, has spreading rhizomatous roots and can be invasive.
microcarpa 'Kelway's Coral Plume' 202
Mahonia Fully to half-hardy, evergreen, shade-tolerant shrubs for well-drained soil, grown for their whorls of deeply cut, spiky leaves and spikes of scented, yellow spring flowers.
Male fern see *Dryopteris filix-mas*
Manna grass see *Glyceria maxima* var. *variegata*
Marsh marigold see *Caltha palustris*
Marsh trefoil see *Menyanthes trifoliata*
Marsilea Mostly tropical aquatic ferns needing full sun, rooting in shallow water or boggy ground.
quadrifolia 180
Matteuccia Fully hardy, deciduous, rhizomatous ferns for moist or wet soil.
struthiopteris 36
Mentha (mints) Fully to frost-hardy, spreading perennials, grown for their aromatic foliage; many are culinary herbs. They are adapted to a wide range of habitats, although only one or two may be grown in water.
aquatica 43
Menyanthes Fully hardy, deciduous, perennial marginal plants, grown for their foliage and flowers. Prefer an open, sunny position.
trifoliata 192
Metasequoia One species, *M. glyptostroboides*, of hardy, deciduous conifer (H to 15m/50ft) that, unusually among conifers, thrives in wet soil and can even be planted in shallow water; in its native China, it is used to stabilize river banks and the margins of paddy fields. Does best in a warm, sunny site.
Milfoil see *Myriophyllum verticillatum*
Mimulus (monkey musks) Fully to half-hardy annuals, perennials, and evergreen shrubs, most preferring sun and moist or wet soil, grown for their brightly coloured flowers.
cardinalis 202
luteus 202
Miscanthus Frost- to fully hardy, moisture-loving grasses grown for their robust, clump-forming habit, late summer flower spikelets, and foliage colours, the latter especially attractive in the many variegated cultivars of the hardy *M. sinensis*.
sinensis 'Zebrinus' 202
Mountain ash see *Sorbus*
Myosotis (forget-me-nots) Small, hardy annuals, biennials, and perennials, grown for their flowers. Excepting *M. scorpioides*, the water forget-me-not, they prefer well-drained soil.
scorpioides 32
Myriophyllum Fully hardy to frost-tender, deciduous submerged plants with attractive foliage, held partly above the surface in shallow water. Require full sun.
aquaticum 27
verticillatum 179
Myrtle flag see *Acorus calamus* 'Variegatus'

N

Narthecium Hardy, rush-like, herbaceous perennials native to acid bog- and moorland. Require full sun.
ossifragum 192
Nelumbo (lotus) Half-hardy to frost-tender, deciduous, perennial marginal plants, grown for their large leaves, exquisite flowers, and distinctive seedheads. Need an open, sunny position.
lutea 188
nucifera 188
nucifera 'Alba Grandiflora' 188
nucifera 'Momo Botan' 189
nucifera 'Mrs Perry D. Slocum' 189
nucifera 'Pekinensis Rubra' 189
nucifera 'Rosea Plena' 189
'Perry's Giant Sunburst' 189
'Perry's Superstar' 189
'Shiroman' 189
Nuphar Fully to frost-hardy, deciduous, perennial deep-water plants, grown for their floating foliage and spherical flowers. Will grow in shade or sun and in running or still water.
japonica 181
Nymphaea (water lilies) Fully hardy to frost-tender, deciduous, summer-flowering, aquatic perennials, grown for their floating, usually rounded leaves and brightly coloured cup- or star-shaped flowers. Need an open, sunny position and still water.
alba 182
'Attraction' 37
'Aurora' 182
'Blue Beauty' 182
capensis 182
'Caroliniana Nivea' 183
'Escarboucle' 183
'Firecrest' 183
'Froebelii' 183
'Gladstoneana' 183
'Gonnère' 183
x *helvola* 184
'James Brydon' 184
'Laydekeri Fulgens' 184
'Lucida' 184
'Marliacea Albida' 184
'Marliacea Carnea' 184
'Marliacea Chromatella' 185
mexicana 26
'Odorata Sulphurea Grandiflora' 185
'Pearl of the Pool' 185
'Pink Sensation' 185
'Ray Davies' 186
'René Gérard' 186
'Robinsoniana' 186
'Rose Arey' 186
'Saint Louis Gold' 186
'Sunrise' 186
'Vésuve' 187
'Virginalis' 187
'Virginia' 187
'William Falconer' 187
'Wood's White Knight' 187
Nymphoides Fully hardy to frost-tender, deciduous, perennial, deep-water plants, with floating foliage, grown for their flowers. Require an open, sunny position.
peltata 181

Omphalodes Creeping, fully to half-hardy annuals and perennials, some evergreen or semi-evergreen. Most prefer sun and well-drained soil; *O. cappadocica* will grow in moist soil, in light or partial shade.
Onoclea One species, *O. sensibilis* (H & S 45cm/18in) of hardy, deciduous fern that rapidly colonizes wet areas in sun or shade.
Origanum Fully to frost-hardy, deciduous perennials and sub-shrubs with usually pink flowers, most low-growing and prostrate in habit. Some are grown as culinary herbs. All prefer sun and well-drained soil.
Orontium One species of hardy, deciduous, perennial deep-water plant, grown for its floating foliage and flower spikes.
aquaticum 193
Osmunda Hardy, deciduous ferns for moist to wet soil. All except *O. regalis* must have a shady site.
regalis 203

PQ

Paeonia Mostly hardy, late spring- and summer-flowering perennials and shrubs for well-drained soil, valued for their bold foliage, showy blooms and, in some cases, colourful seed pods.
Paper reed see *Cyperus papyrus*
Papyrus see *Cyperus papyrus*
Parnassia Fully hardy, mainly summer-flowering perennials, grown for their saucer-shaped flowers. Need sun and wet soil.
palustris 203
Parrot's feather see *Myriophyllum aquaticum*
Peltandra Fully to half-hardy perennial, marginal plants for shallow water, grown for their white, sometimes yellow-margined flower spathes.
undulata 193
Pendulous sedge see *Carex pendula*
Persicaria Fully to half-hardy, moisture-loving, summer- to autumn-flowering perennials, formerly included in *Polygonum*, forming dense clumps with tightly-packed spikes of flowers, mostly in shades of pink to deep red.
bistorta 'Superba' 203
campanulata 203
Petasites Hardy perennials for moist but well-drained soil, grown for their usually large leaves. Make good ground cover, but can be invasive.
japonicus 203
Phalaris Evergreen, spreading, annual and perennial grasses, the perennial species fully hardy, with narrow flower spikelets in summer. Tolerant of dry or wet soil. 'Feesey' is a less invasive, slightly more brightly coloured cultivar of *P. arundinacea* var. *picta*.
arundinacea var. *picta* 204
Phlox Fully to half-hardy, mainly late spring- or summer-flowering annuals and perennials. The taller perennials, such as *P. paniculata* (H 1.2m/4ft, S 60cm/2ft) and *P. maculata* (H 1m/3ft, S 45cm/1½ft), thrive and flower freely in moist, rich soil. *P. paniculata* has many cultivars, with flowers in white, pinks, crimsons, and purples.
paniculata 'Norah Leigh' 204
Phragmites Only *P. australis*, the common reed, is widely grown, a very hardy, deciduous, sun-loving perennial grass with feathery flowerheads that remain attractive through winter.
australis 'Variegatus' 193
Physostegia (obedient plant) Hardy, summer- to early autumn-flowering, moisture-loving perennials, the flowers of which can be moved into, and will remain in, different positions. *P. virginiana* (H 1m/3ft, S 60cm/2ft) can be invasive.
virginiana subsp. *speciosa* 'Variegata' 204
Pickerel weed see *Pontederia cordata*
Pinus (pines) Small to large conifers with spirally arranged leaves. *P. sylvestris* (H to 15–25m/50–80ft) has blue-green needles and attractive bark; the needles of its cultivar 'Aurea' are golden in winter and spring.
Pistia One species of frost-tender, deciduous, perennial floating plant.
stratiotes 181
Polygonum Many moisture-loving perennial polygonums are now reclassified under *Persicaria*; the genus still contains some aquatic species for shallow water or boggy ground.
amphibium 181
Polystichum Fully to frost-hardy, evergreen, semi-evergreen, or deciduous ferns that do best in semi-shade and moist, humus-rich soil.
setiferum 'Divisilobum Densum' 30
Pontederia Fully to frost-hardy, deciduous, perennial marginal plants, grown for their foliage and flower spikes. Need full sun.
cordata 193
Potamogeton Fully hardy, deciduous, perennial submerged plants, with broad, wavy-edged leaves. Best in full sun.
crispus 179
Potentilla Hardy shrubs and perennials for well-drained soil, grown for their clusters of small, flattish to saucer-shaped flowers and for their foliage. *P. fruticosa* is a dense, bushy, yellow-flowered shrub (H 1m/3ft, S 1.5m/5ft), with many attractive cultivars.
Primula Moisture-loving primulas are mainly small, fully hardy to frost-tender perennials, some evergreen, with attractive rosettes of basal leaves and colourful flowers. Drumstick primulas such as *P. denticulata* (H 30–60cm/12–24in, S 30–45cm/12–18in) have compact, spherical flowerheads; candelabra primulas, such as *P. japonica*, have tiered whorls of flowers.
beesiana 204
bulleyana 204
florindae 205
japonica 'Millers Crimson' 205
prolifera 205
pulverulenta 205
rosea 205
Ptilostemon Hardy to half-hardy shrubs and often spiny annuals, biennials, and perennials, with tubular, purple or white flowers and leaves with snowy, white undersides. Mediterranean in origin: prefer dry soil and a sunny site.
Pulmonaria Hardy, mainly spring-flowering, clump-forming perennials, some semi-evergreen. Make good ground cover in shade and moist soil.
angustifolia subsp. *azurea* 206

R

Ranunculus (buttercups) Fully to half-hardy annuals and perennials for sun or shade, some evergreen or semi-evergreen, grown mainly for their yellow flowers. There are a small number of aquatic species, often growing larger than those normally grown in well-drained soil.
aquatilis 179
lingua 'Grandiflorus' 193
Red lotus see *Nelumbo nucifera*
Rheum Genus of hardy perennials that includes the edible rhubarb, grown for their large leaves, borne on robust, fleshy, often coloured stalks. Some species, including *R. palmatum*, are very

large and require plenty of space.
palmatum 'Atrosanguineum' 206
Rhododendron Evergreen, semi-evergreen, and deciduous shrubs of varying sizes, grown for their showy flowers. They need acid to neutral, well-drained soil. The Japanese azaleas are compact evergreens, bearing masses of small, brightly coloured flowers in late spring.
Rodgersia Fully to frost-hardy, summer-flowering, rhizomatous, moisture-loving perennials for sun or semi-shade.
podophylla 206
sambucifolia 206
Royal fern see *Osmunda regalis*
Royal water lily see *Victoria amazonica*
Rubus (brambles) Deciduous, semi-evergreen, or evergreen shrubs and scrambling climbers, some grown for their edible fruits, most preferring moist but well-drained soil and tolerating some shade. The mat-forming, alpine ornamental species *R. pentalobus*, a prostrate shrub, makes good ground cover in sun or shade.

S

Sacred lotus see *Nelumbo nucifera*
Sagittaria (arrowheads) Fully hardy to frost-tender, deciduous, perennial, submerged and marginal aquatic plants, grown for their foliage and flowers. All require full sun.
latifolia 194
sagittifolia 47
Salix (willows) Deciduous, mainly moisture-loving shrubs and trees often found naturally by water, grown for their elegant foliage and silvery catkins.
hastata 'Wehrhahnii' 20
Salvinia Frost-tender, deciduous, perennial aquatic ferns, evergreen in tropical conditions. Do best in warm water, with plenty of light.
auriculata 181
Saururus Fully hardy, deciduous, perennial aquatic plants for shallow water or boggy soil, grown for their foliage. Prefer full sun, but tolerate some shade.
cernuus 194
Saxifraga Small, fully to half-hardy perennials, most evergreen or semi-evergreen, grown for their flowers and attractive, often rosetted foliage. There are species to suit both dry and damp planting pockets between rocks.
Schoenoplectus Hardy, perennial rushes, most with creeping rhizomatous roots. They thrive in shallow water or wet soil. *S. lacustris* subsp. *tabernaemontani* is less vigorous than the species, which can reach 3m (10ft) in height. It has several variegated cultivars, with either vertical or horizontal leaf stripes.
lacustris subsp. *tabernaemontani* 'Zebrinus' 194
Scrophularia Only one species, *S. auriculata*, is commonly grown; a hardy, clump forming perennial for damp soil or very shallow water, grown chiefly for its attractive foliage.
auriculata 'Variegata' 194
Senecio Varied genus, all with appealing, daisy-like flowers. Many prefer well-drained to dry soil, but there are some moisture-loving species.
smithii 206
Shellflower see *Chelone obliqua*
Shuttlecock fern see *Matteuccia struthiopteris*
Siberian bugloss see *Brunnera macrophylla*
Siberian flag see *Iris sibirica*
Silene Fully to half-hardy annuals and perennials, some evergreen, grown for their mass of five-petalled flowers. All need sun and well-drained soil.
Sisyrinchium Fully to half-hardy perennials for moist but well-drained soil, grown for their narrow leaves and slender spikes of spring flowers. Prefer sun but tolerate partial shade.
Soleirolia (mind-your-own-business) One species of prostrate perennial that forms a dense carpet of foliage, green in *S. soleirolii* (H 5cm/2in, S indefinite) golden in the cultivar 'Aurea'. Needs moist soil with good drainage. Dies back in cold winters, but usually regrows vigorously in spring.
Sorbus Fully to frost-hardy, small to medium-sized deciduous trees and shrubs, grown for their foliage, small, 5-petalled flowers, clusters of berries, and, in some species, autumn colour.
Squawroot see *Trillium erectum*
Stinking Benjamin see *Trillium erectum*
Stratiotes Fully hardy, semi-evergreen, perennial, free-floating plants, with rosettes of strap-like leaves.
aloides 179
Sweet flag see *Acorus calamus* 'Variegatus'
Sweet grass see *Glyceria maxima* var. *variegata*
Summer snowflake see *Leucojum aestivum*

T

Tape grass see *Vallisneria spiralis*
Thalia Large, half-hardy, deciduous perennials for wet soil or up to 45cm (18in) of water, grown for their leaves and spikes of flowers, held well above the foliage. Need an open, sunny position.
dealbata 194
Thymus (thymes) Fully to half-hardy, evergreen, prostrate shrubs and woody-based creeping perennials with aromatic leaves. Many are culinary herbs. Require sun and moist but well-drained soil.
Trapa Frost-hardy to tender, deciduous, perennial and annual floating plants. The frost-hardy *T. natans* (Jesuit's nut, water chestnut; S 23cm/9in) has diamond-shaped leaves, often with purple mottling, and small white flowers followed by black fruits. Given full sun, it spreads rapidly.
Trillium Hardy perennials with leaves, sepals, and petals all borne in whorls of three. Most prefer moist, humus-rich soil, in sun or partial shade.
erectum 207
Trollius Hardy, spring- or summer-flowering perennials that thrive in sun or shade beside pools and streams.
europaeus 207
pumilus 207
Turtle head see *Chelone obliqua*
Typha Fully hardy, deciduous, perennial aquatics for shallow water or rich, wet soil, forming dense clumps of narrow leaves and bearing decorative, cylindrical seed heads. Grow in sun or shade.
latifolia 'Variegata' 195
minima 32

U

Umbrella plant see *Darmera peltata*
Utricularia Genus of frost-hardy to frost-tender deciduous or evergreen perennials including several aquatic plants, most free-floating, with modified leaves that trap and digest insects.
vulgaris 179
Uvularia Hardy, spring-flowering perennials that thrive in moist shade, grown for their pendent, bell-shaped yellow flowers.

Vallisneria Frost-tender, evergreen, perennial submerged plants, with ribbon-like leaves. Require deep, clear water, in sun or semi-shade.
spiralis 179
Variegated water grass see *Glyceria maxima* var. *variegata*
Variegated yellow flag see *Iris pseudacorus* 'Variegata'
Veratrum Hardy, clump-forming perennials grown for their pleated leaves and hellebore-like flowers. They thrive in rich, moist soil in semi-shade.
album 207
Veronica Fully to frost-hardy perennials and sub-shrubs, some semi-evergreen or evergreen, grown for their usually blue flowers. Most need full sun and well-drained soil, but there are several aquatic species for shallow water or boggy ground; these also tolerate light shade.
beccabunga 195
Viburnum Fully to frost-hardy, deciduous, semi-evergreen, or evergreen shrubs and trees, with often fragrant flowers. Leaves of many deciduous species, such as *V. opulus* (H & S 4m/12ft), colour well in autumn.
Victoria Tropical, annual or perennial aquatics, with huge, platter-like floating leaves and large, white to pale pink flowers. Require full sun.
amazonica 181
Viola Small, hardy to frost-hardy annuals and semi-evergreen perennials, including numerous popular bedding plants with colourful flowers (the summer- and winter-flowering pansies, for example) as well as the more delicate-flowered violets, mostly forms of *V. odorata* (H 7cm/3in, S 15cm/6in): these woodland plants need cool, moist but well-drained soil and light shade.
Vitis (vines) Deciduous, mostly hardy tendril climbers with handsome leaves that colour well in autumn. Some, such as *V. coignetiae* (H to 15m/50ft), are ornamental plants; others are grown for their edible fruits (grapes). Prefer well-drained soil; foliage colour is best on plants situated in full sun.

Waldsteinia Fully hardy, semi-evergreen, creeping perennials with spreading, runnering stems. Make good ground cover, given sun and well-drained soil.
Wapato see *Sagittaria latifolia*
Water aloe see *Stratiotes aloides*
Water chinquapin see *Nelumbo lutea*
Water clover see *Marsilea quadrifolia*
Water crowfoot see *Ranunculus aquatilis*
Water dragon see *Saururus cernuus*
Water fern see *Azolla caroliniana*
Water figwort see *Scrophularia auriculata* 'Variegata'
Water forget-me-not see *Myosotis scorpioides*
Water fringe see *Nymphoides peltata*
Water hawthorn see *Aponogeton distachyos*
Water hyacinth see *Eichhornia crassipes*
Water lettuce see *Pistia stratiotes*
Water mint see *Mentha aquatica*
Water purslane see *Ludwigia palustris*
Water soldier see *Stratiotes aloides*
Water violet see *Hottonia palustris*
Wild iris see *Iris versicolor*
Willow see *Salix*
Willow grass see *Polygonum amphibium*
Wisteria Deciduous, twining climbers for sun and well-drained soil, grown for their long racemes of pea-like, usually fragrant flowers.

Yellow skunk cabbage see *Lysichiton americanus*
Yucca Fully hardy to frost-tender evergreen shrubs and trees, with sword-like leaves, and usually white flowerheads on tall stems. Must have sun and well-drained soil.
Zantedeschia (arum lilies, calla lilies) Frost-hardy to frost-tender, summer-flowering, tuberous perennials, grown for their elegant funnel-shaped flower spathes. *Z. aethiopica* will grow in moist, well-drained soil, preferably in a cool, shady site, or in shallow water.
aethiopica 'Crowborough' 195
aethiopica 'Green Goddess' 195

General Index

Page number in *italics* indicate illustrations. Individual plants and their common names have entries in the Plant Index *(see pp. 210–213)*.

A

algae 136, *136*, 138, 140–1, 152
amphibians 174
aquatic plants
  buying 154
  containers for 150, 151, *151*
  deep-water 148–9, *148*
    depth of water for 157
  dividing 159, 160, *160*
  free-floating 149, *149*
    functional role 152
  preparing for planting 155, *155*
  selecting 154–5, *154*
  submerged 148, *149*
    functional role 152
  thinning 158, *159*, 160, *160*
areas, measuring 60, *60–1*
arid conditions, plants for 24
autumn
  plant care 163
  pond care *159*
  tasks 141

B

barrels
  as water gardens
    planting plan *27*
    pool in 27, *27*
  lining 79, *79*
  planting depths *27*
  plants in *94*
  waterproofing 94, *94*
baskets
  planting 151, *151*
  plants in 24
beaches 80, *80*
  cobblestone 80, *80*
  informally laid *126*
  pebble *36*, 80, *80*
  shingle 80, *80*
beds, terraced *36*
beetles, pond 174, *174*
bentomat, laying 93, *93*
bentonite, waterproofing with 93, *93*
bitterling 169, *169*
blanketweed 141, *141*
bog gardens 40, *43*, *51*
  draining 82
  independent *78*
    constructing 82, *82–3*
  integral 78–9, *78*
    plants for *152*
  planting 157, *157*
    plan 42, *42*
bog plants, siting 56
boulders, as stepping stones 121, *121*
bricks
  building wall of *69*
  cutting 69, *69*, *87*
  laying, as pool surround 127, *127*
  patterns in 127, *127*
  types *127*
bridges 119, *119*, 122–3
  arched *123*
  handrails for 123
  maintenance 123, 140
  materials for 119
  safety *51*, 123
  timber *123*
    construction 122, *122*
brown spot 164, *164*
bud cuttings 161

C

caddis fly 165, *165*
canals
  advantages of 138
  circulating water in 107
  concrete 106–7, *106*
    construction 107, *107*
    linking reservoir pools 106, *106*, *107*
  formal 97
    cross-section 106, *106*
candles, lighting with 125, *125*
carp family 169, *169*
cast-iron hand pumps 114, *114*
china mark moth 165, *165*
  circuit breaker *see* residual current device
clay
  pond lined with 92–3, *92–3*
    waterproofing 93, *93*
  puddling 92
  testing soil for 92
cobblestone fountains 112
  construction 112–13, *112–13*
cobblestones
  choosing 80
  making beach of 80, *80*
  water running over *38*
composts 150
concrete
  canals 106–7, *106*
    formal, cross-section 106, *106*
  concrete, construction 68–9, *68–9*
  laying *68*
  ponds
    construction techniques 68–9, *68–9*
    repairing 145, *145*
  safety precautions 68
  sunken pools, construction 90–1, *90–1*
  tips for using 69
  wet, working with 69, *69*
construction
  materials 62, 63, *63*
  planning 51
  techniques 64–9, *64–9*
  tools 62, *62*
containers
  planting methods 156–7, *156*, *157*
  for plants 150, 151, *151*
    lining 151, *151*
    positioning 157
    stabilizing 157, *157*
  for water gardens
    shapes 94, *94*
    types 94
  water gardens in 26–7, *26*, *27*, 94–5, *94–5*
country garden
  stream 44, *44–5*
    planting plan 46, *46*
courtyard pool 32
  planting plan 32, *32–3*
crates, for plants 151
crazy paving *77*
  laying 128, *128*
  materials 128, *128*
culvert, formal 103, *103*
curtain of water 102, *102*
cuttings
  bud 161
  leaf-bud 162, *162*
  softwood 162, *162*

D

damselfly larvae 174, *174*
decking (timber) *37*
  laying 130–1, *130–1*
  maintenance 140
  safety 140
  for seating area 129, 130
  securing liner under 131, *131*
  tiles
    as edging *129*, 130
    patterns 130, *131*
deer scarer (*shishi odoshi*) 115, *115*
delivery pipes, preventing backflow *73*, 102
designs 18–47
  site and 50–1, *50*
digging 84
  tips 64
diseases
  of fish 175, *175*
  of plants 164, *164*
division of plants 159, 160, *160*, 161, *161*
dragonfly larvae 174, *174*
drainage
  of bog garden 82
  permanent 59
  temporary 59, *59*
dropsy, of fish 175, *175*
dry beds, plants for 24

E

ecosystem 134–5, 158
  balanced 136–7
edgings 126–9
  for canals 97
  curved, for formal ponds 128, *128*
  for flexible liner 77, *77*, *78*, 126
  formal 127, *127*
    materials for 127
  informal 126, *126*, *127*
    materials for 119
  mixing materials *128*
  timber *129*, *129*
  types 77, *77*
electricity
  installing 51, 72
    in raised pool 87, *87*
  for lighting 119, 124
  low-voltage 72
  mains 72
  safety 72, 108
evergreens, as background 46
excavation 58, *58*

F

fertilizers 150, 158
figwort weevil 165, *165*
filter systems 71, *71*
  installing 73, *73*
  maintenance 135, *141*
finishing touches 118–31
fish
  breeding 173
  buying 170
  care 172–3
  catching 142–3, *142–3*
  checking for disorders 144, *144*
  diseases 174, 175, *175*
  ecosystem and 137
  feeding 172, *172*
  habitat 172
  healthy 170, *170*
  inspecting 173
  pests 174, *174*
  selecting 170, *170*
  signs of distress 138, 139, *139*
  species and varieties 168–9, *168–9*
  stocking levels 171
  in summer 138, 139
  through year 135
  transporting *171*
  unhealthy, signs of 170, *170*, *173*
  water pH for 171, 172
fish lice 174, *174*
fleabeetle, iris 165
flexible liners
  calculating amount 66
  choosing 62–9
  constructing raised pool with 86–7, *86–7*
  constructing simple pond with 76–9, *76–7*
  constructing stream with waterfalls 98–9, *98–9*
  construction method with 66–7, *66–7*
  creating planting environments with 78–9, *78*
  disguising 98, 99, *99*, 126
  edgings for *77*, *77*, *78*, 126
  filling *67*
  folding *79*, *79*
  "hippoing" effect 59, *59*
  mortaring stone on *67*
  multi-purpose 78–9
  overlapping sections 66
  repairing 145, *145*
  securing under decking 131, *131*
  types 63, *63*, 66
  using 76
floating plants 149, *149*, *152*
  placing in pond 157
  role 152
  selecting *154*, 155
  thinning 158, *159*, 160, *160*
flukes, fish 175, *175*
food chain 137, 150
formal pools
  curved edges for 128, *128*
  large
    garden plan with *22–3*
    planting plan 24, *24*
  lining 79, *79*
  materials for 75
  planting *153*
  raised, building requirements 61
  still-water 74–5, *75*
  sunken, building requirements 61
fountain ornaments 110, *110*
  installation 108, *108*
fountains 108–17
  advantages of 134
  cobblestone 112
    construction 112–13, *112–13*
  formal *97*
  height 110, *110*
  installing 108, *108*
  jet types 109, *109*
  lighting *97*
    kit 125, *125*
  millstone fountain 18, *21*, 38, *38*, *39*, 96, *112*, 114, *114*
  ornamental 111
  preventing backflow *73*
  ring fountain, principles of 111, *111*
  safety precautions 108
  separate from pool 22
  spray, principles of 111, *111*
  spray patterns 109, *109*
  styles 110–11, *110–11*
  tiered spray patterns *97*, *109*
  types 97
  wall 116, *117*
    construction 116, *116*
    types *117*
    water flow 117, *117*
frost pockets 57
fungus diseases, of fish 175

G

goldfish, varieties 168, *168*
grass, as edging *77*
grasses
  cutting back *158*
  dividing 161, *161*
great diving beetle 174, *174*

H

half-barrel
  planting plan *27*
  pool in 27, *27*
header pools 102-3, *103*
  formal 103, *103*
  preventing backflow from *73*, 102
health, of pond, maintaining 134–5
herons 174, *174*
honey fungus 164, *164*
hot weather, protecting pond in 138, *138*
hypertufa
  covering glazed sink with 95, *95*
  trough
    making 95, *95*
    plants in *95*

I

ice
  melting 139
  on pond 134, *134*, 137, 139
    absorbing pressure of 139, *139*
India, Mogul garden fountains 110
informal ponds
  building requirements 61
  edging with stones and rocks 126, *126*
  garden plan with 34, *34–5*
  materials for 75
  planting *153*
  planting plan 34, *36*, *36*
  shapes *75*
  still-water 74, *74*, 75
iris fleabeetle 165
iris leaf spot 164, *164*
iris sawfly 165, *165*
Islamic gardens, fountains 110
islands
  constructing 81, *81*
  dry 30, 81, *81*
  wet 81, *81*
    incorporating in existing pond 81, *81*

J

Japanese water garden features
  shishi odoshi 115, *115*
  tsukubai 115, *115*
jetty, construction 131, *131*

K

kingfishers 174
koi carp 157, 169, *169*

L

leaf-bud cuttings 162, *162*
leafhoppers 165, *165*
leaves, keeping pond free of 141
light quality 56
lighting 118, 119, *119*, 124–5, *124*
  bulbs and lenses 125, *125*
  candles 125, *125*
  external 119
  in fish ponds 173
  floating spotlight *125*
  for fountains *97*, 125, *125*
  kits
    fountain lights 125, *125*
    pump and lights 125, *125*
  low-voltage system 72
  positioning 124
  safety precautions 124
  submersible 119, *124*
  types 124
liners, flexible
  calculating amount 66
  choosing 62–9, 76
  constructing raised pool with 86–7, *86–7*
  constructing simple pond with 76–9, *76–7*
  constructing stream with waterfalls 98–9, *98–9*
  construction methods with 66–7, *66–7*
  creating planting environments with 78–9, *78*
  disguising 98, 99, *99*, 126
  edgings for *77*, *77*, *78*, 126
  filling *67*
  folding *79*, *79*
  grades 67
  "hippoing" effect 59, *59*
  mortaring stone on *67*
  multi-purpose 78–9
  overlapping sections 66
  repairing 145, *145*
  securing under decking 131, *131*
  types 63, *63*, 66
  underlay 66, 67, *67*
  using 76
log roll, as edging 89, *89*, *129*
lotus blight 164, *164*

M

marginal plants 149
  dividing 158
  selecting *154*, 155
materials
  for construction 62, 63, *63*
  design and 50, *51*
measurements, of area and volume 60–1, *60–1*
methane 139
mildew, powdery 164, *164*
millstone fountains 18, *21*, 38, *38*, *39*, 96, *112*, 114, *114*
millstones, fibreglass 114
Mogul India, fountains 110
moisture-loving plants 149, *149*
  selecting 155
  soil for 150
moths, china mark 165, *165*
moving water features 96–117
  installation 96–7
  maintenance 135
  planning 96–7
  recirculating, terms 97
mulching 159

N

- netting, over pond *159*
- nutrients in soil 150

O

- offsets, propagation by *160*, 161
- orfe 169, *169*
- Oriental-style water garden
  - design 28
  - garden plan with 28, *28–9*
  - planting plan 30, *31*
- ornaments
  - cast-iron hand pumps 114, *114*
  - fountain 110, *110*
  - installation 108, *108*
  - statuettes 118, *118*
- oxygenating plants 30, 148, *149*, *152*, *152*
  - planting 156, *156*, 157
  - selecting 155
  - softwood cuttings 162
  - thinning 158, 160, *160*

P

- pavers 127
  - making curved edges with *128*
- paving, formal *127*
- pebbles, making beach of 80, *80*
- pests
  - of fish 174, *174*
  - of plants 164, 165, *165*
- pH, of water, testing 151, *151*
- photosynthesis 148
- planning 50–1
- planters, fibreglass
  - planting plan 26
  - pool in 26, *26*
- planting
  - environments 148–9
  - preparations for 156
  - schemes 152–3, *152–3*
  - techniques 156–7, *156–7*
  - time for 158
- plantlets, propagation by *160*, 161
- plants
  - buying 154
  - care during pond cleaning 142, *142*
  - choosing 154–5, *154*
  - colour schemes 153, *153*
  - containers for 150, 151, *151*
  - cutting back 158, *158*
  - deep-water 148–9, *148*
    - depth of water for *157*
  - diseases 164, *164*
  - dividing 159, 160, *160*, 161, *161*
  - essential 152–3
  - feeding 158
  - free-floating 149, *149*, *152*
    - functional role 152
    - placing in pond 157
  - marginal 149
  - moisture-loving 149, *149*
    - soil for 150
  - mulching 159
  - ornamental 153
  - oxygenating 30, 148, *149*, 152, *152*
  - pests 164, 165, *165*
  - planting 156–7, *156–7*
    - preparations for 155, *155*
  - pond designed for *148*
  - protecting 159
  - quantity in pond *141*, 152
  - removing dead leaves 159, *159*
  - routine care 158–9
  - submerged 148, *149*
    - functional role 152
  - tender, overwintering 159, *159*
  - thinning 158, *159*, 160, *160*
  - travelling 149, *149*
  - year-round interest 153
- ponds/pools
  - access to 156, *156*, 158
  - clay 92–3, *92–3*
  - cleaning out 142–4, *142–4*
  - concrete
    - construction 68–9, *68–9*
    - repairing 145, *145*
  - courtyard 32
    - planting plan 32, *32–3*
  - debris in ponds 135
  - designs, for hot, dry gardens 138, *138*
  - draining 135, 142–3, *142–3*
  - ecosystem 136–7
  - edging 77, *77*, 126–9, *126–9*
  - electricity in 87, *87*
  - emptying 135, 142–3, *142–3*
  - exchange of gases in 136, 139
  - formal
    - building requirements 61
    - curved edges for 128, *128*
    - garden plan with *22–3*
    - lining 79, *79*
    - materials for *75*
    - planting plan 24, *24*
    - still-water 74–5, *75*
  - ice on 138–139, *139*
  - informal
    - building requirements 61
    - garden plan with 34, *34–5*
    - materials for *75*
    - shapes 75
  - insulating 139, *139*
  - laying brick surround 127, *127*
  - maintaining health 134–5
  - natural balance in 134–5
  - natural cycle 137, *137*
  - netting *159*
  - overwintering 139, *139*
  - plant care 158–9, *158*, *159*
  - planting schemes 152–3, *152–3*
  - preparing for plants 156
  - raised
    - advantages 86
    - building requirements 61
    - disadvantages 86
    - double 18–19, *18–19*, *20*
    - flexible liner 86–7, *86–7*
    - rigid unit 88–9, *88–9*
    - siting *50*
  - reflections from 56, *56*
  - repairing 145, *145*
  - rigid unit 84–5, *84–5*
    - construction methods 64–5, *64–5*
  - routine care 140-1
  - seasonal care 134, *134*, 135, 137, 141, 163
  - separating areas in 119, *119*
  - still-water 74–5, *74*, *75*
  - stocking levels 75
    - plants 152
  - structural care 140
  - structural repairs 135
  - topping up 140, *140*
  - unhealthy 136, *136*
  - for wildlife 40–3, *40–1*, *42*, *43*, *54–5*
    - constructing 54
- powdery mildew 164, *164*
- pre-formed rigid units 84–5, *84-5*
  - bolted, watercourse of 105, *105*
  - construction methods with 64-5, *64-5*
  - disguising 65, *65*, 85, 104, *104*, 105, *105*
  - excavating for 105, *105*
  - repairing 145
  - semi-raised 88–9, *88–9*
  - stream units 104–5, *104–5*
- primula leaf spot 164, *164*
- propagation 159–62
  - bud cuttings 161
  - division 159, 160, *160*, 161, *161*
  - leaf-bud cuttings 162, *162*
  - offsets *160*, 161
  - plantlets *160*, 161
  - rhizomes 161, *161*
  - runners *160*, 161
  - seed 163, *163*
  - softwood cuttings 162, *162*
  - winter buds 162, *162*
- pumps
  - choosing 72
  - estimating flow rate 72
  - fittings and connectors 72, *72*
  - for fountain, installing 108, *108*
  - hand, cast-iron 114, *114*
  - installing 73, *73*
  - kit with lights 125, *125*
  - maintenance 135, 141, *141*
  - positioning 73
  - preventing backflow *73*, 102
  - remote, installation 108, *108*
  - submersible 97
  - surface, chamber for 73, *73*
  - types 70, *70*

R

- raised pools
  - advantages 86
  - building requirements 61
  - disadvantages 86
  - double
    - garden plan with *18–19*
    - planting plan 18, 20, *20*
  - flexible liner, building 86–7, *86–7*
  - installing electricity in 87, *87*
  - rigid unit
    - installing 88–9, *88–9*
    - planting edges 89, *89*
  - siting *50*
  - still-water *75*
- RCD *see* residual current device
- recirculating water systems, terms 97
- red spider mite 165
- Renaissance fountains 110
- reservoir features 96, 97, 114–15, *114–15*
- reservoir pools
  - canal linking 106, *106*, *107*
  - concrete *91*
  - for streams with bog areas 100
- residual current device (RCD) 72, 108, 124
- retaining walls, on sloping site *58*
- rhizome rot 164
- rhizomes, dividing 161, *161*
- rigid units 84–5, *84–5*
  - bolted, watercourse of 105, *105*
  - construction methods with 64–5, *64–5*
  - disguising 65, *65*, 85, 104, *104*, 105, *105*
  - excavating for 105, *105*
  - repairing 145
  - semi-raised 88–9, *88–9*
  - stream units 104–5, *104–5*
- roach 169, *169*
  - fry *173*
- rocks
  - absorbent *126*
  - edging with 126, *126*
  - informal walls 127, *127*
  - laying 126, *126*, *127*
  - non-absorbent *126*
  - strata lines *127*
- rudd 169, *169*
- runners, propagation by *160*, 161

S

- safety
  - bridges *51*, 123
  - concrete 68
  - decking 140
  - electricity 72, 108, 124
  - lighting 124
  - stepping stones 121
- sawfly, iris 165, *165*
- seed
  - collecting 159
  - propagation by 163, *163*
- setts *77*, 127, *128*
  - making curved edges with *128*
- shade, site in relation to 56
- shelter 57
- shingle, making beach of 80, *80*
- *shishi odoshi* 115, *115*
- shuttering, for concrete construction 91, *91*
- sinks, glazed, covering with hypertufa 95, *95*
- site
  - choosing 50–1, 56–7
  - excavating 58, *58*
  - levelling 58, *58*
- slabs 127
  - cutting 69
  - square
    - laying 128, *128*
    - making curved edges with *128*
- slate, placing *127*
- sleepers, edging with 126–9
- sloping ground
  - digging on *58*
  - landscaping *75*
  - retaining walls on *58*
  - siting water feature on *57*, *57*
- slugs 165, *165*
- snails 165, *165*
- softwood cuttings 162, *162*
- soil
  - blue mottling on *92*
  - composition *58*
  - cross section 150
  - hardpan *92*
  - improving structure *150*
  - nutrients 150
  - structure and composition *150*
  - structure test 150, *150*
  - testing for clay content 92
  - top dressing *151*
  - types *58*, 92, 150
  - wet, working in 158, *158*
- spill stones 96, *102*, 103
- spillways, formal 103, *103*
- spotlights 125
  - floating *125*
- spring
  - plant care 158, *158*, 163
  - pond 135
  - tasks 141
- statuettes *118*
- stepping stones 32, 118, 120–1
  - boulders as 121, *121*
  - formal *118*
    - construction 120, *120*
  - informal *118*, 121, *121*
  - maintenance 140
  - safety precautions 121
  - timber *121*
  - types 120
- still-water features 74–95
  - size *75*
- stone slabs
  - cutting 69
  - square
    - laying 128, *128*
    - making curved edges with *128*
- stones
  - beside watercourse 102–3, *102*
  - cleaning 140
  - cutting *87*
  - edging with 126, *126*
  - laying 126, *126*
  - securing 140
  - types for informal edging *126*
- stonework, watertight *102*
- streams 44, *44–5*
  - changes of direction in 101, *101*
  - creating illusion of *74*
  - creating planting areas 100, *100*
  - depth of pools with 102
  - direction of construction 101
  - edging with stones and rocks *126*
  - informal 97
  - measuring area and volume *61*
  - planting plan 46, *46*
  - rigid units 104–5, *104–5*
  - rocks and stones in 102–3, *102*
  - staircase of stone *100*
  - with waterfalls, constructing with flexible liner 98–9, *98–9*
  - working with site contours 100
- submerged plants 148, *149*
  - role 152
- summer
  - plant care 159, *159*, 163
  - pond care 134, *134*, 138, *138*
  - tasks 141
- sunken ponds, building requirements 61
- sunlight, site of water feature in relation to 56

T

- tender plants, overwintering 159, *159*
- terraced beds *36*
- tiles, decking
  - as edging *129*, 130
  - patterns 130, *131*
- timber
  - cleaning 140
  - decking *37*
    - laying 130–1, *130–1*
    - maintenance 140
    - safety 140
    - for seating area 129, 130
    - securing liner under 131, *131*
  - decking tiles
    - as edging *129*, 130
    - patterns 130, *131*
  - edging water feature with 129, *129*
  - maintenance 140
  - preserving 130, 140
  - securing 129, *129*
- tools, for construction techniques 62, *62*
- town garden
  - informal pond
    - garden plan with 34, *34–5*
    - planting plan 34, 36, *36*
  - stream 44, *44–5*
    - planting plan 46, *46*
- transformer 125, *125*
- trees, siting pond in relation to *57*
- troughs, hypertufa
  - making 95, *95*
  - plants in 95
- *tsukubai* 115, *115*
- tuberculosis, fish 175, *175*

U

- ulcers, of fish 175, *175*
- urns, bubbling 114, *115*

V

- vine weevil 165
- volumes, measuring 60, *60–1*, 61

W

- wall fountains 116–17, *117*
  - construction 116, *116*
  - types *117*
  - water flow 117, *117*
- walls
  - brick, building 69
  - levelling 87
  - retaining, on sloping site *58*
  - rock 127, *127*
- water
  - clear *134*
    - maintaining 141
  - exchange of gases 136, 139
  - green 135, *135*, 140–1, 158
  - health of 136
  - natural balance 140-1
  - pH, testing 151, *151*
  - poor quality 137
  - reflections from 56, *56*, *74*
  - seasonal evaporation 101
- water boatman 174, *174*
- water scorpion 174, *174*
- water table
  - establishing level *58*
  - high, laying flexible liner on *59*, *59*
- water-butt, as topping-up system *78*, 79
- water lily beetle 165, *165*
- water-lily leaf spot 164
- watercourses
  - of bolted rigid units 105, *105*
  - depth of pools with 102
  - header pools 102–3, *103*
  - informal 96
  - rocks and stones in 102–3, *102*
  - seasonal evaporation 101
- waterfalls 97
  - cascading 102, *102*
  - curtain of water 102, *102*
  - double 18
  - measuring area and volume *61*
  - preventing backflow *73*
  - stream with, constructing with flexible liner 98–9, *98–9*
- waterproofing
  - of barrel 94, *94*
  - with bentonite 93, *93*
- weevils
  - figwort 165, *165*
  - vine 165
- whirligig beetle 174, *174*
- white spot 175, *175*
- wick effect 78–9, 82, *148*
- wildlife
  - encouraging 54
  - planning for *50*
  - types of pond for *75*
- wildlife pond
  - with bog garden 40, *40–1*, *43*
  - constructing 54
  - garden plan with 40, *40*
  - planting plan 42, *42*, *54–5*
- windbreaks *57*
- winter
  - plant care 159, *159*, 163
  - pond care 134, *134*, 135, 137, 139, *139*
  - tasks 141

ACKNOWLEDGMENTS

AUTHOR'S ACKNOWLEDGMENTS

RHS Water Gardening has been a demanding title to produce, dealing in depth with the complexities of water-garden design and construction. It has required considerable patience and skill on the part of Dorling Kindersley editorial and design staff. The author would like to thank everyone involved in the book's production, in particular Jill Andrews, Project Art Editor; Cangy Venables, Project Editor; Jane Aspden and Jodie Jones for their input in the book's early stages; Peter Anderson, the project's photographer; and Gerry Adamson, who built the features and acted as model with such patience for the step-by-step photography.

PUBLISHER'S ACKNOWLEDGMENTS

Picture research
Sarah Moule, Fergus Muir

Editorial assistance
Maureen Rissik; thanks also to Francis Ritter

Design assistance
Stephen Josland, Stefan Morris, Rachael Parfitt; thanks also to Derek Coombes

Additional illustrations
Simone End, Malcolm McGregor

Index
Dorothy Frame

Dorling Kindersley would also like to thank:
All the staff of the Royal Horticultural Society for their time and assistance, in particular Susanne Mitchell, Karen Wilson, and Barbara Haynes at Vincent Square, and Nick Fried and Trevor Wiltshire at Wisley.

In the United States, Ray Rogers, Mary Sutherland, Barbara Ellis, James A. Lawrie, and Phoebe Todd-Naylor.

For allowing us to photograph their water gardens and water features:
Barbara and Michael Fitt (Raised Double Pool, pp. 18–21)
Simon Wills (Large Formal Pool, pp. 22–25)
David Everett, Peter Robinson (Water Gardens in Containers, pp. 26–27)
Mr and Mrs H Hills (Oriental-style Water Garden, pp. 14–15, 28–31, 75)
Jonathon and Madeleine Hilton (Informal Pond for Town Garden, pp. 34–37)
Mrs G Barrows (Stream for Town or Country Garden, pp. 44–47).
Mrs B Gillot (Simple Pond with Flexible Liner, pp. 76–77)
Mrs M Parkinson (Rigid Stream Units, pp. 104–105)
Mrs J Piercy (Simple Stream with Waterfall, pp. 98–99 and Installing a Fountain, p. 108)
Mrs G Calder (Cobblestone Fountain, pp. 112–113)
Mrs W Waple (Wall Feature, pp. 116–117)
Mr and Mrs R Baxter (Independent Bog Garden, pp. 82–83 and Cleaning a Pond, pp. 142–144)

Thanks are also due to the following landscape/garden designers:
Julie Toll (Oriental-style Water Garden, pp. 14–15, 28–31, 75)
John Keyes & Graham Rose (Courtyard Pool, pp. 32–33)
The Dale Stone Company (at the Chelsea Flower Show) (Millstone Fountain, pp. 38–39)

PHOTOGRAPHY CREDITS

Key: t=top, b=bottom, c=centre, l=left, r=right, a=above

A–Z Botanical Collection Ltd: 111bl; A Cooper 112tc
Heather Angel: 8cl, 11tr, 32l, 165bl, 165bc, 178tr, 179bl, 181tl, 192tl
Ardea, London Ltd: D Avon 169cb
Gillian Beckett: 207bl
Dr P Bowser: 175c, 175cr
Camera Press: F Rogers 121bl
Bruce Coleman Ltd: 199tl; J Burton 132–133, 166cl; E Crichton 7cr, 169cla; Dr E Pott 180br; A J Purcell 136bc, 137tl; H Reinhard 166tr; Dr F Sauer 137bc; J Shaw 191br; J Simon 26tr; A Stillwell 137cra; K Taylor 137tr, 137bl; H Van Den Berg 174bl; P Van Gaalen 192tr; K Wothe 190bc
Garden Picture Library: B Carter 120tc, 134tr, 200cl; B Challinor 153cr; E Crowe 183bl; G Dann 195bl, C Fairweather 182br; V Fleming 181br; G Glover 128br; J Glover 43b, 52tr, 134cl, 140tl, 153tr, 172tc, 183tr, 193tc, 194br, 201br; G Hanley 153c; S Harte front cover, 193br, 195tl; N Holmes 20br; R Hyam 96br; Lamontagne 128bc, 146cl; G Liston 110bl; J Miller 141br; M O'Hara 153tc; G Rogers 122tc; J S Sira front cover, 120tr, 200br, 202tc; R Sutherland 50br, 78tr, 127, 128bl, 135, 140tr, 140bl, 206br; B Thomas 52bl, 100t, 188br; D Willery 31t, 39t, 202tr; S Wooster 52bc, 77b, 110br, 136cr
John Glover: front cover, 7bl, 8tr, 74tc, 76tc, 84tc, 85b, 96cl, 103bl, 114tr, 114bl, 115br, 116tc, 117tr, 147tr, 177, 185r, 200bl
D Gould: 202tl
Robert Harding Picture Library: 138cr
Jerry Harpur: 2–3, 96tr, 97t, 134br, 167t
Holt Studios International Ltd: 174tl; N Cattlin 164tc, 164bl, 165tc, N Peacock 164bc
Hozelock: 124tc
Andrew Lawson: front cover, back cover, 13bl, 50tr, 74cl, 102bl, 103tr, 118tr, 184tr, 184br, 186cl, 186br, 199br, 200tr, 206tl
Natural History Photographic Agency: A Bannister 174bc
Clive Nichols: back cover, 74br, 102c, 110tr, 123tr
Dr Ed Noga 175tr
Oxford Scientific Films: G I Bernard 146tr, 165cl, 175cl, 179tl; D Brown 108tc, 180bl, 185cl, 188tr, 191bc, 198br; L Crowhurst 178cr; Earth Scenes/Perry D Slocum 189tc; D Fox 174tc; P Gathercole 173cr; M Gibbs 175tc; R L Manuel 179c; C Milkins 92tc, 137c, 174tr, 174cr; C S Milkins 174c; J Mitchell 188bl; Photo Researchers/ J Lepore 21tr; J H Robinson 165cr; P K Sharpe 178bl; G H Thomson 180c
Hugh Palmer: 9, 10tr, 10b, 11bl, 12, 13tr
Photos Horticultural: 165cr, 175tl, 196bl, 198tl, 201tr, 201bl
Planet Earth Pictures: J Perry 164tr
RHS Wisley: Ash 165c; W Halliday 165tr
Perry D Slocum: 164tl, 164bcr, 187br, 189bl, 189tr, 189bc, 189cr
Harry Smith Horticultural Collection: 21br, 24cr, 25br, 25tr, 31l, 39l, 50cl, 104tc, 111tr, 129tl, 179bc, 179tc, 183br, 184tl, 184cl, 186tc, 187cl, 190br, 191bl, 193bl, 194tr, 204tr, 207tr; Polunin 181tr
Stapeley Water Gardens Ltd: 124bc, 182tr, 185bl, 187tl, 187tr, 189tl, 189cl, 191tr

All other photographs by Peter Anderson and Steven Wooster.

AQUATIC SUPPLIERS

The author and publishers would like to thank the following for allowing us to use and photograph their plants and aquatic accessories:

Anglo Aquarium Plant Co Ltd (aquatic plants), Enfield, Middlesex; tel: 0181 363 8548 – thanks especially to David Everett and Katy Dines
Bradshaws (pond liner and underlay), Clifton Moor, York; tel: 01904 691169
Chilstone (wall fountain), Langton Green, Kent; tel: 01892 740866
Civil Engineering Developments Ltd (stones, rocks, and cobbles), West Thurrock, Grays, Essex; tel: 01708 867237
Clandon Park (water-garden accessories, plants, and fish), West Clandon, nr Guildford, Surrey; tel: 01483 224822 – thanks especially to Graham Shred
Cyprio Ltd (pumps and filtration equipment), Frognall, Peterborough, Cambridgeshire; tel: 01778 344502 – thanks especially to Jonathon Hart
Hillhout Ltd (decorative timber and decking), Harfreys Industrial Estate, Great Yarmouth, Suffolk; tel: 01493 440017
Hozelock (pumps and filters), Haddenham, Aylesbury, Buckinghamshire; tel: 01844 291881
H Tisbury and Son (aquatic plants), Noak Hill, Romford, Essex; tel: 01708 341376
Lotus Water Garden Products (surface pump and electric connectors), Burnley, Lancashire; tel: 01282 420771
Maidenhead Aquatics (delivery pipe), North London Aquatic Centre, Mill Hill, London; tel: 0181 201 1999
Marshalls Mono Ltd (walling and paving), Southowram, Halifax, Yorkshire; tel: 01422 306000
Paradise Centre (moisture-loving plants), Lamarsh, Bures, Suffolk; tel: 01787 269449
Park View Nursery (architectural plants), Crews Hill, Enfield, Middlesex; tel: 0181 363 1311
Rein Ltd (reinforcing fibres for cement), Ashbourne, Derbyshire; tel: 01335 342265
Sadolin Nobel UK Ltd (timber preservatives), St Ives, Cambridgeshire; tel: 01480 496868
Trident Water Garden Products (pump and electric connector), Folehill, Coventry; tel: 01203 638802;
Volclay Limited (bentomat liner), Birkenhead, Merseyside; tel: 0151 6380967
Ware Planters (fibreglass planter), Sedgegate Nursery, Nazeing, Essex; tel: 01992 462378
Water Garden Nursery (aquatic plants), Wembworthy, Chulmleigh, Devon; tel: 01837 83566
Wildwoods Water Garden (pond liner and underlay), Enfield, Middlesex; tel: 0181 366 0243